EVERYBODY CAN KNOW

D1531002

Other books by Edith Schaeffer:

L'Abri
Hidden Art

Other books by Francis A. Schaeffer:

Escape from Reason
The God Who Is There
Death in the City
Pollution and the Death of Man
The Church at the End of the Twentieth Century
The Mark of the Christian
The Church Before the Watching World
He Is There and He Is Not Silent
True Spirituality
Genesis in Space and Time: The Flow of Biblical History
The New Super-Spirituality
Back to Freedom and Dignity
Basic Bible Studies
Art and the Bible

EVERYBODY CAN KNOW

by Francis and Edith Schaeffer

Illustrated by
Franky A. Schaeffer V

TYNDALE HOUSE PUBLISHERS
Wheaton, Illinois

Library of Congress Catalog Card Number 73-87127. ISBN 0-8423-0786-9, paper.
Text © Francis and Edith Schaeffer 1973. Illustrations © Franky A. Schaeffer 1973.
First published 1973 in Great Britain by Scripture Union.
American edition by Tyndale House Publishers, Wheaton, Illinois. First printing,
January 1979. Biblical quotations are from the Revised Version. Printed in the
United States of America.

DEDICATED
to our children
and our children's children
of our family and
of the wider L'Abri family

CONTENTS

INTRODUCTION

This book is written to help people of all ages to know something of God's truth, and then to be able to talk together when they are eating together, walking together, sitting in the living room, having a few minutes together at bedtime. Naturally, it may be read silently by individuals, but it is written also that it may be read in a family, and shared with other people. It may be read out loud by a single person who has invited friends for an evening, or invited children living nearby, or nieces and nephews. It may be read aloud to a group of people in a hospital ward, a prison, a retirement home, a rehabilitation home, or any grouping of people who are together because of some circumstance in their lives.

If it is read in installments one evening a week, discussion may take place during the week about what has been read.

It is important that the person who is reading should read with expression and not in a stiff, dry and monotonous voice. It is also important that the variety of "things to do" to illustrate points and make things clearer should really be carried out. Be prepared to need to look for dried beans and peas, old silver to polish, candles to light, cloth to wrap things in, a curtain to tear, jigsaw puzzles to put together and so on. We specially urge you to be prepared to purchase an album of records of Handel's *Messiah*, to listen to at various points. Above all things, be prepared to be involved in the whole period covered by the book of Luke, to "live" in that book as you read and discuss.

It will be best to read the book a chapter at a time. But to help those who may find there is too much in one chapter for one reading, we have put arrows in the margins of the chapters to indicate places where you can stop and begin next time.

One evening a week would be a good way to begin: this way, at the rate of a chapter a week, it would take approximately seven months to cover the book the first time. The second time you read, you may want to read a little each day, along with a portion of Luke, stopping at the arrows in the margins of this book. The discussions which will arise, the trip to an aquarium, the visit to a library with a Bible in your hand, the time spent listening and discussing the *Messiah*, the time spent reading the score of the *Messiah*, can make this book a year's course to help everybody in your family, or neighborhood, or group of friends to know, to consider and to understand the wonder of the existence and reality of the living God.

Centuries ago God told the Israelites something important for us to remember now in this twentieth century. We can read this in Deuteronomy 4:35, 36, 39. "Unto thee it was shewed, that thou mightest know that the Lord *he* is God; there is none else beside *him*. Out of heaven *he* made thee to hear *his* voice, that he might instruct thee. . . . Know therefore this day and lay it to thine heart, that the Lord *he* is God in heaven above, and upon the earth beneath: there is none else." Again in chapter 6 it is recorded that Moses told the people that God had said, "These words which I commanded thee this day, shall be upon thine heart: And thou shalt teach them diligently unto thy children, and shalt talk of them when thou sittest in thine house, and when thou walkest by the way, and when thou liest down, and when thou risest up."

There is a situation in the world today which is like an undertow. Have you ever gone to the seaside and plunged in without knowing that there was a dangerous undertow? Have you felt the sickening strength of the pull out toward the sea, and felt the fright of not being strong enough to get back on your own? There is an undertow in thinking, teaching, writing today which is pulling people out into a sea of despair and blackness. People are being taught that there is no God, no truth, no right and wrong, no purpose in life. People are being affected in disastrous ways by an undertow which catches them—often as they plunge into school or university—or even just into discussion with other people in the village, town, or city in which they live. Help is needed. A big wave is needed to wash them back up on the shore of reality again. Our desire is that this book may be one such wave to help secure many feet on the safety of rock and shore!

1

FIRST THE IDEA,
THEN THE CHOICE . . .

Close your eyes tightly. Yes, I know this is a strange way to
begin but I really want you to close your eyes. Now you can't
see anything in the room, can you? Or if you are sitting on
the grass, or in a boat, or on the sand, or on a rock, or on a
bench in a city park . . . you still cannot see anything that is
around you. Now keep your eyes closed, and let's think of
things. Think of the sun. How brightly it spills warm light into
a room! How beautiful the garden or the park, the beach or
the buildings look in the sun! Think of the moon. Have you
seen a full moon all round and copper-colored in the dark
sky? Have you seen a tiny new moon like a silver half-circle in
a pale evening sky? Have you seen stars and planets on a
clear night, more than you can count? Think of water now.
Think of the ocean, or a lake, or a river, or a tiny stream, or a
waterfall, or a pond, or the water in your bathtub. Can you
"see" water with your eyes closed? Can you imagine it?
     Think of grass now. Think of a lovely lawn with flowers
and bushes and trees. Think of lots of trees in a forest. Can
you "see" grass, flowers, and trees in your head? Can you
"see" daisies and roses, apple trees or banana trees inside
your head? Now think of birds. Think of seagulls swooping
over the seashore or a lake. Think of little sparrows eating
crumbs on your window sill, or pecking at something in the
street. Think of birds. Can you "see" birds inside your head?
Can you "see" pigeons on the roof of a big city building, or a
little red or yellow bird in the country? Try to "see" it as you
are thinking, imagining it in your head.
     Think of a cat now. Do you have a cat? Do you have a

dog . . . or do you know someone else's dog that wags its
tail at you, or barks at you? Think of a cat or a dog, or a little
mouse that runs across the room. Can you "see" a dog or a
cat or a little mouse? Can you see an animal in your head?
Maybe, when I say "animal," you think of a giraffe or an
elephant or a jumping toad or a lion or a cow. Think of a cow
and try to "see" it in your head. Now think of a person. Can
you "see" Mother or Dad in your head? Can you "see" your
sister or your brother, a baby or a big girl or boy in your
head? With your eyes closed, can you think of a person and
"see" the long hair, the beard or the laughing lips of a
person? Can you "see" a friend in your imagination?

Now open your eyes. Let's remember together the
things we have been trying to "see" with our eyes closed.
There is something alike about all of these things. Perhaps
you have guessed what it is. In case you don't know, I'll tell
you. We could not *make* any of the things we thought about,
and tried to "see" with our eyes closed. We could not make
the sun, the moon and stars. We could not make water, not
even a lake full, let alone the big ocean full. We could not
make the grass and flowers and trees. We could not make the
little sparrow, or the swooping seagull. We could not make a
cat or a dog or even a little mouse. We could not make a
person.

Now close your eyes again. It doesn't matter if you are
five years old, or fifteen, or fifty-five, it is important to close
your eyes right now in order to try together to understand
something. With our eyes closed we are now going to try to
"see" things that we *can* make. Think of a tall tower made of
building blocks. Think of sand and something you can make
with it when it is wet. Think of mud or plasticine and of what
can be made from them. Think of paper and pencils, or
canvas and paints and of what you could draw or paint. Think
of sugar and flour, eggs and milk, butter and baking powder
and what you could make out of these. Think of wood and
what you could make out of that.

If you are five years old, or fifteen or fifty-five . . . or
any other age, you have thought of many things you could

make. We have probably each thought of quite different things. But whether it is a cake or cookies (or biscuits, if you live in England), a sand castle or a wooden table, you have "seen" lots of things in your head that you could make. Now open your eyes again. There is *one* important thing for us all to understand. What is it that all of us must do before we start to *make* any kind of thing at all? It is that we must *choose* which thing to make. We cannot make a sand castle and a cake to eat at the same time. We cannot draw on paper and paint on canvas at the same time. No one can make anything without first *thinking* of something, and then choosing to make it. There are lots of things that we think of making that we *never* make.

When one of us was five years old, she thought of making a house that could be fastened to the back of a car and moved when the car went somewhere. At that time there were no "houses" like this, no caravans as they call them in England, or trailers as they call them in America. She "imagined" such a thing in her head. She chose to make one. All she had was paste and cardboard. She cut the cardboard and pasted it together and tried to make a house she could live in. She tried to make cardboard wheels. Did she succeed? Did she really make what she "saw" in her mind? No. She was too young and didn't really know how to make such a thing. Her poor little paste pot and pile of cardboard were not the right materials for making a house. Just seeing something in your head, and then choosing to make it, is not enough. You must really be able to do it. You have to know *how* to do it, and also to have the right materials.

But remember always the *order* of how things are made. Remember what comes *first* is thinking, *then* choosing, *then* making the thing, so that other people can see what was once only in your head.

What happens when we look at each other? Can you "see" the chocolate cake Mother is thinking about? Can she "see" the raft her son is thinking of making? Can we "see" what is in each other's heads? No. We cannot "see" all the things that are being thought about, or imagined in other people's heads. But when a five-year-old makes a building of blocks, then his Mother can see it. When your sister paints a beautiful picture all the family can see it. When Dad builds a cupboard we can see what his "idea" was. When Mother makes the supper we can see what she chose to make. We can see something, or taste it, or feel it, *after* a person has made it.

We look at each other and we cannot see the things in each other's heads. But we can look around the room with our eyes open and see the things other people have made. Everything a human being has made was *first* "seen" in a *person's* head . . . just the way you have been "seeing" things with your eyes shut. *Everything* that a human being (a small child, an older child, a young adult, a middle-aged person, an elderly person) has ever made has been *chosen* from the things they have thought of but have *not* made.

When we first shut our eyes, we thought of the sun, the moon, the stars, the oceans and lakes, the grass and trees. We thought of the birds, a cat, a dog and a little mouse, a lion, a giraffe, an elephant, a toad or a cow. We thought of people, too, of a baby, a child, a grownup or a young person. Remember, we said we could *not* make any of these things. But these things were first seen in the head of someone who *could* make them. The order is always the same. First the *idea*, then *choice*, then skill and ability to *make* the idea take shape so that it can be seen by other persons. A person has to be there to have the idea. A person has to be on the land *before* a house is built. When you see a house in a field, even though it is empty as far as you know, you ask, "I wonder who chose this spot, designed this house, and built it here?" A *person* has to be in the kitchen before the supper is cooked in the stove. A *person* has to be there before cloth is woven on the loom. First a *person*, then the idea, then choice, then the *things* we see. That is the order we ourselves understand every day of our lives. That is the order we *know* to be true, because *we* live that way. We are like a test tube, showing ourselves what the right order is. We are made in the image of a *person*, and we are able to understand the order.

Now I am going to ask you to do something very different. I am going to ask you to think of *time*. What does *time* mean? We can't understand time perfectly, but we do understand something about time. Can you remember yesterday? What happened yesterday? Can you remember a week ago? What did you do a week ago? Can you remember when you were younger than you are now? Can you remember waiting for something, and then having that something come? Can you remember waiting for dinner, hungry as anything, and wishing it was time for the meal? Can you remember that the time did come for dinner, and you ate and were happy eating? Can you remember waiting for a holiday or a vacation, a party or a journey? Can you remember a before and then a during and then an after? Remember waiting for something: that is the *before*. Remember something you loved doing: that is the *during*. Remember what it was like when the party was over, the vacation was finished, the music had stopped: that is the *after*. Old people have a long time to look back on. Old people have a lot to remember. Children can also remember things that have happened during their lifetime. Another way we can find out about things that happened a long time ago is by someone telling us. Old people can tell young people things that happened before they were even born. People who lived a hundred years ago can tell us things because they wrote them down on paper or put them in books.

There was a time before each of us was born. Six years ago, no five-year-old was alive. Twenty years ago, none of today's teen-agers was alive. A hundred years ago grandmother and grandfather were not alive. When you think of all the time there has ever been, not one of us has been alive very long. How long have people been thinking and seeing and imagining things in their heads? As long as there have been people to think, and imagine and then to make things.

What *is* a person? Here is something you need to know.

5

You are a person, and you need to know what a person is ! A person *thinks* (can see and imagine things in his or her head). A person *acts* (can do the things he or she thinks, or make the things he or she imagines). A person *feels* (can long for things to happen, can be happy or excited when it is time to do or make something, can be pleased or satisfied and contented when the thing is finished). A person *thinks* and *acts* and *feels*. A person can communicate. That means a person can talk, can say out loud the things he or she is thinking so that another person can hear and understand and know something. A person loves. There must be at least two persons for one to love another. You love Mother and Mother loves you. Mother loves Dad and Dad loves Mother. A person can have real love for another person; this is even more than liking someone. A person can love. A person can think things in his or her head, and see things in his or her imagination. We did that just now, so we *know* that we can do it. A person can choose what to make by thinking of many things to make, and then deciding on one thing, and making it. That is called being creative. A person is creative!

A very long time ago, there were no human beings . . . no Mothers and Dads and children, like our families. A very long time ago, there was no world! A very long time ago, there was no sun, no moon, or stars, or water, or trees, or grass, or animals. *Everyone* knows that all these things had a beginning. Everyone knows that there was a time before the things we see with our eyes existed. People try to figure out *how* everything came to be. Some people try to imagine that it all just happened . . . just by chance . . . all by itself, that everything just suddenly *was*. They say that because everything is made up of tiny little bits of things called atoms, there was a time when these tiny atoms just flew about as dust flies about (you can see dust particles flying about in a streak of sunshine sometimes) and that those atoms by themselves suddenly decided to form other things. They say that the things they cannot make themselves, and are more complicated than anything they *can* make, were not made at all, but just came into being by chance.

Strange isn't it, that men and women have believed that things could come just to *be* because they are so very complicated that they can't make them. You see, it is because they don't believe there *was* any person to think and choose and make these things. They *know* in their experience that everything has that order, but they try to find another way to explain the beginning of everything they cannot make, and know that no man can make.

People look at things great engineers have made, like space ships and television sets, and say, "How wonderful is the *man* who thought of this in his head, and then knew how to make it." People look at great statues that Michelangelo made, and say, "What a beautiful statue! How great that artist was!" People look at the wonderful paintings of Rembrandt and say, "What a clever *man* he was! How many other paintings he must have thought about that he didn't have time to make." People taste the dinner Mother cooked and say, "How well this rice is cooked! What a fine meal *she* has made! What a good cook she is." People look at something a boy has made and say to him, "What a good idea you had in *your* head! That's a fine raft you have made! You are clever to make something that will float!" "I wonder," we say, "whoever first thought of putting eggs and milk and flour together to make a pancake!" "I wonder how it was that once a small boy watched steam coming out of a boiling kettle and thought in his head about how that could run an engine." Yes, when we see the things people have made, we think about how they thought of the idea in their heads in the first place.

It is sad that so many people look at the complicated things like the sun and the stars and at trees and animals and at other people and have no idea how they were made. People believe that the things human beings could not make must have come by chance, because they do not believe there was anyone there to make them. It is sad that people have to believe something that isn't true, and just take a jump of faith to accept that all these things came by chance.

There is truth. There is that which *really* is. There is the *real* way things came about. There is a *before* and a *during* and an

7

after which is called "history." History really has taken place, and is *now* taking place. What you made yesterday is now history. If you made a fruit cake, or a very nice snowman, you would be angry if someone said you did not make it at all. If your sister made a dress for herself, she would be angry if someone said, "I don't believe it . . . you couldn't have made a dress as nice as that one." If your father made a statue last week and someone came and said, "That clay just happened to look like that. You didn't make it," he would be very upset, wouldn't he? When a thing truly has happened it is history. When a thing really really was made by someone, it cannot *not* have been made! Even the smallest boy or girl can understand this if he or she truly did make a toy house, that is true, not just because he or she is *saying* so; it is true because it *happened.*

The reason people think that things that *were* made were *not* made, is because they do not know, or they do not believe, that the person who made them really exists. That means they do not believe there is any such person.

You see, the *truth* is that God has always lived. There was never a time when he was not alive. The order of things has never changed. First, there was in someone's *mind* everything we now see. God is one God, but God is, and has always been, three Persons. These three Persons are God the Father, God the Son, and God the Holy Spirit. God is infinite. That means God is able to be in every place at one time. We can only be in one place at a time, and we call that being finite. It is hard to be finite when you want to be in two places at once, but you can't change that thing about yourself. You can't be swimming in the sea and walking in the woods at the same time. You can't be in London and in New York at the same time. God is infinite and he *can* be everywhere at once and can also *do* everything he wants to do at one time.

But God is personal too. God can think and act and feel. God can communicate and love. God can think of many, many ideas, and choose, and make things. God is the

Creator. That means he creates things that he thought of first.
We know from the Bible that God made all things. God
created the things that man *cannot* make. God made the
complicated things like the sun and the moon, the stars and
the seas, the trees and the grass, the birds and the animals.
God made man and woman in his own image . . . that means
that God made us so that we could think and act and feel.
God made us so that we could communicate with each other
by talking and writing, singing and painting. God made us so
that we could have lots of ideas and then *choose* what we
would make so that other people could *see* our ideas.

» *God has always lived.* You see, that explains everything, because now we understand how we think and then choose and
then make things, and we know that God also thought and
chose and made things. Of course, he can do anything. We
are "limited"; there are lots of things we cannot do. We cannot make anything that will be like the flowers and have seeds
that will grow more flowers. We cannot make transistor radios
that will have seeds to make baby transistors. We cannot
make airplanes that will have seeds to make little airplanes. There are so many things that *only* God can make.
People who do not believe that there is a God, do not have
any idea how so many complicated things came out of little
particles . . . but they try to think up ways in which this took
place only by "chance." We *can* know how things were made
that we cannot make, that no man can make because we
know God has made them.

 "But I thought this book was going to tell us what Luke
wrote about Jesus." Yes. We are going to tell you what Luke
wrote, but it is very important that before we talk about Jesus
being *born*, we understand that Jesus was the second Person
of the Trinity (remember that we said God is one God but
three Persons) and that he has always lived. It is important
that we know that Jesus created things long before any of us
lived, long before any man lived. It is important that we know
that God created man, that is, that God made *people* in the

first place. Otherwise, we can't understand about God and
the universe, and we can't understand people . . . and since
we are people, too, we can't understand ourselves.

The coming of God's Son Jesus into the world was the
most important thing that has ever happened since God made
the universe. Because it was so important, God made many
preparations for the coming of Jesus. Among other preparations, God at this time had the civilized world ruled by just
one nation, the Romans, and all the educated people who
lived over a very big portion of the world speaking one language, Greek. There were many other preparations, too.

Long ago, before there were any nations or even cities
or villages, Adam and Eve, who were the first people created
by God, sinned. You see, when God made man with the
ability to choose what to *make* (out of all the ideas he had),
man could choose also whether to *believe, love and obey*
God. Think again in your head as you did a little while ago.
But this time, don't think of things you see, or things you
could make, think about whether you *believed* what Mother
said when she told you, "Don't touch the stove; it's hot." Did
you ever say to yourself, "I don't think it is true. I don't think
the stove is hot. Mother is just saying that, but it isn't true"?
And did you ever go and touch the stove and get burned?
That was your *choice*. You chose *not* to believe what Mother
said, and you did something she told you not to do. You had
the choice *not* to touch the stove and not to get hurt, or *not*
to believe Mother and to touch the stove and get burned.

The first man Adam and the first woman Eve were people, just as we are people. They could think and act and feel.
They could love each other and love God. They could communicate. They had ideas in their heads and could choose to
make something. And they could choose to do or not to do
things. They could choose to believe what God told them, or
not to believe it. They were *not* like a doll that you wind up
and that *has* to say what it is made to say. They were not like
the computers that maybe you or your father or brother have
in his place of business, which work because cards are put in
to program them in a certain way. Adam and Eve were not

machines wound up or "programmed" like computers. Adam and Eve were *people*. We can understand that because we are people, too.

God had told Adam and Eve that if they ate of the fruit of a certain tree, they would surely die. The Old Testament tells us all about this, and some day in another book we can find out all we need to about the history of that time. Right now, however, we need to know that Satan, who used to be a beautiful angel and who started to fight against God, wanted to make Adam and Eve fight against God, too. Satan had been put out of the place where he used to be close to God, and he hated God, and wanted to spoil Adam and Eve's friendship with God, so Satan made himself like a snake, and came to Eve and talked to her.

What Satan said was this: "Did God tell you not to eat of the fruit of that tree, or you would die?" And then later he said, "Oh, you won't die, Eve! You will become very, very wise, you will know as much as God and be like God, if only you eat." It was just as if one child came up to another and said, "Oh, you won't be burned if you touch the stove! You'll learn to cook as well as your Mother if only you touch it!" What happened to Eve was that she chose to believe Satan rather than God. So she ate the fruit. And when Eve said to Adam, "You eat, too," he chose to do what Eve told him to do, rather than to do what God had said, and he ate the fruit as well. This was sin. Sin is *not* believing that God is truthful and good and wise and perfect in his love. Sin is choosing to disobey God and to rebel against him. We all know what it means to be a rebel. Someone says, "No, I won't," after he or she has been asked to do something by Mother or a teacher . . . this is rebelling against what they have asked. Adam and Eve rebelled against God. Adam and Eve sinned.

God had said the result would be death. Mother said the result of touching the stove would be being burned. There is a *result* when we do something. God said Adam and Eve and all their children would be separated from God because of sin. But, before a single day was finished (and some day we want to be able to tell you more about what happened at that time), God gave Adam and Eve a promise. God gave them something to look forward to. God said, "Some day someone is going to be born of a woman who will have a victory over Satan." In the Bible the promise is like this: "The seed of the woman shall bruise the head of the serpent." It means that a promise was given that, although Satan had separated man and woman from God, God would give them a way of coming back to him. That *way* of coming back was going to be a very, very important thing in history. It was something that would have a *before* and a *during* and an *after.* There were very many of the *before* years that the Old Testament tells us about.

The New Testament tells us about what happened *during* the time of the coming of the person God had promised would be born of a woman. Luke is one book of the New Testament, and Luke tells us what happened when the right moment in history came, and the person was to be born. Then Luke tells us about this person's lifetime and death. The person is the Second Person of the Trinity. (Trinity just means the three persons in the One God.) Jesus, the Son of God, was to be the Person to have a victory over Satan's horrible work of separating people from God. Jesus was going to take the punishment himself, so that men and women, boys and girls, *people* could be forgiven their sin.

When God made this promise to Adam and Eve, God began preparing the way for the Messiah, or the Savior, to come. This preparation took very many years. God chose the Jews to be the race from which Jesus would be born. God chose the family of David to be the family from which the Messiah would be born. These preparations are written about in the Old Testament of the Bible.

We are ready to start the book of Luke now, and we find that Luke tells us that the things he is going to write about are things many people saw with their own eyes. Luke tells us that he is writing so we can know what took place. He is making it possible for us to be *certain* of what the *truth* is. He is telling us *history.*

2
EXCITED ABOUT GOD

Reading books out loud together is fun, because we are all thinking about the same things together, and later we can talk about them and discuss them. It is a "together thing," instead of everyone "doing their own thing" and never knowing what anyone else's thoughts or questions are. However, as we read together as a family, or friends, it is important to know that there are different kinds of books. We need to remember that there are fairy stories that are fun, like *Alice in Wonderland* or *The Borrowers* (who are tiny little people no bigger than your thumb), and *Peter Rabbit*. We know that these stories did not really happen. They are about pretend people and animals and things, which the author wrote about because he or she had an imagination that could think up fun things to share with other people. Then there are stories which could have happened, but didn't, stories about people like ourselves, which the person writing just "made up." Then there are history books and biographies, which are stories of people who truly lived, and events which really happened.

The Bible is different. Why? Well, people who write have to write from what they have studied, or have seen or heard or experienced, during the short years they have lived. The Bible was written by men who were told things by God which happened before they lived—and some things that happened before anyone lived. The Bible was written also by men who told what they lived through . . . but they were kept from making mistakes in reporting, because God made things clear to them. The Bible was also written about things that were going to happen in the future, and only God could tell men what to write about the future.

You see, God is a Person. We have already learned that

God is one God, but three Persons. He has made us as persons, too. When a person wants another person to know something, he usually tells that person in words. Words are the way we can tell people that it rained last week, or that it is very hot in the sun today, or that next week there is going to be a parade with men playing drums. It is not surprising, is it, that since there are such important things that men need to know, things only God knows, and that since God is fair and just, he has made certain that these things have been written into a book? Human beings can say things in words to each other . . . that is what makes them different from animals, trees, machines, tables and chairs! That is what we are talking about when we say that a person can communicate. God is a Personal God and he communicates (talks in words) with us in the Bible, as well as communicating with us through the beautiful things he has made for us to hear, like the song of the birds, and to see, like the sunset.

Luke, who was a doctor, a physician, who cared for sick people, wrote this book, called The Gospel according to Luke, to tell us things from a doctor's viewpoint, so that we might know of a certainty—that is, be absolutely *sure*—of the things that happened during that period of time. There are four books written about that period: Matthew, Mark, Luke and John. God had four men to write so that each told the same history from a slightly different viewpoint. Each book is accurate. Each book is true history. God did not let mistakes be made, but God did not treat the men like typewriters. They wrote as real men. God always treats human beings as *persons*, as personalities, as important. When God asks us to do things, he is careful to allow us to do things as *people* who are not all the *same*. This is something exciting to know. When you become a child of God, his plan for you will be different from his plan for anyone else. God has made no two things, no two people, no two snowflakes even, exactly alike.

As a doctor, Luke tells us very carefully about the birth of the man who was to prepare the way for Jesus, as well as telling us about the birth of Jesus himself. A doctor is interested in unusual births.

In those days the Jews worshiped God in a Temple in Jerusalem. Today each of us can worship God at any time and at any place, but before Jesus came and died, men had to come to worship God through men who were called priests. One of these priests was named Zacharias. Zacharias was married to Elizabeth, and they were both very old, but they had never had a baby. They had wanted a baby very much, and Zacharias had been praying for one.

One day Zacharias was in the Temple burning incense, when suddenly there was an angel standing on the right side of the altar. Zacharias was very afraid. He was a person just like us, and seeing an angel frightened him as it would have frightened us. But the angel said, "Don't be afraid. I have come to tell you that your prayer is going to be answered."

Now as Zacharias and Elizabeth were so old, they really no longer expected that their prayer for a baby would be answered. They knew that people did not have babies when they were as old as they were. Even though Zacharias knew the Old Testament, and knew that God had given Abraham and Sarah a baby in their old age, he doubted what the angel said. Zacharias listened with his ears to the promises the angel was making, telling him how happy he and Elizabeth would be when the baby was born, but he did not really believe these promises. He did not get excited by thinking that "nothing is impossible to God." Instead of getting excited and saying, "Oh, great!" Zacharias asked for some sort of a sign, to prove to him that the angel was telling him the truth. But as God had sent an *angel* to stand beside him, I think he had already had sign enough, don't you?

However, now that he had asked for a sign, the angel told him that his name was Gabriel, a very wonderful angel whom we shall see one day, and then Gabriel said he *would* give him a sign. The angel said, "Zacharias, you are not going to be able to speak a single word from now until the time the baby is born, because you did not believe me." When God tells us something, we should believe it.

The angel had told Zacharias not only that they would have a baby, but that it was going to be a boy. Parents don't know until the day a baby is born whether it is going to be a boy or girl, but the angel told Zacharias not only that this baby was to be a boy, but that he should be named John. Then the angel said that this child was going to be wonderfully used by the Lord in preparing the way for the Second Person of the Trinity, the Lord Jesus Christ.

John was to be born just before Jesus, and was to grow into the man who would be used by God to prepare the way for his Son. No wonder Zacharias was made dumb as a sign, when he doubted the message God had given him through the angel. This was an announcement to Zacharias that it was time for the fantastic moment in history that all the priests through the centuries had been waiting for. Zacharias not only had been sent a special angel to tell him in *person*, but had been given the privilege of having his little baby boy be the one to do a very *special* thing. People so *often* miss the chance to be excited about what God tells them is coming. People so often don't take the chance to say, "Oh, thank you, God, how wonderful you are to me," *before* it happens.

Well, in the meantime, all the people praying outside the Temple were wondering, "Why doesn't Zacharias come out? He has been in there much longer than usual." Finally Zacharias came out. But he couldn't speak a *word* to them! All he could do was to make signs with his hands, or write if he wanted to say anything. After Zacharias finished his work in the Temple, he went home. Don't you suppose his wife was surprised when she found he could not talk to her? But how happy she must have been when he gave her the message from the angel by writing it out for her.

» Now when Zacharias' wife Elizabeth had been pregnant for six months, the angel Gabriel was sent by God to a city in Galilee, called Nazareth. This time Gabriel was sent to talk to a young girl who was not married, but who was engaged to a man named Joseph. The girl's name was Mary, and she was a virgin, waiting for the time when she would be married to Joseph. The first thing Gabriel said to her was, "Hail (or Hello). You are very much to be honored, Mary. The Lord is with you and he is going to bless you in a very special way among all women." When Mary saw Gabriel, and heard what he said, she was a little upset and worried, wondering what he meant by these words. The angel realized that she was worried, and said, "Don't be afraid, Mary. God is very pleased with you. He has chosen you for a special task. You will have a baby start growing inside you, who will be a boy, and his name will be Jesus. He will be the Son of God, and one day he will be King over the house of Jacob, and there will never be any end to his kingdom."

What a startling and amazing thing for Mary to hear! She was just a young Jewish girl who did believe God, but she was no different from other believing girls. She had not talked to an angel before, and although she knew the Messiah would be born of a woman, she didn't expect that to happen to her—any more than people who believe the Bible today *really* expect Jesus to come back again today! (We'll say more about this later in the book.) Mary was full of surprise and questions! "How can this happen?" she asked. She never had heard of a baby being born without a human father. "I'm not married, how can I have a baby when I have not ever been with a man?" was her question.

Remember we talked about God being three Persons? Jesus has always lived. Jesus had no beginning. Jesus had had many ideas and had created many things after he had chosen to do so. Jesus had talked to the Father, and had loved the Father and the Holy Spirit. Jesus had said with the other Persons of the Trinity, "Let us make man in our image." But now Jesus was going to do something which the Trinity had decided was the *only* way to open a door for people to come to God, and no longer to be separated from God. Jesus was going to leave heaven and all the glorious life there, and to be born as a little baby and to live among men. The only way you can have any little idea of what it would be like, is to imagine someone in the loveliest country you can imagine, such as Switzerland with its glorious mountains and lakes, or Hawaii with its lovely pineapple trees, palm trees, mountains and seashores. Imagine sunsets, and wonderful houses,

beautiful music and kindness, understanding and love. Imagine someone always living in beauty and peace with lovely
sounds, smells, and sights . . . with true understanding and
love and no one being mean. Then imagine that, after always
living in that kind of a place with wonderful people . . . that
person going to an ugly, spoiled place, with horrible smells,
sights and sounds, with people being violent, mean, selfish,
screaming bad words and throwing mud and stones at each
other, and killing each other. Imagine a person saying, "Yes, I
will be willing to go to that ugly place, and live with those
cruel, horrible people, because that is the only way they will
have any way to get out of all their spoiledness."

This gives us just a tiny idea of what it must have meant
to Jesus to leave heaven and to be born and live on this earth.
Mary, as a girl who loved the Lord, but who knew she was the
same as other girls, and had not always done what she knew
to be right, would have been amazed at what she heard the
angel say, as well as afraid. She would have known the Old
Testament promises, like Isaiah 7:14 ("A virgin shall conceive
and bear a son!") and Micah 5:2 (about a "ruler in Israel"
coming from Bethlehem) which were written very many years
before she was born. All the Jewish women who loved the
Lord had hoped they might be the mother of the Messiah,
and now Gabriel was telling her that she had been chosen by
God to be the one.

Did God *make* Mary be the one to be the mother of
the Messiah? No, he treated her as a person with choice.
When Mary asked questions, Gabriel answered her, and he explained carefully to her that a miracle would take place inside
her body, and the Holy Spirit would cause the seed to develop into a baby who would be called the Son of God. Gabriel
also told her about Elizabeth, who was Mary's cousin. The
angel said, "You see, Mary, Elizabeth who was old, too old to
have a baby, is now six months pregnant." Everyone said
Elizabeth could never have a child, but in three months more
her son John was to be born. It was kind of Gabriel, who
spoke with the kindness God had given him, to point out
to Mary that God is able to do anything. Gabriel was really

saying, "Of course, you find it hard to understand, Mary, but although it has never happened before, and never will again, you are to have as your son the Son of God, and to make it a little easier to believe that God is able to do anything, I will tell you of the miracle of Elizabeth and Zacharias having a baby in their old age."

Mary did not ask for a sign. Mary did not doubt. When the angel said, "With God nothing shall be impossible," Mary said, "Behold the handmaid of the Lord; be it unto me according to thy word." That is, Mary said, "I am ready for the Lord to use me for his plan. I trust the Lord's plan that you have told me about." It was a very believing and sweet answer. Mary did not say, "Everyone will think wrong things about me, I don't want to take a risk. " Mary did not say, "I don't believe you." She believed, and said, "Yes" to what God asked her to do. Then the angel went away.

If you were Mary, what would you have wanted to do first after that? Probably just what she did. Mary wanted to talk to someone about it, and as her cousin Elizabeth was having a baby in her old age, and she, Mary, was having a baby in a miraculous way, Elizabeth was the one she wanted to talk to. Gabriel had talked to Zacharias, too, so she knew Elizabeth wouldn't say, "Pooh, an angel! I don't believe it!" She knew Elizabeth and Zacharias had been especially prepared to believe her amazing story. We are told that Mary went up into the hill country in haste. She hurried to get there as quickly as she could, and she went straight into the house of Zacharias and greeted them. I am sure she was wondering just how to tell them her fantastic news, when she had a surprise. She didn't get a chance to tell her news first because something very special happened.

God who made people in the first place, made them so that women could be mothers, and so a marvelous place was made inside each woman, in which tiny babies can grow from cells into real persons. Now on this day two very special women God had chosen to be mothers of two boys met. One old woman whose first baby was now big enough inside her to be kicking and moving, getting closer to the time of being

big enough to be born and eat and breathe outside of her
body. One very young girl who had a baby beginning to grow
inside her, who was to be unique. People sometimes use the
word "unique" to mean just something special, but it should
really be used to mean the only one of a kind. Never before,
and never again, would a young girl, a young woman, have
the Second Person of the Trinity growing into a baby inside of
her. But it was *truly* happening. Stupid, isn't it, to say you
don't believe a thing could *be* just because it is unique? *Some*
people say, "I don't believe Jesus is God. I don't believe the
Second Person of the Trinity ever became a real man by being
born as a real baby boy." And the weird thing is that they say
they don't believe it happened because no one is ever born
without a human father. Of course no one else has been born
without a human father. God made people to be born by two
cells coming together . . . the father is as important as the
mother when a new human being comes into existence.

But this baby is *unique*. This baby is not an ordinary
baby because he is the Son of God. This One had always lived
for ever and ever. *All* human beings had been made in *his*
image . . . to be able to think and act and feel . . . to have
ideas and choose and create . . . to talk with words to each
other. Why then is the Second Person of the Trinity coming to
be born of a woman, to live in a poor little home and to be a
carpenter? We will find out more of the "why" later, but just
now let us think of the fact that he is doing it to help us, to
save us from something terrible. He is doing it because there
is no other way to save us.

So, here are these two women standing facing each
other. They are very ordinary people, just like you and me.
But they have been chosen to do a thing that is most important in history. Don't you think they needed help not to
be afraid? Who needed the most help to be assured that she
had not been dreaming, to be assured that everything was all
right? Mary needed special assurance. And God gave it to her.
She was all ready to tell Elizabeth her news when this special
thing happened. Elizabeth felt the baby in her jump. The Bible
says he "leaped." It would seem it was a special jump that

was different from the way he had moved before. At the same time God the Holy Spirit (remember there is God the Father, God the Son and God the Holy Spirit: three Persons) told Elizabeth what was happening to Mary. So you see it was Elizabeth who spoke next, and she said, "How can it be that the mother of my Lord should come to visit me? As soon as I heard your greeting, Mary, as soon as that salutation was heard in my ears . . . the baby inside me leaped for joy. Oh, Mary, blessed are you because you *believed* what the angel told you. The things that have been told you really *are* going to take place." And as Mary and Elizabeth stood looking at each other, they both were thrilled with the wonder of the *truth* of what was happening, and *excited* about how marvelous God is.

Mary spoke next, and it was like a song, like a piece of poetry. But she wasn't just trying to say something that would sound beautiful; she was spilling out things that were in her mind and heart. It all just *bubbled* out, like a teakettle that is too full, boiling water out over the stove. Mary was putting into words something of the excitement she was *feeling*, and something of the *understanding* she had in her *mind*, of the greatness of God. What she said is in Luke 1:46–55. She really understood and appreciated that God had chosen her to have this baby grow in her for nine months, and then be born the Son of God . . . the Savior, the promised Messiah. Instead of thinking of all the hard things it would mean, instead of thinking of how people would not believe her story, would not accept the baby as God the Second Person, the Savior, instead of thinking of people being mean and nasty to her, and to the Son of God as he lived in her home . . . she just bubbled over with the appreciation of the stupendous thing that was taking place in history—and *her* body.

You know, I love what Mary said because she worships and praises God with such understanding and excitement. But I also love what she said because she doesn't say, "Oh, it's nothing," when she talks about having been chosen to be the one to be the mother of the Messiah. She doesn't put on an act . . . she is so *real* and *true* in her reaction. I don't like it when people aren't excited about what God does for them or through them, or in them. It doesn't seem appreciative or honest. Mary really was honest. She said things that showed she was thrilled that God had chosen someone of such a humble family as hers and that for ever, throughout all the generations of people to come, people would know how God had blessed her, because he had done such a great thing in her. But she goes on to say how great God has shown himself to be in history, and how he has "put down" the proud people, as well as "putting up" the lowly people. She tells of how he has fed the poor, hungry ones, and sent the rich, arrogant kind of people away empty. She tells of how he talked face to face with Abraham centuries before.

Why would she talk about Abraham? Well, what was taking place in her was the *keeping* of the promise to Abraham. God had promised Abraham that from his "seed" (that means from people born to him as children, grandchildren, great-grandchildren, great-great-grandchildren, etc.) the nations of the earth would be blessed. A promise was made to Adam and Eve, remember? A promise that the seed of a woman, someone born of a woman, would defeat (have a victory over) Satan who had separated Adam and Eve from God. A promise was made to Abraham that this One, who would have a victory over Satan and make it possible for God and man not to be separated, would be born from his family . . . somewhere in history. A great-great-great-grandchild would one day be the mother of the Messiah. Mary appreciates that the promise to Abraham is now being fulfilled in her. And Mary declares in her song that you can really trust God to keep all his promises. Mary knows it is all true.

So here are two women being really excited about God and his promises, and sharing their believing and excitement, talking to each other in words that could be understood by anyone listening, that can even be understood by us today. One had a little baby boy jumping around in her, who was to be John, the promised man who was to tell people things to prepare them for listening to Jesus. The other woman had the tiny growing baby in her, who was to be the unique Messiah.

What a fantastic moment in all history! Yet, their conversation was not religious sort of gobble-de-gook that no one could understand: their conversation was in words that could be understood, and about things that God had done that could be understood. This is important to remember, even if you who are five or ten or fifteen years old don't *think* it sounds important, even if you who are fifty-five have never thought about it before.

While you are eating your breakfast together, or having tea together, or walking down a mountain path together, or even just now while you are reading together, you ought to talk about how wonderful it is that God had Luke, a doctor, tell us these things so accurately in order that we could understand. You ought to talk about how marvelous it is that God communicated with people (that means he put into words things he wanted people to be sure to understand)— and how exciting it is that we are a part of this history, too. We fit in, you see. It isn't something that has nothing to do with us. It is *our* history, just as much as Abraham's time was Mary's history.

» Mary stayed in Elizabeth's and Zacharias's house for about three months, we are told, so they had a long time to help each other and talk together. When Elizabeth's baby was born, all the neighbors and relatives came to rejoice with Zacharias and Elizabeth and to look at the baby. I'm sure some sighed and said, "Well, it *was* true wasn't it? It didn't seem possible that old Elizabeth was going to have a boy, but there he is. Isn't he cute? Just listen to him cry!" Some of them said, "Look at little baby Zacharias." We are told they called him that. You see, in those days the first baby boy was always called by the same name as his father. But Elizabeth shook her head. "Not so!" she said, "He is going to be called John!" Then all the cousins argued with her. "There's nobody in our family called John. You can't call him John," they must have said. Then they looked at Zacharias to see what he would say. Well, he couldn't say anything, because for all these long months he had not been able to talk. But he mo-

tioned for a table and something to write on, and he wrote
. . . "His name is John." All the cousins and neighbors were
really surprised at that. We are told they marveled. Can't you
just see their eyebrows going up, and their mouths making
tisking noises, and their heads shaking?

But the next thing surprised them even more because,
as soon as Zacharias had written what he did, he was able to
speak. The promise the angel had made was perfectly kept.
He had had his sign, and now that the baby was born and that
he named him John, as he had been told by the angel to, he
could speak! His voice was heard for the first time in over
nine months. What did he say? Well, he, like Mary, praised
God. The way he praised God was to review some of the
history which made this moment so important. You can read
what he said in Luke 1:68–79. He went over things he knew
from the Old Testament. As a Jewish priest he knew these
things very well, and he believed them to be true. Now he is
saying that the moment has arrived for the Messiah to come.
That is what he means when he says that God has "visited and
redeemed his people."

Zacharias believed what Mary had told him during those
three months as she went over what Gabriel told her. And
together they have understood that the long-waited-for time
in history has come. Now Zacharias is telling his relatives and
neighbors that Baby John is going to grow up to be the one to
prepare people to recognize who Jesus is. He puts it in a very
wonderful way, when he says that John will introduce the
One who will give light to those who sit in darkness. John
was to tell everyone who would listen to him about the Christ
who was coming. Many of the Jews believed him, and so,
when Christ was ready to preach and teach, many were prepared by John to listen.

There is a verse we might all learn together from the
book of John 1:6, 7: "There came a man from God whose
name was John. The same came for a witness, to bear witness
of the Light, that all through him might believe."

Let's turn out all the lights in this room. Or if it is daytime, try in some way to make the room dark. Here we are,

sitting in the darkness. We can't really "see" anything with our eyes open. But now, if you have a candle, light it. That helps a lot, doesn't it? Now if you have other little candles, light them; that makes it even easier to see.

God speaks to us of "light" and "dark" to help us to understand that we can make such terrible mistakes about what the world is, what the universe is, who we are ourselves, whether there is any life after we die, whether there is a place called heaven. We can make such terrible mistakes about whether God made the world or whether it came by chance. We can make such terrible mistakes about all of us just being a collection of molecules or bits of particles, and not really true people at all. We can make such terrible mistakes about whom to believe, and just believe lies instead of the truth. God tells us that believing lies and making such mistakes about life is like sitting in dark darkness, darker than we can possibly make this room. Then he says that because men are in such dark darkness, one of the three Persons, God the Son, came to be born as a baby, and grew up to teach and live so that men would have light to see and understand what a mistake they have made.

John did not talk about himself. He even called himself "a voice crying in the wilderness"! Constantly he told men what terrible mistakes they had made, and what sinners they were in their rebellion against what is *true*, and against God who really exists. John told men that a Savior was coming to save them from the results of all this sin and rebellion. John told men that a "light" was coming to lighten their darkness, and to guide their feet into the true path. John told men the *truth*. At the end of chapter one in Luke, however, we are simply told that John started to grow strong as a little boy, and that as he grew older he went into the desert to wait until it was time for him to start speaking.

All this happened about two thousand years ago. Now it is history. But it is important to us because it is true history. You are a person. I am a person. We are people who have been born into the world, and we are alive today in this time of history. We need to know how we "fit in." We need to know about the past, and we need to know about what is coming in the future, but we need to know what we are meant to do right now. We'll find out more as we go on. But . . . one thing we are meant to do is to give *light* to others sitting in darkness.

Let's make it dark again. If we could each have a candle, we would have a tiny idea of what it is like to light first one, then two, then three, then four, then five candles. We need to be sure we are not making more darkness in the world. We need to be sure what we are saying is *true truth*. We need to *know* the Person who is "light." And we need to tell other people during the time we are alive that Jesus, who is the light, *did* come, and *is* coming again. We need to *understand* as Mary understood, and *believe* as Mary believed, that these things are *true*.

Eve believed Satan's lie was true, so she ate the fruit and was separated from God. Mary believed what Gabriel told her to be true, so she said "Yes," she would do what God was asking her to do, so that people could come back to God. What are *we* supposed to believe and do? We are to believe that what God has had Dr. Luke write for us to read and think about is *true*. Then we are to come into God's family and sit in the light all the time. That is, when we are born into God's family by believing what he tells us in the Bible about himself, and by accepting what Jesus came to do for us, we are children of light. We are supposed to get our ideas and our understanding from *him* so we will not have fuzzy, dark, foggy ideas, but *truth*.

3
A STABLE FOR A LAMB

All through the years and centuries God had been making it very clear that there was no way of coming to him in worship except by coming with a little lamb. And as men brought a lamb, they were to realize that the lamb was picturing a *person* who would one day come to die for their sins.

You remember that Adam and Eve had sinned by believing that Satan's lie was truth, and by believing that God had told them a lie. Now as men had to wait for many years for the promise of a Person to come to take away their sins, a Person to be born of a woman, they needed something to remind them of this. Cain and Abel were Adam and Eve's boys. Abel believed God was speaking truth when he brought a little lamb, as he came to worship God, and put it on a pile of stones . . . an altar. Cain did not believe it mattered at all whether he did what God had explained to his parents. Cain brought a lot of fruit like apples, bananas, pineapple, grapes, and vegetables like peas and artichokes, beans and celery. They made a pretty arrangement on his pile of stones. He thought God should accept his gifts and his worship. But you see, the pretty pile of sweet-smelling fruits and vegetables was *not* what God had told him to bring. In fact God had not said to bring a gift: what he had said was to bring a lamb, which would remind people to *expect* his promise to come true. The lambs that were brought by believing people through the years were a way of saying to God, "I believe that I cannot do anything good to get rid of my sins. I know *gifts* to you cannot pay for my sins to be forgiven. I know someone has to take my place, to take my punishment, like this lamb."

Noah knew about the lamb, and worshiped in this way.

Abraham understood very clearly, as he brought a lamb, that one day the Person who would be our substitute (that means the one to take our place, or our punishment) would do that on a mountain outside Jerusalem. Moses explained clearly the importance of the lamb in saving people from death. Isaiah, in the 53rd chapter, makes it absolutely clear, seven hundred years before Jesus was born, that the coming Messiah was to be "the Lamb of God." Yes, it was well understood that the One coming was to be The Lamb. For many years this had been made clear.

Other things were prophesied years ahead of time. In Isaiah 7:14, men had read for years and years that the "sign" that the Messiah had come would be that a virgin should conceive and bear a son, and call his name Immanuel. And in Micah 5:2 men had read for many years that this Messiah would come from tiny Bethlehem, a village not counted important in Judah. Micah wrote that the one who would come from Bethlehem had existed "from everlasting." No one has existed "for ever and ever" or "from everlasting" except the Triune God: Father, Son and Holy Spirit.

Yes, we know you are waiting to hear what happened next in Luke's account, but whether you are just five, or fifteen, or thirty-five or fifty, you need to know that for centuries God had been preparing people to *recognize* the Messiah, the Son of God, the Second Person of the Trinity when he did come. You need to understand this because it is true, because it is exciting, and because *it matters to you.*

Mary lived in the northern part of Palestine, but at the time the baby was to be born the Lord brought her in a wonderful way to Bethlehem, where so many years before God had said the Messiah should be born. How? Caesar, the Roman ruler, had said that everyone had to go to pay taxes at the city from which their family had originally come. Joseph originally came from the city of David, which is Bethlehem, so he had to go there to pay his taxes. And so it happened that

---

Mary pregnant with Jesus. Luke 2:5

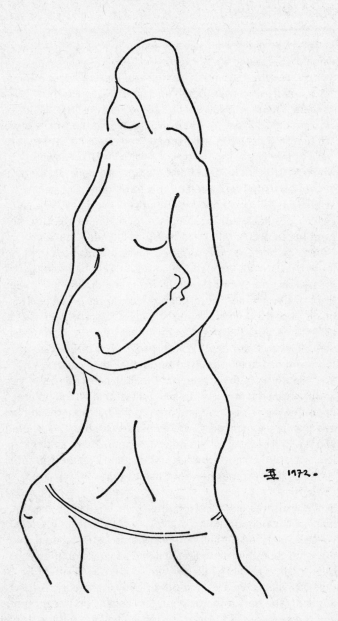

Mary and Joseph went to Bethlehem, so close to the time
when the baby was to be born.

When they arrived in Bethlehem, there was not a single
place left at any inn (or hotel) and no one opened their home
to them. The only place they found to stay was in a stable,
where animals live. The smells would be like the smells of any
stable, not fresh clean smells; and there were no lovely, soft
carpets, nor any beds. Jesus had always lived in heaven,
which is far more beautiful and glorious than any palace or
garden on earth, yet he left all this to be born in a smelly
stable. But do you know something very special? Although a
stable does not seem a good place for a king to be born, or
even for an ordinary baby to be born, let alone the Son of
God to be born, yet it is a *perfect* place for a *lamb* to be
born. You see, all through the centuries God had said the
Messiah would be born in Bethlehem, and that he would be
born of a virgin, and all through the centuries it had been
made clear that he would be *the lamb*. God made every detail
perfect, because he is perfect in all that he does. God made it
very clear, so that people could *recognize* that this was the
One who had been promised through all the years.

So it was in the stable that the little baby was born.
Mary wrapped him in swaddling clothes (that is, long pieces
of cloth wrapped around and around the baby), and laid him
in a manger. A manger is where animals eat, but also where
you could easily put a little newborn lamb. There among
lambs, the little baby gave his first cry, and breathed air into
his lungs just as other newborn babies do.

» While Jesus was being born in the stable and laid in the
manger, a wonderful thing was taking place out on the hills
which are around Bethlehem. Shepherds were gathered together around their little fires, talking as they would on any
other night. On these hills away from the city all would be
quiet. The stars would stand out brightly in the dark sky.
Suddenly the darkness was gone—an angel stood near them,
and the glory of God made a bright light all around them, and
they were afraid. In the midst of this, the angel spoke to them

30

in words they could understand. God did not want them to be afraid; he had something wonderful to tell them. The angel said to them, "Fear not: for behold, I bring you good tidings of great joy, which shall be to all people. For unto you is born this day in the city of David a Savior, which is Christ the Lord. And this shall be a sign unto you; you shall find the babe wrapped in swaddling clothes, lying in a manger."

Can you imagine that the most wonderful message that has ever been given at any time in history, or in any part of the world, came to these shepherds sitting in their rough robes around little fires, on the rough ground of the very ordinary hills above Bethlehem? Don't you suppose they were excited? They could hardly believe it, but they would no longer be afraid, they would be full of amazement that the promises of the Old Testament were being fulfilled right then. You see, they were Jews, and they would have known what was written in Isaiah and Micah. They would have known many of the promises about the Messiah. Can't you imagine them hitting each other on the backs, and saying, "Oh, wow, imagine that we have been chosen by God to be told these things! What a night it is, isn't it? It is the night the promised Messiah has been born."

And while they were reacting to the angel's message, something else took place, for they had not yet seen all that God was going to show them. Suddenly many angels were all around them . . . Luke calls them a "multitude." The Light must have been brighter than ever, and the words were a song such as had never been sung before, because it was a song sung by excited angels praising God for the Savior's birth, at the moment in history when he was *being* born. It is one thing to look forward to something for a long time, *expecting* that something, and knowing it will come. But it is another thing to be able to say, "This is it!" This was a song sung by angels who were thrilled that the Savior had come to open the way for men to come back to God. "Glory to God in the highest, and on earth peace to men of good will." After the angels had gone back into the heavens, the stars were the only lights left in the dark sky, and the shepherds must have looked up to where all the glory had been, blinking their eyes, wondering if it could have been real. But they showed they *did* believe it had been real, and that they believed what the angel had told them.

How did they show this? By doing something they would not have done if they had not had the message. Some people do *nothing* when they get a message. That is because they don't believe it is true, or they are too lazy to do anything about it, or they can't be bothered to find out if it is important, or they feel it will make no difference to them, no matter what they do. Lots of people are like that today. Lots of people sit in a field, or on a hill, or in a room, and just stare . . . not even at the stars, perhaps: they just stare, and try to see things in their own minds, and don't really listen to any message from the outside. If God sent an angel to some people like this, they wouldn't do anything except stare straight ahead, and perhaps be rude to the angel. God sent the message to humble, poor, working shepherds who were ready to believe and to do something about what was told them.

What did the shepherds do? They made some arrangement for their sheep, I am sure. They said to each other, "Let's go down to Bethlehem now, and see this thing which God has just told us about, through that angel." We are told by Doctor Luke that they hurried. Probably they walked very rapidly . . . jog, jog, jog down the hill, with the smaller boys perhaps having to run and jump down rocks to keep up. While they hurried they must have talked; each one would tell some detail he remembered from the Old Testament. Maybe one of them knew the verse in Micah and recited it to the others.

Anyway, they hurried to the stable and there they found Joseph and Mary and the baby. They knew it was the One the angel had told them about because, sure enough, he was wrapped in swaddling clothes and lying in a manger, just as the angel had told them he would be. You see, the "signs" that God gives to reassure people are *clear*. These signs given to the shepherds are meant to make it clear to us, too. We can read the Old Testament, and we can then read the New Testament, and we can know that the prophecies and promises came true exactly as they had been prophesied and promised hundreds of years before. Then all *that* is meant to help us to believe what God tells us about the things we are meant to be doing *now*, and about the future, because God has told us very much more about what is still to happen.

Once, a little boy said with a big sigh, "Oh dear, when I grow up there will be nothing left to discover. Everyone has gotten ahead of me." But this is nothing you need to worry about. You see, there are so many things left to discover about what God has made already in this universe. There are many things to discover about the things we have seen or heard about already. But God tells us that eyes have not seen, nor ears heard, nor can anyone imagine in their minds the absolute *wonder* of the things God is preparing for us in the future. God says they are so much more glorious and marvelous than anything we have yet seen, that we can't even imagine them. No words we understand could describe them. So don't worry about everything having already been discovered. If you believe in God, and act on what he tells you, there is so much that is exciting ahead that you can say to yourself, "I haven't seen anything yet to compare with what God is preparing right now!" God is a fantastic artist, scientist, architect, landscape gardener. He is a wonderful Father to have. He is the Creator of all things. And he *keeps* his promises.

Can you imagine the shepherds standing there together, looking down at that tiny baby. Have you ever seen a newborn baby? It's a wonderful sight . . . to see such tiny hands and feet, and little nose, eyes all screwed up shut tight, or open but not focusing, not able to see much yet. Do you suppose these men felt a little disappointed that this baby looked just like other newborn babies? He didn't have a bright light around him, he looked just like any baby. He had left his glory behind in Heaven. There was nothing about him to make people kneel and worship, unless they had believed what they had been *told*. These men believed the angel, and they believed the Old Testament, and they must have looked down with awe and great wonder, knowing that this was the Person for whom believers had waited thousands of years, the One who would take away the sins of those who believed on Him.

》 After the shepherds had looked and looked, until they would never forget the sight of that little baby in the manger, they went out to tell everyone who would listen to them of the wonderful things they had seen and heard on the hills that night. They told of following the angel's instructions carefully and finding them to be accurate and true. Then Doctor Luke reports to us that the shepherds returned to their flocks that night, praising God for all the things they had *heard* and *seen*, as it was told to them. Did you pay attention to that? It was not an airy-fairy mystical experience they had had . . . they had not had some strange vision. These shepherds praised God for what they had *seen* with their eyes, and *heard* with their ears, which proved to them that what the angel had told them was truth!

Don't ever forget that Doctor Luke felt it was important to make sure we know these things to be true, and not just a story. Can't you just imagine the shepherds sitting around their fire until daybreak brought streaks of light into the sky, and the sun came up? Can't you imagine them talking and talking, interrupting each other, all eager to speak? They would have wanted to talk about the angels, the light, the baby in the manger . . . and also all they could remember from the Old Testament. They also would have talked about the future, wondering what would happen next. It was a night that would have been remembered by each of them as long as they lived.

This is the story of the first Christmas. We think of it as "The Christmas Story," but to these shepherds it was the most wonderful night of their lives. To us, it should be more than a story, even more than a true story; it should be one of the most important things in our lives that this is true, and that it can make a difference to everything.

For Mary and Joseph it was also a wonderful night. Mary had had the baby safely in that stable. Joseph, who loved her, would be glad that all had gone well. Mary needed to begin to care for the baby, in the same way as any mother. As a gentle, sensitive person she would have had mixed feelings as she looked at the baby in her arms. As a loving mother she would have been full of love for the helpless baby, and she would have been thankful that she had milk coming in her breast to be able to give him clean food. How wonderful it is that God made mothers to have clean milk with all its food value so that mothers in stables as well as mothers in hospitals or palaces, mothers in deserts, in jungles, in icy-cold Alaskan snowfields, mothers anywhere in history and in the earth's geography could *all* have clean, nutritious food for their babies.

Yes, Mary would have been glad that being shut out of a hotel did not mean being shut away from having the proper food for the baby. But, even as she cared for him and fed him, she would be remembering all the angel had said, and all the Old Testament sayings she could remember about the Messiah. She *knew*, you see, that she held her own Savior in her arms.

What a night that first Christmas was—for the angels as they watched and had the glad task of telling and praising with words; for the shepherds as they saw and heard and ran out to tell; for the people the shepherds told; for Joseph and Mary; for Jesus who had emptied himself of the glory and much of his power to become a real baby. Yes, what a night it was for us, and all who have become a part of God's family, to look back to. It was a night when many could *know* that God had kept his promises.

Do you know why we give gifts at Christmas? The real reason should be because we are so thankful that God gave us a gift, that we want to celebrate that by giving things to other people, as well as thinking of what we can do to show God our appreciation. We are told that God loved the world so much, that he gave his only Son—so that anyone who would believe in him (that means anyone who would believe

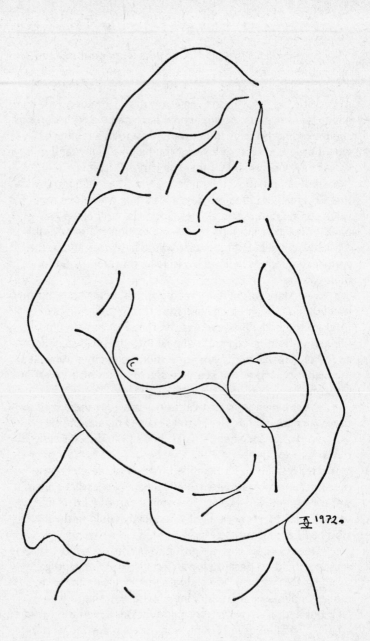

what he said in words, and also who would believe that what he did was for them, too) would have everlasting life. What a gift! The first part of the gift is that the Trinity agreed to be separated for a time, so that Jesus could be born, and live and teach and help people to know about him, and then *die* so that *anyone* who would believe him could live.

The second part of the gift is that as Jesus died in the place of anyone who believes in him, then he gives his righteousness in place of their sins. It is as if we had a dirty cloth around our shoulders, covering us with filth and rags, and then someone came along with a snowy white table cloth and said, "Look, I'll take the dirty cloth, and cover you with this sparkling white cloth." Perhaps in your reading out loud together, you could do just that, to see what the exchange would look like. The *gift* of the white cloth is *real* because we are told that whoever believes and accepts what Jesus came to do for him has his sins taken away, and is covered with righteousness (that means the good things Jesus did). Then, on top of all that, he gives us everlasting life. Everlasting is for ever and ever. He promises us that his gift is a wonderful life ahead of us!

But when you get a gift at Christmas, or a birthday, or some other day, there is something that you have to do about it, before it is really any good to you. You have to accept it, to *take* it in your hands and make it your own. Perhaps it would be a good thing if right now one of you got a plate of cookies (or biscuits, if you live in England), or a basket of oranges or apples, or a few nuts and raisins, or whatever you have in the house that you would enjoy eating as you finish reading. One of you pass it around. If one of you shakes her head, or his head, and says "no" they *they* won't *have* the thing. You have to *take* a gift to have it. Just because someone kindly prepares it for you does not mean you have it. When you take a gift, you say, "Thank you" or "Thank you very much," don't you?

God tells us that he loved the world so much that he sent his Son, to make it possible for men and women, boys

---

Mary feeds Jesus.   Luke 2:1–20

and girls to believe him and then to have everlasting life. When someone loves you very much and gives you a gift that costs them a lot, not just money but a lot of time, you would hurt that person very much if you just kicked the gift and said, "I don't believe you love me." Just think for a while of how God feels as men turn and kick away his gift.

People often worry about how other people don't care about hungry, sick, poor people in places like Bombay, or other parts of the world. We should care about trying to help people who have great need, and are suffering in different ways. But, you know, we ought also to remember that God is a Person, and he feels, as well as thinks and acts. How do you think God feels when people just say, "I don't believe God loves people," or "I don't believe God is even there at all"? We ought to spend more time telling God how much *we* appreciate *him*, and ask him to help us make other people *understand* how great and wonderful and loving he is. He is our Father, when we have come to be his children, and we ought to tell our Father how much we love him, as well as tell other people what a wonderful Father he is!

It is great to be able to tell people about the gift that is possible because of the first Christmas. It is great because we can tell people that gift is *free* to people of any tribe, or nation or kindred or tongue. The gift is not shut up to any one sort of nationality, or race, or language group or family. We know this from Rev. 7:9 and other verses. You see God really does love *people,* and he really *is* love. It is because God is holy and perfectly just that sin needs to be punished. The way Jesus paid for the gift was by taking the punishment himself. Jesus loved us enough to die in our place.

We have a lot more time in which to understand this, however, because Luke goes on to tell us so many things that are true. Today lots of people are teaching that there is no such thing as truth at all, or that if something seems true today, it won't be true tomorrow. You see, this is Satan's special lie today, and so since all of you will meet some people who believe nothing is true, or will read books, or hear TV programs that say this, it is more important than ever to know not only that there *is* truth, but to know what the truth *is*. That is why it is important for families to read together what God says in his written Word, the Bible, and why it is a good thing for us to study one of the books in the Bible together.

4
RUNNING AROUND IN THE DARK

When Jesus was eight days old, Mary and Joseph had the usual special time of giving him his name. It was the name the angel had told Mary he should be given: his name was to be Jesus. All Jewish mothers went to the Temple when their first baby boy was forty days old, because this was part of God's law, to be followed until after the Messiah came and died. Mary and Joseph were true believers and so were faithful to the commands of God in the Bible. Jesus was brought to be presented to the Lord, and the sacrifice brought at that time by his mother Mary, and Joseph, was what any poor family would bring—not what a rich family would bring.

You see, Jesus, the Son of God, the Second Person of the Trinity, was born and brought up in a poor family. That means he did not have any kind of human luxury, and as a little boy he would have known what it was to have *less* than many other boys of that time, even though he had had more than anyone on earth has ever had in the place he left to come to earth. He was willing to become really poor in every way, to eat poor man's food, sleep in a poor man's kind of a house, to have the kind of clothes and other things that poor people had. We are told in another place in the New Testament that he became poor for us, so that some day we can become rich. You see, he did become poor in every way—not just poor as compared with the marvelous riches of heaven, but even poor by men's way of judging. And because he became poor, and died to take our punishment, we can accept what he did for us, and we will become rich for ever and ever in the life that is ahead of us in Heaven. It isn't often you see a rich man willing to be poor, so that other people can have what they need, is it?

But now we are thinking of the little five-and-half-week-old baby Jesus being brought to the Temple. Could anyone recognize this poorly-dressed little baby as the King of Kings, and Lord of Lords? Well, certain things did happen at the Temple that showed he was no ordinary baby.

There were some Jews in that day who were faithfully looking for the Messiah promised all through the Old Testament. The name of one of these was Simeon. God had given a special message to Simeon, telling him he would not die until he had seen the Messiah. On the day when the baby Jesus was being brought to the Temple, the Lord led Simeon there. God is able to lead his children to be in the place he wants them to be, at the time he wants them there, in order that they may meet other people, or do things that God wants them to do. God is able to do all things, but when we become his children, he does not move us around like dolls or puppets or little machines, but as we ask him to lead us and help us, he does answer. Simeon was the sort of man who was close to the Lord, and was led by the Lord, so he was in the right place at the right time to see the Person God had promised he would see before he died. Simeon, when he saw the little baby, reached out and took Jesus in his arms and looked down at him, and as he looked he knew who he was. We know he knew, because God gave Doctor Luke the words Simeon said, for us to be able to read.

We are told that, as Simeon gazed at the baby, the first thing he did was to bless God. He must have felt overwhelmed with thanksgiving that God had kept this special promise. He said to God, "Lord, now you can let me die in peace, as you said you would, because now my eyes have seen your salvation!" Imagine that . . . Simeon knew that tiny forty-day-old baby was his salvation! He knew this was the One promised for so many years throughout the Old Testament, and then promised especially to him. The promise to him was that the Messiah would be born in his lifetime and he would see him. Simeon went on to say that he knew God had prepared this salvation to be before the face of all people. And that this One would be a light to give light to the Gentiles as well as to be a glory to Israel.

What Simeon said as he held that baby in his arms showed a marvelous understanding of what Jesus had come to do, as well as of the fact that this was the Messiah. You see, Simeon understood that this Messiah, Jesus, was a special glory to Israel because he was the One promised to Abraham all those years before, the One who would be born of the Jewish nation and of the house of David. He also understood that the Gentiles were in very great darkness, because most of them did not have the Bible, and did not even know about the Messiah's coming.

Who are Gentiles? Gentiles are just all the other people in the world, the ones who are not Jews.

Who are the Jews? Well, many years ago a man named Abraham believed God, and worshiped God . . . although everyone else in the place where he lived believed Satan's lies, and worshiped the moon and idols. God called Abraham to come out of that place, and live as a shepherd. Abraham not only believed God, but did what God told him to do. A promise was made to Abraham that because of his faithfulness all his children, grandchildren and great-great-grandchildren would be called God's people. A promise was also made that the whole world would be helped, blessed, given something special, through someone who would be born from Abraham's family. So the Jews are Abraham's descendants.

The Gentiles are the people who are children and grandchildren and great-grandchildren of the *other* people living at the time of Abraham. These other people had turned away from God. They were like Cain, and did not worship in the way God had explained. In fact they were not even worshiping God at all; many of them were worshiping the moon!

So Simeon stood there with the promised Messiah in his arms, and showed that he remembered and understood what the Old Testament said about what was going to happen. He said that this baby was not only going to be a glory to the

Simeon holds Jesus and blesses God.   Luke 2:28

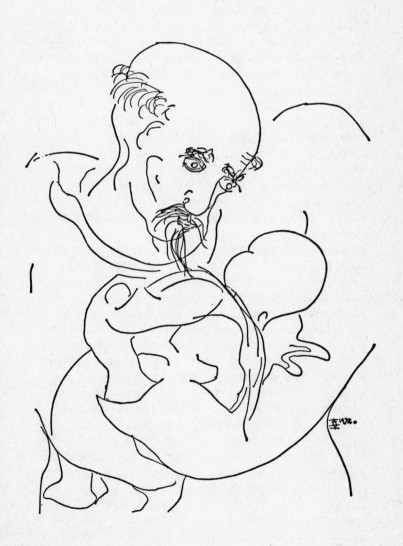

Jews, but that he would be a light to lighten the Gentiles. You remember how we lit candles in a dark room . . . well, Simeon said that Jesus had come to give light to people who do not know the truth, and who do not even know there is such a thing as truth. People with wrong ideas who have believed lies about the world, the universe, and about who they are . . . need light to light up their dark thinking, their dark ideas. They need light to show them what ideas are *really* true, so that they can live on the basis of truth.

Do you find this difficult to understand? Let's pretend that this room in which we are sitting is our life. Now let's pretend we each have ideas of what truth is, that all of us have *different* ideas. Let's pretend all the furniture in the room is the true way things are in the universe. All right now . . . let's pretend we all go out into the hall together, and someone makes the room very dark. This is a pretend, because if we really did this we would get hurt. Let's pretend that the game is to go in one at a time, and run as fast as possible around the room, across it and down the length of it in the dark, according to our *own ideas* of how the furniture ought to be placed. Ouch! ouch! . . . ooooooh . . . aaaaahhhh . . . ouch!! What has happened? Well, if we have *really* run through the room according to our own ideas and not the way the furniture really is placed there, we have bumped our shins, we have bruised our shoulders, we have fallen over a stool, we have run our head into the edge of a cupboard, we have knocked over a lamp and cut our hands!

Do you understand what it is to try to live life in the dark, to live according to the way *people* think, rather than according to the way things *really* are? It is like running through rooms full of furniture, in the dark.

Simeon understood when he said Jesus was going to be a light to lighten the Gentiles. Joseph and Mary were amazed at all Simeon said, and marveled at what he spoke concerning the little baby living in their home. Simeon turned to bless them, and then he went on to say that this baby would be spoken against by many people, and that Mary would suffer because of what would be done to him. Simeon showed that he understood that Jesus was going to have to die, just as Isaiah had written in chapter 53 of his book.

Wonderful old Simeon! There are lots of people we'd like to meet in Heaven, and Simeon is one of them. These are all real people, and just as with *all* real people, we are going to enjoy talking to some, more than to others. People always have differed all through the ages, some are personalities we enjoy especially, and others are personalities others enjoy. Since we are finite, and limited, and that means we can only be alone with one person at a time, we could never spend time alone with more than one person at a time—so we don't *need* to enjoy everyone equally. We just need to learn what it means to have feelings of love and kindness toward the ones we don't enjoy, as well as the ones we do enjoy.

God is infinite and unlimited, which means he can be with each person in Heaven and in the world as if he were alone with them, all at once. We can't understand that perfectly, but we can be very glad that God *can* be alone with each of us . . . and that we don't have to wait in a long line for our turn, nor do we have to be afraid that he won't enjoy being with us, because he says, "He that cometh unto me I will in no wise cast out." That means if we come to him, he won't push us away.

》 Let's get back to the Temple now. While Simeon was speaking, a very old lady came in. This old lady, we are told, was eighty-four years old and she had been a widow for many years. Her husband had died after they had been married only seven years. Ever since her husband had died, she had spent all her time in the Temple, coming there to pray for long periods of time. Her name was Anna.

We want you to notice something. Many times in the Bible God tells us of women who faithfully were doing what God planned for them to do, and God shows us carefully how important the lives of these women were. If anyone tells you that the Bible makes women appear unimportant, that just isn't true. We could have a whole book showing what God led women to do through centuries of history. Anyway, Anna

was an old woman whom God brought to see the baby
Messiah. She was as thrilled as Simeon, and we are told she
went out to tell all the people living in that area, who were
really "looking for redemption in Jerusalem." What does that
mean? Well, it means that the people in Jerusalem who believed the Old Testament and were really expecting the Messiah and looking for his coming, *knew each other.* That is very
natural, isn't it? People who really believe God like to pray
together, talk together and study the Bible together . . . so
very often they discover each other when they live in the
same city. Also *God* helps people find others who will help
them. People who believe God need friends who also believe
God, so that they can help each other discover wonderful
things in the Bible, and help each other grow strong as people of God.

So Anna, who knew the others who were waiting for the
Messiah, hurried off as quickly as an eighty-four-year-old person can hurry to visit them and tell them about having seen
Jesus. She must have said, "Oh, he has come, he has come, I
have seen him. He has been born, and is now a baby of forty
days old." They would all have been excited, don't you think?
And they would have said, "Thank you" to God for letting
them be alive when he came. Never forget that all the first
people who believed that Jesus was the Messiah, the Savior,
were Jews who knew their Old Testament and were looking
for him to come.

After this time in the Temple Jesus was taken by Mary
and Joseph to their old home in Nazareth of Galilee. The
Gospel of Matthew tells us that for a time Jesus was taken to
Egypt, but the Gospel of Luke does not tell us this part of the
story. When you and your brother or sister say what happened at school, or at a picnic, or during a game, one of you
leaves out one thing, and the other something else. People
always tell things a bit differently, because one thing is more
important to one person, and something else to another.
Remember, God treats his children as people, not as
machines. This is clear in the way the Bible is written. God
made sure that everything he wanted us to know was in-

46

cluded, but he allowed men to write in a very personal way, with their interests as well as their manner of writing showing through.

In Nazareth Jesus grew, just as any other child would grow. We know that Joseph was a carpenter, and as the family was poor and help would be needed by Mary and Joseph, we can be sure he learned to help in the carpentry work, and in other ways. We have no reason to think that he looked any different from any of the other boys around him. However, although he *looked* the same as boys his age, we know from Luke 2:40 that he was different. This verse tells us, "And the child grew, and waxed strong, filled with wisdom: and the grace of God was upon him." Jesus had come to earth to be born as a baby, to grow as a boy in an ordinary home. He had put aside his glory and his power. He stayed in one place at one time, like any human being, He was hungry and needed to eat, tired and needed to sleep. He had put aside much of what he had been accustomed to throughout all the ages of endless eternity. Yet still, he was different. He grew spiritually, and was strong in spiritual things at an early age, and he was filled with wisdom. That means he was much wiser than ordinary little boys, and the grace of God was upon him.

All this means that he was, indeed, very special, although he lived through all the difficulties, the hardships, of a poor home and the need for hard work. He was different, although he experienced hunger and cold, and temptations of every kind. He knew what it was to have people "despise" him . . . It's no fun to have other people dislike you, and even harder to have them hate you. Jesus knew these feelings that you have, whether you are five, fifteen, thirty, or fifty-five! All this means he can understand you better than anyone else can. He can understand because he is God, but he can also understand because he lived as a boy and an adult.

》 The next thing the Bible tells us about Jesus is an event which took place when he was twelve years old. Because Mary and Joseph were believers and loved the Lord, they went up to Jerusalem year after year to the great Jewish feast, the feast of the Passover. In Old Testament times a boy began to have a part in these ceremonies when he was twelve years old, and so we can be sure that Jesus was very happy when he was old enough to go to Jerusalem with Mary and Joseph. It isn't hard to imagine twelve-year-old Jesus walking with Mary and Joseph and their friends from Nazareth down into the Jordan Valley and then climbing up the steep mountain road to Jerusalem. When all the special things that they did during those Passover days were finished, Mary and Joseph started homeward. They thought that Jesus was somewhere in the crowd walking along with them. But he wasn't! He had stayed behind in Jerusalem. They went on their way for a whole day, confident that he was among their relatives or friends. However, when night came and they could not find him, they grew concerned and went back to Jerusalem to look for him. They searched for three days. We can be sure that by that time they were *very* upset; just as mothers always are when they don't know where their children are.

Many people came to Jerusalem during the days of the Passover. There must have been many attractions which would have been of interest to a twelve-year-old boy. Mary and Joseph looked in all the places where they thought he might be, and they didn't find him anywhere. Then, on the third day—where do you think they found him? He was in the Temple, surrounded by the religious leaders, both asking and answering questions. We are told that everyone who heard him was astonished at his understanding, and his answers. That would have been a fascinating discussion to have been able to hear, wouldn't it? Yes, Jesus at twelve years old was really involved in a deep discussion with mature religious leaders . . . people much older than he was.

When Mary and Joseph found him there they were very surprised. Mary said to him, "Son, why have you treated us this way? Look, your father and I have been looking for you with sadness." From this we know that, in their family, it must have been common for them to speak of Joseph as the father of the home. However, you will remember that Joseph was not Jesus's father. Mary was the real mother of Jesus, but

Jesus, as the Second Person of the Trinity, did not have any
earthly father. God alone was his Father.

He said, "How is it that you were looking for me? Don't
you know that I must be taking care of my Father's business?"
Jesus was reminding Mary that he was the Son of God, and
that he had come into the world with a specific purpose. He
had come into the world to bring "light." We have already
thought about the fact that some people are, as it were,
"sitting in the dark," because they can't see or know, or
understand the answers to their questions about life. Here
was Jesus, at twelve years of age, in discussion with men who
first answered his questions, but then sat in astonishment as
he began to give *them* answers. If you are very young, maybe
you won't understand the importance of what follows—but if
you are older, you *must* think about this: Jesus was involved
in discussing ideas. He got so involved in discussion that he
stayed three days and three nights without noticing the passing of time, because the conversation was more important. It
was more important for him to make clear some things to
those men, and to discuss and clarify some questions and
answers with them, than simply to be a twelve-year-old be-
having the way the neighbors and friends and Joseph and
Mary wanted him to behave.

We are told that Mary and Joseph did not understand
him at all at this point. Strange, but they seemed to have
forgotten the wonder of all they had been told about who
Jesus was, and they did not expect him to be doing the things
he had left Heaven to come to earth to do. It was because of
this that they didn't understand what he meant when he said
he had to be "busy taking care of his Father's business."

You see, I am sure Jesus was so much like other boys,
just as later he was so much like other men, that people
would not believe he was God, and even his closest friends
did not really expect the things he told them, to come true.
As a boy living in a carpenter's home, Joseph would expect
Jesus to think that learning carpentry was the most important
thing. Jesus knew that he had come to do more important
things, but as he was still just a young boy, he did go back to

49

Nazareth with Joseph and Mary, and obeyed them, just as it is
right that we should obey our parents at that age. There does
come a time when we may have a problem—a problem of
being sure that God is leading us to do something which our
parents do not understand. When you believe in Jesus as your
Savior, God does become your Heavenly Father, and he does
have a plan to unfold to you for your life. However, as
children, we are told to be obedient to our parents.

Think of Jesus, walking back to Nazareth to continue the
life of a twelve-year-old boy. He had just astonished the most
learned and educated leaders of his day with his questions
and wonderful answers. He was the unique Son of God, and
yet *that* day he returned to his home in Nazareth to continue
to live in obedience to Mary and Joseph until he became a
man. The Bible tells us that Mary did not forget these things,
but thought much about them. Luke tells us, "His mother
kept all these sayings in her heart." The next verse, Luke 2:52,
tells us all we know of the life of Jesus from the time he was
twelve until the time he was thirty. "And Jesus advanced in
wisdom and stature, and in favor with God and men." Way
back in the Old Testament, when Isaiah in Chapter 11 verse 2
is explaining what the Messiah will be like, he says, "And the
Spirit of the Lord shall rest upon him, the spirit of wisdom
and understanding, the spirit of counsel and might, the spirit
of knowledge and of the fear of the Lord." And later in the
Bible in Colossians 2:3 the Apostle Paul says that in Jesus are
hidden all the treasures of wisdom and knowledge. Yes, Jesus
who had always lived, and who is infinite and perfect in his
wisdom . . . had really put aside much of what he had always
had, so that it is true that he grew, and increased in his
wisdom, yet—he was like no other twelve-year-old, nor were
the next years without wisdom and understanding being
shared, though we have no report of them.

Jesus knew what it was to grow physically, as well as in
knowledge and wisdom, because he came to be born as a
baby . . . and then grow. As for us, we have to be born *two*
times. We are born physically as babies, and we can say, "My
birthday is November 3rd"—or whatever date it is. It is easy

to see that ten-year-olds are a lot bigger and stronger than five-year-olds. It is easy to see that five-year-olds are bigger and stronger and more capable than a five-day-old baby. To grow physically, babies, children, people have to eat properly. They have to eat the right kind of food, and the right amount of it, to be healthy and strong. They have to exercise their bodies so that their muscles develop. They have to study so that their minds develop.

But no one can grow without being born first! Jesus spoke later, when he was teaching, about people's need to be "born again." To be "born again" means to be born into God's family, through believing what God has told us in his Book, and accepting what Jesus came to do for us as he took our punishment when he died. When we are "born again" we are babies in God's family and we need to grow. The "food" we need is the Word of God, the Bible. To be healthy spiritually (that means to be healthy as children in God's family) we need to have spiritual food, good fresh air and exercise. We need to read the Bible as our food, talk to the Lord in prayer so that we can be in the fresh air of his presence, and then do what he wants us to do, as our exercise.

God made us as whole people. So when sin came into the world, and things were spoiled, nothing was as it should be. That is why there are so many sad things. When Jesus came to be born, and grow as a boy and then to die—he came so that we could be born the second time. Think of it! If he had just stayed in Heaven, we wouldn't have had any way of being "changed" or of getting rid of our sin. Jesus had never been born before! He had always lived; he did not *need* to be born. But he came to be born, and it is pretty humble to be willing to be a little boy, a little child, a twelve-year-old boy . . . when you have been Infinite God, Second Person of the Three Persons for ever and ever! He came to be born the *first* time, without needing to be born in order to be alive, so that we could be born the *second* time. We couldn't live for ever with him, unless we could be born the second time.

We are told in Romans, Chapter 5, that because of

Adam's and Eve's sins, we all die, but because of Jesus being obedient, and never sinning, and then dying for us—we can have eternal life. It's a terrific exchange, isn't it?

Don't you think that if it was important for Jesus, who was the Son of God, to be willing to be obedient to Joseph and Mary as he was living in their home as a growing boy, then it is important for children to obey their parents? This twentieth century we live in is a time when many children won't obey parents, and young people won't obey their teachers and older students won't respect their professors, and people pay no attention to anyone in authority over them. Why? Well, because so many don't think there is any truth at all. They don't think there is a personal God, so they don't think there *is* any person in the Universe who is absolutely right. This wrong idea is like a damp fog settling over a city, getting into houses through the cracks under the doors and windows. Because people hear this teaching of wrong ideas on every side, they *act* as if it were right. You see, if people believe nothing is true, and nothing is *really* right or *really* wrong—they don't obey, and they can't make anyone else obey.

We know there are things that are true, and things that are false. We know there are things that are right and things that are wrong. We know that God is perfect in his wisdom and knowledge, in his love and his justice. When God gives us absolute commands—we know that to obey them is right, and to disobey them is wrong.

One thing God had told us to do is to obey our parents. So we know there is something *important* about obeying our parents, instead of just doing anything we want to do! *One* important thing is that God has *said* we are to do this. *Another* important thing is that it helps us to learn what it means to obey *God*, when we are born into *his* family and *he* is our Father. Parents also need to obey God, to be good parents. They mustn't order their children to do things against God's commands.

How do we know what we should do to obey God? Well, that is what he gave us the Bible for. His rules are all written in his Book. Yes, we can pray and ask him to show us what to do day by day . . . but he never shows us something that is against what he has written in his Book. This is what "absolute" means. An absolute is something that is right at any time in history anywhere in the world. If God has said something is wrong, it is wrong at *any* time for anybody. It is important to know the difference between what God has said, and what man has said. This is why it is so important to keep reading the Bible.

5
SHOW YOU ARE REALLY SORRY

Luke next tells us about John. You remember the angel Gabriel had told Zacharias that this baby John would grow up to be great in the sight of the Lord. The angel said that, as he would preach and teach and speak to people, he would have the same kind of power that Isaiah had had hundreds of years before. He had said that John would turn back many of the Jewish people, the children of Israel, to the Lord their God. People would change their ways of life, fathers would be more concerned about their children, and rebellious and disobedient people would study and be interested in the things *believing* people were saying. John would prepare people to listen to Jesus. All this had been promised before John was born, and as Elizabeth and Zacharias looked at baby John they must often have wondered how he could do all these things!

When Luke starts to tell us about John's preaching and teaching, he tells us first what was going on at the same time. He wants us to be sure we aren't reading some kind of a fairy story, so he tells us things that make us remember once more that this is all true history. He states that it was the fifteenth year that Tiberius Caesar had been ruler, and that at the time a man named Pontius Pilate was governor of Judea. Luke explains that Herod was ruler of Galilee, and his brother Philip was ruler of Iturea, and that another man named Lysanias was the ruler of Abilene. He tells us that Annas and Caiaphas were the high priests at this time.

Perhaps you are saying . . . "Oh, pooh . . . I don't care, why don't you just say what happened next?" Maybe you think you don't care, but please think again. If you were being told something that happened when Abraham Lincoln was president of the United States, or something that happened when Henry VIII was king of England, or even an event that happened when De Gaulle was president of France, or something that took place when Mao was writing his Little Red Book in China . . . two things would come to your mind. First, you would have some idea about the period of history that was being talked about, and secondly, you would know that the events happened in this world (that is, in space) and in time (that is, time that can be measured by months and years) and in history (that is, that can be put in some order in your mind because it fits into a sequence of other things that have taken place).

If you came home and someone said, "There was an earthquake in Tokyo," it might not seem very *real* to you. But if someone said, "Jane, while you were having your music class in school, and Dad was plowing the field, and mother was making a sponge cake, and Johnny was playing football, the news came over the radio that right at that moment a big earthquake tremor was shaking Tokyo," then this has more connection with real time. And, as you think of Tokyo on your map, it makes it more real to you as something going on in history, the history of *your* time.

This is why it is so important to realize that the Bible was written in enough detail to help us understand that it is talking about real people in real countries on this earth, in a period of time that is real history. It is important also as we think of the future, because where the Bible tells us about the future, it is going to take place in just as real a way . . . and the people who will be a part of that future are just as real as people, persons, personalities. The past is not a fairy story, the present time is not unreal and far off and impossible for us to find out about, and the future is not an airy-fairy bit of imagination. It is all real.

All this is bound up with Luke's account of John's work. It really is very exciting, because Luke tells us that when these men were ruling, John had come out of the wilderness where God had been preparing him for this time of speaking, and he had gone into the country around Jordan. You could find

Jordan on your map easily, and often you hear about Jordan in the newspapers. It is a place where people still live today. As John walked around the Jordan area, he began preaching to people, telling them that they ought to be baptized to show they repented of their sins. The exciting part is this: not only had the angel told his parents before he was born that he would do this, but 700 years before, Isaiah wrote in the Old Testament about what John would be doing! God had made it clear to anyone who would listen, that the prophecies about the Messiah were all coming true.

In Matthew 3:1–12 Matthew writes about this time, too. It would be good if you would look up these things in the Bible yourselves. Matthew says that John preached these words: "Repent ye . . . " and then he says that John is the one written about by the prophet Isaiah. Look it up for yourself in Isaiah 40 where, in the third verse it says, "The voice of one that crieth, 'Prepare ye in the wilderness the way of the Lord.'" John was to prepare people of that time to know that this was the Messiah, and to prepare them to listen to Jesus, if they really understood what John was saying. But he should prepare us to believe, too. We are meant to read, ask questions, understand, and then believe. God gives us enough information really to know . . . not everything . . . but enough to be convinced that he is speaking to us. So here was John, outdoors, walking around, coming to the river, talking, explaining, answering questions. Yes, people asked questions. "Repent," he said. "Do something to show that you are really sorry for your sins. Don't just say Abraham is your father. That isn't enough . . . something has to be real in you today." This was the sort of thing John said. And someone asked, "What shall we do then?" Some wanted to know what he *meant* by showing they were sorry, by saying, "bring forth fruits worthy of repentance."

So John gave examples. He told them that they could do things like this: if one man had two coats, he could give one to somebody who didn't have any at all. If another person had a lot of food, he could share that with someone who was hungry. Then a tax-gatherer asked what he could do, and

John's answer to him was very practical: he said, "Don't cheat people. Don't take more than you are supposed to take." And when a soldier asked what to do, John answered, "Don't falsely accuse people of things they didn't do; don't be violent with people; be content with your wages." What was John saying? He was saying that to *repent*, to be *sorry* for doing something wrong and sinful, which is something that takes place inside your head, as you think of how wrong you were and inside yourself as you *feel* sorry—to *repent*, you should do something practical outside yourself, something to show you really mean it, something that will cost you something. Just to say, "Sorry," doesn't cost much.

You see, John is pointing out that real repentance for greediness and covetousness, anger and violence, selfishness and hate, will cause people to do something different. There will be a change in things people see from the outside, if there is a change inside us. Let's say a brother has been fighting with his sister, and has pulled her hair and broken her string of beads. Let's say he mumbles, "Sorry" and she mumbles, "Mmm." Has he shown anyone that he really feels sorry? How could people see that he means it? Well, he can't put her hair back in, if he's pulled some out, but he could take all the money he had saved up to get a model airplane and buy her some beads instead. Or he could try to get the right kind of strong thread, and take a lot of time and patience to try and mend the beads, and do some other very kind things to show that he is sorry. But some of the things we need to repent of are not as easy to show we are sorry for, because it is not something like one person's beads that we have broken. This is why John said we should share what we have with poor people, because it is the kind of selfishness and greediness that we feel that has made such a difference in history. People have been mean to other people, ever since sin came into the world, and the greediness and selfishness and mean violence of some have made so many people miserable. John says that, to show you are sorry for your part in all this, you are to share things, even if you haven't taken anything away from that particular person.

» John said he would baptize those who wanted really to show their repentance. It was a baptism that was special to that particular moment. For hundreds of years people had been waiting for the coming of the Messiah who was to be the Lamb of God. We saw how the lamb was used in worship for so many years, to remind the people what the Messiah was coming to do. Now John is helping people to be ready . . . to get jogged out of the rut of just thinking that the Messiah would come some time in the future. John is to make people think. He is to make them think of how sinful they have been, and of how much they need first of all to be sorry, and then to have some real way of getting rid of that sin. He is preparing them to understand their need and to be ready to receive the Messiah. To whom did he speak the loudest and strongest? To the Pharisees and Sadducees! When they came to be baptized, he called them vipers, or snakes! Matthew tells us this in chapter 3:7 of his Gospel.

Who were the Pharisees and Sadducees? They were two different groups of religious leaders. They had the Old Testament, so they ought to have known the truth and to have been waiting for the Messiah, but they were all filled with wrong teachings, wrong actions and wrong beliefs. They were harming other people because they were like cooks that mix poison with the food they are serving. People expect good, nourishing food from a cook's hands . . . but when they get poison mixed in their food, they've been fooled into eating something that makes them really sick. Religious teachers that mix up things that are *not* true, with bits and pieces of the truth, hurt people more seriously than poisoned food, because it is a matter of "life and death" for ever, rather than being sick for a little while.

The Pharisees were very right in certain things, and very proud of being moral and self-denying. They kept all sorts of little rules that had been added to what the Old Testament taught, and they were very proud of keeping these little rules. They didn't see their own sinfulness at all, and thought that they were perfect. Later on, we will see that they were the ones that tried in all sorts of ways to harm Jesus.

The Sadducees were men among the Jews who did not believe in the existence of angels. So they would not have believed that an angel spoke to Zacharias and told him John was to prepare the way for the Messiah. The Sadducees did not believe in the resurrection either. They would have been something like the rationalists of today. This just means the kind of people who do not believe in the supernatural, such as miracles, or angels, or that Satan and the demons exist. The interesting thing was, though, that as John stood near the river Jordan, on the ground where ants and bugs were, where the water was no different from usual, where ordinary people were coming around to hear him . . . he simply shouted at these men and he told them that they, too, needed to repent. Just "being religious" does not get rid of sins. He wanted them to realize that there is punishment coming to men, unless they listen to God and believe.

We know that John did not tell them that the baptism that showed their repentance, would take away their sin. We know that John did not say that giving your second coat away and sharing your food would take away your sin. John the Baptist told those people, and he tells us, something fantastic that is reported in chapter 1 verse 29, of John's Gospel. (The John who wrote the Gospel was another John.) When John the Baptist saw Jesus walking toward him, he cried out loud enough for everyone to hear: "Behold the Lamb of God, who taketh away the sin of the world."

That was clear, wasn't it? It might not be clear to anyone who didn't know about all the lambs that had been brought to the place of worship from the time of Abel, Noah, Abraham, and Moses onwards, to remind them that a "Lamb of God" would come. It might not have been clear to people who didn't know that the lamb was to represent the fact that Someone had to *take our* place, and be punished for us. But it should have been clear to the men who stood there then. And it should be clear to all who have the Bible and can read the Old and New Testaments today. "Behold the Lamb of God, who taketh away the sin of the world!"

What a glorious thing to know! What a marvelous thing

to hear! How wonderful it should have been that day for people to see him with their eyes! But did they get excited and believe? Did they all bow down and say, "Oh, thank you for coming to save us, to take our sin away"? No. Only a few people like John, and Simeon, and Anna and the shepherds and others whom we do not know, and some we will hear about later on—only a few people believed and were glad.

And the Pharisees and Sadducees just scowled. They had been called vipers, and they were furious. They were full of pride about themselves and their own ideas, and they really didn't care at all about the Messiah, the Son of God, the Second Person of the Trinity standing in front of them. They wanted to keep on being religious and arguing about how to do it. They were getting ready to criticize God. But all who believed John's message, and were sorry for their sins, were baptized by John in the Jordan River that day. Remember this was a preparation for listening to, and understanding, Jesus.

» Jesus had walked from Galilee to Jordan on that special day, to be baptized by John. But Matthew tells us that John was astounded and said, "I have need to be baptized of thee, comest thou to me?" John knew that, although he had a special task to do, he was only a sinful man himself who needed the Lamb of God as his Savior, too. Jesus simply answered John, "Suffer it now, for thus it becometh us to fulfil all righteousness." Jesus did not have to be baptized to show any sorrow for his sin, because he never sinned. Not once! He was baptized to show all the world that from this time on he was representing us in his life as well as in his death. That means he wanted to make it clear to people then who were trying to understand, and to us now, that he was *living* for us, as well as going to *die* for us later on. It is wonderful to think that Jesus took our punishment as he died on the cross—so that we need not be punished for our sin if we accept what he did. But it is also wonderful that at this time, when Jesus stood in the Jordan River to be baptized by John, he began a special period of living his perfect life for all who will accept him as Savior.

A fantastic thing happened while Jesus was there in the water being baptized. It was one more way in which God was making certain that people would understand who Jesus was, so that they could not be mixed up by people like the Pharisees and the Sadducees. You see, John had said that Someone was coming who would have power to prepare them for heaven, with what John called the baptism of the Holy Spirit and of fire. John meant that only the death of Jesus would give people cleansing from their sin and the Holy Spirit to dwell in them. John had also said, "Behold the Lamb of God."

And now the One he had pointed to, was standing in the water as they had all done, looking no different. In fact, we are told in other places in the Bible that Jesus did not have any special *look* about him to make people want to come to him. He did not look like a big hero or a president or a king or somebody that people rush to hear sing. He was just a man who mixed with the crowd of men, and didn't *look* anything special. And here is this Jesus, being baptized by John. How could the people know that this was not at all like *their* baptism to show they were sorry for their sin?

When Jesus came up out of the water to the shore of the river, we are told in Luke, and in Matthew 3:16–17, that "the heavens were opened unto him, and he saw the Spirit of God descending as a dove . . . and lo, a voice out of the heavens, saying, This is my beloved Son, in whom I am well pleased." Everyone there had proved to them that there is one God but in three separate Persons. Jesus, the Second Person of the Trinity, stood there on the shore of the river; the Holy Spirit, who is the Third Person of the Trinity, came down in a shape like a dove, so that people could see him come to be with Jesus; and the Father, who is the First Person of the Trinity, spoke in a voice that everyone could hear, with words they could understand, telling people in their own language that this man is his very much loved Son in whom he is well pleased.

Do you know something? Anyone who was there that day and did not believe was really calling God a liar, as much

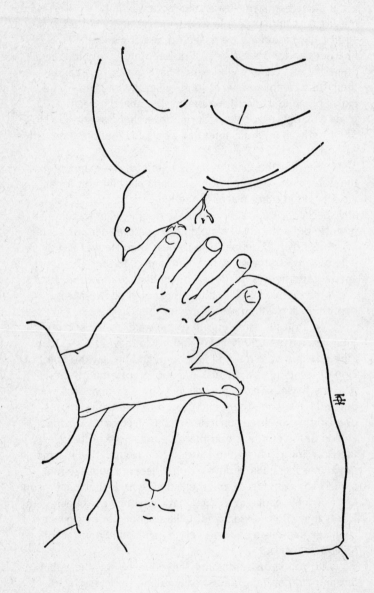

as Eve and Adam ever did. Right in the midst of the Three Persons of the Trinity anyone who did not believe was just defying God. How frightening it is to think of the way people spit at God, and turn away when he is making the truth so clear, and when he is opening a way for them to come to him and have eternal life!

We weren't there at that time, but God made certain that we could have an account of all that went on, in our own language. This account is meant to be passed down from one generation to another. There is a promise in the book of Revelation that there will be very many people in heaven, even though we get discouraged as we read of how few believed Jesus when they saw and heard such marvelous things. It is a promise that will help us when we get discouraged about how few people today believe that the Bible is true. The promise is a description of a day we will see, and be a part of, if we believe: "After these things I saw, and behold, a great multitude, which no man could number, out of every nation, and of all tribes and people and tongues, standing before the throne and before the Lamb, arrayed in white robes and palms in their hands; and they cry with a great voice, saying, Salvation unto our God which sitteth on the throne, and unto the Lamb."

This is one of our favorite verses in the whole Bible. This means that there will be children of all kinds of colors and language-groups and hidden-away tribes who will hear and find out and understand and believe . . . even though Satan tries to tell such lies that people will be blinded. There will be children who have been taught the wrong things by unbelieving teachers and parents who will discover the true truth, understand, and believe. There will be some from *every* kind of "impossible" background who will be there with us.

As you finish this chapter, why don't you get that filthy, dirty cloth and a white tablecloth again. Put them in front of you and look at them. Make the exchange . . . remembering that as he was baptized into his life for us, he lived a perfect

The baptism of Jesus. Luke 3:21–22

life to give his righteousness to cover us. As his death takes away our sins because he became our substitute, so his life is for us . . . covering us with the good things that he has done. Have one of the family stand, cover that one with the white tablecloth or sheet. There is a hymn that speaks of being "*clothed* with his righteousness." It goes something like this:

When He shall come with trumpet sound,
Oh, may I then in Him be found;
Dressed in His righteousness alone,
Faultless to stand before the throne.

There *is* a trumpet sound coming. There *is* a time coming when we will see the Lamb of God, Jesus, ourselves. We can be there and be a part of it, because all this is true. And because God keeps his promises.

6
THE FIGHTER AGAINST TRUTH

After Jesus had been baptized, and the Holy Spirit had come down to him in a way that other people could see, in the form of a dove, and God the Father had spoken, saying very clearly to everyone there that this was his Son and that he, the Father, was very pleased, we are told that the Holy Spirit filled Jesus, and led him away from Jordan into the wilderness.

What does it mean—that the Holy Spirit filled Jesus? The Holy Spirit is the Third Person of the Trinity, so he is God, too. Jesus as the Second Person of the Trinity could do things in his own power, and could do things in his own wisdom and strength. But remember we said that Jesus was in a very special way living for us. Also, he was teaching us things about how we, as human beings, can live under God's direction. Jesus showed us that the Holy Spirit can live within people and help them to do what God the Father has planned. Jesus, himself, was led by the Holy Spirit who was within him. Jesus was doing what he did with the strength of the Holy Spirit.

This is important as well as amazing. It is important because later we will find that the Holy Spirit comes to live inside every person who is "born again." We have talked a little about how we have to be born a second time, born into God's family, to have eternal life. When we believe what God tells us, and accept what Jesus came to do for us, the Holy Spirit comes to live in us, to help us. He doesn't sit inside, driving us like a driver of a train, but he comforts us, helps us when we are sad, and if we ask him, he helps us to know what we should do. None of us will ever be perfect. None of us will do what the Holy Spirit leads us to do perfectly, because we not only make mistakes, but we also get rebellious at times! At times we all say, "I don't want to do that, and I won't." We say that to our parents when we are little, we say it to our Heavenly Father at many ages, we say it to the Holy Spirit many times. We all have a way of bringing a funny little list of things to the Lord, and saying, "I'll do any of these things," but of hiding another list somewhere in our minds, and saying, "But I won't do any of these other things, even if you want me to." One day, when Jesus comes back again, sin will be over, and Satan won't be tempting us any more, and we won't be sinful. But at present, no one is perfect.

As Jesus left Jordan to go off into a wild, country place where he was alone, with no human beings around him, he was led by the Holy Spirit, filled with the Holy Spirit, because he willed the will of the Father always. But although Jesus, as God the Son, was perfect, yet we are told he faced every kind of temptation that we have ever had. In the book of Hebrews 4:15, we are told that we must remember when we pray, that Jesus understands our weaknesses and temptations, because he was "tempted in *all* points." That means Jesus was tempted with all the kinds of temptations Satan tempts *us* with, so he understands how hard it is for us.

As Jesus went out into the wilderness, someone else was coming to that wild place of rocks and bushes, with wild animals as well as little lizards crawling around; with flies buzzing, as well as birds and butterflies fluttering in the air That someone who was headed for the same place was Satan!

Had Satan and Jesus ever met before? Do you remember that in the first chapter we said that Satan used to be one of the angels in Heaven? Satan's name was Lucifer and we are told in Isaiah 14:12–20 that he wanted to be like God. He wanted to be as high as God and to have the other angels worship him, and he started a rebellion against God. Some of the angels followed him. From other places in the Bible we know that Satan has special power in the world today, and that he knows that one day his time of power will be over. Since he hates God, and wants to destroy everything God has made, he is fighting very hard.

66

So Jesus had known Satan as Lucifer, the beautiful angel who became the proud, arrogant, egotistical angel who coveted being equal with God. We are told in Exodus 20:17 that we are not to covet. Coveting something means to want what someone else has so much that we are prepared to harm them in getting it. We are not to covet what other people have, but above everything we are not to want to be God. Lots of people really show that they want to be God, by the way they act. Satan wanted to be like God, and to have the angels worship him. And Satan hated to see Adam and Eve having such a close relationship with God, that he wanted to stop it! Satan wanted Eve to sin as he had, so he tempted her to want to become like God by eating the fruit God had said they could not eat. Satan tried to get Eve to believe his lie—and she did. Jesus had seen Satan doing that to Eve, and the whole reason that Jesus had come to earth was to have victory over Satan. Jesus came to make it possible for people to come back and be in God's family and have a close relationship with God.

Why had Satan come to this wild country place to be alone with Jesus? Satan was trying to spoil what Jesus had come to do. He was wickedly plotting to try to make Jesus sin. We are told that Jesus was in this wilderness place, surrounded by wild bushes and rocks, wild animals and insects for forty days and forty nights. What did he eat? We are told he did not eat during that time at all. For forty days and forty nights Satan was whispering temptations to Jesus. And then we are told what the last three temptations were.

You can imagine how hungry Jesus was by this time. Perhaps you have never been forty days without anything to eat, but you probably know what it is like to be very, *very* hungry. Maybe you know what it is like to rush into the room where the bread is kept, and to start eating bread before it is time for the meal. Luke tells us that after those forty days, Jesus was hungry!

At this point Satan said, "If thou art the Son of God, command this stone that it become bread." What a nasty phrase . . . "If thou art the Son of God . . . ." Have you ever had anyone say something like, "If you're *big* enough to climb over that fence, why don't you steal those strawberries," or "Why don't you steal the cherries if you are strong enough to climb up that tree." It is horrid to have someone challenge you with a nasty "if," and then ask you to do something wrong to prove that that "if" is true.

Over and over again people tried to make Jesus prove that he was the Son of God by doing something that would have spoiled what he came for, that would have given Satan the victory. This time as Satan stood there in person, sneering or leering or just giving a falsely sweet smile, he added this very tempting idea. "If thou art the Son of God, command this stone that it become bread." Could Jesus have turned the stones into bread? Yes, of course he could. Did he ever do miracles like that when he was on the earth? Yes, he did. Then why would it have been sinful to do it right then? Bread is not a wrong thing. It would not have been wrong for Jesus to eat when he was hungry. But it would have been sin for Jesus to obey the Devil. Sometimes the Devil tells us to do something which seems right to us, and we "rationalize" . . . that is, we fool ourselves into thinking it is the thing to do! He is very subtle that way. He tries to twist us.

Do you know how Jesus answered Satan? Luke and Matthew explain that he answered him by quoting from the Bible! Jesus quoted from the Old Testament, from the book of Deuteronomy, 8:3. He quoted from the place where Moses told the Israelites to remember how God fed them with manna (food) which dropped from heaven every day, to feed them and to teach them that although God could provide food for their bodies, the really important thing for them to do was to listen to his Word. God told those Old Testament people that man "lives" by listening to the Word of God. So Jesus quoted this verse, saying, "It is written, Man shall not live by bread alone, but by every word that proceedeth out of the mouth of God."

Why did Jesus quote from the Bible? Once again he is making it very clear to anyone who has doubts about it that the Old Testament is God's Word because he, Jesus, says so.

Also he wants us to know that the Word of God, the Bible, has real power over Satan. In the book of Ephesians where it tells us how to fight against Satan (Ephesians 6:11–18), we are told to take the sword of the Spirit, which is the Word of God. So you see it is made clear to us that quoting from the Bible when Satan tempts us is like thrusting him with a sword. Jesus did this first of all because he knew this would defeat Satan with what is really a sword thrust, because Jesus knew that the Bible has that power. Secondly, Jesus is showing us what *we* can do when Satan tempts us. Satan tempts people no matter what age they are. The temptations may be of different sorts, but they really are not all *that* different. And the wonderful thing is that any one of us who are Christians can do what Jesus did, no matter what age we are.

This is one good reason for memorizing Bible verses, because then we can have them ready in our minds when we need them. In Psalm 119:11 it says, "Thy word have I laid up in mine heart, that I might not sin against thee." It speaks of memorizing, as "hiding in the heart," so that we have the Bible at the center of our lives.

» Then Satan tempted Jesus again. He took Jesus up into a high mountain and showed him all the kingdoms of the world (that means the nations and tribes and countries). As they looked out over the world (Luke says it was "in a moment of time . . . "), Satan said to Jesus, "If thou therefore wilt worship before me, it shall all be thine." Satan said that he could give power over the world to anyone he wanted to give it to. Now the Bible does call Satan the prince of this world (John 12:31). One day Satan will be cast out of the world, but that day has not come yet. So Satan could have given the world in a certain way to Jesus. And Satan said he would do that . . . *if Jesus would bow down and worship him.*

What a temptation to rationalize! *But* if Jesus had obeyed Satan and worshiped him, then not one single person could have gone to Heaven. The way to Heaven, for each person who will be there, depended on Jesus. The possibility of having sin forgiven, and of having that white "robe of righteousness" covering us, the possibility of being born into God's family—all depended on Jesus not sinning, not bowing to Satan, and on his taking the punishment for our sin. If he had sinned, he could not have taken our place. Satan, out there on that mountain, was trying to put out the light altogether, and plunge the world into terrible darkness for ever. Satan is always trying to get people to do something bad by promising a good result. People get caught in his trap so often. Some people even worship Satan, and build churches in which to worship him, now in this twentieth century, about two thousand years after he stood on that hill with Jesus.

Jesus did not worship Satan, but quoted from the Bible in answering him. He quoted from Deuteronomy 6:13, saying, "Thou shalt fear the Lord thy God; and him shalt thou serve." That is a good verse for us to memorize. It is a serious thing to worship anybody or anything other than God. Satan never stops trying to get people to worship something else for just a little while, in order that some good may come. This is always wrong. In some parts of the world, people are urged to bow down to an idol, or to pray at a shrine, or to take part in some kind of worship in a false religion, in order to be allowed to go afterwards to a Christian church.

Before the last great war, in Korea during the Japanese occupation, people were told they must put a shrine, called a "Shinto Shrine," in a corner of the church, and that before they had their church service they must bow down to the shrine; then they could worship God afterwards. If they would not bow down before the shrine, they were put in prison. Some people "rationalized" (that means they excused themselves, and made up reasons to themselves to feel all right about it) and bowed, and said they were still Christians. Others, some who were only fourteen and fifteen years old, would not bow, because they said they would only worship the true and living God. We need to be careful, whether people are asking us to do something they say is just "amusing" but is really false worship, or false religion, or whether it is something like putting a Shinto Shrine in church. We need to be especially careful in this twentieth century, because there are lots of ways in which people are worshiping Satan and getting mixed up with his sneaking ways of turning people into the dark, and getting them away from the light which is true truth. It's no joke to fool about serious things. In your parties (or in your "pretend" games, if you are younger) don't ever get mixed up in playing with ouija boards, or in any weird sort of falsely "spiritual" kind of stunt or game. Satan is a mean enemy.

After this, Satan gave Jesus one other temptation. He took him to Jerusalem and set him up on a pinnacle of the Temple. He started this temptation with the same nasty phrase he used in the first one, "If thou art the Son of God. . . . " The reason Satan was fighting so furiously was that Christ is the unique Son of God. He was trying to get Jesus to sin so that all that Jesus was going to do as the Son of God would be cancelled out! And today, Satan continues to try to cancel out the effect of Jesus being the Son of God by causing people to doubt that this is true. When Satan succeeds in getting people to say that Jesus is just a man, and not the Son of God, then he is pleased with his victory. When people teach this, they are bringing more darkness into the world.

If we had our candles lit in a dark room, and we thought of each of these candles as churches where the truth has been preached, and then we thought of *new* ministers coming who did *not* believe that Jesus is the unique Son of God . . . we could illustrate what happens just by blowing out first one and then another candle. Try it. If you have a dozen birthday candles, scatter them round a dark room, then pretend these represent places where the truth is being taught . . . but as first one and then another gets doubts, and teaches that Jesus is just a man, and the Bible is just a fairy story . . . blow out first one and then another. These are Satan's victories.

But that day Satan had no victory over Jesus, and we are very thankful he did not and will not. Jesus came to do something, and he did it! Satan said on the pinnacle of the Temple, "If thou art the Son of God, cast thyself down from hence." And then Satan did something he often does to people: he quoted a Bible verse, from Psalm 91:11, "It is written, he shall give his angels charge over thee, to keep thee in all thy ways. They shall bear thee up in their hands, lest thou dash thy foot against a stone." Jesus, in answer to this wrong use of the Bible by Satan, quoted from Deuteronomy 6:16, "Ye shall not tempt the Lord your God." It is the same thing again; Satan is trying to trick Jesus into obeying him. Of course angels could come and protect Jesus, just as Jesus could make stones into bread if he wanted to, but to obey Satan, in order to prove that he, Jesus, was God . . . that would mean defeat.

We should be warned by all this, because Satan is not very original. He continues to do the same kinds of things year after year. Often you will have people who do not believe the Bible, quoting some verse in a wrong fashion to try to get you to do something that would be wrong. It is very important to study the whole Bible carefully, so as not to be led astray by people who take verses or parts of verses "out of context." What does that mean? Well, for example in Proverbs we are told, "But the foolish despise wisdom and instruction." And if you just took the last four words in that sentence and said that they came from the Bible, they would clash with everything the Bible teaches. If people try to prove something quite opposite to what the Bible as a whole book teaches by quoting something separated from the entire teaching, they can lead you astray. After we have become a part of God's family by accepting what Christ did for us, we can ask the Holy Spirit to teach us the true meaning of the Word of God as we read it, and pray that he will keep us from Satan's attempts to fool us.

When the Devil had ended these efforts to make Jesus sin, we are told he "departed." He went away for a time. How exhausted Jesus must have been after all the pressure that had been put upon him, and after not eating for forty days, too! How relieved he must have been to see Satan turn away

Jesus tells Satan not to tempt his God.   Luke 4:1–13

and go. Then a special thing happened. In Matthew 4:11, we are told that after Satan left, angels came and took care of Jesus. It says they "ministered unto him."

When we were very tired and hungry in Japan, in Hong Kong, in Singapore and other places in the East, we would go to a restaurant, and the first thing they brought out was a lovely hot face cloth! What a wonderful custom that is, to have a tightly rolled-up, hot face cloth taken from the tray by pincers and handed to you so that you can shake it out and put it over your *face.* How good it feels to be refreshed in this way, before tea and food is brought to you! Perhaps you have had a face cloth brought to you at the end of a long air trip. Somehow this takes away some of the tiredness.

We don't know what those angels did, but we know that Jesus had the refreshment and food he needed at the end of that hard time. How glad the angels must have been to be able to do something specific for him! How thankful the angels must have been that he had the victory over Satan! They would have been thankful for our sakes. We can imagine them talking about it. We aren't told what their reaction then was, but we do know that angels rejoice in heaven every time someone accepts Christ as his or her Savior. So if you have believed, you can be sure that is one time the angels talked about you! We may be certain that it was a special moment for these angels who took care of Jesus' needs right then. It would be a time they would always remember.

》 The account of Jesus's temptation, given to us so clearly, shows us that Satan is a person. He is not infinite, because only God is infinite. If he is not infinite he can only be in one place at one time, but he *is* powerful, and he does have other persons who do whatever he commands. These are the demons. He is always trying to fight against truth, always trying to make people believe lies, so that he can spoil not only what God has made, but any relationship between God and *people.* Satan hates it when anyone has a relationship with God.

This account also shows angels can come and do things in this world. We know the angel Gabriel came to talk to both Zacharias and Mary, and now we also learn about these angels who came to take care of Jesus when he was tired and hungry. We are told about what some other angels have done and will do. But there are people who, like the Sadducees in Jesus' day, don't believe there are any angels or demons or anything "supernatural" so if they were reading this account, they would just cut out about Satan and about the angels.

What is "supernatural"? That word just means *anything* that God has made and that God can do, which men do not see every day around them, and men cannot do themselves. Things like Heaven, and angels, and Jesus making water into wine and a little bread into enough for many thousands; like Jesus' body rising from the dead, and Elijah being fed by big birds dropping meat, and Daniel caged with lions and not being eaten up or even bitten, like the fiery furnace not burning the young men whom the king threw in, and like Jonah being swallowed by a great fish that God had prepared to be there, and like the Red Sea rolling back so the Israelites could walk through. Promises of God for the future are "supernatural," such as Jesus coming back and people being raised from the dead, and our bodies being changed to be like his body . . . all kinds of wonderful things promised for the future are supernatural.

But people today who are like the Sadducees do not believe in anything supernatural. Now Sadducees were religious men, and they would have read the Scriptures, and have claimed to be good Jews. What did they do when they read about anything supernatural? They just cut it out! Maybe not with scissors, but with their minds.

Will you all play a serious game, or give yourselves a serious illustration? It may seem ridiculous, but really it is something you should do. Get a pair of scissors and an old magazine or newspaper that you don't mind destroying. Look for a story that talks about certain things or kinds of people quite a bit. For instance a story, or a news article, telling about the problems of foreigners, and foreign products. You are going to decide that you don't believe foreign countries or foreign people exist. You believe that only your own country exists. So you have to cut out everything that talks about another country, and everything mentioned that was made in another country, and every mention of a person from another country. Maybe one of you should prepare this "game" for later in the day, or for tomorrow night, but do prepare well for it. Let's say this article talks about bananas, and about the people in that country that grow bananas, and about some things made there. You have to cut out the word "banana" from any recipe mentioned, as well! You don't believe the country, the people, *or* the bananas exist, so how can you talk about a banana pie or tart recipe? You can find a lot of better illustrations if you just get a newspaper or a magazine. Get scissors, a large sheet of paper or cardboard, and with the scissors literally cut out everything that you have said you don't believe exists. Then paste what remains on the large piece of paper, full of gaps.

Now try to read the article. Does it make sense? If you don't believe the country or the people who make rubber, or the rubber trees exist, you have to cut out everything that speaks of making rubber tires or foam rubber, etc. Even if a synthetic imitation is made, who would have thought of the imitation if there hadn't been the thing to imitate? Please do this at least one evening, and try reading what is left, out loud. It is just like the Sadducees of Jesus' day and the liberal theologians of today cutting the supernatural out of the Bible and then acting as if the rest made sense by itself.

How can you make something known to people if they are going to cut out the things that are essential to your reporting? If you decide that everything outside your own country does not exist, how could anyone tell you the truth about what they have experienced and seen in their travels? The Bible is God's Word to us. The Bible is God making known to us things that happened before man lived, things that happened centuries ago, things that happened at different periods of history, and things that are coming in the future. God is very fair in having put into words these things men need to know, but cannot experience, or find out for themselves, in their own short lifetimes.

Men try to find life on other planets, to see what is on the moon, to discover things they have not known before. When the newspaper reports came out about men walking on the moon for the first time, grandmother said, "They are just making that up, I don't believe it." So she "cut out" everything about the men going to the moon. How could she find out what was going on? She could not! It was useless to show her pictures or stories about it, or even to have her listen to the radio. She had "cut it out," you see.

God tells us about the reason we are separated from him, and tells us what happened to change the perfect world he made into something with suffering and sorrow. He tells us about the battle that is going on now with Satan and the demons, and he tells us about the angels who remained with him, and some of the things they do. He tells us about the future, and he tells us about how we can talk to him now, and he will answer us. *He could not tell us the truth if he did not tell us of the supernatural.* When people cut out part of what the Bible gives, they not only destroy that part, and make it impossible to understand what God is telling them, but it spoils all the rest too. When half the report or story is cut out, what is left is just plain nonsense.

At the very end of the Bible, in the next to the last two verses, a warning is given. It is serious and solemn. We are told that no one is to add anything to the Bible. The Pharisees did this by adding their own little rules and saying that these had to be obeyed as if they were equal to God's rules in the Bible. We are also forbidden to take away from the words in the Bible, as the Sadducees did by cutting out the supernatural. Never forget your lesson with the scissors. Don't cut things out of the Bible. God commands us not to, and warns us that there is a punishment for doing it. Also, you are destroying your possibility of understanding any of the rest of it. And don't judge the teaching of the Bible by either "Pharisee" kinds of teachers, or "Sadducee" kinds of teachers, because that isn't *fair* to what God is wanting you to know. What kind of a school would it be if you had to study out of textbooks that had half the words cut out of every sentence! It is important to be sure you are reading God's Word the way he meant you to have it.

7

PEOPLE ARE NOT JUST PEBBLES

After the temptation was over, and the angels had cared for his needs, Jesus returned to Galilee (Luke 4:14). And we are told that on one Sabbath day in Nazareth, where Jesus had been brought up, he went into the synagogue, as he had always done. (The synagogue is where the Jews worshiped on the Sabbath day each week. That is our Saturday.)

Luke tells us that Jesus stood up to read out loud, and they gave him the book of Isaiah. The exciting thing is that you can turn to your Old Testament and find the very place where Jesus read from that day! Doesn't it give you a thrill up your spine to think that you can read from the very same place Jesus read? It is in Isaiah 61:1 and 2. We are told that when Jesus had opened the book and had found the place where this was written, he began to read. Just think of listening to Jesus, the Second Person of the Trinity, read a paragraph that had been written 700 years before, that had been written about *his* coming! Wouldn't Simeon and Anna have been excited if they had heard him read that? I wonder who was there that day who *was* excited. Let us read what he read: "The Spirit of the Lord God is upon me; because the Lord hath anointed me to preach good tidings unto the meek; he hath sent me to bind up the broken-hearted, to proclaim liberty to the captives, and the opening of the prison to them that are bound; to proclaim the acceptable year of the Lord,"

Yes, comma! That is not the end of verse two. Jesus stopped and closed the book of Isaiah after that comma, because he was being very accurate, and letting people have a chance to realize that there was a big break in time after that comma. We have already thought about how different the Bible is from other books, because it is God's book, and because God can tell us things to come in the future. Well, this place in Isaiah told about what the Messiah, Jesus, would do during his first time of coming to the world, and then it went on after that comma to say some of the things which will happen after his second coming. (Jesus is coming back again, you see, but we will talk about that later.)

At this time Jesus just read out loud to all those who were in that synagogue in Nazareth, the things that the Messiah would do. He then told these people that he *was* the Messiah, and that later he would do these things. That was all the proof they should have needed. It was all so very fair. After he finished reading, and closed the book, he gave the book to the minister, and sat down. Luke says the eyes of everyone in the synagogue were upon him. No matter where they were sitting they all turned to stare at him. Something must have struck them about it, and *some* must have been excited. I am sure there were a few who were filled with a kind of expectancy, a kind of breathless feeling of "Oh, I wonder what is coming next!" Those who were ready to listen would have felt differently from the others about what came next. Jesus began to say to them, "This day," (that is, today, that's clear enough isn't it? *Today*). "Today is this scripture fulfilled in your ears." He said that what they had just heard read really was going to take place in *their* lifetime. He told them that what they had heard about ever since they were children, and their grandparents had heard about since they were children, was going to happen right in their time, and they could see the things happening with their own eyes! Do you think all the people were happy when they heard this? Do you think they were all *excited* to find out that the prophecy of Isaiah would now be fulfilled? Wouldn't you expect them to start praising God together for sending their Messiah, for keeping his promise to them all through the years?

No, sadly *none* of these things happened. It was sad for Jesus, who had waited for the right moment in history to come, and who had left everything to come. I am sure the Holy Spirit was grieved too. We know that God the Father is saddened as men turn away from his true word. How more forcibly could the Word of God be given than to have it written by inspiration as God gave it, then to be *read* by the Second Person of the Trinity who *said*, so that men could hear, that it *was* the Word of God, and was to be fulfilled right then? I am sure the angels were sad at the men's reactions. And any who *did* receive Jesus' word and believe it that day, would have been sad to see the others react. Only one supernatural group of people—Satan and the demons—were glad that day. They are always glad when people turn away from God's truth. You see Jesus had been speaking in the synagogue in Nazareth, his home town, where he had come as a boy, and as a young man. So the people now cried out, "Is not this Joseph's son?" They were saying, "Why, this is just Joseph's and Mary's boy. We know *that* family!" Then Jesus answered them by saying that he knew they would tell him just to go ahead and heal himself. He said that a prophet is not accepted in his own country. In other words that even in the *past* when God had sent prophets, men who were especially prepared to give a message from him, the people who lived where they grew up would not believe them. Now they were doing the same with the Son of God.

Jesus reminded them that it was a widow from another part of the country who believed Elijah, when Elijah told her her barrel of meal would never be finished, and that there would always be a little oil in her pitcher, if she made a pancake for him. It was a Syrian, a man of *another* country, named Naaman, who believed that Elisha really *was* sent from God, and who was healed of his leprosy as a result. As Jesus reminded these men of this, they should have realized what a terrible thing they were doing in turning away from One who was *more* than a Prophet of God, who was God the Messiah himself.

But instead, when they heard him explaining and telling them things that should have made them understand, Luke tells us, "They were filled with wrath." They were furious. Can't you hear the angry roar of words and ugly sounds of fury pouring out of their throats? Have you ever seen an

angry mob? When lots and lots of people get angry at the
same time, they make each other angrier and angrier. And
when lots of people get angry against one person, they make
each other feel important by deciding that the one person is
bad, and they are all good. There is nothing that makes
people feel more proud than to scream together against
someone. It can happen over little things when brothers and
sisters are playing together, or it can happen to adults too. If
you have ever been the person that everyone is against, you
will know what it feels like.

When one of us was nine years old, some children in a
small town where she lived decided to gang up against her
and to call her names and laugh at her every time they saw
her. So she knows a little bit of what it feels like, because this
went on for months. But never has anyone stood alone for
the truth, without Jesus understanding exactly how they feel.
He came to his own people, the Jews, his own village people,
his own synagogue people. And we are told in John 1:11, 12:
"He came unto his own, and they that were his own received
him not. But as many as received him, to them gave he the
right to become children of God, even to them that believe
on his name." Yes, Jesus, the Son of God, who—as John says
in John 1:3—made everything, and who came as a light shining in a dark place, was *not* welcomed by the people of his
village, during the time he lived among them, nor does the
world as a whole receive him. But to everyone who does
receive him, and believes what he says, and accepts what he
offers, as he offers to take our punishment, he gives the
power to become the sons of God. He said so and he keeps
his promises.

» Back to the angry mob. What did they *do*? Well, they rose up.
That means they stood up, but I think it was a threatening
kind of standing up. With ugly, hateful, angry-looking faces,
they stood up and rushed at Jesus, forced him out of the city,
and led him to the brow of the hill on which the city was
built. You can picture a mob pushing a man, surrounding him
on all sides and then forcing him along in the way you are

82

forced along in the sea, with an undertow pulling you and a big wave pushing you. The city of Nazareth was built on a hill, and a "brow" of a hill is like a cliff . . . a sudden, steep drop! They were all ready to throw him over that cliff, and they expected to see him crash on the rocks beneath. "Now we'll get rid of him," they must have thought. A violent mob against one man! Could he escape?

Jesus truly is God, and although he came to die in our place, this was not the right time, he was going to *live* for us for a period of time first. Also, he came to do all those other things Isaiah wrote that he was going to do—to preach to the poor, to heal the broken-hearted, to make blind people see. And he was going to do some of these things in a way people could see and understand, as well as other things *inside* people, where other people could not see. No, it was not *time* for Jesus to die, and this was not the place, or the way for him to die. So he did what he *could* have done at any time, but did not do always. He used his power as the Second Person of the Trinity, as God who had always lived and who could do anything, and he just slipped out of that crowd, out of their sight. Suddenly he was not there. Suddenly there was nobody there to throw down.

As Jesus just slipped out of their sight, he went on down to another city to continue his work. He went to Capernaum, a city of Galilee, and taught the people there. In Capernaum they were astonished at his teaching because his word came to them with such power. There they must have said to each other, "This man certainly preaches differently from any rabbi we have ever heard. He speaks with terrific power." Remember that Jesus was speaking with the power of the Holy Spirit. Jesus wants us to notice this. There is more he wants to teach us later on about the Holy Spirit being able to speak through us with power, when we become Christians, believers, and are born into God's family, and restored to a place of relationship with God.

In the Capernaum synagogue, there was a man who had an evil spirit in him, that is, one of the demons. And this demon, speaking to Jesus, cried out, "Let us alone, what have we to do with thee, Jesus of Nazareth, you have come to destroy us. I know who you are . . . you are the Holy One of God." Now the men in the synagogue heard this demon screaming against Jesus, and recognizing him as the Son of God who had come to have a victory over Satan. That was something for those men to remember, wasn't it? Then Jesus, who felt sorry for the poor man who had the demon in him, rebuked the demon and commanded him to come out of the man. And we are told that the demon made the man fall down, but then he came out of the man—and when that happened the man would really have looked different, calm and peaceful and quiet.

Then the synagogue men were really amazed, and said to each other, "What kind of a man is this who speaks with such authority and power that he can command unclean spirits to come out of a man?" And we know they talked about this all over the place, because we are told that the fame of Jesus now went out over every place in the country around there.

As soon as this had taken place, Jesus got up and went out of the synagogue, and went to the home of a man named Simon Peter. When he got into the house, everyone there began begging Jesus to do something to help Simon Peter's mother-in-law. They told Jesus she had gone down with a very high fever and they begged Jesus to help in some way. So Jesus went to stand beside this very sick woman and he spoke, telling the sickness to go away. Luke, who is a doctor, is of course very interested in these cases of Jesus healing people. As a doctor he knew that these really *were* miracles. Jesus, according to Luke, "rebuked the fever: and it left her and immediately she rose up and ministered unto them." I think Luke was impressed, as anyone would be, who knows anything about people who have had a high fever and a serious illness, that she not only got better, but that there was no period of convalescence. You know how it is: you begin to feel better, but you still have to stay in bed for a time, or you will have a relapse. But when Jesus made someone well, he made them completely well right away. Peter's wife's mother got up and prepared something like afternoon tea, or supper, for the other people, rather than having them make her something: no wonder Luke was impressed.

As the sun went down that day, and the working day was over, so many people in that area had heard about Peter's mother-in-law, that crowds came to Jesus and brought their sick husbands, wives, children, mothers, fathers, uncles and so on—Luke says, "All they that had any sick with divers diseases brought them unto him." "Divers diseases" just means a great variety of different kinds of illnesses. And what did Jesus do? He touched every one of them with his hands, and each one was healed. During that same long evening, many other people who had demons living in them came there too, and Jesus rebuked the demons, scolding them, telling them to come out and leave people alone. It is interesting to notice that Luke tells us that, as the demons came out, they cried out, calling Jesus the Son of God. It is no problem to Satan and the demons to know that Jesus is the Son of God. Later on in the Bible, James says that just believing that there is one God, the true God, is not in itself enough, because even the demons believe this, and *tremble*. The demons know that God is really there. They know that God is powerful, more powerful than Satan, so they "tremble" with fear when they are face to face with Jesus, the Son of God. It is only human beings who go around during their lifetime saying that "there is no God," or who choose to make some other God out of their own imaginations to worship. Satan lies to people about God, but he doesn't fool himself, or the demons! He is just fighting, and trying to hurt as many people as he can.

Jesus must have stayed there helping people all through the night. We are told that when day came, he left and went out into a desert place, but that people followed him out there, too, looking for help. He told them he had to preach in other cities, too, because he had come to let many people know the truth. So now Jesus is doing just what the verse he read in the synagogue said the Messiah would do—he is preaching the gospel to the poor, healing the broken-hearted,

85

making blind people see. Remember that people could hear
Isaiah read in the synagogue; they knew this prophecy; they
were being given proof that Jesus was really fulfilling what the
Messiah was supposed to do. They should recognize who he
is!

What would you expect people to do when they heard
of Someone who could do such miracles? You would expect
them to rush to see him, wouldn't you? Curiosity would make
a lot of them come, and wanting to get over a deformity or
blindness or something else wrong in their bodies would
make others want to come. Yes, crowds would come. And
this is just what happened when people heard of what Jesus
had done in Capernaum.

》 One day the crowds grew so great that, as Jesus was standing
by the lake of Gennesaret, he saw two empty fishing boats,
and it gave him an idea of how to get a little way away from
the crowds, so that he could speak and yet not be pushed.
The fishermen were washing their nets in the shallow water.
Have you ever seen fishermen washing their nets? They stand
up to about their knees in water and slush the nets up and
down to get the seaweed and shells or anything messy out of
them. Jesus stepped into Simon's fishing boat, and called over
to Simon, saying something like this, "Simon, would you
mind pushing your boat out a little way from the land?"
Simon did this, and there Jesus sat down in the boat, now
separated from the pushing crowds, but near enough for
them to hear him. And he began to teach the people. What
a wonderful pulpit! There in the boat with the little waves
lap-lap-lapping against the sides, with the ripple of the waters
catching the light of the sun, and the skies—with perhaps
clouds drifting past, people could look at all the beauty of
sky, water, green plants, sand and rocks, and listen to the
One who made it all, telling them things he knew it was
important for them to know.

When people say, "Why doesn't God come and *tell*
people the truth!" remember that he did. Not only did he
come in history, right on this earth to die, but he came to talk

and explain. And then—he had it all carefully written down. Not *everything* Jesus said as he taught was written down, but the central things that are important for us to know were, and what was written has been preserved through hundreds of years—and kept from any serious mistakes that copying could have made. It is all so very exciting, and yet not enough people are excited about it now. And I wonder that day how many of these people were excited about hearing the teaching of Jesus, and how many were just wanting to have something right then, like healing, or an immediate *gift* of some sort.

There is a big difference between just wanting to get something that God might *give* for right now, and wanting really to *know* God, and listen to him, and learn how to become his child. As Jesus taught and spoke that day, he knew the difference inside the people. He didn't just have to look at their faces to see different reactions and different desires. He knew then, as he knows now, who we really are inside, what we are thinking about, our struggles and our longings. And if we are just putting on an act and not being really real, he knows that, too.

Now when Jesus had finished teaching and speaking to the crowd, he turned to Simon and said, "Launch out your ship into the deep water, and let down your nets for a catch of fish." And Simon answering said, "Master, we have worked all night long, and we have caught nothing in our nets. However, if you tell me to, I'll let down the net again." This was just what Simon did, and as soon as he did so, there were so many fish enclosed in the net, that it began to break. Simon, and the others with him, beckoned to the men in the other ship. You imagine that beckoning as rather frantic—saying, "Hurry, hurry, there are so many fish! Out net is breaking! Hurry, they'll all get away." The others got there in a hurry, I'm sure, and as expert fishermen they would soon have hauled in all they could. Luke tells us there was enough to fill both ships. They were so loaded with fish that they began to sink down lower into the water.

When Simon Peter saw what was happening, he fell

down at Jesus' feet, saying, "Depart from me; for I am a sinful man, O Lord." He was so astonished at the catch of fish, as a fisherman who knew what it was to fish all night for a small fraction of that number, that he recognized the miracle involved in Jesus supplying that many fish at the right spot at that moment. It made Simon Peter recognize that Jesus was truly the Lord, and it made him afraid because he thought of his sins. We are told that James and John, who were sons of Zebedee, and were partners with Simon, were afraid, too. Jesus, who knew their thoughts and fears, said kindly to Simon, "Fear not; from henceforth thou shalt catch men."

Simon Peter and his partners had been fishermen for many years. They knew what it was to make their living from fishing, and they were filled with the realization that Jesus could enable them to do a week's fishing in ten minutes, if he so willed. They must have been struck with the reality of the power of the One who was speaking to them.

But what had he said? He had said that from now on they were to catch men! What did that mean? They were to have a long time with Jesus ahead to learn *more* of what it meant. Right now, however, these three men brought their boats to land, and really followed Jesus. Luke tells us, "They left all, and followed him." This means they stopped their work of fishing for a living, and followed Jesus. At first it meant sitting at his feet, listening to him teach, walking around with him, coming to know and understand him better. They were not immediately ready to be fishers of men. It took time for them to be prepared. They had much to learn, and many difficult as well as wonderful things ahead of them.

Does Jesus ask everyone to leave their little ships, their nets, their professions and their work to follow him and be fishers of men? Does he ask every dentist to leave his drills, every business man to leave his office, his store, his factory, every artist to leave his easel, every printer to leave his printing press, every doctor to leave his hospital, every farmer to

Simon Peter at Jesus' feet.   Luke 5:1–11

leave his fields, every violinist to leave his orchestra, every nurse to leave her nursing home, every baker to leave his bakery, every candlestick maker to leave his melted wax, every airplane pilot to leave his plane, every photographer to leave his camera, every bus driver to leave his bus? No, he has a *plan* for each one of his children, and has a *place* where each one is meant to be, but that plan is individual, and the place to be and things each one is to be doing are different. The important thing is to be *willing* to do what he asks. And wherever we are, as those who are following Jesus, we are meant to "catch men" for Jesus.

Let's think together. All these things we are finding out in the Bible are true, aren't they? And if they are true, then isn't it very important that people find out about them? How can people find out things? By reading, and by hearing things explained. Some people don't like certain kinds of buildings, and would never go in a church. Other people would never understand anything if they had to go to big meetings. They get "turned off" by crowds. Other people can't stand a certain kind of music, and would never go to hear it. There are people who differ in their language, in their customs, in their education, in the kinds of houses they choose to live in, in the things that interest them. We could go on and on about *different* kinds of people. Well, you see Jesus is comparing people with *fish*. Think how many kinds of fish there are. This evening, or another evening this week when you have more time, try to find pictures of fish: perhaps out of old magazines, nature magazines . . . or if you are an artist or a naturalist draw, paint, crayon a lot of pictures of fish. Maybe you have an aquarium in your town you could visit. Maybe you have a fish bowl or an aquarium in your house. Spend some time gathering pictures of great varieties of fish. Spend some time talking together as a family or group about fish. Hunt up information and read it together about how different fish live—the difference in habits of salmon and trout, for instance—the difference between salt water and fresh water fish, the difference between tropical fish and fish in northern waters.

Jesus is making a comparison to make us *think* as well as to make Simon Peter and James and John understand. These three men knew about fish, so when Jesus said, "Follow me and you will catch men," they understood that men will slip away out of the net, and will swim in the opposite direction, and will be very difficult to "catch for the Lord." We are to realize something else too. What will "catch" some fish, would never catch others. If we are to be "fishers of men" we are not to have little tiny rules and say, "One, two, three . . . what you do is get a hook, put a worm on it, sit by the water for a while and presto . . . a fish!" You may catch something in a pond or lake that way, but a great big tuna fish needs some expert equipment and some expert understanding, and a bit of training and strength of a certain kind, to land! Fishing is complicated, and how you go about it depends on what kind of fish you are out to catch.

Of course, as Jesus uses this illustration to make us *think,* he expects us to realize that the comparison does not completely fit. I mean, we don't catch men to fry them and eat them. All the illustrations Jesus uses are to bring out clearly certain points. People are not meant to be *unintelligent* about where the illustration must stop. Of course, what Jesus is talking about is catching men in the sense of bringing them to know about him, to know about how to be born into God's family by accepting him as Savior.

Remembering that now, let us bring our information about fish together, and look at our pictures together, and remember that we need to understand the kind of people with whom we are meant to be talking about the Lord. We need to know something about them, and their likes and dislikes, their ways of thinking and acting and feeling. Because, of course, they are people, and not fish, and so they think and act and feel . . . they have ideas and make choices, and we need really to communicate with them. That means talking in a way that they understand. Let the difference in the fish help us to understand that to make the important truth known, we need to be willing to understand the difference in people.

Can any one man fish for every kind of fish in the world? I think not. We need then to pray that the Lord will help us to be prepared, to know where he would have us live, what sort of things we should be doing (whether farming, or doctoring, or engineering, or nursing, or typing, or baking bread) in order to be able to catch the kind of "fish"—men and women, boys and girls—that *he* wants us to.

We are meant to have people in for dinner, tea, lunch, supper, or take someone on a picnic with us because we are told Christians are to be hospitable. Naturally they are to be *people* we *meet* . . . people with whom we can communicate with some sort of real understanding. We cannot talk to everyone in the world. We need to ask God to help us to find the people of his choice, for us to talk to (or to help those people to find us). We need to pray that he will send them to us, in the way Jesus showed Peter he could send fish near the boat. Yes, some of us will be pastors, ministers, missionaries . . . but that does not mean these people are more important fishermen than others. Everyone has the responsibility to ask the Lord to use them right where they are. Everyone is to be a teller. Why? Because God is not sending an angel to people to tell them. He has chosen to send human beings to tell other human beings. Jesus started this in a special way by taking these men to train them. But what he said to them he says to us. There is no one better to talk to an artist than another artist, no one better to talk to a ten-year-old than another ten-year-old, no one better to talk to a philosopher than another philosopher, no one better to talk to a violinist than another violinist. There is training needed first in knowing the Lord himself, or we cannot tell others about him. Then we need to know his Word, so that we can tell what it says.

But . . . it is important to know the "fish" . . . that is, to know and understand and care about and love *people*. Because we are "catching" people to give them something to help them now, and for ever, we need to *care* about *people* as *people* . . . not just to *count* them as so many in a "net." We need to understand that people are important, are significant in a really personal universe. Big words? Yes, but before this book is finished, you can come to understand that people are *not* just bits of atoms stuck together, they are not just pebbles that sink into the ocean out of sight . . . they *matter.* They matter to God, and they matter in history. You need to understand that you are important to God, as well as others. Then you can learn to love others as yourself!

8
A MATTER OF LIFE AND DEATH

Jesus healed many different people of all kinds of diseases
when he was on the earth. He had only to speak a word, and
the worst diseases were healed. He did it that men might
know that he was God, and he did it to give men very *vivid*
illustrations of how sin is like a horrible virus and disease
which needs to be completely cured, cleansed, taken away.
Sometimes when a person has a disease, it actually destroys
portions of the body. Even if they get over the disease, the
portion of the body cannot be given back to them by doctors,
or through medicine. Where did disease come from?

   You remember that God had told Adam and Eve that, if
they ate of the fruit of that tree, they would surely die. It was
a promise. All they had to do was to believe God, to believe
his promise, and not eat that particular fruit. Instead they
believed Satan when he said they would *not* die. All right.
They ate—and death started.

   What is death? It is a separation of the soul from the
body. The soul is the person, *and* the body is the person.
Each of us is one whole person, made up of the soul (we
think, we have ideas, we love, we have feelings, we have
thoughts and feelings about God when we come to know
him, as well as thoughts and feelings about other people) and
of the body—we have hands, feet, noses, tongues, eyes, brain
cells, voice boxes, lungs and hearts. The things of the soul
cannot be seen with the eyes of our bodies—but our hands
and feet, tongues and eyes can be seen. Without our bodies
we cannot express to each other the things which are going
on which people cannot see.

   Adam and Eve died spiritually right away; that means

they were separated from God. They had to leave that beautiful garden where they were able to talk with words, and
walk along real paths, with *God*. They were cut off from *him*,
and they could *not* come back without some way of being *rid*
of their sins. We have talked a lot about how the lamb was
the illustration. The lamb was the way God helped people to
understand that only through the Lamb of God, the Messiah,
would there be a way to come back to God. Adam and Eve
were separated from God right away. But there were other
things that happened as a result of sin. Other kinds of death
began right away. Adam and Eve were not as happy together.
They were not as close to each other. People are separated
from people because of sin. There is so much talking about
black and white people not understanding each other, about
Europeans and Asians having differences; there are so many
divorces between men and women, so many children in families who fight with each other. All the troubles between people are a kind of separation, a kind of disease, a kind of
death.

Then there is no one who is always easy to live with
himself or herself. People often say to themselves, "I'm tired
of me. I get so mad with myself. I wish I were different. I am
sick of me." Yes, people are separated from themselves. That
is a part of the death that came. Then, before Adam and Eve
died, before anyone dies, there are things which cause the
body to become spoiled so that it is getting ready to be
separated from the soul. All the diseases. All the viruses and
germs. All the things which can happen to bodies came because of sin. It is a vicious circle, physical sickness, death,
and more sin, more diseases, more death.

Everyone in the world is troubled in one way or another
by the disease, or the accident, the sickness of body or mind,
that touches someone they *know*. *Some* people are troubled
about *all* the sickness and suffering in the world. But most of
them do not understand the connection between these things
and the whole problem of sin separating them from God.
Most people do not get as concerned that they are separated
from God, and that everyone is separated from God, as they

do about being separated from a leg when it is amputated, or being separated from their eyes, when they go blind.

Of course, we are clearly told all through the Bible that individual people are not always ill because of their individual sins. Job's friends had that wrong idea. They thought he had been very wicked because he had so *many* troubles. This was not true. Satan was trying to make Job hate God. Job trusted God in the middle of his troubles and illnesses. This won a battle God was waging against Satan. It is fantastic that, when we just keep on trusting God, we can be involved in fighting on God's side. No. Sickness is not God's punishment to individuals; it is part of the whole spoiledness of the universe after sin. History matters! There is cause and effect. If you eat a dirty bun with germs of intestinal flu on it, you will have intestinal flu. The germs in the world are a result of sin spoiling things, but your intestinal flu is not "sent" by God.

Remember the story about the little child whose mother said, "Don't touch the stove, you will be burned." The child touched the stove because someone said, "Don't believe Mother! You won't get burned! You'll learn to cook as she does." And so the child touched, and was burned. Now suppose that mother said, "Come now, here is a bowl of cool water, come, soak your hand in it, it will take the pain out and help the burn to heal." And the child ran away and played in the garden in the dirt. What would happen? Infection! Yes, and more infection, until perhaps blood poisoning set in. Can you see what we are trying to illustrate?

Of course, sin bringing death is far more overwhelming in the way it affects history, and all people, than is the story of the child being burned. But, don't you see, God did give a solution. God did tell people what to do. And throughout the centuries most of them have not listened. So the effects of sin and separation resulting from it, are getting worse and worse in the way men are treating each other, as well as in all kinds of new viruses appearing. It is like a burn becoming more and more infected.

Some day there will be an end to it all. God the Father has told us so; Jesus clearly teaches about that future time;

the Holy Spirit has helped men who were writing the Bible to write it accurately. The *promises* about the end of all the battle that Satan is continuing now *are* going to come true in the future. But right now we need to understand what God has made so plain to us, for the *now* of our lives, as well as being prepared to have a part in the future.

Jesus, as Luke the doctor tells us, healed people while he, Jesus, was living among them. Why? Because sickness and all the things death has brought into the world make Jesus sad and angry. He came to bring a victory over all that Satan introduced into the world. To heal some people at that time was a comfort to Jesus himself, I am sure, as he pushed their diseases aside in compassion. But this is *not* what was most important to Jesus. He made it very plain that he wanted people really to understand two things. First, that he was the Messiah and that the promises of God were being kept. He healed so they would know he was God. But, secondly he wanted to make plain to them that there was something he can do that was more important than healing their physical diseases. He knew that if he healed people of pneumonia they might get measles next week. He knew that if he healed people of chicken pox, they might get polio next month. He knew that if he healed people of blindness they might be deaf in another year. Jesus knew that there was only *one* permanent thing he could do for people, one thing—that would never change and would last for ever and ever. He knew he could give people something that could *not* be *taken away* from them, that would give them life for ever in perfect bodies, in a perfect home, in perfect surroundings, in a perfect condition mentally and spiritually. He knew he could do something that would eventually give a complete victory over Satan for ever.

Knowing this, do you think Jesus *only* healed people in order to make them happy and comfortable for a few days, weeks, or months? As he healed, he talked, he taught, he demonstrated (that is, he gave examples) so that they could *understand.* And *some* of them did listen, understand and believe.

One day Jesus was in a certain city, and a man with leprosy came and fell down before him, begging Jesus to heal him. Do you know what leprosy is? It is a disease which was thought to be incurable. People stayed far away from men with leprosy, and never touched them. This disease causes fingers and toes to drop off, and is very deforming. It is a terrible example of the separation of parts of the body from the rest of the body in disease. What did the man with leprosy say to Jesus? "Lord, if thou wilt, thou canst make me clean." Do you hear him? He really believed Jesus could heal this incurable disease. He said, "I know you can, Lord. If you only will, you can cure me completely." To be "clean" was something especially connected with leprosy at that time, because a leper was put outside, away from other people. Now Jesus put out his hand, and said, "I will, be thou clean." As with the woman, Peter's mother-in-law, this man was immediately clean, well and full of energy. The man had come believing Jesus had the power to do this, and Jesus had answered his pleas, had done what the man begged for. Now Jesus told him not to go and tell, but to go and worship God, according to a way given in the Old Testament. However, after that, more and more people heard about what Jesus could do, and we are told that great multitudes, or huge crowds, came to hear him speak and to be healed of the various things wrong with their bodies.

Luke tells us that Jesus went off into a wilderness place, away from the crowds and alone among just rocks and trees, to pray. God is continually helping us to understand that there is one God, but three Persons. Jesus, who is the Son of God, goes away from people, to talk alone with God the Father. We are never meant to forget that there are three Persons. Why must we not forget? Why is it important? Well, because it helps us to understand the whole universe. How can that be?

Any of you who are studying in school know that many are being taught that everything started with just atoms, or energy particles . . . just bits of particles flying around! This theory makes it impossible to explain where personality came from. That means it makes it impossible to explain where you and I came from. Where did thinking, acting, feeling, having ideas, choosing, making things, loving, writing, painting, making music . . . all the things that people *do*, come from? We are not machines or animals; we are people. If everyone came by "chance" out of particles, if it isn't a personal universe in the sense of being created by a personal God, it isn't a universe really for *people* at all. And all the things we feel and all the things we do just don't make any *sense,* and there is no purpose or reason for being here at *all.* It would mean we are just an accident. It would mean that just by accident the particles formed together in the pattern that is us. This would not be a "people universe," it would not be a personal universe, not a universe really made for mothers and dads, children and homes, friendships and love, talking and singing, playing music together, making beautiful poems and gathering flowers into an arrangement for the supper table. You are being taught that there is no real meaning in any of these relationships.

Why do people believe and teach this? Because they don't know how it *could* be a personal universe. Why don't they? Because they don't know, or believe, that God the Father, God the Son, and God the Holy Spirit have always been there, and that there has always been loving and talking, thinking, acting, feeling and choice. They don't know that people were made in the image of a Person, to be people.

Jesus, when he was on the earth, made it clear in many different ways, at many different times, that he and God the Father communicate, talk together. Jesus spent time with God the Father in prayer, over and over again. We will find out more about this later. But remember that Jesus is helping us to be ready to take what is true out of what we learn in school or at university, and helping us to recognize things that are not true, that are part of Satan's lie. One of the biggest lies of Satan is that people are not people at all, that there is no personality in the universe. Many young people are believing that lie, and feel it just isn't worth going on and doing anything. It has spoiled everything for them.

》 One day Pharisees, and doctors of law, and all kinds of people had come out of every town of Galilee and Judea, and Jerusalem. You can imagine these people walking along dusty roads, getting hot and perspiring, hearing animals' noises, smelling animal smells and the smell of food, and the fields, and manure. You can imagine them talking. Perhaps some were arguing. "I don't believe all those things. I am going to see for myself." "Have you heard about Jo? Well, he had leprosy and I saw him . . . he is perfectly normal now, just like anyone. I know it happened, because I saw him for years getting worse and worse." "Oh! Guess what Priscilla said? She knew Simon's mother-in-law and she said it was fantastic what happened to her. She is sure this must be the Messiah we've been waiting for!"

Yes, some would be coming excitedly, believing, some would be arguing, others would have dark, murderous ideas. See in your imagination the scowls of the Pharisees. These men were the religious ones who felt so proud and sure of themselves. They felt better than anyone else. They had their little rules they followed perfectly. They didn't bother to think about some of God's laws that they had broken; they had made up a list that was fairly easy to keep. As far as they were concerned, Jesus did not fit the pattern of religious ideas they had, and they were angry, and because people were coming to hear Jesus, they felt threatened. They not only had scowls; they were thinking, and probably saying to each other, very ugly things about Jesus. They were coming hoping to catch him doing something they could criticize. They were coming hoping to prove Jesus wrong.

Crowds of people. "A multitude," Luke calls it. People walking from all directions, all coming to crowd into a house. But all with the *same* motives? All with a *real* desire to know God? All seeking for *truth*? No. Some coming with curiosity. Some coming for a thrill. Some coming to get rid of blindness. Some really coming to find out if this were the Messiah. Some coming believing Jesus was the promised One. Some coming with excitement. And others . . . others coming to make a plot to get rid of him. Others coming to scoff and laugh. Oh, yes, a mixture of educated and uneducated, sick and well, old and young, men and women, rich and poor, seeking ones, and sarcastic ones. They were a mixture of pushing, hot, tired, dirty humanity as well as some beautiful to look at in fresh clothing. I am sure you would have been fascinated . . . but you would not have found the mixture of people very different from a crowd pushing down 42nd Street, New York, or down Nathan Row in Hong Kong, or down the Ginza in Tokyo, or down one of the crowded streets in Bombay. They were poor, needy human beings, with one thing alike about them all. They were sinful. As all people are.

As Jesus looked at them, crowded around him in this house, squashed together so that some heads were hidden behind others, not only could he see them, hear them, smell them, feel them pushing against him . . . but he could do something we cannot do. He could *know* what they were really thinking about, and what they really *cared* about. He could know the selfishness, the greed, the false motives, the twisted ideas that they had in their minds. He could know who was honest and serious in seeking truth. He really knew whom he was facing.

Now four men came hurrying along, carrying a bed with a sick man on it. They were disappointed that people were pressed in so thickly that there wasn't even room at the door. You can imagine the sick man's feeling of disappointment. Perhaps he said, "Oh, it's no use." And perhaps it was just one of his friends who had the good idea. Anyway, whoever had the idea, it *was* a clever one. The bed, by the way, would be an eastern bed—not a wooden one, but a kind of thin mattress that would be rolled up and put away during the day, so the room could be used as more than just a bedroom. The four men went up to the roof carrying their friend who had palsy (a crippling disease). The houses in that part of the world have outside steps leading up to the roof, which is flat, so don't imagine a peaked roof with a ridgepole! Up on the roof they went to carry out their good idea.

"Here," one of them must have said, "I think *this* is a good spot. Right *here* we are probably immediately above him; I can hear his voice, I think, in *this* location." They began to take the simple roofing off that spot of the roof. In the book of Mark it says (Mark 2:1–12) that they broke up a place in the roof. Gradually they would have made a hole, and they could see Jesus, and hear him clearly. Can't you imagine the daylight showing through that hole, and people wondering where the sudden blast of heat had come from, and where that streak of light was coming from. Some would be too far back to see. Some would look up and almost cry out when they saw a head looking through the ceiling. Maybe a little girl put her hand over her mouth to keep herself from squealing. "Oh!" a boy might have said to himself, or whispered to his mother, "What is going on up there?" Gradually the hole got bigger, and the four men would finally have said, "There, that's it, we can manage now."

Now came the good idea. They put ropes on the four corners of the mattress-bed and began lowering it down like a slow elevator (or lift, if you live in England) without sides. Now you can imagine everyone was looking! I wonder if Jesus stopped talking and just waited for that mattress to land at his feet, or if he kept on talking without paying attention. Anyway Jesus did not stop the men. He did not seem to be at all disturbed that they were putting this man down right in front of him, and forcing him to see him. In fact, it was quite the opposite. Luke says that when Jesus *saw* their faith, he spoke to the man. What does it mean he "*saw* their faith"? Well, he saw the work that they were doing that showed they believed that Jesus was going to be *able* to do something for this sick man. All that work taking off the tiles and making a hole, and lowering the man down, all that *showed* they believed that Jesus had power. Putting the man down at Jesus' feet showed that they believed that Jesus had love and compassion and would *care* for the man.

Later in the New Testament, James says that a person needs to show his faith by doing something based on faith. That is, you *do* things differently if you really believe that Jesus is the Son of God, and if you really believe that he died for you, and that as you have accepted him you are now in

God's family. You do something differently if you believe that God is able to answer prayer and that he cares about your problems and troubles. You do something that is based on your faith.

The examples that James uses are Abraham and Rahab from the Old Testament, and what they did to show that they believed. Abraham believed that God would take care of Isaac when Abraham took Isaac up a mountain to make a sacrifice. Abraham believed that God would take care of Isaac . . . and God did. God showed Abraham a little ram, like a lamb, caught in the thickets and that this was to be substituted for Isaac. Abraham showed his faith in God's love and God's keeping his promises by obeying God and doing what God had told him to do.

Rahab was the woman who kept the spies in her house, and who did that because she believed the God of the spies was the true God. She *did* something, something dangerous, because she had faith that God *is* God. The letter to the Hebrews, in the 11th chapter, tells of lots of people who did things, based on their faith. What does "based on their faith" mean? Well, it just means that because they believed that God is love, and is all-powerful, and is truly there, they did things such as walking around the walls of Jericho seven times, believing that God would keep his promise, and fighting thousands of people with a tiny army of three hundred as Gideon did, and not being afraid to be thrown to the lions as Daniel allowed himself to be. One thing was the *same* in all these people's lives. They did things that showed that their faith in God was *real*.

So Jesus "saw their faith." Jesus saw by what these men had done, that they really believed in him. He could also see deep into their hearts and know that this was real faith in him. He had the double reality. But God has made plain that the *inner* reality will show up in a different kind of *outside* reality. The lives and actions of believers are supposed to *show* that they believe that God is real, and that what he says in the Bible is true.

When Jesus "saw their faith," what did he say?

He said, "Man, thy sins are forgiven thee." What a silence there must have been among the people! What a shock to them! What a surprise! "Man, thy sins are forgiven thee." But he had palsy! But he was crippled! But he couldn't walk! Had Jesus done *anything* for him?

Now please remember what we thought about together earlier in this chapter. Remember what we said about where disease comes from, and how temporary the healing of physical disease is, even when Jesus healed. Jesus, full of love and compassion for this man with such real faith, skipped the temporary thing altogether at that moment. He wanted this man to know that his sins were forgiven, that he would have eternal life. Jesus would have seen beyond that poor little bed, that poor little room, that poor little house, that dusty village, the spoiled countryside. Jesus could see in his memory, and in a special way, the glory he had left. Jesus could see into the glory of the future, and see the wonderful things being prepared for those who have "faith," who believe in him. And his deep desire and first thought was to tell this man that his sins were forgiven. Were his sins forgiven because he had been let through the roof? No, they were forgiven because he believed. His coming to Jesus in that hard, persistent way, simply showed outwardly the faith that was there.

What was going on in the crowd? Maybe some were whispering. Maybe all were quiet. There was a kind of shock among them. Perhaps some understood, and their shock was a shock of thrill, of wonder, of worship, of thankfulness because of the power of Jesus to forgive sins. We know there were those there who were furious again. Yes, those same Pharisees who were so angry before. Maybe not the same men, but men of the same group. Pharisees so proud of being religious. They didn't say anything, but they were angry inside, and thinking thoughts that made ugly, angry faces. Jesus not only saw their faces, he could read their thoughts as

---

The Pharisees began to reason, saying, who can forgive sins but God alone? Luke 5:17–26

they began to say things like, "This man is a blasphemer. No one but God can forgive sins. This man is *blaspheming.*"

Jesus answered them in this way. He said, "Which is it easier to do? To say, Thy sins be forgiven thee; or to say, Rise up and walk? But that ye may know that the Son of man hath power upon earth to forgive sins (he said unto the sick of palsy), I say unto thee, Arise, take up thy couch, and go unto thy house." Jesus makes it very clear that to be able to forgive sins is far harder than to be able to heal a very crippled man. Of course if you were just *saying* something with nothing happening, it isn't any harder to say one thing than another. When Jesus says, "Which is it harder to say . . . " he means harder to say with a *result* taking place. Now the result of the sins being forgiven could be seen by Jesus, but the people in the room could not see this change. But the results of saying, "Get up, pick up your mattress-bed, and go down the street to your house . . . " *could* be seen, if there *were* any results! So Jesus is really saying: "It is harder to forgive sins than it is to heal a sick body, but so that you will understand who I am, I will tell the man to get up, fold up his bed, and walk away."

I imagine you could have heard gasps . . . "Ooooh . . . Aaaah . . . Wheeee . . . Sssss . . . " Little noises as people took in their breath, or made surprised little sounds. Because, you see, the man sat right up, stood up, leaned over and rolled up his bed, put it up on his shoulder, and walked out of the house. People probably pushed back to make way for him. People were flabbergasted. Off he went, down the street where men were pulling loads heavy enough for horses, down he went past girls with big water jugs on top of their heads, balanced so well they could turn around and look at him . . . "Oooohh . . . isn't that crippled Bert?" (or whatever his name was) they would have said. "Look, he is walking, and carrying his bed . . . he looks strong. Whatever has happened to him?"

What they could *not* see was that his sins had been forgiven, and that he felt joyful with a joy that was more than just the joy of walking. Perhaps he couldn't sort out all the excited feelings. But he knew that he *belonged* to the Lord.

He had been forgiven, and accepted by the Lord. We're told he went away glorifying the Lord. We are told they were all amazed, and they glorified God, and were filled with fear, saying, "We've seen some strange things today." Some would really have been convinced that Jesus was the Messiah and could forgive sins. Some would just have been confused and afraid. What do you think the Pharisees were thinking, the Pharisees with their scornful faces, and hateful thoughts? They were waiting. I think we know this from what happens next. They were waiting to criticize the next thing they could find against Jesus.

» Jesus went out into the street after this. In Mark 2:13, 14, you'll find that he walked along the seashore. As he was out walking, he passed a publican (a tax collector) named Matthew (or Levi) sitting at his custom table where he took taxes from people. The publicans were not very popular at that time. They had a reputation for cheating and getting as much out of people in taxes as they could. The scribes and Pharisees linked the word "publican" with "sinner" and stayed as far as they could from them. As Jesus came close to Matthew, he spoke to him and said a surprising thing. "Follow me." Just that. "Follow me." And Matthew just got straight up, left his table, and followed Jesus! It doesn't mean he just followed him down the street, for that one afternoon. It means he followed Jesus, and left his taxgathering, and became one of the Apostles. Matthew is the one who later wrote the Gospel of Matthew.

Just think—Matthew, who had been one of the publicans who, by the way, paid the Romans a sum of money to gather the taxes, and then grabbed and kept everything they could—Matthew now left his way of earning a living, and followed Jesus in just the same way that Simon Peter, James and John had followed him. It was *real*. I mean that they followed him because they believed that he was the Messiah, and they realized something of what it meant to have the privilege of being with the Son of God. I say "something," because later we know that they sometimes had periods of fears and doubts. In the end, however, Matthew not only faithfully followed Jesus, and wrote the Gospel of Matthew, but was finally killed as a martyr for his Christian faith.

Matthew left that place where he had been gathering taxes, and gave a great dinner to all his friends so that they could eat and talk with Jesus. Of course, his friends were other publicans and people who were not ones with a reputation for being honest, good or religious. When Mark tells the story, he says that "there were many, and they followed him." Yes, they followed along to the dinner, but I am sure Mark means that many of them truly became believers, disciples of Jesus, and followed him. *Now* the Pharisees and scribes felt that they really had found something to criticize, and gossip about. They began to make murmuring noises, and to make criticisms about Jesus and his disciples eating with sinners and publicans. These religious leaders felt they were too good to associate with men they regarded as sinners, so they said some very harsh things, you may be sure.

It was Jesus himself who answered them. He said, "They that are whole have no need of a physician, but they that are sick: I came not to call the righteous, but sinners." What is he saying? Are there any righteous people? Any completely good people? Any perfect people? No. The Bible clearly tells us that there is no one perfect, no one righteous with his own goodness, *not one.* So Jesus is saying that it is only people who *know* they are sinful who realize how much they need to be rid of their sins. He is comparing it with illness; only people who know they are sick and need a doctor will send for a doctor.

Jesus is saying that he has gone to eat dinner with people who know they are sinners, and who are more ready to listen to him, more eager to find out what he has to say, than these proud Pharisees who are filled with "self-righteousness" . . . that is, filled with pride about their goodness, a goodness they think makes them better than and different from all other men, and also better than Jesus. Terrible, isn't it, but it is a trap people fall into in every period of history—

men feel they are better than God, and quite capable of
telling God what to do!

Jesus spoke in a parable after this. A parable is a story to
illustrate a truth. He said that if you sew a new strong piece of
cloth on to an old weak piece of cloth, the old cloth will tear
as you wear it. This can happen today with a shirt or a pair of
pajamas. I think he meant us to realize that these Pharisees
had an old set of ideas. They weren't God's ideas. They didn't
come out of the Old Testament. They were their own ideas
which they were hanging on to, and they were trying to "sew
in" the fresh understanding which Jesus was bringing them,
without putting their old ideas aside. We need to put aside
our strong prejudices, the ideas that are not from God as he
speaks in the Bible at all, but are things people teach *as if*
they were as important as the Bible. You know, you might try
getting an old soft, worn, linen handkerchief, or a very worn
almost-tearing shirt or something. Ask Mother before you
take the wrong thing! And sew a patch on to it . . . just to see
how a strong, new piece of cloth causes weak, old cloth to
tear. It is something we need to think about today, in the
century in which we live, two thousand years after Jesus
taught that parable.

Are we ready to have a whole fresh way of helping
people? Or do we have to try to fit everything into the way
we have always done things? Jesus ate with the publicans and
sinners, to help them. They needed his help, and he judged
that it was the thing to do to go to that dinner to talk to them.
The Pharisees would never have gone near these people . . .
it didn't fit into their idea of being properly religious. But—
would the people ever have been told the Word of God that
way? The Pharisees were not ready to recognize Jesus, nor to
follow him, nor to listen to him.

9
A MIRROR TO SHOW THE DIRT

One Sabbath day Jesus and his disciples were walking through grain fields. Have you ever seen a ripe field of wheat, blowing in a breeze? It bends in ripples, looking very much like waves in a sea. If the sky is blue, and the sun is shining on the golden-beige-colored grain, it is one of the most beautiful sights of any countryside, anywhere in the world.

Would they be walking in file, one after another, or side by side? I wonder. Anyway, I am sure they were talking together, discussing some of the things they were learning from Jesus. Remember that none of them had been his disciple for very long.

As you walk through grasses, have you ever pulled one, and chewed the end that slipped free from the stalk? Have you ever eaten wheat, ripe and ready to harvest . . . a grain of whole wheat? It is a natural thing to do, to pick grasses or a few blades of grain, even if you are not hungry. But as these disciples of Jesus were really hungry, they pulled some wheat, rubbed it in their hands to loosen the chaff from the wheat, and ate it. Whole wheat would be filling and nourishing when they had not had a meal for some length of time.

Who do you think was near enough to be watching what they were doing? Some of those proud, critical Pharisees. They started right away to be cantankerous and to find fault. They called out to Jesus, "Look at your disciples breaking the laws we have made for the Sabbath day!"

When you think of it, it is almost too much to believe. Here are men, supposedly men who believe in the God of the Old Testament, supposedly concerned about worshiping him, and what are they using the Sabbath day to do? Just think, the Sabbath day was given specially for worshiping God, and here

is God, God the Son, God the Second Person of the Trinity,
standing right before them, with the wheat blowing in the
breeze, with the sun beating down on their heads. Here is the
One who made the wheat, who made the sun, and who made
them. Instead of worshiping him, or trying to find out who he
really is, *they* are telling *him* what his disciples should do on
the Sabbath day.

Jesus answered them by asking them if they had not
heard of the time David, in Old Testament days, had eaten
bread in the Temple, which only priests were supposed to eat,
and that David was not rebuked for that. Jesus said to them
(Matthew 12:6), "But I say unto you, that one greater than
the Temple is here" (right in front of them in the wheat field,
that is).

What was he saying? Well, *they* were so very concerned
about the holiness of the Temple, and the keeping of laws
they had added to the laws of God. Jesus is saying (so it
seems to us) that all this which has been made by him, the
world and the wheat field they are in, is where God dwells,
and that in fact the Maker of it all is in the midst of them right
there. It reminds us of verses in Isaiah (66:1-2), "The heaven
is my throne, and the earth is my footstool: what manner of
house will ye build unto me? and what place shall be my rest?
For all these things hath mine hand made, and so all these
things come to be, saith the Lord: but to this man will I look,
even to him that is poor and of a contrite spirit, and that
trembleth at my word."

Jesus was saying to those Pharisees that day, and to
anyone who will pay any attention today, "It is no use making
temples, church buildings in which to worship, nor is it any
use making up all kinds of little rules of your own to judge
people as to whether they are religious or not . . . if you are
not concerned about *my Word*." Jesus that day stood in front
of these religious men in *person,* but they paid no more
attention to him than some people do today to his written
Word. Jesus was speaking to them in language they could
understand, but they paid no attention to him. Can't you see,
they were judging Jesus? They were setting themselves up as

111

better than God. *They* were making the rules and telling God what the rules were.

Do people do that now, two thousand years later? Oh, yes. People have not changed. All the varieties of people are in the world today. People judge the Bible, the Word of God, and try to tell God what should be in it and what shouldn't. They judge what they think is acceptable to the twentieth century, and what is not! It is just like the Pharisees and Sadducees making up their minds about what they will and will not accept from God's Word. Basically, underneath, people have not changed.

Jesus goes on in Matthew (Matt. 12:7) and tells the Pharisees that if they had really understood what he was saying, they would have understood that God is more interested in people having mercy, compassion, loving care for others, than in merely doing religious acts. He says that if only they had understood this, they wouldn't have been condemning, judging, and critical and have said things against those men who were eating wheat on the Sabbath day. Then Jesus said, "The Son of Man is Lord of the Sabbath" (Luke 6:5).

Why does he say "Son of Man"? After Jesus, who is the Son of God, came as a baby, he often called himself Son of Man, because he is truly man as well as truly God. So you see, Jesus is telling them that *he made* the Sabbath day. No one can tell him what he should do on that day.

Do you think the proud Pharisees learned anything that day? We don't have any signs of that, because in the very next verses in this sixth chapter of Luke, we are given another story of what they did. It was another Sabbath day, when Jesus entered into the synagogue and taught. While he was teaching, he noticed a man there with a withered hand. This means that his hand was in some way paralyzed and useless. It was his right hand, and as most people use their right hand to do things, it must have been very hard for him to dress himself, hammer, eat, write . . . do anything, in fact. Now the scribes and Pharisees who were there in the Temple saw the man with the withered hand, and saw Jesus looking at him as he taught. They began to wonder what Jesus would do, and they watched him very closely. You can be sure that they did not have friendly expressions on their faces, because they were watching for one reason—only in order to catch him. They were looking to see whether Jesus would *heal* that man or not, because if Jesus healed him they wanted to accuse Jesus of working on the Sabbath day. But Jesus knew what they were thinking. They couldn't fool him. None of us can fool God. If we say one thing, and think another . . . God knows we are false. We can fool other people, and we can even fool ourselves, but we cannot fool God.

Because Jesus knew their thoughts against him, he said to the man with the withered hand, "Stand up." Yes, he told him to stand up in the middle of the synagogue, in front of all the people, Pharisees and everyone else. Then Jesus said to everyone: "I ask you, is it lawful on the Sabbath to do good, or do harm? to save a life, or to destroy it?" We are told this same story in Matthew 12:9–14, and Matthew tells us that Jesus also gave an example. Jesus asked: "What man shall there be of you, that shall have one sheep, and if this fall into a pit on the Sabbath day, will he not lay hold on it, and lift it out? How much then is a man of more value than a sheep! Wherefore it is lawful to do good on the Sabbath day." Jesus, you see, is saying that even if it *is* work to take care of people's needs on the Sabbath day, the law was not meant to make people *suffer*, and to stop people from doing good. After this, Jesus said to the man, "Stretch forth thy hand," and the man stretched it straight out. He was able to because it was healed immediately, and worked as well as his good hand. How excited the man and his real friends would have been! Others there who were really trying to understand would have been glad to have had Jesus' explanation, and to know that the Sabbath day, the day of worship, was not to be a selfish day, a day when people cared only about resting and being quiet themselves.

Sometimes worshiping God means being alone with the Bible, being alone in a field, or the woods, or sitting by the ocean on a rock, or by a waterfall, or under a tree, or in a

room, reading his Word and praying, talking to him and
hearing his Word, just loving him and telling him so. But
sometimes it would only be selfish to do this—when doing it
meant hurting people who need you to take care of their
wounds, or illnesses. For instance, if you run past a hurt and
bleeding man to get to your place of quiet . . . that is not
really worshiping. If a nurse doesn't answer the bell of a very
ill patient because she is reading her Bible, that isn't really
worshiping the Lord. If a mother doesn't care for her sick,
feverish, crying baby because she is reading her Bible, that
isn't really worshiping the Lord. If a person is carried into
your house, hurt in an accident and you shut yourself in a
room to read your Bible, waiting for the next day to take care
of that one—that isn't worshiping God. Jesus is helping the
ones who really *wanted* to understand the true meaning of
worshiping God on the Sabbath day.

But the Pharisees didn't try to understand. Luke says
they were filled with madness. The Pharisees and scribes got
together as soon as the service in the synagogue was over.
Can't you just see the sneers and satisfied smirks as they
looked at each other and motioned with their heads? "Come
on, let's get together and talk about this. What will we do
about this terrible man who is breaking our rules for the
Sabbath? Come on over here, where we can talk, plan, plot,
scheme. We'll think of a way to hurt him. We'll destroy him,
get rid of him" (Matthew 12:14, Luke 6:11).

» Soon after that time Jesus went up into a mountain to pray.
He did go away from people, to be alone with God, his
Father. Here again we have Jesus the Son talking to God the
Father. We are told that at this time Jesus spent the whole
night in prayer. The whole *night* praying? Does that sound
like a long time? Really a night doesn't take long to pass by.
Have you known people who have spent a whole afternoon
or a whole evening talking? Perhaps you have spent half the
night talking to someone when you had lots of things you

Jesus in prayer on a mountain. Luke 6:12

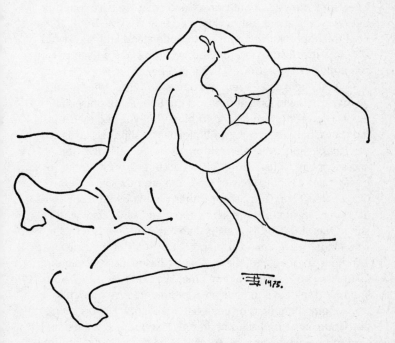

wanted to tell. When people are in trouble, or have questions to ask, or don't know what to do next, they can spend a lot of time trying to get help from another person. When someone loves another person very much and is talking to that person, time goes by very quickly. When someone admires another person's work, they can rave about it for a long time.

Prayer is talking to God. Prayer is telling God you adore him, you love him, you admire him, you think his creation is fantastic. Then prayer is telling God you trust him, and you know he is all-wise and that his plan is the only plan you want for your life, and it is asking him please to show you that plan. Prayer is also telling God your problems and difficulties and asking for specific help. Prayer is asking for definite things for yourself and for others, with faith that God will keep his promise to answer. If we were really going to tell what the Bible says about prayer, and what we have found in our own lives about prayer, it would take a whole book. But here the important thing for us to understand and be excited about, is that Jesus, God the Son, when he was on earth, spent much time in prayer, even all night at times.

You might say, "Well, of course God the Father would be interested and care about God the Son, as he prayed all night. He was his Son talking to him." But you see that is just the point that it is exciting to understand. Although Jesus is the *Unique* Son, after *we* are born again by believing God, and accepting Christ as our Savior, accepting what he did for us—we also become sons of God. We are now children in God's family. He, God, is *our* Father. You know, the children of a king can run into the king's room and say, "Dad" and talk to him. But God is greater than any king—he is the One who made Heaven and Earth and is the Ruler of the Universe. And he is so open and loving, that he has made it possible for us to run into his room at any time. We don't have to wait in line. We don't have to have an appointment. We don't have to pay something first, or get a bill afterwards. How is it that every human being has to be in only one place at a time, and God can be everywhere at once? It is because God is infinite and we are all finite. We should be very thrilled and excited to understand that, because God is infinite, he can be with anyone in any country, with everyone who wants to be alone with him—all at the same time, and with each one alone.

The unique thing about God the Father and God the Son and God the Holy Spirit is that each One is infinite. One God—Three Persons—infinite. It *means* something very important and real to us every single day of our lives, that we can talk to God without waiting for him to have time. How despairing we get when we feel we need someone, and that someone is busy with another person! But God is always able to be with us when we need him, because he is infinite. We would often like to be in three or four places at once. To be sleeping as well as typing at a typewriter! To be skiing as well as packing dishes to move! To be talking alone to ten people in ten different places at once! But you and we can never be in two places at once. How glad we should be that God is really God and is so different from us in being able to be alone with all of us at the same time.

If the boy next door came to your father and asked, "Dad, please buy me a pair of shoes, and give me money for my lunch tomorrow at school," your dad would probably say, "You've made a mistake; I am not your father." Before you can come to God as your Father, and ask him for things, you must know that you have been "born again," born into his family.

Jesus had something very important to be praying about that night, because the next morning he was going to be selecting from the disciples twelve men to become his special ambassadors, to be specially close to him during the rest of his life, until his death, resurrection, and ascension, and then to be his special messengers in the world. When morning came, Jesus called those who had been following him, and out of them he chose twelve. They were Simon Peter, and Andrew his brother, James and John, Philip and Bartholomew, Matthew and Thomas, James (the son of Alphaeus), and another Simon. Then there was Judas, the brother of James, and Judas Iscariot. Eleven of the twelve did what Jesus called them to do. Judas became a traitor. These twelve were called the apostles, and they were chosen to do a special task during a certain time of history. We can never be apostles because that time of history is over, but each of us who is born again can be an ambassador who represents the Lord, and tells others about Jesus, God the Father, and the Holy Spirit.

After this, Jesus came down to all the people, and many were healed by him. He also preached to them. Part of what he preached in that sermon is given to us in Luke 6:20–49. It is very much like the Sermon on the Mount which you will find in Matthew 5, 6 and 7. People sometimes think they can get to Heaven by doing all the things Jesus tells them to do in these verses from Matthew and Luke. But to do all these things that Jesus tells them to do, they would have to be perfect, just as a person would have to be perfect to keep the Ten Commandments. No person can get to Heaven, or earn eternal life, or get rid of their sins, by trying to keep the Ten Commandments or the Sermon on the Mount, or by trying to copy the life of Jesus, because no one is good enough to do these things. How thankful we should be that we don't have to keep these things perfectly to get to Heaven, because if that were the only way to eternal life, it would be hopeless for us all. As it is, we have hope and assurance, and certainty, because Jesus came to take the punishment for our sins, he lived for us, and died for us. Do we then say, "Well, we can skip the Ten Commandments. We can skip the next verses in Luke, and the Sermon on the Mount in Matthew"? On, no, quite the opposite. First of all, we need those parts of the Bible very much to see what our sin is, to see a little of what God sees when he looks at us.

I want you to do something. Choose one of your family or group to illustrate what we want to understand. That person will sit right there where he or she is. On the couch, on the floor, on the grass—it doesn't matter. Now get a bit of black chalk, or a bit of coal dust, or some charcoal . . . something that will quickly make some dirty smudges. One of you go and make that chosen person dirty (just the face) with some smudges. Now can that person see what you see on his or her face? Get a mirror and show him or her his or her face in the mirror! You might try putting the smudges on the faces of everyone in the group but one. That would be a better illustration really. Then pass the mirror around the room. *The mirror represents this section of Luke and Matthew.* What Jesus is giving now, and what God gave to the Israelites in the Old Testament, can be represented by a mirror, a mirror to show the dirt that is there.

We won't put all these verses in this chapter and discuss them all together now, but do read them and discuss them as a family. "Do good to them that hate you." "Love your enemies." "Pray for them that despitefully use you." "Lend, hoping for nothing again." Will you understand all that Jesus means in these things he is saying? No, it will take years of living, praying, reading the Bible, to come to a new and deeper understanding, and never will it be perfect in this life.

Yes, we should read these verses often, and read them looking honestly at ourselves. If we begin to feel proud of ourselves and critical of someone else, we need to look into this "mirror" as Jesus has told us to do in a very vivid way. In Luke 6:41, 42, he is talking about a man who wants to take a "mote" out of his brother's eye. A mote is a small thing. Jesus says this man is a hypocrite, because he has a beam in his own eye that needs to come out before he can see clearly enough to take any speck like a mote out of his brother's eye. He is saying that so often we are in danger of seeing somebody else's faults, when what we need is to see our *own* faults.

It is a very good thing, any time we pray about someone else's sin, or fault, or mistake, or bad habit, even if we love the person and don't think we are feeling superior to them, to ask the Lord, "Oh, please, if I am not seeing my own sin, please show me what I ought to be asking forgiveness for, before I pray about my friend's sin, or mistake, or fault." It is a good thing to picture it in your mind, or draw a little picture on a piece of paper. Draw an eye . . . draw two eyes . . . put a tiny speck in one eye . . . put a big stick in the other eye. Then pray—thinking of yourself with a big stick in *your* eye, asking the Lord to take *it* out first!

Yes, ask the Lord to help you to use the mirrors he gives us in his Word, to help us see how many "smudges" we have as we live day by day. We mustn't compare ourselves to the children next door, the girls in our school, the fellows in the hockey team, the men at the office, the women in the club. We are to use the mirror God prepared for us. It is the only one polished enough really to show up "dirt."

» At the end of this sermon, Jesus told a very wonderful story about two men who built houses. Before we hear about these men and their houses, we want you to do something. Perhaps you will have to wait until another day to do this, but it would be good if you could do it right now! Get two baking pans, or large bowls, or even soup bowls—two containers that are rather shallow yet will hold water. Get a rock that will fit into one of these containers (if it is only possible to get a small saucer, get a small stone or pebble). In the other container, pile up a pile of sand, or earth that is about the same size as the stone, or rock! Make it piled up to look almost as solid. Now take a teapot, a jug or a pitcher of water . . . and watch what happens when it is poured over the stone, or rock . . . see how it splashes in the bowl, or pan . . . but the rock remains as solid as it was before, doesn't it? Now pour a stream of water over the earth or sand. Now you will understand why you need sides on this container . . . as there will be more than water in danger of running out! See how the sand disappears into a puddle of dirty water? There is nothing solid left.

Jesus says, "Anyone who comes to me and hears my sayings, and *does* them, I will show you whom he is like. He is like a man who built a house, and digged deeply into the ground until he found a good rock base, and laid his foundation on a rock. Later a flood came, water rose up and lashed against that house, but the water in all its fury could not shake the house, because it was firmly fixed, built upon strong rock."

There are other men, Jesus says, who hear what he says,

but who do not do anything about it. A man who listens just with his ears, but turns away from doing what Jesus says, is like a man that built a house on the earth, or sand. When the flood rose and the stream of water beat violently against that house, immediately it fell—and Jesus says, "The ruin was great of that house." Have you seen pictures of houses split apart and all ruined with flood waters? The chimney is just a pile of bricks somewhere in the mud, the windows are in splinters, the rugs are a mess of caked mud, with bits of sticks and stones and torn curtains and broken chairs all mixed up with a broken kitchen stove and some children's toys. It is a terrible sight—a house destroyed by flood.

Jesus is talking about something more important than the houses we live in as families. We know we wouldn't like our house and furnishings all spilled out into mud, and everything we enjoy together broken. But what Jesus is wanting us to "see" in our imaginations, to understand with our minds, is that *our lives* are like houses. And as we "build" our lives, we must first of all have a foundation. The foundation must be solid, so that when the storms and floods come, it will not be just swept away. What are the storms and floods of life? Well, all sorts of things; troubles, problems, big questions, sickness, other people being mean to us, disappointments of many kinds, and a sudden fear that there is no purpose to living at all. When these "storms" come, our little house, which is "me," our little house must be built upon a rock to be able to take the storms, and still stand unbroken!

What is the rock? What is the sand? We are told clearly in the Bible that God is the rock. In the Old Testament, in the Psalms, David says, "Lead me to the rock, that is higher than I" (Psalm 61:2b) and in Psalm 40:2, "He brought me up also out of an horrible pit, out of the miry clay, and set my feet upon a rock, and established my goings." And in Psalm 18:2, "The Lord is my rock, my fortress, and my deliverer; my God, my strength, in him will I trust."

So the foundation must be on the rock, and the rock is the Lord. As Paul says very certainly in I Corinthians 3:11,

"For other foundation can no man lay than that which is laid, which is Jesus Christ." In the Old Testament, God lets men know that *he* is the Rock. David sang with happiness that he had been taken out of the mud, clay and sand and had his feet safely on the Rock. Jesus, in the story of the two houses, taught that "anyone who comes to me and hears my sayings and does them is like a man building his house on the rock." And in his letter to the Corinthians Paul explains that there is no other foundation on which you can build your life as a Christian. It all hangs together. It fits. The Bible is a unity, even though it was written at different times of history, even though men are fuzzy in their understanding. It is all there. God is unfolding to men the *truth* that is the *same* truth year after year, century after century.

And the house built on the sand? The house with a foundation that is so easily torn apart by flood waters? What is that? This is the picture of those who do not do what they hear the Lord telling them to do, those who turn away to their own ideas, like Cain, near the beginning of the Old Testament and like the Pharisees and Sadducees in the New Testament as well as like the "fool" who says there is no God.

"But," you may say, "I thought we just saw that all those things Jesus is teaching we should do cannot be done by anyone who is not perfect. What is the use then of his saying, 'do'?" Some men asked Jesus what work they could do that they might work the works of God. John tells us about Jesus' answer (John 6:28, 29), "This is the work of God, that ye believe on him whom he hath sent." Jesus taught this over and over again, in many ways, to help different kinds of people to understand. He has said we are in darkness, and he is the light. Now he has said we are on sand that will be washed away, but he is the Rock. We must "do" his teachings, he says, and now again he makes it clear that the work we must do first of all is to believe on him.

How many there listening that day understood him? How many *really* believed? We don't know. But we can know that Jesus was very patient as he went on teaching and explaining, and as it became more and more clear. We have an advantage: we can just turn to the next chapter and keep on reading. We can find out "what happened next." We should find it easier to be sure our life is built on the *Rock*, Jesus.

10
HIDDEN TREASURE

Have you ever had a treasure hunt? It is a fun game to arrange
for the family. Each little hidden note tells you where to look
for the next clue, and you go from one hidden clue to
another until you find the "treasure." It would be fun in the
summer time to have all your bathing things in a box as the
treasure, and then you would know that the family party was
going to be a swimming party. Or the treasure could be boat
tickets for an afternoon's boat ride, or it could be a big
watermelon for a treat. If the treasure can't be shared, then
everyone else who has taken part in the hunt is disappointed.
You can think up lots of different kinds of treasure hunts.

In many ways, the truth God gave is like hidden treasure.
It is the Bible, and he has given his Word for everyone to
find, but to many people in the world it is a hidden treasure.
If the treasure is found, it opens the way not just to a swimming party, or a special afternoon on a boat with your family
or friends; it opens the way to knowing God himself as a
Father and Friend, and having special times ahead that will
last forever and be so much more wonderful than any day's
outing we have ever had.

As you read and study the Bible and discuss together,
you are finding this treasure, and perhaps some day you can
give the clues to others. Some clues have helped you to rush
to the place where you "dig up" the understanding, and
maybe you will find other people who need *you* to explain to
them the "clue" that helped you the most. This is one reason
why it is so valuable to do this reading, discussing and discovering *together* as a family or in a group . . . because if one
person is running off in the wrong direction in their thinking
and understanding, someone else who realizes that can be a

help! We are *meant* to be helpful to each other in finding the treasure that is there for us, the Word of God.

After Jesus had finished speaking to that audience of people, we find him coming into Capernaum, a city by the sea of Galilee, a place which he often visited. An officer in the Roman army, called a centurion, lived in the city, and his servant was very ill. We are told it was a servant of whom he was very fond, and that he was very near death, so that the centurion was feeling heavy hearted. When he heard that Jesus was there, he sent some of the Jewish leaders to him to beg him to come and heal his servant. As the men talked to Jesus, they explained that the centurion was not Jewish, but that he had shown real love for the Jews and had built a synagogue for them with his own money. These Jewish men wanted Jesus to come to this centurion and help him, because they felt he was such a worthy person.

Now as Jesus came near the centurion's house, some of the centurion's friends came, bringing a message from the centurion himself: "Lord, don't take the trouble to come into my house: because I'm not worthy to have you under my roof. I really didn't feel worthy to come directly to you myself, either. But I know it isn't necessary for you to come into the house, because all you would have to do is say one word, and my servant will be healed. The reason I feel certain of this, is because I am a man who has authority over soldiers under me—and when I say 'go,' the man goes, and when I say 'come,' that person comes; and when I say, 'do this,' then my servant does it."

You see, this Roman military leader was saying that he recognized that Jesus had real authority. He realized that Jesus had a special authority, and that he could command sicknesses to go away, that he could say that a person should be well, and it would happen just as quickly as when a military leader gave a command to someone under him.

The centurion realized the difference between himself as a sinful man, and Jesus as good. Speaking of himself as "unworthy" was not a kind of politeness, nor just an insincere compliment. He had some understanding. Jesus said about him, "I haven't found faith like this among the Jews here in Israel." Jesus was amazed at his understanding and his belief—so amazed that he told the people who were standing around him because they had been following along down the street, that this Roman soldier had special faith.

Does that mean the centurion understood everything? No, but he had really believed the amount he understood, and he understood that Jesus was special and had a unique ability. And Jesus, who could see into people's minds and hearts, said he had faith that was deeper, or in some way more complete, than any of the rest of the men he had met. And when the friends went back to the centurion's house, they found that the sick servant was perfectly well again!

It was the day after that, in a town called Nain, that a whole procession of weeping people were walking down the street near the gate of the city. It was a funeral procession following a dead man whose body was being carried out of the city gate, and the mother of the man was weeping with great sorrow because he was her only son—and she was without a child at all. Her husband was dead, so she really was very alone. Picture the two large groups of people meeting there at the gate—the funeral procession, and Jesus with a crowd following him, on their way into the city. When Jesus saw this heartbroken mother, we are told he had compassion on her, which means he felt very sad for her and wanted to help her. Compassion mixes the feeling of being sorry and wanting very much to do something to help. Jesus said to her, "Weep not." But he didn't just *say*, "Don't cry," he *did* something to stop her crying. What a surprise that woman had! She heard his words, "Don't weep," in her ears, and then saw Jesus touch the bier (that was the sort of stretcher on which men were carrying the body). The men carrying the bier stood still. They must have been curious as to why Jesus had touched the bier in that way. And then everyone heard the startling words, "Young man, I say unto thee, 'Arise!'" People didn't have time to say, "Is he crazy? Doesn't he know the fellow is dead?" People didn't have time to laugh or make sarcastic remarks at all, because Luke, the doctor, reports to us that the man who was dead sat up on his own funeral bier and began to speak.

That is fantastic, isn't it? I mean, if he had just moved and slowly opened his eyes, it would have been the impossible coming-back-to-life that would have caused people to jump and clutch each other! But can you imagine the gasps and the jumps of people? Can you imagine a young wife suddenly tightly hanging on to her husband's arm, and a child wanting to be picked up, and an old man suddenly putting his arm about his nephew? Why? Well, the dead man they had been about to bury was *talking* to them. We aren't told what he said. *That* would have been interesting to hear, wouldn't it? Maybe he just said he was thirsty, or maybe he asked what he was doing out there by the gate on a bier? Anyway, we are told that Jesus gave him back to his mother, and it isn't hard to imagine that she hugged him and cried and cried, but this time for joy—joy that she could hear her son's voice, feel his body warm and alive against her again. Full of joy that she was no longer separated from her son—because his soul was no longer separated from his body.

What reaction did the people have? We are told they were afraid, and they glorified God in the same way as they had when the man who had been lowered down into the room in front of Jesus, had been healed and took up his bed and walked. Some of them said, "A great prophet has risen among us." Some said, "God has visited his people." Did they all know now that Jesus was the Messiah? Did they connect him with the promises in Isaiah and other parts of the Old Testament? Some may have. Surely some understood much more than others. These people had the Old Testament. They had the teaching in the Old Testament that should have helped them, *if* they had really been remembering it, and talking about it day by day.

You know, it is only God who can raise people from the dead. In the Old Testament, and in the New Testament, too, God used some of his servants to raise people from the dead, but they never did it in their own name, but in God's name. It is only God's power that can bring people back to life. Jesus is God. As Jesus raised people from the dead and did other miracles, he did it with his own power. You notice how easily he did it? He just spoke the word, and immediately the thing was done. He is the Lord of life, and he can raise from the dead anyone he wishes.

Some day Jesus will speak the word and *all* those who have taken him as their Savior, and who have died, will be raised from the dead as easily as this man whom we have just read about. Jesus will speak the word on that wonderful day, "Arise," and the bodies of all the believers, no matter how long ago they lived, will come out of their graves. Some from India, some from China, some from South America, some from Africa, some from Australia, some from England, some from all the European countries, some from America, some from the depths of the sea, wherever in the world people have died, believing, having been born into God's family—when the word is spoken for the resurrection from the dead, they will arise.

If your grandfather, your great-grandfather, your great-great-grandfather were believers, they will be raised from the dead along with the people who lived centuries before that. When Jesus said to the dead young man, "Arise," he sat up *immediately* and talked! It didn't take any length of time for him to become alive again.

And the Bible tells us in 1 Corinthians 15:51–52, "Behold, I tell you a mystery: We shall not all sleep, but we shall all be changed, in a moment, in the twinkling of an eye, at the last trump: for the trumpet shall sound, and the dead shall be raised incorruptible, and we shall be changed."

All of you wink an eye. If you can't wink, just close and open both eyes! How long did that take? We are told that in a very short time, in as long as it takes to wink, when the trumpet shall sound . . . the dead shall be raised.

Handel wrote a marvelous piece of music, the *Messiah.* You ought to have that whole album of records to listen to until you know it by heart. This one, "Behold I show you a mystery; but we shall all be changed, In a moment, in the twinkling of an eye . . . " is sung in a wonderful deep bass voice. If you have a copy, listen to it right now. Listen to it and read 1 Corinthians 15:51–55 and read verse 57, too. You will see that verse 57 says thanks to God who is the One who gives us a *victory* over death through our Lord Jesus Christ. Handel's music is wonderful praise to God, and the words are straight from the Bible. It isn't just beautiful music and poetic words . . . it is the true Word of God being sung. You know, thousands of people hear it every year in concert halls all over the world. Yet how terrible to think of so many hearing those words, even singing them, and not believing that they are true. If you listen as a family or a group to the music, and believe that the words are true, you might stop right now and pray for all the people who have the records in their homes and who listen as if it were a fairy tale. Pray that their "eyes of understanding" will be opened, and their ears will be opened to understand. This is doing something practical, not just shaking our heads and saying, "How awful!" This is what we *should* do when things trouble us about people.

Well, that day when the boy was raised from the dead followed the day when Jesus spoke a word, and the centurion's servant became well . . . although Jesus had not even gone into his house. So one day his authority was shown in this way, and the *next* in his raising the man from the dead. Now some men come and ask a question. To us the answer seems clear, but they are confused, and although some are stubbornly objecting, others are seeking to find out who Jesus really is. They say the question they ask comes from John the Baptist: "Are you really the one that should come or do we look for another?" They are asking whether he is the Messiah, the Son of God, yet so much has been given to them to understand—even God the Father directly speaking at the time of his baptism.

Perhaps you know how easy it is to want more and more proof of things that seem almost unbelievable to you. You may say, "Did Uncle Joe *really* come last night?" and your mother might reply, "But you saw him, don't you remember, when you looked over the banister?" And you might say "Yes, I did. But he had a beard, and I thought he would look different from that. Anyway I thought maybe I dreamed it last night."

>> The people who were following Jesus—even including John the Baptist—were ordinary people, and they kept asking for more proof, for things that would help them know. What did Jesus answer? He said, "Go on now, and tell John what you have *seen* and *heard*; how that the blind see, the lame walk, lepers are cured, the deaf hear, the dead are raised, and to the poor the gospel is preached." Jesus had just cured several more people, and the dead man had just been raised—so the men *knew* these things had happened. Jesus had given this list to show that he was fulfilling the prophecies of what the Messiah would do, to show that he really *was* the Messiah promised for so long.

At the end of the list, Jesus mentioned the greatest thing of all that he would do . . . "to the poor the gospel is preached." What *is* the gospel? It is simply the good news. But what good news? The best news of all. It is the news that God has prepared a way, opened a door, given a light, that we might step out of the place where we were lost and wandering, in mud and dark fog and swamps, into a place where we can breathe a deep sigh because we know that all that is *behind* us, and we are *certain* of being *home*. We are home in the family where we belong, with the knowledge that nothing can take us back to the awful swamp again, and that we are going to be safe and happy with our Father for ever.

The gospel is the good news of salvation. It was good news to that man and his mother that he was going home with her, instead of being buried in the grave outside the city. However, I think that in the list of things he was doing, Jesus put the preaching of the gospel *after* raising the dead, because the good news of the gospel is that we can have our bodies changed one day so that we will never die again. Listen to the singing of those words on your record of the *Messiah* . . . or sing it yourselves, "The trumpet shall sound and the dead shall be raised incorruptible, and we shall be changed." Do we believe it? Do we believe it with our minds, with our feelings, with our expectations? Do we *live* as though we believed it to be true truth? The fact that Jesus preached this good news to the people who lived then, that now two thousand years later it has not been squashed out, and that we still can read it, hear it, come to know it, is a greater miracle than the boy sitting up on his funeral bier in the city gate of Nain.

All down the centuries people have tried to burn the Bible and to get rid of it. Even today there are parts of the world where it is banned. Think of how Satan has tried to get rid of truth, and has tried to stop people from believing it. Yet today the Bible is written in more languages than ever before, and the good news has not been squashed out. We ourselves have found it. And we are responsible for seeing that other people are led to it. We are supposed to be giving "clues" to them. It is not to be a selfish hunt! The treasure is to be shared.

Jesus speaks to the Pharisees again, giving them a picture of how unreasonable people are when they don't really want to find truth, but just want to find fault with everyone but themselves. He says they have accused John the Baptist of being filled with a demon, because he ate a limited diet of plain food, and stayed out in the desert alone for so long. He then says these same men have called him, Jesus, a glutton, one who eats greedily, because he ate dinners with publicans and sinners! Jesus says this is the way people rationalize (try to excuse themselves, make themselves feel they are right) when they are rejecting God, when they are turning away from the truth God gives them. They do not do this with logic and reason. They don't have reasons for this that make sense, or that *fit* things as they really know they are.

Let's give an example. Look around this room, as you did when we read the first chapter. Pick up something. The lamp? A chair? A tray? A teapot? That vase? Right. Who made it? Someone who first had the idea in his or her head. Someone who chose to make that thing. Someone who then designed it on paper . . . and then searched for materials to make it. Perhaps you have picked something you, or Mother, or Dad made. Try to remember what it is like to see that thing in your mind, to choose to make it from other ideas you have had. Then to make it, and have other people see it, talk about it. Other people understand something about you, or about the person who made whatever you are looking at. They understand something about the kind of color, shape and texture you find pleasing. There is something they understand when they look at what you *make* that they cannot understand when you just talk. Making things is a way of communication . . . a way of letting people know what kind of a person you are. We *know* this is the way a person can be known to other people. Day by day we can find that to be true. It fits things as we know they really *are*.

Think again of the fact that people first of all declare that they do not believe there is any *Person* to have had ideas, before the universe was made. They make up their minds *first* that God is not there. They make up their minds *first* that there never was a Person who saw the sun, moon and stars in his mind, before making them. They make up their minds that there was no Person to have an imagination that could think and choose and design all the variety of trees, bushes, fruit, flowers and vegetables. They make up their minds that there was no Person to have thought of the wonder of the different kinds of fish, birds and animals. They make up their minds that there was no Person *to* make people who could also think and act and feel and choose, who would be able to love and communicate. So they will not listen or try to think whether or not the existence of God the Father, the Son and the Holy Spirit, and God's universe, and God's Word (his explanation) to them, really fit things as they know they are. They won't look at what God made and recognize that he must be there because the things he made are there. They won't look to see something of what he is like in the beauty of what he made. And they won't read what he has explained carefully in his Word, the Bible, and believe what he has said.

Those Pharisees that day stood there rejecting what God had said that "hit" them, that was against them. They rejected what they should have understood from the Old Testament.

They rejected what John the Baptist had said. They rejected what Jesus was saying and doing day after day in front of them. People are doing the same thing today. One day all that the Bible tells is coming, *will* come. Are *we* believing not just bits and pieces of the Word of God, not just the past history of the Word of God, not just the teaching on how to be born again, not just the teaching on how to live day by day, moment by moment, but also what he tells us of the future, too? We need to be *thinking, acting,* and *feeling* as if we truly believed all that God has given us. We need to live in the midst of the whole truth, and remember that *this is real.* What the Bible teaches us gives us a perspective of *reality.* Living outside of that means living a life that doesn't fit things as they really are!

What is perspective? Each of you get a piece of paper and a lead pencil, or a crayon or a charcoal pencil. Now decide on something to draw—a chair, a table, a whole room, or a house with some trees. Each of you draw the same thing, the thing you decide upon. Now compare the drawings. Do some look more real than others? Do some look flat, and not as real? What makes the difference between a chair in one drawing that looks as though you could sit on it, and one that looks like a flat thing on a piece of paper without a seat there at all? It is what is called perspective. When you learn to draw the lines to make it all look more real, to have more depth as things really do, then you are drawing with perspective. The Bible teaches us the real-life perspective, as an art teacher should be able to teach you how to draw with perspective. As we come to understand and believe the truth of the Bible and to understand a little more all the time, then our lives are more *real* in the midst of the *real* universe, in the midst of the way things really are.

» Now as we come to the end of Chapter 7 in Luke, we find in verse 36 that one of the Pharisees invited Jesus to his house for dinner. As Jesus sat there at the meal in the Pharisee's home, his feet would not be under a table, because it was the custom at that time, in that part of the world, to eat lying on a kind of chaise-longue or couch, so that a person's feet would

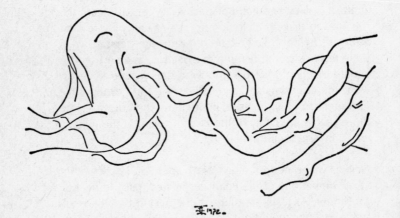

be stretched out away from the table. This is the picture you should have in your mind, as we tell what happened next.

If we were looking through the window or the doorway into that room that night, we would have seen a woman coming toward the spot where Jesus' feet were resting. He would have been looking at the table, or the food, or at one of the men with whom he was talking. As we watched, we would see that the woman had her head bent with her hair probably falling around her face, because she was weeping, with tears rolling down her cheeks. Her hands probably shook a little, because you know that when you are crying it makes the whole of your body a bit trembly—and in her hands you would have noticed a beautiful box. It was a box carved out of stone called alabaster, a lovely soft yellowy-white or pinky-white stone. Vases or lamp bases are often made out of alabaster, particularly in Italy. Then the woman bent over and, as her tears fell on Jesus' feet, she wiped them with her hair, and opened the box to take the perfumed ointment out of it and pour it on his feet.

What do you suppose the Pharisee was doing? Well, even if we had been there looking, we couldn't have seen into his mind, could we? He was thinking things inside himself. How do we know? Because Jesus knew, and Jesus answered the Pharisee's thoughts without the Pharisee speaking! Jesus knew that the Pharisee was thinking, "If this man were a prophet, he would have known what a sinful woman she is, and he wouldn't let her touch him because she is so bad." Notice that the Pharisee did not even believe Jesus is a prophet of God, let alone the Son of God. He was judging by the fact that he himself would not associate with someone he thought to be sinful because he thought that by contrast he was a good man. Jesus said, "Simon," (that was the Pharisee's name) "Simon, I have something to say to you." Simon replied, "Say on."

And Jesus told Simon a parable, a story to illustrate

A sinful woman washes Jesus' feet with her tears.   Luke 7:41–50

135

something. Remember what Jesus had said to the Pharisees who had so very harshly criticized him for eating with sinners and publicans? Jesus had told them that he had come to save sinners, not good people. He did not mean that anyone is good enough to save himself. He meant that no one can be saved, unless he knows that he (or she) needs saving. In other words, a person must recognize that he needs to be forgiven before he can understand that Jesus came to make it possible for him to be forgiven.

Jesus told a parable to illustrate the very same thing. You will find it in the next verses. He told the story of the two men who owed another man money. One owed five hundred pennies, and one owed fifty pennies. The man said to the two men, "You don't have to pay me. I forgive you this debt." Jesus asked Simon which one would love the man the most. "I suppose," answered Simon, "the one who owed the biggest debt, the one who owed the greatest amount of money." Then Jesus began to talk about the woman. Jesus said something like this, "This woman understands she has sinned much. She has come to me in faith, believing. She has brought an expensive ointment to pour on my feet, and she has washed my feet with tears. She has done these things because she had faith." Jesus said to the woman directly, "Thy sins are forgiven." He made it clear that she had come to him believing, because he said, "Thy faith hath saved thee; go in peace."

The men who sat at the dinner table went on thinking and questioning. "Who is this who forgives sins?" What a contrast again! The sinful woman left the room with her perfume box empty, but her heart full of joy. Her sins had been forgiven her by the One who had come to die in her place. Did she understand this perfectly? No, but she had come believing all that she *could* understand.

And the men? There they were, so good in their own eyes, so religious in the eyes of the city people, not despised as the woman was, secure in their reputations. They sat despising the woman, feeling so much better than she was, counting on their religious good deeds to be enough. The

woman left the room—saved. Jesus said so. The men were
sitting so close to Jesus they could look into his eyes and hear
him speak—sitting there relying on their own "goodness"—
lost.

Was Jesus saying it is better to be very bad, than to try
to be good? No, that is not the point at all. The point is that it
is better to *know* you need forgiveness and to come to him
believing, than it is to *think* you are good enough yourself,
and that it is only other people who are bad. This woman with
her box of perfume and her tears is picturing to us the need
to weep and be sorry, and to show Jesus that we appreciate
what he came to do. Some day we shall see her. That day
when Jesus comes back.

11
ASTONISHMENT AHEAD

Perhaps you live in a city and have never seen anything grow from seed. Perhaps you live where you see vegetables in rows and rows, but you have never seen a field planted with wheat. But wherever you live, I think it would be helpful if you could make a little model of a plot of ground where four different kinds of conditions exist. This would help you to understand the parable Jesus told about the sower. Take a large box with fairly shallow sides, or a shoe box, or whatever you are able to find. If you live in a city where you cannot get dirt, some weeds and a few stones easily, then you'd better take a small box no bigger than a shoe box.

Fix the box with soil in it, earth, dirt . . . from the garden, or from a flower pot if you can't get any other soil. Pat it down. Now fix a part of it with some weeds, or some grass representing weeds, or if you have some bits of fallen leaves, or dried up leaves from the house plants, use those for weeds. Take a few pebbles and little stones to make another part of it stony. Now take a flat stick like a ruler, or a toy block, and pat down a hard path. A portion of the soil should make up the fourth section, and it should be brown, smooth and without any sticks or stones. If you wanted to do one more thing to make it complete, you could take a little doll house man, or make a man out of wire pipe cleaners, and make a tiny bag on a string to hang over his shoulder. There you have the scene all set for the story!

Jesus said that a sower went out to sow his seed. Now you must imagine a man with a pouch hanging over his shoulder, a bag full of seed. He is taking seed in his hand and throwing it, scattering it from side to side. He is not sowing vegetable seed in rows, but something like wheat seed over a large area of a field. As he scattered the seed, first on one side and then the other, it fell on different kinds of ground.

Some of it fell by the wayside and was trodden down, and the birds swooped down and ate it up. Look at your model now. The "wayside" is represented by that little path you patted down with the block, and you must imagine that it has been walked on so often that it is very hard. The birds would find it there and snatch it up as quickly as they take food from a bird feeder, or crumbs from the street.

Then some of the seed fell on a rock. This was a rock with a tiny bit of soil on it, because this seed sprang up and began to grow, but withered away almost immediately because it had no place for the roots to go down and get moisture. Plants soon dry up without moisture. Have you seen what happens to a plant in a shallow pot in the house, when you forget to water it?

The next fell among thorns and weeds. As quickly as the seed grew, more weeds and thorns grew too, until they choked it. Any of you who have ever planted or watched a garden, know that weeds will choke a little plant and stop it from growing. Weeds always seem to grow faster and thicker than the plants that you have planted. If the weeds and the plants grow in the same spot, the weeds win. And others fell on good ground and sprang up, and bore fruit a hundredfold. What does that mean? Well, if you have planted one seed of corn, and it really grows, when the time comes for the corn to be ripe, you will pick two or three ears of corn from the one plant, and if you count the number of grains of corn, it will come to more than a hundred. When one seed grows into a plant, the "fruit" is many times as much as the one you began with.

As we have said, a parable is a story to teach a spiritual truth.

When Jesus' disciples asked what this parable meant, Jesus explained it to them. The first thing he said was, "The seed is the Word of God." What is the ground then? The ground is made up of the people of the world. Jesus went on to explain what happens when different people hear the Word

of God. He said that those by the wayside (they are represented by the hard path you patted down) are people that
hear, and then the devil comes and takes the word out of
their hearts immediately. These are the people whose re-
sponse is so hard that it is as if the "seed" is lying right on
top to be eaten by the birds. In other words, Satan finds it
easy to take away any memory of what they have heard. It
does not sink in for a minute.

The second kind of people are like rocky ground. They
seem to hear the truth of God's Word with joy. (We've seen
people like this, and hear their warm voices in our ears
still in memory, yet remember that after the first seeming
interest they never came back to hear more, or even wrote
a letter.)

This kind of person, Jesus says, seems to believe for a
very short time, but has no real roots. He or she has what we
would call a shallow, surface kind of interest. A seed can put
forth a tiny shoot of green, but if there is no soil and moisture and no real root forms, it is not really growing. This kind
of person is like this. Perhaps they hear a sermon, or read a
book, or have a conversation with you. You think, "How
interested he or she is! I must invite him or her around for a
Bible Study, or an evening's discussion." But you will find that
their *interest* is one of being entertained, as a person would
be entertained by reading a novel, or going to a concert, or
seeing a boat race. There is a flurry of interest in the author
who wrote the novel, in the violinist or guitarist who played
in the concert, or in the oarsman rowing; but then the names
are forgotten and they turn their attention to something else.

These people who are the rocky soil are like that. No
roots. No real plant at all. It is not age that makes the soil
rocky. People like rocky soil can be of any age. Jesus says
they "fall away in time of *temptation.*" The temptation does
not need to be to do something very wicked, but simply to
put anything and everything ahead of going on with their
study of the Word of God. A child who says, "No, I'd rather
play, run, eat, talk to the child next door, but I don't want to
hear any more about the Bible," may not be wanting to do

something wrong, but he or she is rocky ground. The interest *was* there, but it is not deep enough to provide the "plant" with any moisture or food, so the roots don't grow, and without roots there are no leaves . . . and it goes on this way!

》 The next seed fell among weeds and thorns. You can look at your "model" plot of ground to get the idea here. But it is better actually to plant a small vegetable garden yourself. Keep all of it weeded, watered and cared for, except one small patch. Let that patch get overrun with weeds; let the weeds grow along with what you planted. You will have all the illustration you need! A long time ago we planted a very big vegetable garden in orderly rows, with the names of each vegetable at the end of each row. Then we had to teach in a children's summer Bible School for four weeks, and we had not a minute to be in the garden. At the end of four weeks, it was difficult to find the plants! The weeds were much higher than they were! We couldn't get the garden in order as we had to go away again to run a children's camp. When we got back some weeks later we found little stunted pieces of corn, a few hard, green tomatoes, a tiny bit of evidence that other vegetables had tried to struggle along. But the weeds were too much for them. There was no "fruit" . . . there was nothing to pick, and eat! It was a lesson to us in gardening, but it helped us to understand some spiritual things, too, including this parable of the sower.

What does Jesus say the weeds are? Those who are being portrayed here are people who believe, and then go on living without realizing that certain things will "choke" their growth. The things Jesus calls "weeds" are two very opposite things . . . but both will make it difficult for us to grow as Christians. They are cares and riches and pleasures. Opposite things. First, the worries and anxieties of making a living, of paying taxes, of getting a bigger car, of having a summer home as well as a winter home, of sending children to college, of paying bills, of having a larger bank account, of making investments, or having more and more expensive holidays or vacations. If we are poor, of never being sure there is enough money for little things. If we are richer, of never being sure there is enough for extravagant things. Worries such as quarrels in the family, troubles at work, neighbors not being friendly to the children. Worries and anxieties can come at any age. A child can be worried by grown-ups who do not understand him, by not having the same things as other children, and always comparing himself with someone who has more. Some people can be worried about not having enough to eat, or being too poor to have a dentist care for their aching teeth, or about their sheep being eaten by animals. There are enough possible "worries and anxieties" in the world to take up a whole book just listing them.

We are talking about *growing* plants now, little plants that are really growing as the weeds choke them. The danger is that the weeds will so push out the air and light, that the plants will never have flowers and fruit. The weeds have to be pulled out in some way. Does that mean they will never come back? No, but the plant has a chance to grow a bit more, and the next weeds won't take over quite as easily.

Does a growing Christian (because this is what the plants illustrate to us) *never* have cares and worries, anxieties and troubles? Paul, whom you will study about later on in the New Testament, was a very great Christian. But we are told he had all kinds of troubles—like shipwrecks, being put in prison for preaching about Jesus, being hungry, being hated and persecuted by other people, having people hit him with sticks, getting so tired that he felt he couldn't keep on with his work. Once he wrote to the Corinthian Christians, "For out of much affliction and anguish of heart I wrote unto you with many *tears* . . . ." He is as unhappy as all *that*, because of his worry and concern about how the people in that church were living. So it is not that a Christian should jump around clapping his hands all the time saying, "Oh, I am so happy," when there are troubles to make him sad.

But—and there is a very big *but*! There is a difference between what Paul did and letting all your thoughts, energies, feelings, time and strength to be taken up day after day with your troubles. Everyone will be tempted to do this, but letting troubles small and great, difficulties, anxieties, fears and worries fill our minds is definitely letting the weeds of the cares of the world choke our growth as Christians, and there will not be fruit.

What are we to do about it? There is a verse you should know. It is Philippians 4:6; "In nothing be anxious; but," and here is the *but* that makes the difference—"but in everything by prayer and supplication with thanksgiving let your requests be made known unto God." Let us be sure we understand what this says and do something. When we begin to worry about something, like people being mean to us at school, or having a pain we fear is appendicitis or cancer, or worrying about being popular with our fellow-students, or worrying about the bills coming at the end of the month, or what other people will say about our children, or worrying about our business growing constantly bigger—or about losing our job—whatever our age, whatever the worry, and whatever area of life it is in, we are told what we are to do about it as Christians. The worry is meant to take us *towards* spending time with the Lord, not *away* from spending time with him. We are meant to pray, to talk to the Lord, to tell him all about it. We are told how to pray about our worries, and first to think of all the things we are thankful for. And when you begin to tell the Lord what you are thankful for, it can take a long time.

When we have been walking together in the woods recently, we have been praying out loud. And to begin by saying "thank you," and just to relax and think of all the things we are thankful for, can take *miles*! Yes, the Lord wants us to remember what he has given us in the past; he wants us to name the things we remember that he has done for us. We bring him joy when we say "thank you" in detail. He knows us very well; he knows that this will help us to stop thinking about our trouble in such a lopsided way. He knows that it will help us to get the right perspective on things if we balance our trouble, problem or difficulty against the things we are *thankful* for. Then he tells us to *ask*, to make our requests known to him. Prayer is asking, supplication is begging, making a request is telling in detail something you want done. Yes, the God who made the universe and all the things in it, the God who can do anything, has said we are to come to him, as his children, as born-into-his-family people, as Christians, and spend time with him when we are worried. We are to be with him. We are told that in his presence is joy. In his presence we are in the light, not in the fog.

It is foggy and grey day after day as this book is being written. How lovely it would be to go up higher into the mountains! Those who have been skiing these last few days say that there is sunshine up there and sparkling snow-capped peaks are to be seen against a blue sky. But we have to stay down here in the fog to write.

When we are in a fog of difficulty, we don't have to take a train up to the top of a mountain. What we do to change the surroundings is to go for a time, even a few minutes, into the sunshine of God's presence. No, this isn't just "romantic slush" as some people today might be thinking. It is *real.* Just being in the presence of the Lord as we talk to him, also takes us away from the danger of the "weeds" of cares choking us. Then we are given a practical help . . . we are told to *ask in detail.* Every single thing we worry about should be talked over with God, and we should ask him for help. This is how Christians should, day by day, pull out the weeds of worry.

Just before this verse in Paul's letter to the Philippians, chapter four and verse five, is the warning, "The Lord is at hand." What does that mean? It means that Jesus is coming back some day; it may be soon. It helps to warn us, to shake us up a bit, to cause us to think whether what we are asking for is really the only thing to be asking for. It helps us to remember other things we should be praying for.

Right after this verse, and in verse seven, we are told that if we *do this* when things worry us, then "The peace of God which passeth all understanding, shall guard your hearts and your thoughts in Christ Jesus." How exciting! You see, we are told that if we pray like this when we are worried, then our emotions and thoughts will be peaceful. Peaceful for ever without a break? No. But right after we have brought the difficult thing to him in conversation, in prayer, zip . . . the weed is out. The soil is ready for the plant to grow, till the next weed appears!

What are the other kind of weeds? They are the pleasures and riches of this life. Pleasures and riches sound good. It sounds as if it would be easy to grow as a Christian if there were not many troubles, and there were lots of pleasures and riches. But, it doesn't work that way. Very often the richer a person becomes, and the more free time that person has just to play games, travel, be entertained, the less they think about other people's needs. And the less they ask God what they should do with their time and money, and the less time they spend talking to God in prayer. The pleasures and riches are choking out the growth, just as much as the other kind of weeds, the weeds of worry.

It's a strange thing, but the more a person has, the less, usually, they give to the Lord. The Bible warns us about this over and over again. Later on in Luke we will be thinking about treasures in heaven, and how to store them there. God warns that where your treasure is, your wealth, your money and things, that will be where your "heart" will be too . . . that is, your interests, thoughts and feelings. So often it is the people who do not have much who give to the Lord more money than those who have a lot! Why? Well, the Bible shows us that if your riches are being put in heaven, they won't choke you and it is the *proportion* of what is given to what is kept, that matters. It is the riches and pleasures of *this life* that are a danger.

Does this mean that no one can be a Christian and be rich? No, God says that with him all things are possible, but that it is much harder to grow as a Christian if you are rich and that as much care must be taken then as when people are crushed with fears and worries. Riches are more dangerous, because it is harder to recognize that you are being choked! Selfishness and greediness grow as a very fast growing weed, along with riches. It is so easy to want one more thing and one more and one more, and to stop thinking about other people's needs.

Christians *ought* to be the people who are weeping over the needs of hungry and suffering people. Christians ought to be sharing what they have, and thinking of others who have physical as well as spiritual need. But so often riches and pleasures choke out such compassion, and people get more and more selfish. Just as much prayer is needed about what to do with riches, and with free time as is needed when people are worried about sickness, or not having enough money, or being in other kinds of trouble. We will study this more later, but right now, do remember that this weed is one that stops fruit from coming on the little "plant."

When you take a walk, try to look for weeds in gardens. If you come across a garden that is not weeded, take a good look at it. Put yourself in the plant's place, and pray . . . ask the Lord to help you to notice the weeds when they are small and not let them stop you from growing. Talk together as a family about keeping a balance in your lives together. Yes, we are to enjoy things that God has given us, and made for us to enjoy. But day by day we are meant to be growing, and the things the Lord has planned for us, the things the Lord is giving us, will not stop our growing.

What is the good ground like? Jesus explains that good ground consists of the people who have an honest and good heart, and, having heard the Word of God, they keep it, and bring forth fruit with patience. Lots of things are there in the good ground, things we could talk about for hours! Honesty and sincerity are involved in our first listening to God's Word, and they are important day by day as we ask for God's plan. We can be honest and sincere one minute, and then be deceiving ourselves another. Is anyone *perfectly* honest and sincere? No, but it is important to ask God to help us recognize this when we begin to try to fool ourselves and others, and God! Jesus speaks of good ground in the same way he spoke before of those who *hear* and *do*. In this place it is the ones who have *heard* the Word, and *keep* it. It is a matter of listening, reading and asking God's help to understand, and then doing what he tells us to do. And patience will be needed, as it is whenever it takes a long time to do something. Growing as a fruitful plant—takes a lifetime! Does the good ground never have a weed? Well, if you have a garden, you know that even the best ground suddenly has weeds springing up as if from nowhere. Yes, weeds need to be pulled out even of the good ground, but that's nothing like sowing seeds in the thorn patch!

A question you might ask youself is, "What kind of ground am I?" The wonderful thing is that if you care about it, and pray, the Lord can soften the hard ground, break up rocks, pull out weeds . . . and really help you, if you care to ask him.

» Jesus went on that day to tell another short parable. He told of a man who really wanted to see, lighting a candle, and putting it up on a candlestick. Jesus said that no one who really wants to see, or to give light to other people in the room so that they can see, would ever *cover up* a candle with a vessel. Right now, get the tallest candlestick you have in the house and put a candle in it—right there on a table. Next to it put a low candle, maybe a fat little one that will sit on a plate. Now cover the lower one with a metal bowl turned upside down, something that will not burn, but will cover it for a moment . . . if it is something with holes, the candle will burn longer under there. Now light the two candles, cover the low one, and let the one on the candlestick burn away up there! It doesn't take long to get the point. We are meant to give forth light to others. We learned before what light represents . . . truth—and the truth is the Word of God. How are we going to give any light if we hide under something that keeps the light from being seen by anyone?

While Jesus was talking to the crowd, his mother Mary, and his half-brothers, Mary and Joseph's children, came to see him, and couldn't get near him because of the crowd. You remember that Jesus had no human father; God alone was his Father, but he did have a human mother, Mary. After Jesus was born in this unique and wonderful way, Mary and her husband Joseph had children. These were the brothers that Doctor Luke is speaking about here.

Jesus loved his mother very much, but when someone came and told him his mother and brothers were wanting to see him, he said, "My mother and my brethren are these which hear the word of God and do it." Jesus is pointing out something *very* important, and he is using this moment to make it real. Here were his earthly mother and his half-brothers in the family in which he had grown up, but he is saying that they are not any closer to him even then, and will never be any closer to him, than each one who is born into God's family, and in that way becomes part of Jesus' family. We sometimes wish we could be close friends of the great people of the world—like kings, or great artists, or wonderful musicians, or famous doctors, or brilliant scientists. But Jesus is the *greatest* of all who have ever lived on earth, and when we believe in him, we cannot only be his friends, but a part of his family. Some people try to pray to the mother of Jesus because they feel that she is closer to Jesus than anyone else, but Jesus tells us this isn't so, because he himself says that all saved ones, all born-again ones are his "mother and his brothers." We don't need anyone to help us to talk to God the Father except Jesus himself. We belong to God as his children. He is always ready to hear us because Jesus died for us, and we come only through Jesus.

Soon after this Jesus walked down to the shore of the lake and stepped into a boat. "Come on," he said to the disciples who were with him. "Let us go over to the other side of the lake." So the men pushed the boat out into the water, and off they went. As they sailed along, the boat must have rocked softly, and Jesus, who was very tired, fell asleep. Suddenly a wind storm blew up. Any of you who live near a lake or sea, know how suddenly the sky gets black and the wind whips up a calm water into a froth of waves! The waves must have rocked the boat, and caused it to toss up and down, with water spilling in to make puddles in the bottom. How frightening it is to see waves get higher and higher and to feel the wind sweep you along as you are in a little boat!

As the boat began to fill with water, it was in danger of sinking, and the frightened men woke Jesus, saying, "Master, Master, we are perishing." Mark in his Gospel tells that they also said, "Don't you care if we are lost?" Then Jesus stood up, and spoke! Imagine, he could speak to the wind and sea! He rebuked the wind and sea, and immediately there was a calm. No wonder the men were amazed. They had never in all their years of fishing, sailing, handling boats, living by the lake, seen a storm become calm in a moment of time. It shocked them so much that they said to each other, "What manner of man is this? For he commandeth even the winds and waters, and they obey him." Jesus told them they should not have been afraid. He told them they should have faith that he could take care of them. You see, he is teaching them little by little not only who he is, but what the power of God is like. We must remember as God's children, that our Father can take care of us in storms at sea, in the air, and so on. We must pray, asking his help, believing he is able to do all things.

However, Jesus is also teaching that when we are his children, *he is always with us* just as if he were in a boat with us. Take your chalk, drawing pencils and sketch books, crayons and paper, whatever you have, and sketch a picture of a small boat. Put yourself in it—just a little stick figure if you can't draw—and put in another stick figure representing Jesus. Think of that boat as your day by day life. Remind yourself that Jesus is in the boat with you; he is with you day by day. You are not alone in this twentieth century storm! You are not alone at the university, in the discussions that rage about you like fifty-foot waves. Ask *him* to keep your little boat from sinking.

There was a man by the name of Jairus who was a ruler in the synagogue; that meant that he was very important in that town. His important position meant nothing to him on this particular day, however, because his only daughter, who was only twelve years old, was very ill, and he thought she was close to dying. Can you picture Jesus with crowds of people around him on the street, and Jairus pushing his way through until he fell in front of Jesus' feet? That means that he bowed down very low, with his head just about touching the ground, begging Jesus to listen to him, begging Jesus to come to the house where his daughter lay dying, and heal her. But, as Jesus walked along with Jairus in the direction of his house, the people pushed against Jesus, making it hard for him to walk quickly.

In the midst of this crowd, there was a woman who had had a sickness that had caused her to bleed for twelve years. Luke tells us that she had spent all her money on doctors, but that none of them could cure her. This woman came up behind Jesus and touched the border of his garment. Immediately she stopped bleeding! Now Jesus said, "Who touched me?" And everyone said, "I didn't, I didn't." And Peter said, "Master, really now, in the midst of all this pushing crowd around you, how can you ask who touched you?" Peter thought it was a foolish question. Jesus repeated, "Someone touched me, because I was aware that something had taken place!" You see, he knew very well that this woman had touched him believing that he could help her, but he wanted her to acknowledge that fact, to say so. When the woman realized she could not hide from Jesus, she trembled, but came up to him and told him what had happened, so that the whole crowd heard and knew why she had touched him, and that she had been healed immediately. Jesus spoke gently to her, saying, "Daughter, thy faith hath made thee whole; go in peace."

While he was saying this someone from Jairus' home came to Jairus saying, "Thy daughter is dead, trouble not the Master." What a blow to Jairus! He must have felt overwhelmed with sorrow. Too late! Quickly Jesus comforted him by saying, "Fear not, only believe, and she will be made whole." It is a promise. "Don't be afraid, Jairus. Just believe

Jesus restores Jairus' daughter to him and his wife. Luke 8:41–56

in me, and she will be no longer separated—body from soul—she will be whole again, body and soul, alive." When Jesus arrived with Jairus at the house, he didn't allow anyone else to go in except Peter, James, and John and the father and mother of the little girl. All the people in the house were crying and saying how terrible it was that she was dead. As Jesus passed by them on his way to the girl's room, he said, "Weep not; for she is not dead, but sleepeth." They laughed him to scorn, Luke says; in other words, they mocked him and made fun of him. Jesus put them all out, and then went over to the little girl and took her by the hand, saying, "Maiden, arise," or "Little girl, get up." Her spirit came into her right away, and she got up immediately. Jesus said, "Now get her something to eat."

Can't you imagine how amazed her mother and father were? Luke says they were "astonished." And so they would have been! Death is a shock to watch. It is very difficult to realize that the body does not have the soul there any longer. It is hard to see someone not "whole" any longer—only a part of them there, the body. But it would be even more of a shock, more astonishing, to see a dead person get up and eat supper—suddenly whole again, suddenly laughing and talking. Jesus had kept his promise to Jairus, hadn't he?

This same Jesus, our Savior, will keep all his promises to us. He will keep his promises to all who come to him believing. The more time men spent with him during those years on earth, the more they got to know him. Now we can get to know him by reading his Word, the Bible, and talking to him in prayer, and finding out what his promises are. What he tells us about the future *will* take place. In a way, we are walking down the street of life with him, just as Jairus walked down the street that day. The astonishment is ahead of us!

12
JESUS IN SPACE AND TIME
AND HISTORY

One day, Jesus called his twelve apostles together and gave
them special power to heal people's sicknesses and to preach.
He told them to go on a preaching journey, from place to
place. He said they should not take money or food, because
the people to whom they would preach should take care of
their needs, feed them and give them a place to sleep. They
left and did what Jesus had told them to do, going from town
to town preaching the gospel, and healing sick people everywhere.

So you see, a lot of towns had the possibility of hearing
the gospel, and of knowing about Jesus during that time.
Jesus, because he had come as truly man, did limit himself to
being in just *one* place at a time. So when the apostles went
out like this, it made it possible for more people to find out
that Jesus had come. Herod the ruler heard about all this, and
he was very puzzled as to what was going on, because he had
beheaded John the Baptist, and some people told him John
had come back to life again. Others said it was Elijah, the Old
Testament prophet, who had come to preach again. Herod
was intrigued by all he heard, and wanted to see "this man,"
as he would have called Jesus. For to Herod at that time Jesus
was a mystery man.

When the apostles returned, they must have been very
tired from the long walking trip, and from all their talking.
There is nothing more tiring than talking to people about
intensely important things. So Jesus took the apostles away
for a short rest to a desert place outside the city that was
called Bethsaida. But the people found out where they had

153

EVERYBODY CAN KNOW

gone, and followed them! Now when you imagine them following Jesus and the apostles out on to the grassy hills about
the lake, you mustn't imagine just fifty or a hundred people.
This time we know how many there were in the "multitude,"
because we are told that there were at least five thousand.
What a crowd! Instead of chasing them away, Jesus welcomed
them, and spoke to them about the things of God, and healed
those who were ill. When the sun began to cast long
shadows, as it does in the late afternoon, the twelve apostles
came a little anxiously to Jesus and said something like this:
"You'd better send these crowds away now to the towns and
villages around here, because we're in a desert place and
there is nowhere to get food."

Can you imagine what Jesus answered? He said, "*You*
give them something to eat." They must have been shocked
at that answer, for they quickly said, "But there are five
thousand men, besides women and children." (Matthew
14:13–21 is where we find there were women and children in
addition to five thousand men.) "Where are we going to get
food for that many?" In John 6:1–14, we read that it was
Andrew, Peter's brother, who suddenly said, "There is a little
boy here, who has five barley loaves and two small fish: but
what are they among so many?" Imagine what you would
have thought if you had been one of the twelve men. What
impression would you have had if you had looked at the
crowd of five thousand men, plus a lot of women and children, and then looked at five little loaves and two fish?

Do you have any rolls in the house? I don't suppose you
have two fish! If you do, it would be a good thing to put five
nice-sized rolls or muffins or scones (that would be about the
size of those little loaves) with a napkin in a basket, or on a
plate . . . put it there in front of you all, to look at. Then if
you don't have fish, one of you draw a picture of a fish, a
boiled trout maybe, . . . and cut out two alike. It is good to
just sit and *look* at that small amount of food for a minute.

Jesus accepts food from a little boy.   Luke 9:10–17

154

After all, the apostles were just ordinary people . . . this didn't look like any more food to them than it does to you.

Now look at it, and think of the boy. His mother had prepared this lunch so that he wouldn't be hungry; we don't know whether he got caught up in the crowd, or whether his mother knew where he was going, but she was a thoughtful person who provided for her boy. He was pretty special in the kind of trust he had in Jesus, wasn't he? He was asked to give *all* that he had right then, and he gave it all. He had a choice, but he didn't keep back one bit. It is important to know that God is no man's debtor. What does that mean? That if you give something to the Lord, it is wonderful what happens. He doesn't "owe" it to you; he cares for *your* need, as well as using what you give for other people's needs. This boy learned that in a fantastic manner, which I am sure he never forgot. He had trusted his lunch to Jesus.

Try to imagine you are there on that hillside with all the people milling around, and Jesus standing there now with the five little loaves and two fish. What happened next? Jesus told the apostles to get the people to sit down in groups of fifty. Can't you imagine them counting? One, two, three, four, five, ten, fifteen, twenty, thirty, forty, fifty—no more in *this* group, come over here, now we'll start over *here*, one, two . . . and so on. I wonder if the boy sat in the group nearest Jesus, or if he walked around with the apostles as they counted people out and got them all quietly sitting down? Remember that the apostles had trust and faith at that point to do *exactly* as Jesus told them, without arguing or making any more references to the fact that there was no food. They were obeying, without seeing what was coming next. So very often in life, we need to do what God is leading us to do *now* without seeing what is coming *next*. We never pass the stage where we need to learn the lesson of not worrying about what is coming *next*. The little boy didn't know what was coming next either, but he had already obeyed and given his lunch.

How many groups of fifty? Well, it would take a hundred groups of fifty to make five thousand, but there were more than that because of the women and children. All sitting on the green grass in the sunset now, all waiting expectantly! Jesus had the food in his hands—the people had nothing, the apostles had nothing, the boy had nothing. Jesus then looked up to heaven and blessed these five little loaves and two fish, he gave thanks for the food the boy had given, and prayed that God would multiply it. Then he started to break it into pieces. Look now at what is on your table, if you have put bread and fish there. How many pieces would they make? Not many! But as Jesus broke the bread and fish, he handed the pieces to the disciples to pass around. Soon one man had more than he could put in his basket, so he started serving people; then another had his basket full; soon twelve were passing out food, and as they came back for more, more was broken into their baskets. Fifty were eating by now, then a hundred were eating, then five hundred, and then six hundred.

It would take a long while, breaking and handing it out as quickly as possible, for it would still take time to walk around, lean down to let people take all they wanted, go back for more, and continue. Five thousand men, plus women and children and the little boy and the apostles and Jesus . . . everyone that was there had enough bread and fish. Jesus kept breaking and breaking and breaking, and always there was more. We know they all had enough to eat, because we are told that the disciples gathered up the pieces that were left so as not to waste anything, and they gathered twelve baskets full.

How could Jesus do this miracle? He could do it because he is God. He had made the world in the first place. Would it be hard for the Creator of all things to make the waves and wind stop tossing a boat? Would it be hard for the Creator of all things to multiply bread and fish into more pieces of bread and fish?

In Colossians 1:16, 17, Paul tells us about Christ as Creator, and he says, "For in him were all things created, in the heavens and upon the earth, things visible and things invisible, whether thrones or dominions or principalities or powers; all things have been created through him, and unto him; and he is before all things, and in him all things consist." That is pretty complete. That takes in everything, doesn't it?

That says that the Second Person of the Trinity, the Son of God, Jesus, the Messiah, Christ (all names for the same Person) made everything, and that he existed before anything was made. Can't you see that the people who say, "I don't believe in miracles," are just like the people who try to find some way of explaining how *everything* came into being by *chance*? It is because they do not believe there *is* a God. They do not believe there is a Triune, personal, powerful, infinite, everlasting God! It is because people do not believe there *was* a Mind to *have* ideas, choose and create, that they think everything *had* to come by chance. And it is because people do not think there is a powerful Creator God, that they do not believe that there are miracles. You see they don't believe there is anyone to *do* the miracles! It is not hard to believe that the Creator of everything could multiply the bread and the fish. And Jesus, as Creator of everything, was showing more than five thousand people that day, that he could do such a thing. They *saw* what he did, and they *tasted* what he did, and they were *filled* with what he did! Their stomachs were full of the bread and fish, and it nourished them.

Centuries before, Moses had called out to God in prayer at one time, beginning like this: "O Lord God, thou hast begun to shew thy servant thy greatness, and thy strong hand: for what god is there in heaven or in earth, that can do according to thy works, and according to thy mighty acts?" Some of the more than five thousand people that day would have known Deuteronomy 3:24, where this is written down, and they would have know other parts of the Old Testament which might have come to mind. I wonder if some of them *did* remember Moses' prayer, and did pray right then, realizing that God was *beginning* to show his greatness in *their* generation.

» On another day as Jesus was praying alone, away from the crowds of people, he turned to the disciples who were near-

by and asked a question. "Whom do the people say that I
am?" They answered Jesus by saying, "Some say you are John
the Baptist. Some say you are Elijah, and others say you are
one of the old prophets risen from the dead." Then Jesus
must have looked very searchingly at his disciples as he
asked, "Whom do *you* say that I am?" It was Peter who
answered. Peter was always quick in rushing to speak or to do
something. Peter said, "The Christ of God." John (in chapter
6 verses 68 and 69) tells us that Peter spoke very clearly of his
conviction as to who Jesus was: "Then Simon Peter answered
him, 'Lord, to whom shall we go? Thou hast the words of
eternal life. And we believe and are *sure* that thou art that
Christ, the Son of the living God.'"

Jesus wanted his disciples to be sure in their minds, to
be able to put into words, who they thought him to be. In the
Old Testament, over and over again, God did things that men
might *know* in their minds, and tell others in words, that he is
indeed God. We would need a whole book to look at all the
places we are thinking about in the Old Testament, but let's
remember together at least *two* places.

Do you remember Joshua speaking to the Israelites,
after the Jordan river had separated into two so that they
could walk over on dry ground? Joshua instructed men to put
twelve stones out of the river Jordan on the ground east of
Jericho, and said to the people, "When your children ask you
what these stones mean, you are to let them *know*, telling
how God dried up the river so that the Jews could walk over
on dry ground, just as years before he had done that to the
Red Sea." Joshua said they were to tell this story over and
over again, so that "All the people of the earth might *know*
the hand of the Lord: that it is mighty: that ye might fear (that
means to have awe for, a feeling of worship towards) the Lord
your God for ever." (Joshua 4:19–24.) Yes, God has always
wanted people to *know* that he is God. And he wants all of us
to know this, too.

The other thing we can remember together from the
Old Testament is in 1 Kings 18:21–39. Elijah stood before the
Israelites, many of whom were worshiping the false god,

Baal. This heathen religion had four hundred and fifty priests, and many were following these priests in their worship of false gods. Elijah stood before them on this particular day, and asked how much longer they were going to be mixed up, arguing, having two opinions as to whether *Baal* or the living God is the Lord. Elijah said he alone was the prophet of the living God, but Baal had four hundred and fifty prophets there. So Elijah proposed a test. You will remember that the test was that each would prepare an identical altar, and put an identical sacrifice on it, but that the God who was truly God must send fire to burn up the sacrifice. Do you remember that the four hundred and fifty men danced around in "square circles" all day, lashing themselves till blood ran, trying to beg Baal to send fire down? But nothing happened. Elijah was a little sarcastic, saying maybe their god was asleep or out for a walk. Anyway . . . when Elijah prayed that God, the God of Abraham, Isaac and of Israel, would send down fire, he said, "Hear me, O Lord, hear me, that this people may *know* that thou, Lord, art God." And then we are told that the fire fell and not only burned up the sacrifice, but licked up the water that was in the trench, the dust around the stones . . . it was a terrific fire! And the result? When the people saw it, they fell on their faces and they said, "The Lord, he is God; the Lord, he is God!"

Centuries have passed since that day. Now Jesus is talking to Israelites; he has come, the promised Messiah, to fulfil the promises, and to tie the teaching he is now giving them into the history they already know. These disciples are all Jews. They are ordinary men. You may be sure they have read, discussed, argued about the Old Testament. Now they are following the Messiah. Can't you see how it is? The days of the week follow one after another. They get sleepy, they get a toothache, they stub their toes, they get dusty. Spring comes, summer is hot, flies buzz around, the milk goes sour. What are we saying? There were everyday things going on, as always. There were the same smells, tastes, noises, feelings, reactions to people in the family, people on the street, a girl walking by, a beggar whining, and it would not be easy to *stay certain* all the time about things they were seeing Jesus do, hearing him say, and being convinced were truth. *They* were in a moment of history when they were *with* Jesus, yes, but it was a *harder* time to believe than now, because they couldn't see things as clearly as we can.

We have the whole Bible to tell us the complete teaching, and we have more of history that has passed. Sometimes people say, often to little children, "Wouldn't it have been wonderful to have been there when Jesus was teaching, and healing people?" But I think even the youngest in the family listening to this book can realize that perhaps you would *not* have found it as easy to know who Jesus really was, even if you had been eating some of that bread and fish. Anyway, you were *not* living then, and you *are* living now, and the time is coming in the future when you will look back on this moment of history and think, "Why didn't I live every day asking God to go ahead and do what *he* wanted with me in the twentieth century? Oh, why did I live so much of the time as if *all* I said I believed was like a story, and not true. Why did I use up so much of my time, energy, money, talents, emotions on things that didn't matter?" When the future day comes, and Jesus returns, we won't be able to go back to today, but right now we can ask him to help us to have our "eyes of understanding" opened. It would be a good idea to stop and pray for that *one* thing, pray for more understanding of *him*, and of his Word, and of what he wants us as a group or a family, and as individual people to *know* now, and to *do*.

Jesus told his disciples that he was going to suffer many things, that he was going to be rejected by the elders and chief priests of the synagogue, and that he would be killed, and on the third day he would be raised. He told them as clearly as that, but it seems they heard only with their *ears*, and whatever they thought as they heard, they did *not* imagine these things really happening, they did not picture at all what it would be like, nor think what they would do and what their reactions would be if he did die. They probably said, "mmmmmm," with a kind of "Yes, I hear," sort of sound, but we know what happened later on, that they didn't *then* understand. I am sure we cannot really imagine what it was like to have been walking day by day with Jesus, hearing him speak, watching him do fantastic things, getting to love him as a person, and even coming to be sure he was the Messiah . . . but *not* expecting his death.

Jesus was preparing them, but they had to *live through* the days ahead to come to a conviction and understanding that *really* prepared them to believe, understand, preach, teach, live and die as they later did. Jesus was preparing some of them also to write accounts of what happened, so that we could know what it *really* had been like. He prepared them to write about how slowly they were convinced. Their accounts are not accounts of a smoothly "made up" story. They are real history, just as the Old Testament is real history.

Now Jesus told them about a "test" for them which is the same for us. Jesus said, "If a man is really going to follow me, let him deny himself and take up his cross daily and follow me. For whosoever will save his life shall lose it, but whosoever will lose his life for my sake, the same shall save it." What does he mean? Well, it takes a lifetime to understand this and we never *do* understand perfectly, but Jesus means, partly at least, that we are not always to be taking care of our "rights," our material things, our physical needs, our own interests—and then just giving to him what is left over around the edges. We have to know something of what it means to put the Lord *first*. That has to have some real place in our day-by-day living. John says in his Gospel that we are to become as corns of wheat planted in the ground. That is like the seed we talked about, isn't it? Except that this time *our lives* are the grains of corn. We have to be willing to lose everything in the eyes of men. We have to be willing *not* to do the clever thing, the brilliant thing, the wise thing, the sharp thing, in the eyes of other people. We have to be willing *not* to be a huge success, *not* to be first in everything, *not* to save all our money for ourselves, *not* always to go from a smaller thing to a bigger thing, and then an even bigger thing.

Let's give an example. One day an English student studying in Paris was approaching the time of some important

162

exams. As he walked down a Paris street, he must have been thinking of his studies. But suddenly he met a man from South America who looked very depressed and sad, and who very obviously needed someone to talk to. The English student got into a conversation, and realized the situation was serious. He felt the South American man could be helped if he took him to a tiny place in Switzerland, where he could discuss his problems about humanistic philosophy and where he could get some real answers to life. The English person felt he had a decision, to turn away from this man, who after all wasn't his responsibility, or to turn away from his exams, and drive the fellow to Switzerland, right then. At that moment, it seems to me, that English student denied *himself,* became a corn planted in the ground . . . he turned away from what "men" would all judge to be wise, and did what he was sure God wanted him to do. He drove the South American to L'Abri in Switzerland. It would take too long to tell the whole story, but the South American man is one whom you will meet in heaven some day, and you can talk to him about it yourself, if you are going!

Of course it is important to do well in exams and all school work. It is important to be a good engineer, a skilful doctor, a fine artist, a productive farmer, an accurate secretary, a creative housekeeper, a well-trained athlete—because if we want to make it clear to people that they are created in the image of God, it is silly to do things sloppily. Often people excuse poor work by saying they are busy talking to other people about Christianity. But their poor work cancels out what they are saying!

It is in extreme moments that we face the decision involving the sacrifice of putting aside our normal responsibilities. Putting God first, or seeking first the Kingdom of God, *does* however, need *some* real demonstration.

Whether we are five, fifteen, thirty-five, fifty . . . we have all kinds of places in which we can demonstrate to the Lord and to ourselves that we are choosing *him*, rather than protecting ourselves. It doesn't matter about other people watching; *we* are meant to be caring about the Lord. We

163

need also to ask him to help us to recognize the places where he means us to do a practical thing that will be "losing our lives for his sake, rather than saving our lives for our own sake." His promises do come true. He promises that anyone who does lose his life for the Lord's sake will be, in the end, saving it! Remember that we said that before, God is no man's debtor. He also promises that the one who is always saving his life, protecting it, getting his rights for his own sake, will lose it. Then Jesus explained it a bit more by saying, "Whoever is ashamed of me *and* of my words, that same person will the Son of man be ashamed of when he shall come in his glory." People are ashamed of being Christians at times. People are ashamed to believe the Bible, ashamed to say they believe it is true, ashamed of what Jesus has claimed concerning the Old Testament, and concerning the future. Peter was later himself to be ashamed, and to deny *knowing* Jesus.

Can we never be forgiven if we are ashamed? Yes, we can be forgiven of all sin. But we have really to be *sorry*, and to come asking forgiveness, and then—because Jesus died for us—we *are* forgiven. But we need to know that being ashamed of God and his Word *is* really very sinful, and we need to ask not only to be forgiven, but to have that taken away, and to be more concerned about Jesus not being ashamed of us! Later on, some of the things Jesus taught will make this part more clear!

》 About a week after Jesus had been telling the disciples these serious things, which perhaps they didn't understand as well as you do because they lived *before* things you know about had taken place, Jesus chose three men to go for a walk up a mountain with him. Peter, James, John and Jesus climbed up a high mountain where Jesus wanted to go to pray. This was not unusual for the three men, as in fact they fell asleep as they waited, having often been with Jesus as he prayed. But suddenly as Jesus prayed, they must have looked up with astonishment. Their sleepy eyes would have widened and their mouths dropped open. For they saw Jesus looking completely different. His face had changed and become not only beautiful but glowing. Matthew in chapter 17 of his Gospel says it shone like the sun. Jesus' clothing became glistening. Mark says (9:3) that his clothing was as white as snow, whiter than any cloth they had ever seen.

Have you seen fresh snow after it has been falling all night, and when the sun suddenly comes out, making the snow sparkle like a million diamonds? Have you seen the sea, or a lake, with sunlight sparkling on little ripples? That is a kind of glistening, too. Have you seen a stone with little sparkly bits in it when the sun catches it? Have you seen real diamonds being displayed in a jeweler's window? Well . . . the whitest, most sparkling thing you can think of, is what the disciples used to try to describe this glory. Jesus' face—as bright as the sun, his clothing white and sparkling. They must have thought they were dreaming!

Then they saw that two men were with Jesus . . . Moses and Elijah. How did they know them? Well, we think they recognized them, just like that. But they had never *seen* these men because Moses and Elijah had lived long before this time. But, you see, God is letting us find out something very interesting. He is teaching us that we will recognize people in heaven, even people we haven't known, *without* being introduced first! Yes, there were Moses and Elijah talking to Jesus. What were they talking about? Luke says they were talking about the decease of Jesus. What does that mean? It means they were talking about the fact that Jesus was soon going to die. They were discussing his coming death. This shows us what a really exciting moment in history it was.

We have already traced the fact that the Old Testament people all came to God with a little lamb, representing the Lamb of God, the Messiah who would one day come. Well, think of this fact—*all those people* who *had* believed, and died looking forward to the coming Messiah, *all of them* needed him to come and fulfil his promise to die in their place. All those lambs were just representing the Messiah. He really *had* to come in space (that means on the earth, somewhere you can find in your maps, on your globe, in the atlas . . . geographic space); and he had to come in time (that

165

means in time that could be counted on the calendar, recorded on the clock, time that had a "before" and a "during" as well as an "after); and he had to come in history (that means in the weaving together of space and time of human lives as fathers become grandfathers, and grandfathers become great-grandfathers, and children become fathers—and the weaving of one generation affects the next). Jesus *had* to come in *space* and *time* and *history*, and *die* in history, so that Moses and Elijah and Peter and James and John, and you and I . . . could be forgiven our sins, and could be born again. God does things so perfectly. He is so marvelous in the *way* he does things with such perfection! The baby Jesus born in a stable where lambs are born! And *now* Moses and Elijah come to talk to Jesus about his death for *them*, and for all the people they represented who had lived before, and believed, and who were waiting for his death for them, too. What an opportunity James, Peter and John were having! They were seeing Jesus as we one day shall see him, when he comes back in all his glory. He will be all-glorious like that when we see him. And they were seeing Moses and Elijah, so they saw what it will be like to be with all those people we are reading about, people who will be with us some day.

Peter got so excited about it that he said, "Let's make three tents, one for you, Jesus, one for Moses and one for Elijah." Peter just wanted to stay there with all this glory and excitement, and you can hardly blame him. Moses, the law-giver who had received the Ten Commandments from God, was now talking to Jesus who was going to die as his Savior, and the Savior of all because no one could keep the Ten Commandments perfectly. Elijah, the old prophet who had so faithfully preached and taught, and who had been taken up to heaven in a fiery chariot, was also talking to Jesus. Peter's excitement and wish is understandable. Then, while he was still speaking, a cloud came over the mountain, and they were in the mist, and we are told they were afraid as the cloud drifted all around them (Luke says they entered into a cloud, Luke 9:34). Suddenly a voice came out of the cloud saying, "This is my Son, my chosen: hear ye him." And when the voice stopped speaking, Jesus was standing there alone with them. All the glory gone. Moses and Elijah gone. Just the grass, rocks, their plain, old clothing, and the climb back down the mountain path ahead of them.

Jesus told them not to tell anyone what they had seen until after he had died, and risen from the dead. Mark (in 9:10) says they kept talking to each other and wondering what rising from the dead meant. They had been given such a lot that day, but they weren't clear as to the meaning of the death and resurrection of Jesus. They had much ahead to live through.

A little later Jesus said to them, "Let these sayings sink down into your ears: for the Son of man shall be delivered into the hands of men." But they simply did not understand that he was talking about really dying, and rising again. Do remember, though, that it was all taking place in such a short time. The time that Jesus was preaching, teaching, healing people, answering questions, bringing some dead people back to life, explaining things about the future, calling men to leave their work and follow him . . . all this took only a little more than three years. Three years isn't very long. If you have been in school five years, you can remember most of what took place in the last three years, and it doesn't seem that long, does it? And older people think back to three years ago and it seems as if it were only last year. You can imagine that the disciples were just getting used to being *with* Jesus, so to think of him dying was not very real to them.

In middle of all this, one day Jesus found his disciples arguing about who was going to be the greatest one of them all. They were thinking of who would rise some day to the "top." When Jesus knew what they were thinking, he took a small child, and put him beside him, saying, "Whosoever shall receive this little child in my name receiveth me." And he added to that "He that is the least among you all, the same is great." *That* should hit *us*, as hard as it should have hit those men. What is he saying? "Lose your life if you want to save it." "Receive an unimportant little child in my name, if you want to receive me." "Take a small place and be satisfied, because the one who is least shall be the greatest." It is all backwards from the way men judge. Don't you think it is important to *try* to stop looking at things in just a *human* way? Each day we need to ask ourselves if we are in some small way living by God's rules.

We are supposed to be waiting, and expecting Jesus to come back at *any* moment. How long *do* we have to live the way he told us to live? We need to start now!

13
THE MAN WHO REALLY CARED

Do you have a lot of nearby objects that you can use to illustrate something? Beans? Dried peas or lentils? Pebbles? Shells? Pine cones? Birthday candles? Any of these things would do, but candles would be best. If you have plasticine, or some sort of clay or something spongy, or earth in little pots, take seventy candles and put them two by two in the clay, or in something which holds them separately. Group them on a table some distance apart from each other. Thirty-five twos will take up quite a bit of space, so perhaps you could spread them over several tables in the room. If you are using pebbles, shells, or pine cones or something else, put them in twos in the same way. Whatever you are using, group more of these things around each set of two.

What are these things representing? The candles or shells or beans or pebbles are people. The two-and-two groupings are the disciples going out two by two, and the others represent the villages and towns they are going to. Naturally if you want to go to more trouble, you could get some small building blocks and build a few villages—and if you are using candles, be sure you have a lot to represent the people in the villages. That would be quite a sight, because of course the two-by-two groupings would be lighted, and gradually as they "talked" other lights would come on. The main thing is to use *something*, even dried beans, to give some idea of the multiplication involved!

Yes, multiplication. You may think you are not interested in arithmetic, but multiplication is something everyone is interested in. How? Well, you like to see your piggy bank, or your bank account, multiply and increase, don't you? And if you are a farmer, you like to see your crops grow and your harvest increase. If you knit, or crochet, you like to see how your flying fingers, plus wool and needles or hook multiply the garments or blankets as time goes by. And if a man is building houses, or making furniture, he likes to see how his time, skill, wood and tools combine to increase the furniture or houses that "flow forth" from his fingers. It really is amazing at times to see how much can come forth from the efforts of *one* human being in a variety of areas of creativity and work.

Jesus multiplied bread and fish; that was a miracle of creativity accomplished by the Son of God. You can imagine what happened right after that—people came crowding around, hoping for more bread. Remember that Jesus knew what people were thinking, so one day when they crowded around him, John (Chapter 6:26, 27) tells us that Jesus said, "You aren't seeking me because of the miracles, you are coming because you ate the bread and were filled. I want to tell you the important thing is not working for that which perishes (that means something that is soon gone, something that will not last), but for that which endures for ever and ever." Then Jesus went on to tell them that the work of God they must do was to believe on the One God had sent. He told them they must believe on him. They argued that God had sent manna from heaven to feed the Israelites, and asked what sign God would give now, to prove that what Jesus said was true. Wasn't that amazing, when they had just had the "sign" of the bread and fish being multiplied? It was as if they were coming around from another side, trying to get more bread and fish.

Then Jesus told them that God his Father had sent them the true bread, which if they would eat, they would never perish, never die. In other words, they would have eternal life. And he went on to say, "I am the bread of life: he that cometh to me shall never hunger; and he that believeth on me shall never thirst." That is a wonderful verse, and you should memorize it and never forget it. It can be a comfort and joy to *you* many times, as well as a help to other people.

People are hungry spiritually. People are depressed because they have no hope. People are desperate because they have no meaning in life, and find no reason to go on. People feel empty and have no Person to go to; they think there is no one in all the universe who could fulfil their needs, or who would care about them. People need to know about the Bread of Life and the Water of Life, that Jesus is and that people may have if they believe him. Here in John 6:37, Jesus says that anyone who comes to him he will in no way cast out. So many people need to know about him.

How are they going to find out? Jesus multiplied the bread and fish because the people were tired and hungry, and the sun was going down, and there was nowhere to buy food. Very practical physical reasons. But God does so many things at once. He was also teaching them that he is able to multiply the supply of everything we need, first in this life (so what have we to fear about giving him our little "lunch," or our anything else, in order to follow him?), and then in giving us that which is eternal, the Bread of Life and the Water of Life.

Many of them could have found this out directly from Jesus and his preaching at that time. Many people today could find it from reading the Bible in their own language. But Jesus made it possible for people to find out in another way what they needed to know so badly. He began to teach that human beings should tell other people. It was very simple. People who know are to tell others who don't know. Right then, as we read in Luke 10, Jesus appointed seventy of the disciples who were following him, and sent them out two by two. Now look at your beans, or candles, or pine cones. Two by two, thirty-five couples—even on foot—would cover a lot of territory and inform many people quite quickly in that area of the world. Hitchhikers who roam around all of Europe these days, find out things from others that they meet in youth hostels . . . it is amazing what gets around by word of mouth today, and today the world has as many people living in it right now, as have ever lived from the beginning of the world until just a few years ago.

Sending seventy out by twos was effective in preparing

the way for people to hear about the fact that Jesus had come as Messiah, and that prophecy was being fulfilled in their time. Jesus gave them special power to heal people in his name, and he told them to enter people's houses and tell them the kingdom of God was coming near. They were not to take any money or food with them, for he said that people would take care of them. Jesus didn't call what the people would give "charity." He told the disciples that people would feed them and give them a place to sleep because, "A laborer is worthy of his hire." In other words, a person who works should receive something for working. This journey was to be their work.

It is very interesting that as Jesus sent them out he compared the people to fields of grain. Jesus said to the seventy before they went, "The harvest is plenteous, but the laborers are few; pray ye therefore the Lord of the harvest, that he send forth laborers into his harvest." If you stop to think about what Jesus said, it is really quite fantastic. He said to them, and to us, that one of our responsibilities, as we see the people of the world, is to realize that there is a "harvest" to be gathered which is far more important than harvesting your wheat or corn. This is a harvest of people—people to be "picked" like corn, if you want to picture it like this, for eternal life. But, Jesus said, although the harvest is great, there are few willing to go to do this.

We are responsible to pray that the Lord will send the ones he would have go. Prayer will make a difference, or Jesus would not have said so. We are to pray to the Lord of the harvest. Are we doing it? John 4:35–37 speaks of the harvest too, "Lift up your eyes, and look on the fields, that they are white already unto harvest. He that reapeth receiveth wages, and gathereth fruit unto life eternal; that he that soweth and he that reapeth may rejoice together. For herein is the saying true, One soweth, another reapeth." Yes, sowing the Word of God among people, and reaping the harvest of people who will believe, is the picture given. *We* have some responsibility. Supposing the seventy had said, "No, I can't . . . " There wasn't long in those days for people to be prepared to listen to Jesus while he was on earth, because the whole time of his ministry was only a bit more than three years. And now? Do we have unlimited time now?

A lot of people are afraid that atomic warfare will finish off the people of the world, or that some other calamity like the sun flaming up and getting hotter, will wipe out civilization, but God has told us what is coming. There *is* an end. There *will* be a last baby born some day. There will be the last martyr killed some day. Life—as it is now—will not go on for ever. *Jesus is coming back.* Later in Luke's Gospel Jesus talks about it in detail, but just now, as you look at your seventy candles, or pine cones, or beans, or peas, remember what a short time they had!

Paul says something in Romans 10:11 that fits together with this. Perhaps you could discuss it as you go for a walk together in the fields, or wherever there is a harvest, because it is worth thinking about. "For the scripture saith, Whosoever believeth on him shall not be put to shame. For there is no distinction between Jew and Greek: for the same Lord is Lord of all, and is rich unto all that call upon him: for, Whosoever shall call upon the name of the Lord shall be saved. How then shall they call on him in whom they have not believed? and how shall they believe in him whom they have not heard? and how shall they hear without a preacher? and how shall they preach, except they be sent? even as it is written, how beautiful are the feet of them that bring glad tidings of good things." That is quite clear. We are meant to *be doing* something about people. Are lights coming on in people's understanding in the area where you live? Do people sit and discuss at your supper-table, your lunch-table, your tea-table? Do some come seeking you out for answers? Do they know you are interested? Unless the Lord is sending you somewhere else, he has sent you where you are as farmers, dentists, lawyers, engineers, fishermen, doctors, bankers, clothing store owners, grocery store keepers, directors of businesses, artists, bakers, candle makers, creators of furniture, architects, nurses, telephone girls, deep-sea divers, wig-makers, whatever you do now. If you are where the Lord meant you to be, in school, on the basketball team, playing your guitar or violin, dyeing batik, teaching in school, doing research in a laboratory . . . whatever it is, please do something now.

Take as many candles as there are people in the room reading this together. Light them. Put other unlighted candles around the three, six, eight, or however many there are. Are there more than two? Right where you are, *people* need to be "harvested," given light, fished for, however you want to see it, and you are there!

Pray the Lord of the harvest to send out laborers into the harvest. Yes, do think of other parts of the world, and of the need to give money to send people, so that others might hear . . . but pray also that the Lord of the harvest will send some of the "harvest" into your garden, house, apartment, tent, boat or wherever you live. You are supposed to be one of those with beautiful feet, right where your feet have taken you, as you bring glad tidings of good things *there*!

Multiplication? Yes, Jesus multiplied five loaves and two fish to feed many more than 5,000 people, but the disciples passed the food around. Jesus has said *he* is the bread of life. In a very real sense we are meant to pass the bread around. The multiplication is not our problem. *He* has given us a task. He is able to fulfil his promises: "I am the bread of life: he that cometh to me shall never hunger."

》 When the seventy people came back, they were full of stories of the wonderful things that had happened during their time away, things that had taken place in the name of Jesus. When Jesus replied, he said that the important thing for them to rejoice about was not the miracles they had been able to do in his name, but the fact that their names were written in heaven. What does Jesus mean, about names being written in heaven? There are several places in the Bible where we are told about a Book of life, in which the names of those who are going to have eternal life are written one by one. That is why it is called the book of *life*. Every person whose name is in it has *eternal* life. We believe the names are recorded, just

as names are recorded when a child is born and the government registers the birth—there are papers that are important
to the child's legal status in this life. So then, when a person
accepts Christ as his or her Savior—having believed and
bowed before God and having understood something of his
or her guilt, and having understood something of Jesus taking
the punishment as he died—that person is born again, and
that birth is registered in the "book of life."

Listen to what Paul says in his letter to born-again Christians, at Philippi: "I beseech thee also, true yokefellow, help
these women, for they labored with me in the gospel, with
Clement also, and the rest of my fellow-workers, whose
names are in the book of life." Paul calls all who have worked
hard with him to explain the gospel to others, those "whose
names are in the book of life." To Paul it is just another way
of saying, people who are born again. We'll look at one more
place where this book is mentioned, in Revelation 2:27. There
we are told that no one can come into the heavenly city to
spoil it; the only ones who can enter are those whose names
are written in the Lamb's book of life. Who is the Lamb?
Jesus, the Lamb of God. It is his book of life. He died so that
people could be born again and have their names recorded
there, so it is very logical that it is the Lamb's book of life.
One day the names will be read, and everyone whose name is
there, will be there! This, said Jesus to the seventy, is what
they ought to be rejoicing about, and so should *we*!

Now a lawyer spoke to Jesus, asking him, "What shall I
do to inherit eternal life?" In Matthew 22:34, 35, it would
seem that we find the same lawyer speaking, and Matthew
says he is a Pharisee. Anyway, in Luke we are told he
"tempted" Jesus with this question. In other words, it was
not an honest question coming from a seeking heart; it was a
"catch" question, testing Jesus on the Ten Commandments.
Jesus answered him, "What is written in the law, how readest
thou?" or "What is your understanding of the law?" The
lawyer had studied law, it was his day by day life, so he had a
quick answer for that, and said, "Thou shalt love the Lord thy
God with all thy heart, and with all thy soul and with all thy

strength, and with all thy mind; and thy neighbor as thyself." Jesus answered him, "Thou hast answered right: this do
and thou shalt live." Now what should the Pharisee who was
a lawyer have said to that? He should have asked at that point
what he could do about his sin—because he should have realized that he had not kept and never would be able to keep,
that summary of the commandments. But instead, we are told
by Luke in Chapter 10, verse 29, that he felt he could justify
himself. This man felt in his egoism that he could be good
enough himself and did not need a Savior to justify him. The
question he asked Jesus was, "And who is my neighbor?",
but Luke makes it clear he asked this because he felt he could
do anything required of him. He could even love his neighbor
as himself, if he only knew who he was.

Jesus answers this question by telling a parable. A certain man went down the mountain from Jerusalem to Jericho,
when suddenly a band of thieves attacked him. They stripped
him of all his clothing, beat him up, and left him naked,
wounded and half dead. A certain priest happened to be
walking down that same mountain road and, if you had been
behind a rock, hidden, watching this take place, you would
probably have said to yourself, "Oh good, a Jewish priest will
take care of this poor suffering man." Instead, however, when
he saw the man was naked, bleeding, probably filthy and
looking horrible, the priest passed by on the other side of the
road.

Try to imagine what it would have been like to be the
poor man: so many sharp pains, dizzy and faint, listening,
listening for footsteps. How hopeful he must have been as he
heard footsteps coming closer, and closer, and closer, and
then how disappointed as the sounds became fainter and
fainter and farther away. Have you ever had a bad fall, or
been hurt in some way and waited for someone to come and
help you? Have you ever waited and longed to hear mother's
footsteps coming, when you were sick in bed, and hoped she
would come to wash your face, put on clean sheets, or bring
a cool drink? Perhaps you have a little idea of how this man

felt, except he did not know whether any one would ever stop to help him.

Soon he heard more footsteps approaching. This time we are told it was a Levite, and that he came and looked at the hurt man, and then went away to the other side of the road and continued on his way. This time the hope would have been even more real. Closer, and closer, came footsteps until they stopped right by him. And then imagine the crushed feeling when instead of a voice, or a hand touching him, the only thing that happened was the sound of footsteps going away again. What a hopeless, lost feeling must have been added to the pain! A Levite was also a religious leader among the Jews, and you might think he would have been glad to help this poor man who had been coming from Jerusalem, but like the priest, he had just passed by.

It would seem that the attacked, half-dead, naked man was Jewish, and that Jesus was emphasizing that the priest and Levite had more reason to help him, because the next man who came along on his beast was a Samaritan. The Samaritans were not friends of the Jews. In the Gospel of John, Chapter 4, when Jesus asks for a drink of water from a Samaritan woman drawing up a bucket from a well, her amazement is shown in the question she asks: "How is it that thou, being a Jew, askest drink of me, which am a Samaritan woman? (For Jews have no dealings with Samaritans.)" Jesus told the parable to teach a very strong lesson as to whom we're to love, as neighbors.

So the Samaritan came along, riding a donkey or a horse, clop, clop, clop, clop. He saw the poor, beaten-up man, stopped, got off his animal, and because he had com-passion on him, he not only came over to him, but brought with him some oil and some wine and a piece of cloth, to do something about his bleeding wounds.

What is "compassion?" It is feeling sorry with a real desire to do something to help. This man felt sorry, and right away went through the things he had with him, and brought them over to the man's side. He used up his own oil and wine and clean cloth, for this perfect stranger, and probably a man of a group no one would have expected him to care about. He not only used his own things, but he knelt down and got dirty. His knees probably got all full of little stones and scratchy sticks as well as dirt. He couldn't have put oil and wine on wounds without wiping them a bit . . . and getting his hands bloody and having to touch the broken, torn skin as he tried to help. He also had to look at the unpleasantness of a broken, torn, bleeding, dirty and naked body. He didn't shrink from that because he really was compassionate.

So often we hear people say, "Oh, I can't stand to look at blood, I can't bear to see an injured person." So with a prim feeling of being too sorry to help, they stay away when someone needs them. Or you hear someone say, "I can't visit Mazie in the hospital now I know she has cancer. I can't bear to think of it." Is that compassion for Mazie, when she needs a friend? Or they say, "I wouldn't know what to talk about, so I'm not going to visit Mrs. Q in the Old Folks' Home," or "I feel too badly about that little Timmy's burns so I can't go to his home any more," or, "I have to avoid being with the Z's since the accident . . . I feel too sorry." What people often feel is sorry for themselves, and they shrink away from any kind of unbeautiful situation.

Then there are the other kind of "crossing over to the other side" happenings today, that cause people in American cities and many other places, to leave people half dead and bleeding and torn in the street without coming near them. There are even hospitals that won't admit people when they are hurt. All over the world this story Jesus told is being lived over and over again, without the Samaritan ever coming!

But we haven't finished the story yet. This good Samaritan did all that he could for the man as he lay there, and then carefully picked him up and put him on his animal, a donkey or a horse . . . and now the hurt stranger was being given the ride, while the Samaritan walked along beside him. Jesus says he took him to an inn, a little hotel, and not only did he get a bed for him for the night, but he stayed there with him. I am sure he stayed up much of the night caring for him, until he was sure he was sleeping naturally, and beginning to be better. He gave up his own comfort and sleep for this stranger. He not only gave his *things*, the oil, wine, cloth and his own place on the animal, he also gave him his *time*: all the time it took to do all those things before they got to the inn, and during the night he stayed there.

He used up energy, and emotion—he must have felt angry at the robbers, felt indignant that no one else had stopped to help, and felt sorry for the man, and almost felt the pain with him. And he risked hurting his own back lifting him, and dirtying his own clothing. It would have given the Samaritan a very tiring night. There is a word being used a lot today that applies to what the Good Samaritan did—he got *involved*. What does "involved" mean? It means giving part of your real self to the thing that you are doing, not just staying apart and looking on from the outside.

Right now, remember Jesus was telling this story to the proud lawyer who thought he could earn eternal life by keeping the law. Jesus finished the story by telling how the Samaritan spoke to the inn keeper the next morning and paid him for the man's room for some time longer, saying, "If it costs more than this, never mind, I'll come back another day and pay it. Just spend anything that is needed to care for this man."

When Jesus had finished, he asked the lawyer a question. "Which of the three men was a neighbor to the man that fell among thieves?" A simple question? Don't forget that the hurt man was probably a countryman, belonging to the same country as the first two men who had passed by. What would the lawyer answer? "He that showed mercy on him," answered the lawyer. I wonder if the lawyer knew the verse in Proverbs 14:21 that says, "He that despiseth his neighbor sinneth: But he that hath pity on the poor, happy is he." He should have known that verse from the Old Testament, but so should the priest and the Levite.

Jesus told him something very vividly. If you want to work your way to heaven, you would have to love everybody of every race, country, language group, family, tribe and nation . . . as much as yourself. If you want to show perfection of love to your neighbors, you would have really to love, and show that you love, everyone as much as yourself. No sinful man can do this, and so no one can get to heaven by what he does. When Jesus said to the lawyer, "Go and do likewise," he didn't mean just *once*, to one man. He meant that the lawyer must live this way without stop, with no day off from loving his neighbor. There is something very serious for us to learn in this chapter, whether we are five, twenty, or fifty years old.

Look first at the objects you still have on the table. We started by thinking about the seventy going out two by two, and thought of our responsibility to use our lives, and to use our homes as places where the people around us can find out the truth while they and we are still living. Look, think, and feel some responsibility about making truth known.

» But *now* where are we? What has Jesus been teaching in the parable of the Good Samaritan? He has been teaching that no sinful person can be good enough to get to heaven by virtue of his good works to other people. He has also been showing that he, Jesus, is like the good Samaritan in that he has done everything for us, for each one who believes in him. We can learn these lessons well. But there is a danger that as we learn the lessons from the story of the Good Samaritan we will become proud, and think, "I'm right. I know the truth. I am not like the lawyer who thought he could earn his way to heaven. I know I need to believe in what Jesus did for me!"

We are also in danger of just going on, turning a page, and not realizing that Jesus is speaking also to *us* . . . yes, to us *after* we are born again, after we have become Christians. For there are two big divisions of people in the world.

Take some green split peas, and some yellow ones. Or take two different kinds of beans. Put the green dried peas in one bunch on the table, and put the yellow in another. Let us say the green ones represent the Christians, and let us say the yellow ones represent the ones who do not yet know the truth, or who have turned away. Now take two white cards, or cut out two pieces of white paper which are stiff enough to stand when folded, and whoever can print nicely, print clearly on one: "Neighbors," and on the other: "Brothers and Sisters." Then put the card saying "Brothers and Sisters" by the pile that represents Christians, and put the card saying "Neighbors" on the side you have used to represent the ones who are not born again.

What are we as Christians now to do about our living among *people*? How does the Lord tell us to act? Because we are born again, are we then to say we can break the commandments? Not at all. Quite the other way round. There is meant to be a change in us, so that people see something of the reality, the truth, the fact, that we have the help of the Holy Spirit, and so that we can do things that those who are trying to do things in their own strength, can't do. We can't be perfect, but we are to ask the Lord day by day to do what he has taught us we are to do, as well as to ask him for guidance.

Let's look at our two piles of peas or beans. There are "Brothers and Sisters": these are in the family of God with us, and we are to love them in a way that makes people say, "Look how they love one another!" Is that what people say about the way we treat our Christian friends? Well, it is supposed to be obvious. "By this shall all men know that ye are my disciples, if ye have love one to another." (John 13:35) So, we have a special responsibility to show our love to the pile of peas or beans in which *we* are.

But what about the rest? Only one name covers them all: "Neighbors." And Jesus, in the story of the Good Samaritan, is talking to us as well. We are supposed to be "involved." We are supposed to be taking time, money, energy, doing something for our neighbors.

Does that mean we are to run up to a bleeding, naked, half-dead, beaten up man and say, "Here, read this New Testament! Look at this tract, man, it will give you the way to eternal life?" What does he need? He needs his wounds to be cared for, a clean bed, food, hot tea, someone to be really gentle and loving. Later, perhaps, you can talk to him. And if not? You have been loving him as you love yourself. What do you need when you are injured, ill, starving, cold, exhausted, dirty, without clothing? Do you need to sing a hymn? Do you need a sermon? No, you need help in every area where you have that special need. Jesus is giving very practical teaching as to what our way of life as Christians is to be. We are supposed to be involved in doing something about our neighbor's physical needs. That doesn't mean we stop caring about going out two by two, about discussing with people in our tent or house or apartment or boat. It doesn't mean we stop giving money to help others tell, but it does mean that we have responsibility for the hurt, sick, starving ones. We do have responsibility for poor widows, orphans, people in slums. The *world* is our neighbor.

But I am finite! Yes. Each of us is finite. We cannot do everything. God knows we are finite. He made us that way. But because of our finiteness we cannot pull away and say "that ends it."

We are meant to do our size thing. Five-year-olds can share and care for someone. A ten-year-old can decide to give away something to some other ten-year-old, in their village, school, or city slum near them. Fifteen-year-olds can find someone who has *real need* and give time, something of their *own* to someone else. Twenty-five-year-olds can do something *personal* for some person who is in the "neighbor" group. When we are told *all* men are our neighbors, it doesn't mean we are to do nothing about it because there are too many. We are to do something.

We may get overwhelmed, as *we* did when we visited Bombay and felt hopeless about helping so many people in need; we may feel *too small*, too finite, too inadequate. But look at those piles of peas. If every Christian would look at his bank account, his food, his clothing, his house, his time, his strength, his skills and say, "Lord, what do you want me to do for my neighbors? I want to do something very *real* . . . not only a check to missions, or a church, but something involving *me*." Well, the beans, peas, whatever you have

THE MAN WHO REALLY CARED

chosen, aren't in two piles like that . . . *throw them together!*
Yes, there are far more of the neighors, than there are of the
ones in God's family, but as the mix is scattered (not just on a
plate on the table, scattered around the world) *something*
should be happening to show people the difference.

But what are Christians, the ones on their way to heaven
and eternal mansions, the ones who are alive, doing for the
"neighbors" who are in darkness of a kind of death right
now? *Are* we treating them as ourselves? Too often it is the
Samaritan, the one who has not the background, the base,
the preparation for it, who shows the compassion.

14
DARK LIGHT AND LIGHT LIGHT

Some people think that prayer is just meditation. That means sitting and thinking with a kind of concentration that shuts out other things in order to see what comes into your heads. Others say it is a telephone conversation with another human being. Some believe it is like taking an aspirin pill—it helps you with some kind of a headache in life, taking your mind off your problems for a while. Yet others think it is just psychological help . . . that means it helps you feel better, just as listening to music or arranging some flowers might, but that there is no one there to hear you. These people really don't believe that the living God, the Triune God, the Creator God of the universe, exists. Yet they talk about "prayer." You hear the word "prayer" and it means *so* many different things to different people, that it is confusing. That is the way lots of words are today. People take words, and they use them to mean something completely opposite, so that you have to define the words, or you may be saying one thing, and they will be thinking another.

The word "God," for instance. In India there are thousands of gods being worshiped in the Hindu religion, but those thousands of gods have no connection at all with the one true God in three Persons that we mean when we say "God." People worship the sun, or the moon. Some say the word "god" and they mean some big electric force. Just *saying* the word "God," is not enough for us to understand what people are talking about. When you realize how many different things people mean by the word "god," and how many different things "prayer" means to people, you have to be sure you are *communicating* when you talk about praying to God. Some people write a sentence in a language they

don't understand, and they call that a "prayer"; then they
take that piece of paper and put it on a prayer wheel, that
turns around and around, so many times a minute. They think
some god will give them what they want if the piece of paper
with this prayer in a strange language goes around many
times. We were recently in a Buddhist temple in Singapore
and were shown the many different idols by an old man. One
idol was shown as stepping on people. The old man said, "If
you pray to that idol, he will help you to get rid of your
enemies." What did he mean by "pray?" He meant if you buy
some sticks of incense and light them and put them in a bowl
in front of the idol, that perfumed smoke will be "praying" to
the idol, and you will have some kind of a victory over your
enemies. That has *no* connection with what the Bible means
by the word "prayer."

One day Jesus was praying in a certain place, and when
he finished praying, and looked at his disciples, one of them
said to him, "Lord, teach us to pray." So Jesus began to teach
them. His teaching took time. It was not given all at once, but
in this chapter of Luke he gave important, basic teaching to
the disciples who wanted to know *then,* and to us as we ask
now. We never finish learning more about prayer and, as with
so many things, we learn by doing it. If you are learning to
swim, or ski, or play the piano, or skate, or row a boat—it is
important to listen when someone teaches you, but the
growth of your understanding and your *ease* in swimming, or
skiing, or playing the piano, or skating, or rowing a boat,
comes as you do it. The same is true of painting, or singing,
or planting a garden, and with most other things. Too many
people are always wanting to study about prayer, without
taking much time to pray.

Matthew, in chapter 6 verses 5–7, first tells us some of
the things Jesus said we were not to do. Don't be like the
hypocrites who love to pray standing out in a street, or in a
synagogue, so that men will see them praying. They were
praying to show off, in pride, and they already have their
reward. Our prayer is to be something between God and
ourselves. We are having a real conversation, and we are

doing it to be with the One we are talking to, not to perform a religious rite to be seen by other people, or to show off in front of them.

But this does not mean that we are never to pray where we can be seen praying. Sometimes it is the very opposite. It is being ashamed of being a Christian not to thank the Lord for our food when we are in a restaurant. It is being ashamed if we refuse to pray when others make fun of us when we pray at night. Sometimes it is good to pray with other believers, for each one to pray, and to join in with each other. Sometimes it is good to pray with just one other person, so that the two can agree to pray together for something. It is helpful to have someone pray in a meeting, or service, as we can worship together in this way. So remember that what Jesus is saying is not that we should *never* pray in front of anyone else, but that we should not pray with wrong, false spiritual pride. We should not pray feeling that the praying *in itself* makes us better than others. This is the prayer of the hypocrite Jesus is talking about.

To make a contrast with the hypocrite, Jesus said that the way to pray is to go into your closet (a little place shut away from other people), close the door and pray in secret to your Father. He said that as you pray in secret, your Father will reward you. That means that as you are really asking your heavenly Father for things, he will answer, . . . because the prayer has been not false, but real.

Then Jesus warned against another thing. Don't use "vain repetitions as the heathen do," when you pray. He was speaking of the very kind of things we just talked about, those papers going around on the prayer wheel, for instance. People say the same words over and over again, thinking that if they say the words twenty-five times, God will be more pleased than if they say them ten times. Jesus said that the heathen pray to false gods and idols this way, but that this is not the way to pray to the true, living God. You are not earning something by praying. Prayer is not like doing a hard thing, like saying words very quickly, or walking on spikes, or on hot coals, or kneeling on dried peas in order to make some angry god do something for you, or to work some sort of magic. Jesus made it plain there are lots of mixed up ideas about what prayer is, and he did not want people to think they could "try out" one kind of thing, and then "try out" something else. So many people think they can mix up a lot of religious-sounding ideas and come out with some sort of magic, like rubbing a genie's lamp. All these things must be put away—and you must never "try out" any kind of "formula" to get what you want by saying certain things so many times. All this is connected with false gods.

With all that warning, we can go on to see what we *are* taught to do. Jesus gave an example of what our prayer should be. It is a short example, but there are a number of things we can understand from it. We know that when Jesus prayed all night, and for long hours, he did not just repeat these words. He had just told the disciples they were *not* to keep repeating the same words. So remember, what he gave is an example, or a pattern.

"Our Father, which art in heaven." First of all, we are to talk to our heavenly Father, God the Father, whose children we are because we have been born into his family by accepting Christ as our Savior. Jesus is his unique Son, but we are his children too, so we come to Someone who is a Person, and who is our Father and who loves us and will treat us as children, who will listen to us tenderly. But some people have never had a happy home, and have never known a good father, so these people would think of harsh and ugly things connected with the word "father," perhaps. It is important to realize that this is our heavenly Father, perfect in his love, who said he so loved the world that he gave his only begotten Son that whosoever believeth on him should have everlasting life. He is the One who is preparing to arrange things so that when we get into his presence there will be "fullness of joy," joy so full that there won't be room for more! He is also the God of the Universe, who made all things, and he is able to do anything, so we are coming to someone not only more loving but also more powerful than any human father.

187

But to begin to pray by calling God "Our Father," a person needs to be his child by accepting Christ. Otherwise a person ought to say, "O God, please help me to find you . . . or to know if you exist." If we come by saying, "Our Father," it ought to be true. How many, many people say these words without ever once thinking that it is wrong to say something that is not true? Many people think they are doing something religious—for which they should get some sort of a reward—by just repeating, "Our Father which art in heaven . . . " We are his family, coming to him.

"Hallowed be thy name." In this pattern we are shown the need to worship God for his holiness. We shall also worship him for his majesty, his greatness, his wonderful Person and his wonderful power. Part of our prayer time should be spent in worshiping and thinking of the greatness of God and the great things God has done and telling him our appreciation, admiration, adoration. He is a holy God.

"Thy Kingdom come." Here we are to pray for the second coming of Jesus. In other places, too, we are told to pray for his second coming. Almost any child wants to find out what it will be like to be grown up, to be doing some special thing, to have their own home and their own children. This is natural. Everyone wants to know what every age in life will be like. But some day Jesus will come back again, and then some ten-year-olds will find out what it is like to be changed in a twinkling of an eye when they are only ten years old! Only one generation of children will ever have that experience for all eternity! That will be a discovery bigger than any other kind of discovery!

"Thy will be done, as in heaven, so in earth," is teaching us to pray for God's will to be done, not just in the earth as a whole, but particularly in our own lives. When we are praying as we ought, we should spend part of our prayer time asking the Lord to show us his will, his plan. God never hands us a blueprint, or a map with all his plans for us spread out for a long period ahead. It is a matter of asking every day, and many times a day, for the Lord to guide us and show us the next step. It isn't just the student getting ready to go to college who needs to ask the Lord for his plan to be shown, for guidance as to what university, and what area of studies. It isn't just the girl who is being asked by someone to marry him, who needs to pray that the Lord will help her in her decision. It isn't just the couple who need to pray where the Lord would have them live, or what position or career they should be involved in. It is not in just the major decisions in life that we need to ask God to unfold his plan for us, but hour by hour, day by day.

The five-year-old can pray for help in his or her day with some real understanding that the Heavenly Father cares. The ten-year-old can pray about his or her schoolwork, or what children to play with. A fifteen-year-old needs guidance in when to say "no" to things that seem to be trivial but can make a whole difference in the future, like trying out drugs or doing what "everybody is doing," or to find out the Lord's will in doing something very original. A businessman needs to pray for the Lord's will in decisions he makes day by day, just as a mother needs to ask the Lord's will in the use of her time, her ideas and creativity to make the home something that will be exactly what each other person of the family needs at that time. Just as needs change in a home because no two years running do you all remain the same age with the same needs, so do our personal needs for knowing the Lord's will change. How tremendous to be able to call on the help of the living God who has lived for ever and who knows the future . . . to call on him as Father, asking him to show you his will for each day!

"Give us this day our daily bread." Does that mean anything to you? Jesus said that we may ask for our *material* needs. We need food day by day. We are told we may ask for it. It is not wrong to ask for things in the material, physical realm. It is not wrong to ask for bread, milk, food of all sorts. It is not wrong for a child to pray for a toy, nor for a man to pray for a house. It is not wrong to ask for various needs at various times of life, because God is our Father. He is interested in our needs, and has opened the way for us to talk with him, as a proof that there has been a victory over the separation Satan brought about when he persuaded Eve and Adam and all men and women since to sin.

We learn through experience as we pray that God does answer, and that we are in touch with him, but that there is a battle going on, and Satan is trying to spoil our relationship with God. Sometimes prayer is a battle! Of course, God wants to give us food, but when we ask him for food, there is a much bigger, deeper reason for his answering us. Let us say, for instance, that you are a child but you have been taken to another country, or you are older in a far off place where an enemy is making life hard for you, as is true in parts of the world, such as China, Russia and parts of Africa right now. Somehow you get in touch with your family afar off and ask for some clothing, some food, some medicine. A package comes. Two important things have happened to make you happy. First, you know your message got through, and then you have an answer proving there is love and care for you. That is the first big thing. Secondly, you have some of the things you so badly needed. The "things" won't last long, but the comfort that you are "in touch" means you can get in touch again, and means that the loved person is *there*. Of *course*, with the Lord it is even more "certain," because not only do answers to prayers give us comfort we need, but we know he is preparing a perfect future for us, and we will be out of the enemy's reach altogether some day.

"Forgive us our sins, as we also forgive everyone that is indebted to us." God forgives us all our sins because Jesus died for us. There never has been and never will be anyone who will earn eternal life by forgiving other people, or being good. But after we become God's children, he wants us to come to him every time we have sinned and tell him we are sorry for what we have done wrong. And he wants us to remember what he is doing for *us*, and to forgive other people for what they are doing against us, *even* when they cheat us or are unfair to us.

Let's take the case of a little girl. Suppose a little girl broke her mother's beautiful crystal dish, and her mother said, "I forgive you, dear, but please try to be more careful another time." Later that day, the little girl's younger brother or sister broke one of her doll's tea set dishes that she had just been given for her birthday, and she said, "You'll have to pay for that. You buy me another one! Give me the money right now! Oh, I don't want to play with you any more!" And she screamed and cried, stamping her feet.

Now who did the greatest damage? It was the little girl, wasn't it, when she broke the expensive crystal bowl? Her mother forgave her for the big thing, and yet she did not forgive her brother or sister for the little thing. When things happen in business, in the home, in the university, among our friends, in our school, in play, in sports . . . we are to remember that we have been forgiven by God, because Jesus took our punishment for us, and that therefore we are to be forgiving and kind to others. Not an easy way to live! But this is what the Bible tells us makes a difference in the closeness of our relationship with God day by day. It is very practical and *real*.

"And lead us not into temptation; but deliver us from evil." If mother tells you not to eat a sweet (or candy in America) before supper, and you find a whole big dish of sweets on the dining-room table where you are sitting to do your school work, you are tempted to disobey! A temptation is something that makes it easy for you to do a wrong thing. Jesus told us, in this example of how to pray, that we are to *ask* that temptation does not come to us. It would be like asking mother to put the sweets on a high shelf, so that they would be out of sight. Then we would not be tempted to disobey.

We should ask the Lord day by day to keep temptation from us. So often we go to a party, or out with people, or we arrange to meet someone, when we know it is going straight into temptation. It is often too late to ask "Help me" when we have walked into the temptation, *wanting* to be tempted. God tells us to ask all the time, day by day, and all through the day, "Lead me not into temptation." And then we are deliberately to walk in the other direction, or to ask for the sweets to be put up out of the way, or to say "no" to the invitation. But sometimes temptation is thrown at us, put before us deliberately by some other person, or Satan sends a very clever temptation to deceive us. It seems that this is what the Lord meant by the next phrase, "Deliver us from evil." We are to ask God to give us his strength in our moment of weakness to say "no" to the thing that is right there in front of us. It is good to learn from a very young age that we must not think we can keep from doing wrong things because we have a strong character or a naturally strong will, but must realize we need to ask the Lord to help us. He tells us in the New Testament that his strength is made perfect in weakness. That means that when we recognize our weakness, or realize we are weak, and ask for his strength, he gives it to us.

Isn't it amazing to think of these disciples sitting there listening to Jesus giving them this example to teach them something about prayer, and now 2000 years later to know it as "The Lord's Prayer"! And that the central teaching has been kept all through these years for us to learn from.

》 When we talk to someone, what do we want? An answer. When we ask for something or when we make a request, what do we want? An answer! Prayer is asking, requesting, talking, calling, speaking, making desires known, giving our reasons, seeking a plan . . . all these things and many more, as well as worshiping and adoring God. An answer is important. Jesus goes on to tell us two stories about how God answers. The first is in Luke 11:5-10.

Supposing one of you were to go to a friend's house at midnight, and everything was all locked up and the lights out. Obviously everyone was asleep, but you felt you really *had* to ask for something important. So bang, bang, bang, knock, knock, knock . . . you made so much noise in the quiet darkness of the night, that there was a danger of waking the neighbors, let alone your friend! Suddenly you saw a light go on in his room, and his voice came out of the window saying, "What do you want?" Well, you answered, "Sorry to bother you, but a friend of mine has just arrived. He has come from so far away, and has been traveling so long, that he really is hungry, and I don't have a thing to give to him. Friend, please lend me three loaves of bread!" Your friend in the window said, "Don't bother me now. The house is all locked up, my children are asleep in this room too, and I don't want to rattle around now; I might wake the whole family."

The house Jesus was referring to would probably have been very small, and you know how it is when children get wakened; the family risks having no more sleep that night! Jesus went on to say that perhaps the man would not give him bread because he was his friend or because he felt touched by him, but that if his friend kept rattling around and asking, he would give him the bread to get it over with. The word Jesus uses is "importunity." It is a long word, but it means keeping on, or continuing to ask.

It is in connection with this story that Jesus then said in Luke 11:9–10, "Ask, and it shall be given you; seek, and ye shall find; knock and it shall be opened unto you. For every one that asketh receiveth; and he that seeketh findeth; and to him that knocketh it shall be opened!" You really should memorize these verses. God will answer prayer. Jesus used the illustration of the man asking his friend for bread at midnight to illustrate the fact that if you ask, as the man did, God will answer you *more* quickly, and will not mind if you keep on asking. Then Jesus said, "Knock"—as the man in story knocked—"on the door into God's presence, and he will open the door to you." He won't send you away without responding, without paying attention. Then Jesus said, "Seek"—the friend was seeking bread, not for himself, but for another friend. We are to seek for ourselves not only things we need for this life, like bread, but also things that other people may not see we need, like comfort when we are sad, strength when we are weak, ideas when we don't know what to do. We are to *seek* for ourselves, but also for other people. God will answer, as the man did, by giving something to us that we can share with others. Bread? Well, the picture of the man with the loaf of bread should remind us to ask for bread to give to others, money to give others, things to make it possible to help other people, like a house to invite people to come into, enough food to share, enough land to share. Jesus is teaching that we are to really seek for things from God with which to help other people. God *will* answer.

The second story Jesus told is one you could illustrate on your table if you have the things. Take two dinner plates. On one put a fried egg, or an omelet, or just a hard-boiled egg. Also put a fried fish, or a fish cake, or a fish finger, or even a fresh fish, or a picture of a fish! Next to that put a piece of bread, or toast. Make it look pleasant, something nice enough to eat. On one dinner plate you now have a meal. On the second dinner plate put a toy snake, or a snake made out of green plasticine or clay, or a real dead garden snake! Next to that put a *stone*: and some kind of an ugly bug—either a dead spider or a cockroach, or a picture of one. Put both plates on the table, each of them with a knife and fork, or a spoon, or chopsticks, so that both plates look as if they were there for a meal. Put a glass of water, or a cup of tea beside each plate and maybe some flowers in the center, as if the table were set for two.

Now listen to what Jesus said in Luke 11:11–12; "And of which of you that is a father shall his son ask a loaf, and he give him a stone? Or a fish and he for a fish give him a serpent? Or if he shall ask an egg, will he give him a scorpion?" Now look at the two dinner plates. Would a good earthly father give his son a meal of a stone, a serpent, and a scorpion? If you were given a plate like that when you were really hungry, would you think it was the loving provision of a real father? Now there are some pretty bad fathers in this sinful world of people, and some pretty bad mothers, too, but a dinner plate like that isn't often set before a hungry child who has asked for egg, fish and bread. Jesus said that he thought a father would give the child the food he had asked for. Look at the other plate; that is the one all the disciples sitting there imagined they would give to a hungry child. I am sure that they thought, "Of *course* a father would give the real food to his child."

The importunate friend. Luke 11:5–10

Then Jesus went on to say in Luke 11:13, "If ye then, being evil, know how to give good gifts unto your children, how much more shall your heavenly Father give the Holy Spirit to them that ask him?" In Matthew 7:7–11, Matthew reports that Jesus said, "How much more shall your Father which is in heaven give good things to them that ask him?" Jesus is teaching that if we ask for the Holy Spirit's help, the Heavenly Father is not going to give us the opposite thing, and if we ask for other kinds of good things, God is not going to give us bad things. Jesus is saying that our Father in heaven is far too loving and gentle and kind to do that. He will answer us.

Will the answer be a package of everything we have asked for, like we get when we send a list to a department store? No. He answers, knowing a lot of things we do not know. He sees this moment in our lives as a part of the past and the future, and he knows what it would be dangerous for us to have, and what would be a help. If an earthly father knows his child has diabetes, he will not give that child cake or sweets or anything else that will be dangerous for him. But lots of things earthly fathers do not know, hinder them making the right decision about any request. God is perfect in his knowledge, and in his wisdom, and in his plan for us and the way we fit into his plan. It is more complicated than handing a list to a store! You see, God is a Person, and he answers on the basis of what real love and knowledge of us and of history have to do with the answer, and he answers knowing what lies beneath our request. He knows better than we do what we are *really* asking for. When we look back over life, we sometimes shiver or shudder as to what would have happened if certain prayers of ours had been answered exactly as we asked them. We realize we were asking for something that would have hurt us, hurt others, and hurt the glory of the Lord.

But, with all that being said, the fact remains that God *does* answer prayer, and he does tell us to *ask*, and if you begin to live this way, you will have answers to encourage you, and to look back on and remember when you come to another different place.

This chapter would be much too long if we stopped to give you some answers to prayer we have had in just the last weeks, let alone months and years. You could understand some of the answers we are talking about if you read the book *L'Abri*. And, since that book was written, there have been many, many more!

》 To finish this chapter in Luke, there are two other things Jesus spoke about that must be included, even though it would take too long to study every verse.

One is something we can illustrate with two cups. Take two cups which look alike, and make sure the outsides are clean. One must be also clean inside, and the other should have a lot of tea or coffee stains, or mud, smeared in it. Now as Jesus spoke to the Pharisees, he told them they cared only about cleaning the outside of the cup. He said they did things which they thought were keeping the law religiously, but really they were only sticking to a few easy rules. Underneath, they had hearts that were wicked, greedy, selfish, not loving or compassionate at all, so that inside they looked like the dirty cup. Tip the cups so you can see the clean outsides, then tip them the other way, so that you see the insides. Jesus said that this was the way God looked at men, and that when he saw the Pharisees, he saw men filthy and *not caring about filth*, not worried about their sin.

How many people are like that today! People who are religious. People who want to have everything "just so" as far as certain of men's rules are concerned, who keep the outside of the cup clean. But inside they are filled with envy, pride in their own goodness, gossip about other people, hateful thoughts, desire to have the top places, discontent, lack of faith, no real desire to worship, no expectation that prayer will be answered, no compassion for the hungry, lost people of the world. Inside they are dirty, and the problem is that they couldn't care less!

Perhaps it would help us to understand if we pictured it in this way. Think of two churches, each filled with 200 people. In one church, all the 200 are primly dressed in clothing that fits the rules of proper dress for church—shoes and stockings, dresses of the right length, suits and ties—and all looking very much as if they wanted to keep the rules perfectly . . . on the outside. But let us suppose that *inside*, many of the 200 people in this church are empty of love and compassion, do not put God first, are worrying about their jobs, are filled with thoughts about getting more money, are envious and greedy, and are thinking critical thoughts about other people, particularly criticizing the sermon and *not* worshiping at all really. They are just sitting in their fine clothes looking right on the outside.

In the other church are 200 people looking very strange in their mixture of clothing. Some have bare feet, blue jeans, long hair; some of the girls have slacks on; some are in short dresses, and others in long dresses with shawls; some of the men are in suits and ties and others with turtle neck jerseys. Some of them have not even had a bath for a long time. But *inside* they are seriously seeking to know God personally. Some are wanting to find him, if he exists; others love him and trust him and have brought friends to hear the truth. Others are praying for some who have just wandered in, and are planning to invite them to lunch. Some are weeping over their own sins. Many are *really* worshiping.

Now do you begin to understand? Jesus is saying to the Pharisees *and* to us, that he looks *inside* to see what we *really* are. He is not concerned about how well we keep the little rules that aren't in the Bible.

That is why this teaching belongs with our thinking about prayer. We are to care about the inside of the cup that is "me." As we pray we are to say, and mean, "Lord, help me to let you wash away the dirt inside. Help me to have the inside even cleaner than the outside." Jesus said to the Pharisees in Luke 11:39–44 that they loved to be greeted in the synagogue as men of importance, as religious leaders. He said, "Woe to you, if you are walking around as cups that are dirty inside, and everyone is looking at the outside and praising you for that. You are like *graves* walking around, and people think you are alive and don't notice that you are *dead*." What a warning! Let us thank God that our insides can be washed clean by Jesus and his death for us, and ask him to help us to care about being cleansed where people *don't see it*!

The other thing in this chapter that we must connect with the rest is in Luke 11:33–36. Here we are back to light again. Do you have two candles? Two oil lamps would be even better, or two candles with glass chimneys around them. First, Jesus spoke of the fact that we are the light of the world. Yes, we are meant to be giving light (the true truth) to those who are in darkness, so we are not to hide our light. Do you remember the time when we put the candle on a candlestick, and not under a thing that hid it? Jesus said we are not to hide our light with evil works either, because if we are doing sinful things, people can't pay much attention to what we are saying about truth: the light is being hidden by the dirt of our wrong doings. So in a way this is saying that the actions which are seen by people are going to make a difference to the light we give out. This is very important.

Light your two candles or lamps now. One candle, or lamp, should have a very sparkling clean glass lamp chimney around it, or it should have a piece of glass held in front of it that is clean. The other candle or lamp should have a very dirty lamp chimney, or a very dirty piece of glass held in front of it. If all you have are electric lamps, use a very weak bulb in one, hidden by a dark shade, and a bright bulb in the other with a white shade.

One light is light now—and the other light is dark. Do look well at the light that is light, and the light that is dark. Draw pictures of lamps that are sparkly light, and lamps that are dingy and dark. Get this fixed in your mind, and "see it" in your memory, or imagination . . . dark light, light light.

Jesus said, "Watch out that the light which is in you is not darkness." In Matthew 6:23 it is even clearer . . . "If therefore the light that is in thee be darkness, how great is that darkness!" Remember what we talked about at the beginning of this chapter? That some people talk about prayer, and God, and they don't mean the true God at all, and they aren't talking about true prayer, true talking to the true God at all? Think carefully now. If people *think* they have the truth, something true when they talk about hundreds of thousands of gods and prayer being incense sticks or prayer being pieces of paper going around on wheels; if people *think* they are giving truth to others when they teach that Jesus is just a man; or that God did not create man in the first place; or that the Bible is not true when it speaks about the universe and about history; or when they teach that you get to heaven by being good, and you don't need to have a Messiah or a Savior; if people then *think* they have a light and walk by that light and try to get other people to walk along with them in that light, and if all the time the light is *darkness*—Jesus said that that darkness is very terrible indeed, it is a great darkness. How dangerous it is to think you have a light, and then walk by a precipice, with a gorge thousands of feet below, or a slippery cliff with the sea pounding below . . . when your light is darkness.

"It doesn't matter," some people say. "It doesn't matter what you believe, just as long as you believe something. If it makes you feel good inside, it doesn't matter what religions, philosophy, rules, you live by."

Does it matter if there is such a thing as truth? Yes, says Jesus, it matters, because there is truth and there is that which is the opposite, not true. There is true light, and there is darkness acting as light. Be sure, Jesus says, that your light is the real light.

15
STOP WORRYING!

Have you ever made a loaf of bread? There are lots of recipes, and lots of kinds of bread, but yeast is the thing that makes bread rise. It would be a good idea to make a couple of loaves of bread, and watch them rise while you are reading this chapter together. Then you can bake it and eat it together later. Perhaps while you are eating it, you can discuss the various things we will be studying in this next part of Luke.

Here is an easy recipe for oatmeal bread which does not need to be kneaded and which rises quite quickly.

(1) Stir $1^1/_2$ cups ($^3/_4$ pint) of boiling water, into a large bowl with
   1 cup (4 ozs) raw oatmeal
   $^1/_3$ cup ($2^3/_4$ ozs) of margarine
   $^1/_2$ cup (8 ozs) of treacle, molasses, or honey
   1 tablespoon (approximately 1 oz) salt.
(2) Cool until it is lukewarm.
(3) Combine 2 packages of dried yeast (each package approximately 1 oz each) or 2 squares of moist (live) yeast (or if you have a large block of moist (live) yeast slice an inch cube, or measure by pressing it into tablespoons . . . measure 2 tablespoons of moist (live) yeast with $^1/_2$ cup ($^1/_4$ pint) of lukewarm water and stir until the yeast dissolves.
(4) Add this yeast and water to the warm oatmeal mixture you have made and mix well.
(5) Beat 2 eggs lightly, and add them to the mixture. Then stir in $5^1/_2$ cups (1 lb. 6 ozs) of flour, cover and let the mixture stand for 15 minutes.
(6) Grease 2 bread loaf pans, about 9 by 5 by 3 inches in size, separate your bread mixture into two

amounts and put into the two pans. Pat down until
it is even in the pans.
(7) Let it rise for about 1½ hours, or until the bread is
about double the size it was at the beginning.
(8) Bake in a moderate oven, about 350°F., for one
hour.

Use this, or another bread recipe, to prepare the pans of
bread, or bowl of dough so that as you read the book it is in
a nice warm spot in the room where you are reading. The
whole idea is to watch it rise, as you look at it from time to
time. You see, some people never make bread, and when you
talk about "leaven" or yeast, they don't know what you are
talking about. The leaven, or yeast, is very small compared
with all the other things you put in bread dough, but that
small lump of leaven, or yeast, is what makes the bread rise
up to double the size it was before, and it goes all through
the bread until there isn't any part of it that is not affected. Be
sure each person has seen the small lump of leaven or yeast.
Cut another piece or put the same amount of dry yeast on a
plate to show how small it is by comparison. You will see as
you watch the bread rise, that it rises all over. The big
"lump" of bread had only a little lump of leaven in it, but it
has spread all through the bread, and it has had an effect
on all of it.
   At the beginning of Luke chapter 12, we find Jesus
talking to a crowd of people. In fact there are so many people
pushing together to hear him, that Luke says they were "in-
numerable," which means that he couldn't count them. They
were stepping on each other because they were so crowded.
Jesus began to speak by saying, "Beware of the leaven of the
Pharisees, which is hypocrisy." What could he mean? Well, as
we look at the bread, we realize that leaven is something that
will filter through to every part of the loaf, and affect it all.
Hypocrisy, pretending to be something you are not, saying
one thing and living another, trying to hide bad things underneath good things, Jesus said, will go all through a group
of people, and all through any one person, if it is allowed to

get a good start. Jesus went on to say more about this: there is nothing in our lives that is hidden that will not be known. Whatever we have done in the dark, will be known in the light. Things that have been whispered in the ear in a tiny closet, will be shouted from rooftops.

That would be frightening, if it were the end of Jesus' message. What Jesus is saying is very powerful. It is making sin into something that everyone recognizes they have in their lives, even if it is hidden where they think no one knows about it. There is real danger, said Jesus, of being like the Pharisees, who carried out all kinds of rules for being religious, who felt very good and were proud of their goodness and of being better than other people, yet who had so many things they were doing that they would not want to be known. This kind of double life could not continue without becoming known. But who wants the double life, the life of hypocrisy to continue? Satan does. Satan is the great enemy of God, and Satan does not want men to find out the truth, but instead to live a hypocritical religious life.

Jesus said, "Be not afraid of them which kill the body, and after that have no more that they can do. But I will warn you whom ye shall fear: Fear him, which after he hath killed hath the power to cast into hell." It is Satan who *wants* men in hell, and will do everything he can to deceive them, and to make men deceive other men. Jesus had been talking about the awful influence of the Pharisees, and the effect they could have if men were not warned to stay away from that influence. They were to examine their own lives and be sure they were not continuing to live in the same way.

But what is there to do about it? Can anyone get rid of all the things they have done in the dark? Or whispered and wish they could "unwhisper"? Can anyone get rid of the things they have done which they don't want shouted from the housetops?

This is exactly what Jesus came for: to take the punishment so that sin could be forgiven. In the Old Testament, in Isaiah 1:18 we are told, "Come now, let us reason together, saith the Lord: though your sins be as scarlet, they shall be as white as snow; though they be red like crimson, they shall be as wool." Later, in Isaiah 53:5, we read of the coming Messiah who will make it possible to get rid of sin like that, because "he was wounded for our transgressions, he was bruised for our iniquities. . . ." Another Old Testament prophet put it like this in Micah 7:19, "He will turn again and have compassion upon us; he will tread our iniquities under foot: and thou wilt cast all their sins into the depths of the sea." Do you realize how *wonderful* it is? All the sin that is so serious that it cannot be balanced by doing something religious or good, all this sin that has been hidden from men, can be cast into the sea, washed away so that the "inside of the cup" is as white as snow! How? Peter, in 1 Peter 2:24, says very simply about Jesus, "His own self bare our sins in his body upon the tree." Jesus, when he died on the cross, took our sins, and took the punishment for them, so that we can have forgiveness that will get rid of them. We don't need to be afraid. What we need is to come to Jesus and accept what he did.

》 Now in Luke 12, we read that Jesus went on to encourage people as to how gentle and loving and fatherly God is. He wanted people to understand. He told them that sparrows are birds that no one really thinks of as important, but not one of them is forgotten by God. God knows every sparrow, and what is happening to it. Jesus pointed out that *people* are of much more importance than sparrows. In fact, God knows exactly how many hairs are on each person's head. So don't be afraid. It is the ones who turn away from the truth, who deny God, who will not accept the Son of God and turn away from the Holy Spirit, that are the ones who are lost. But, Jesus said that he would tell the angels about every person who was not ashamed of him and told other people that he or she believed in him.

Can you imagine people thinking over these things? How wonderful it would be to have Jesus telling the angels about *them*, how wonderful to be sure they were going to be forgiven! Some of them would have been certain they wanted to belong to the Lord, not to be hypocrites, but to have their sins forgiven and be unafraid to belong to Jesus. Then Jesus gave them both a warning and an encouragement. "The day is coming when you will be taken into the synagogues and made to stand before religious officials and powerful men in government. Don't try to figure out what you will say at that time, or what sort of answers you will give to their accusations. The Holy Spirit will teach you, and give you the right things to say at that very time." For those who believed, it must have been a bit of a shock to realize they were going to get into trouble with important and powerful men because of their beliefs. Yet they had seen how the Pharisees were always trying to trick Jesus, so they would realize that it would be these same men who would try to make it difficult for them, if they continued to follow him.

Can't you feel how *serious* the conversation was, how much some of the crowd would be trying to understand the really important things Jesus was teaching them? Suddenly a voice piped up from the middle of the crowd, "Master—" Every head would turn in that direction to see what deep question this person could have. "Master—" And a silence would fall so that everyone could hear. "Master, speak to my brother and tell him to divide his inheritance with me." Here, while Jesus was saying such serious and even frightening things, this person had been thinking of something else—and those thoughts were all about wanting a share of his brother's money and things for life right now. He hadn't bothered to listen to any of the serious warnings! Can't you just imagine some of the others feeling a bit disgusted? "*What* a time to be thinking about that! Wasn't he *listening*?"

But what about us? Do we listen to all the Bible teaches with only a small part of our brain? Is the rest of our brain taken up with what we are going to *get* next? With where we can get some money and what we can buy with it? It is such an easy thing, at any age, to think so very much about what we want in this life that we get all out of balance. To be standing in front of the Son of God, the Messiah, who was talking about things that made a difference in the *for ever* of the future, and to ask that Messiah to divide up some money for him, so that for a tiny space of a few years he could have more, showed how out of balance that man was. Just think of being able to say, "Master, I have a question . . . " and asking *that* as your only question! But if we are honest, aren't we in danger of doing that as well?

What was Jesus' answer?

First Jesus asked him a question, "Who made me to be the judge of your affairs, the one to divide your things?" There was a legal judge for men's business affairs, and Jesus had not come from heaven to divide money equally. Then Jesus turned to everyone, and since they had all heard the man's request, he spoke to them *all*, saying, "Beware of covetousness." Then he said, "Watch out for covetousness, because a person's life does not consist (or is not made of) the *things* which he possesses." Life is not made up of houses, cars, clothing, money and the like. Life is quite different, and Jesus is speaking to us, as well as to those people, to shake us into realizing what life is all about.

To do this, Jesus told a parable.

There was a certain rich man who had wonderful crops from his land. One year he had a particularly good harvest of whatever he grew. "What shall I do?" the rich man thought. "I don't have room in my barns and storage places for all this fruit and harvest." Then as he thought, with no thought for anyone else but himself, and no thought of asking God what to do, he had this idea: "I will pull down my barns (storage buildings) and build larger, better ones, and in these new great buildings I'll store up all my big crop of fruit and grain and other things." *Then* the man said, "After that I will say to myself, 'Soul, you have enough wealth of things laid up for many years ahead. Don't do a thing now. Retire, take it easy, and just eat, drink and be merry.'" He stood there looking over his success and thinking only of himself and his opportunity for ease and luxury. He pictured himself sitting by a bowl of fruit, drinking, putting his feet up and looking at a

---

"Soul, thou hast much goods laid up for many years: Take thine ease: eat, drink and be merry." Luke 12:16–21

good view, listening to water tinkling from a fountain, or waves on a seashore, as he sat in the sun! He may have started to think of how he would amuse himself, to be "merry" as he ate and drank.

What a completely *selfish* picture, and what a picture of someone not seeing anything that really *exists* in the universe, except his own little circle! Here is a man who did not bother to think about the existence of God, or his being in relationship with God, or the purpose of life. He never thought of any responsibility he might have to use his prosperity for something very special in *his* moment of history, nor of the effect his life would have on other people living at the same time, or in years to come. All he thought of was his own comfort. But that night God said to him, "Thou fool, this night thy soul shall be required of thee: then whose shall those things be, which you have provided?" Yes, the very night he made big plans for *himself*, to enjoy his riches, he died. What God said was, "Then who is going to have all these things?" There is an Old Testament verse in Psalms where David speaks of just such a foolish man: "Lo, this is the man that made not God his strength; but trusted in the abundance of his riches, and strengthened himself in his wickedness."

This man is the example Jesus gave to shake the young man who had just that one question to ask. But it also shakes us. We need to stop and consider how foolish it is to pile up riches and things that have to be left on the earth. God asked the man in the story who was going to use all the things he had spent his lifetime gathering together. He had spent his whole life *preparing for life on the earth,* and had completely put aside the thought that life on the earth could come to a sudden end. Death finishes the possibility of using the things that are in the barn, the house, the car, the boat, the bank. There it sits, and the person who has died cannot use it. Jesus ended this story by saying that anyone who lays up all his treasure on this earth, is just like the foolish man. The only way to be rich for ever is to be rich toward God.

Is there some way of laying up treasure in heaven? Is

there some way of preparing for life there? The Bible teaches in several places about treasures to be put in heaven, but on this particular occasion, Jesus went on to talk about a way to live which will demonstrate that we really believe what he is teaching. How can we show the Lord, angels, other people, the demons, that we consider God's promises practical and dependable, and not just something to sing about, or to say solemnly in church as the sun comes through the windows and we feel worshipful?

Let's really try to think about what Jesus has said.

"Be not anxious for your life, what ye shall eat; nor yet for your body, what ye shall put on." Philippians 4:6 says the same thing in another way: "In nothing be anxious; but in everything by prayer and supplication with thanksgiving let your requests be made known unto God." We are not to worry about what we are going to eat, or about our clothing. We are not to make it the *first* thought, the thing that drives us. We are to recognize that we can pray for the Lord to give us food and clothing, and our *first* concern should be to do what he wants. Dr. Luke tells us that Jesus went on to explain a little more. He said that life is more than just food, and the body is more than just what clothes to put on. He is not saying we don't *need* food, or that we don't *need* clothes, but that we are to realize that there are more important things to think about, and to *do*. He wants us to understand that he is not expecting us to starve and go around in rags, so he teaches us to learn from the birds. Birds don't have houses and barns and they don't plant fields and harvest them, but they have food because God provides food for them. You are better than the birds, Jesus said, and God will take care of your need for food.

» Now, will the shortest person listening to this, stand up. Put a piece of paper or a ruler or stick eighteen inches long on top of your head, or let someone else put it there and hold it. Imagine growing eighteen inches taller by thinking about it! Jesus said that, if you can't even control how tall you are, why use all your time worrying about food, clothing, money for a

209

house, money for the other things you need. *Stop worrying*, Jesus said, and use your energy and thinking to do something more *lasting*. Let God do for you the things he has promised, while you do the things he has told you to do. Jesus went on in more detail about the daily things, so that no one of us could mistake what he is talking about.

Could one of you get some flowers and put them here in front of everyone who is listening. If you are in Hawaii, you may be able just to pick up a lei (a necklace made of hundreds of little flowers on a thread). If you are in Singapore, you can go into the garden and pick an orchid. If you are in Switzerland, you can pick a wild flower from the field, before the cows eat it!! Get a lot of flowers of different colors if you can, but have some sort of a real flower if it is possible.

Look for a minute at the petals, the texture, the color, the amazing blend of shades, the stamen, the leaves, the lovely lines and shapes. Think of the *diversity* of flowers. No two of even one kind of flower are alike, and there are so many hundreds of varieties. Then think of different grasses. Think of the wonder of the mosses with their delicate fronds like miniature ferns, or the long grass that bends in the wind, or grasses with leaves of different colors, shapes and sizes. What differences there are! Now look again at the flowers you have in front of you and listen carefully. Did Jesus say— "Don't worry about clothes; think of grey gunnysacks, potato bags and rags . . . that is all you need on this earth." No. He said, "Think of the lilies, how they grow, they do not spin or weave and yet I tell you that King Solomon, with all the gorgeous clothing he had in his rich days, didn't have clothing to compare with these beautiful lilies." Then after everyone had thought about that for a time, Jesus stated, "If God dressed the grass of the fields so beautifully, which is so wonderful to look at today, and tomorrow is cut down, how much more will he dress you, O ye of little faith."

Jesus asks us to think of the grass of the field. What happens to grass? When the right moment of summer comes, the farmer takes his curved scythe, and swish, swish, the flowers and grass are cut, turned with a big fork, and left to dry, then put in piles and later gathered into the barn for the cattle to eat in the winter. If God makes such beautiful flowers to live a short time, and then be cut and dried and eaten, don't you think he can dress you just as beautifully? Don't you think he cares about dressing his children, the ones who have been born into his family by accepting Jesus as their Savior? We have a Father who is sensitive to beauty. He designed the flowers. He designed the variety of birds, the trees that change in color, or have amazing blossom. He designed the fantastic colored fish of so many shapes. Don't you think he will provide clothing for you?

Jesus said, "O ye of little faith" in the same way that he said, "O ye of little faith" when the disciples became so afraid in the storm on the lake. He wants us to *trust* our Father to take *care* of our needs, when we put our thinking and energy and time into his plan for us and consider his teaching as the most important thing.

Then Jesus said, "Don't seek first the things you are going to eat, and drink, don't have doubts about being able to have these things. You are supposed to be *different* from those who do not believe in God, and to put first the things God is leading you to do in your life, and then all these things shall be added to you!"

What does this mean in practice? Suppose you just have enough meat to last your family for two days, and you aren't sure any money is coming for some time because your pay isn't due. You feel you must be careful to make the food last, and you have ideas of how to "stretch it" for the *family*, but that is all. Then six young people come in to ask questions about Christianity. They might be friends of the teenager in the family, or they might have heard they could get in on some really good discussion at your house. The conversation is going well, and questions are coming thick and fast—and you know it wouldn't be right to stop it then. It is supper time. What do you do? Save the food for the family, or invite them all to stay? Make something to stretch the meat a bit,

211

and pray that the Lord will supply your food for the rest of
the week in some way, because you are doing this for him.
His truth is most important in this situation.

Suppose you are just getting along week by week on
your pay but you hear about a family which is not having
enough to eat, where there is a sick child who needs special
food and medicine. You also know they need blankets. You
are sure the Lord led you to know about this and you can't
put it out of your mind. What do you do? You share some of
your money to buy what they need, and pray that the Lord
will supply what you need to get through the week.

How does he do it? By sending you a lot of money
suddenly? Not necessarily. You may receive a special gift, or a
bonus from the work, or sell something, or receive a gift of a
turkey from someone, or a crate of oranges! Or the ideas may
come as to how to "stretch" your food by making your own
bread, for instance, or making soup out of boiling the bones
after you finish eating the chicken, or economizing in some
other way. But you can't ever understand his promise to
supply if you always put yourself first.

Jesus said that we are to be concerned about whether or
not we are following the plan God has for us as individuals.
We are *not* to waste our time and energy in worrying about
the money, food, clothing, house, etc., when our time is so
precious for the thing he has planned. "All these things,"
Jesus said, "your Father *knows* you need." Then Jesus said
"Fear not, little flock." Isn't being called one of a little flock
wonderful? Can't you see a shepherd taking care of his flock?
We are one of the lambs in a little flock, and Jesus says, "Fear
not! for it is your Father's good pleasure to give you the
kingdom." Don't be afraid, our Heavenly Father is planning all
sorts of marvelous things for us in the time ahead. The same
One who designed the flowers is planning the time ahead.
Don't worry, because he won't forget what we need now,
either.

Jesus went on to say even more. "Sell what you have,
and give alms: provide yourselves bags which don't get old, a
treasure in heaven that faileth not, where no thief comes

near, and where moths can't spoil it." Do we really understand that? He is saying give of things that belong to you,
don't save it all here like that foolish man. It is possible to
have your treasure where it won't get eaten up by termites
and moths. How? Jesus stated that what we *give away, we
have*! It is like saying that, if we lose our life for his sake, we
will find it! If we give to poor people who need it, if we give
to the Lord's work, making it possible for others to hear
about him, if we provide food and clothing for starving, cold
people, this is put into heaven, Jesus says.

God is teaching us the amazing fact that we can use the
same ten dollars, or ten pounds, or ten francs, or whatever
money we use, to do three things at once! If we give it, it
helps the person or the work we give it to, now in this world.
But as we give it because we love the Lord, and are giving it
to *him* in a very real way, then he accepts it, and says it is just
as if we had given it only to him. Then thirdly, we are told it
is saved for us as a treasure in *heaven.* Perhaps we don't
understand the meaning of this completely, but it is something very real. God warns and warns his people that they are
to lay up treasure in heaven and not on the earth, and if every
Christian had really followed this carefully, things would be
different in the world. There would be fewer hungry people.
And—there would be more people hearing the truth, too.
There'd be more candles lighted, more of those "beans" put
two by two earlier, as we read together. Things would be
different on earth and things would have been different in
heaven for those people, for us, for anyone who is a child of
God.

I wonder what the difference *will be*? It will be something. Some of us will say; "But why didn't you tell me?" and
God will only need to point to his word. It *does* tell us.

Jesus ended this part of his teaching with the words:
"Where your treasure is, there will your heart be also." People are very interested in and think about their treasures. If
you have bought investments, lands, houses, you have an
interest in that particular part of the world, wherever it may
be. If you have given money to people for the Lord's work,

213

those people and that work take up part of your interest, your "heart" and then, because it is also a treasure in heaven, your thoughts are concerned more about the things the Lord tells us of heaven, than if everything had been "invested" here on earth. You can't grow spiritually if your thoughts are always on earthly investments. It makes a difference to your spiritual growth when you are laying up treasure in heaven. It makes heaven more like a home you are preparing to move into.

Each one of the family could make their own special "bag," or a place to put aside money that is to be the Lord's tithe or the portion to be given the Lord. A draw-string bag could be made out of cotton, linen, chamois, or leather. A special tin or wooden box could be prepared. Wood or leather can be burned with a special electric needle, cloth can have embroidered words, tin can have words painted on it, something knitted or crocheted can also have words placed with another color of wool. A bank book, which an older member of the family may prefer, for a separate account for the Lord, could have the same special words printed on it.

What words should be on your "bag that waxes not old"? Choose the words that make it mean the most to you—such as "The Lord's money"; "Treasure in Heaven"; "The part to take with me"; "No moth or rust will spoil this"; or just "My bag that will not wax old." This is your secret account you are investing in heaven. The amount in it is between you and the Lord . . . but as you put money *in*, then you must pray as to where it is to be given. It is as you give that it is stored in heaven. The bag will fill up, and then be empty, over and over again . . . but as it empties, the account is filling up! Jesus says so. It is one of his "backwards" rules. Let us each prepare to be acting in a way which shows we believe this to be *true*, and that we expect to be going to Heaven and therefore are "packing" our bags!

Immediately after this teaching, Jesus went on to tell a parable about his second coming. He had come the first time, to be born, to live, to preach and heal people, to raise the dead so that people could recognize who he was, but also to die. If he had not died, then there would have been no way for people to have their sins forgiven. However, he explained that he was coming again. He did this so that people wouldn't be mixed up after he died, and so that everyone living then, and now, would know it is important to live in a state of getting ready. Getting ready for Heaven and our home there, but also getting ready for the moment when Jesus comes back. Be ready, be prepared, be watching, be expecting him.

Jesus told the story of servants whose master had gone away, and who said, "Oh, he's been gone so long, he'll never come back. Let's not bother to take care of the things he told us to do, let's not bother to be ready for his coming; let's just have parties." So they did, and when the master came they were all drunk! Suppose you were going to have a family reunion, a lovely big dinner with everyone in the family coming, your cousins and aunts and uncles and grandmother and grandfather, and you were looking forward to it very much. Then suppose your mother asked you to take a bath, get dressed, and do the things she wanted you to do, because you were going to go as soon as Dad could come home. But instead of taking a bath or putting on nice clothes, you got into the treacle, dark molasses, got it all over your face, hands, clothes . . . and then thought of rolling in the sand, mud or coal dust to see what it would feel like, and to fool people into thinking you were a clown. Then suddenly—your father came in the car to take you to the beautiful dinner where there were flowers, candles, gifts at each place and a wonderful time of meeting the people you love, people you had been waiting a long time to see. But you were not ready!

In Luke 12:40 Jesus said, "Be ye therefore ready also; for the Son of man cometh at an hour when ye think not." Some day he is coming. In a twinkling of an eye we will be changed and be with him, meeting everybody we have wanted to meet, going to a time of eating together and having rewards, gifts. How are we to get ready? *Not* by sitting around dressed up in our best clothes, but by doing what Jesus has been telling us to do, by putting first the things of the Lord, and by studying and *doing* what the Bible teaches.

215

16
RIGHT AND WRONG, ALWAYS AND EVERYWHERE

If people think they are just a collection of molecules that came together, or that they are simply particles of energy that formed themselves in these patterns by chance, it isn't surprising that many of them have no compassion for other people. At least, it seems strange that a machine-like collection of molecules would behave much differently from a computer with other computers. Computers are very efficient at solving arithmetic problems if the cards are fed into them properly, but you can't imagine them feeling sad, or loving other computers. Of course, people who think they are just a collection of molecules don't really always act in this way, because they keep saying, "That's wrong, you shouldn't do that." Or they say, "That war shouldn't be going on, it isn't good." Or they say, "That man was bad to kill all those people."

But if the whole universe is made up of little energy particles, and the way things got together by *chance* caused molecules and atoms and the things men discover as various patterns which they describe with formulas; if rocks, plants, birds, fish, animals and people are just *chance* combinations of particles; if the only thing that is coming in the future is some sort of wiping out of all that there is; *how* can people say something is good, or bad, or that there is something right and something wrong? And also, what is the difference finally between someone being very cruel and someone being very compassionate and taking care of people?

All this is *if . . . if* there is no person who created, and who not only made the universe, the plants, fish, birds, animals, sun, moon, stars, oceans, but who also made men and women. Where, then, can you get a standard for what is kind and what is cruel, for what is good and what is bad? Think for a moment. Should each person make up his own mind and act the way he wants to? Some people think it is good to annoy all the rich people and throw stones at their windows because they are rich and others are poor. Some people think it is all right to treat poor people badly. Some people think it is all right to be rude to old people just because they are old. Some people think it is right to be cruel to anyone who is different from them, who speaks a different language, has a different color of skin, or different customs. Some women think it is right to be nasty to men because they want to prove they are better.

Who makes the rules? Who tells other people what is right and what is wrong? It is a good thing to think about. No one enjoys living where there are no laws or rules, and no people to enforce, or make people keep, the rules. If the government tells people what to do, what is there to make the men in the government make the right rules? People who think there is no one in the whole universe watching them, treat other people with cruelty very easily, just as boys and girls often kick each other or knock each other down when they think no teacher or older person is watching.

If there were no Creator God who really made all things and all men, then the religions of men are only made up by men, and are of no use whatsoever. The only thing that would be worth anything would be trying to have as good a time as possible for the short time you could live, before someone ruined your good time with their idea of an opposite way of living!

What a mess it would be if all the crying and seeking for help, just ended in an empty echo, like calling into a cave and hearing an echo. Happily this is not so!

As you already know, there is God the Father, God the Son, and God the Holy Spirit, and the Bible, God's Word, has been given to us to give us explanation as to what the universe, and our lives are all about. We have been talking a lot about *sin*. What is sin? Is it just something a lot of men have decided is wrong? Is sin just something seventy-five per cent of people voted we shouldn't do? No. We have a perfect God, who is perfect in his holiness, and perfect in his love. He is holy, and he is love. He has made the rules, he has made the laws. Anything we do which is against the *character* of God is sin. It is breaking the laws of God, yes, but in breaking his laws we are doing something against his character.

People say God is harsh, but that is because they don't know God. They say his laws are too harsh, but that is because they haven't really thought about what God's laws are. Jesus said that the summing up of all the law is, "To love the Lord your God with all your heart and soul and mind, and to love your neighbor as yourself." Did you ever realize that all the law is *love*? It is breaking the law of love when we sin. When we sin we are being unloving to God, or to some other person. What is a person? A person thinks and acts and feels. That is what makes a person different from a molecule! And God made the rules to fit with his character of love, so that thinking, acting and feeling that is not full of love toward God and toward people, is sin. God is *holy*, and he cannot have sin in his presence. God cannot have people close to him who are thinking, acting and feeling in ways that are without love.

When Eve and Adam sinned, by thinking, acting and feeling that God was a liar (which was obviously *not* loving God with their hearts or souls or minds), and when all people since then sinned, it meant they could not be close to God. God as perfectly holy could not break his own character and law of love. If God had said, "It doesn't matter," he would have been saying that his promise that death would result if they ate of that fruit, was going to be broken. But also, God would have been saying that it didn't matter if they called him a liar, and went on to live unloving lives. So God had to put Adam and Eve away from the garden where they had walked with him and talked with him every evening when it grew cool and the sun went down. He had to show them the results of their sin. God could not be a holy God, perfect in every way, and not keep his promise.

You could say, "Why didn't he make them just to act and think and feel the very same way all the time?" But don't forget, God did not make computers, or mechanical dolls. He made personalities who had choice, to think and act and feel, to have ideas and to be creative. Adam and Eve chose to do the thing which God said would bring a certain result, and the result followed.

So we *do* have someone to tell us what the laws are. We do have an absolute right and wrong—and the basis of this is the character of God, which is holiness and love. Right and wrong are absolute: that means they are always the same and never vary from generation to generation. We can feel secure in the certainty that the things that are right and the things that are wrong do *not* change with every country, every mile we walk, every lake we swim, every ocean we cross. The things that are right and wrong, are the same wherever we are. We do not need to feel afraid that the things that are right and wrong now will change when we grow older. Sometimes laws made by people change. In some countries it is wrong to drive on the left side of the road, and in some countries it is wrong to drive on the right side of the road. In some countries you must count your money and say how much you are bringing in, and in other countries it doesn't matter how much money you bring in. In some schools children are not allowed to eat an apple in school, and in other schools children may have an apple or cookie (or biscuit) in school. These things are rules made by people: they change depending on who is making the rules.

God is always the same. He is always God. The three Persons of the Trinity always agree. The rules never change. That is what absolute means. "Absolute" means something that does not change with time, or space. If all people just came from particles, no person is any more "right" than any other person. It is the same as the fact that *thinking* came first. People know they think, choose and *then* make, or create something, but because they do not believe there is a

Person, God the Trinity, they make up *another* explanation for how all things came to *be*. It is the same with right and wrong. Today in the twentieth century people are saying there is *no* right and wrong. You will hear in schools, universities, TV programs and plays, and read in magazines and books that there are no absolute rules, that there is nothing that does not change. All this is called relativism. People do not believe there is a God, who is holy and who *is* love, and so they do not accept the rules which are all *based* on love. People do not believe there is a God who is absolute to make rules which do not change. This is why the world gets into a worse mess all the time, and why people get so mixed up. Sometimes even Christian people think nothing of breaking God's rules. They become affected by reading newspapers and magazine articles, watching television programs, seeing films, listening to radio broadcasts and lectures day by day, so many of which are based on relativism (on the belief that everything is relative).

All that has been said thus far is to help us to understand God's love, and to realize that since his rules do *not* change, and since everyone has sinned, Jesus had to teach about sin, and show us true compassion. Jesus is compassionate because he came to do something for the people he loves and feels sorry for.

》 Let's study some of the things that show us how loving and compassionate Jesus the Son of God is. Luke chapter 13 tells us some of these things.

The first thing we're told is about some of those people who were trying to shock Jesus and trip him up. He was always talking about sin, so they thought they would tell him about people who were *much* worse than they were. They probably rolled their eyes and made great shocked noises as they talked. Some Galilaeans were sacrificing at their worship, and Pilate came along and killed them right there in the middle of it, along with the lambs. Now, thought the men to themselves, as they smacked their lips over this horror, Jesus will know how wicked these men were; the awful way they died proves that they were more wicked than we are. Jesus read the thoughts in their minds, and asked them a question. "Think ye that these Galilaeans were sinners above all the Galilaeans, because they have suffered these things?" As the men waited for the answer they must have been surprised, because it was just what they had been thinking. Jesus said, "I tell you, Nay, but except ye repent, ye shall all in like manner perish." Then Jesus goes on to say that eighteen men who died when a tower in Siloam fell and killed them, were not worse sinners than any other people living in Jerusalem either. And he finished by saying again, "I tell you, Nay, but except ye repent, ye shall all in like manner perish."

Did he mean these men would die a violent, sudden death? No! What Jesus was doing was to give men an opportunity of understanding that sin is sin, and that dying is dying, and that being lost is being lost, and that they should not be judging other people, and feeling better and safer than others, because there is only one way of being safe, and getting rid of sin. Jesus spoke these strong words because he loved people.

Will you take a pencil and paper, or a crayon and paper, or a notebook and a pen, and "listen with your eyes" as well as your ears? Draw a lot of paths, but have them all end at a cliff, or a gorge, or a precipice . . . a dangerous place. Now draw *one* path that leads to a house. We'll read on as you draw. If the people who are on those paths shouted at each other, and argued about which is the better path, and who was going to get to the end first—and suddenly you noticed that they were all blind, would you think it loving or *un*loving if someone said very loudly and strongly, "Stop, listen to me . . . you are all blind. You are all on the wrong path. You are all going to fall into that gorge, over the cliff, if you carry on. But there is *another* path that leads to a beautiful, safe warm house—where there is a dinner, friends of yours, family, rooms enough for each of you. Please stop and change your path. I'll do what is necessary to get you from where you are, on to this right path. Just stop and listen to what I will tell you—don't go on that way. I am willing to pay the greatest price, to suffer, to get you on this path to the house."

Would you think it loving to have the person who could see what was happening just shrug his shoulders and say, "Let them go. They will find out, after it is too late; they're enjoying themselves now, why bother them?"

Jesus came to tell, and then to die to make it possible for people to get on the path to the house. Over and over again in many different ways, he told the people this.

Before we go on, all stand up and stretch a little. Now get a scarf or a soft cloth and tie it around your eyes so that you cannot see. Whirl each other around a bit, then select a spot that is "home" and a spot that is the cliff. There should be all sorts of things you would fall over, but of course we don't want anyone to get hurt. The important thing is to get some small idea of the situation of being blind to truth and rushing off in a direction where vague "voices" say, "come here, come this way" but . . . when all "ways" are leading to where you would fall down. Don't forget there is an enemy (the devil) who is trying, by whispering wrong directions and putting a variety of hindrances in the way, to keep people from finding the path to the house. So with the blindfold, and with someone trying to push you in the wrong direction, you need someone to come along and shake you to listen to the truth.

Jesus, in John's Gospel chapter 14 said that in his Father's house were many rooms, and that he was going to prepare a place for all of us who are coming. Thomas asked the very question about the path, the way to get there, that we should *all* be asking. Thomas said, "Lord, we know not whither thou goest; how know we the way?" Then Jesus said, "I am the way." He said it clearly while he was on the earth, and he left a record in the Bible of what he said, so that

---

A woman who had an infirmity eighteen years and was bowed together.   Luke 13:10–16

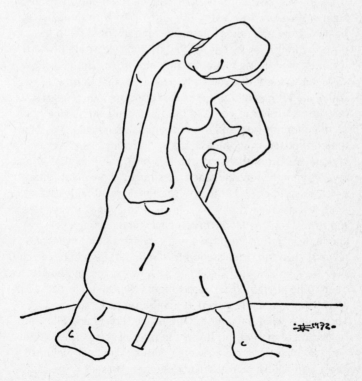

generation after generation would know. He is the way: we can be sure of going as we believe in him.

Jesus came, because God in his holiness had planned a way for people to come back to him, to come back to the wonderful home he is preparing for ever.

Can't you see God is *love*?

Jesus showed his compassion, his love, over and over again. Luke tells us in chapter 13 of an old woman who had a disease which she had had for eighteen years, and which caused her to be bent over. One of you stand and bend over from the waist as if you were doing a bending exercise. Now stay that way a minute. Suppose you could *never* straighten up. Now keep bending over so that your head is down fairly close to your knees . . . walk across the room and try to drink a glass of water. It gets very tiring if you try it for long. Imagine how frustrating and exhausting it would be to have to do everything, day by day, in that position. It would be hard for one day, for one week, for one month . . . but imagine eighteen years of that difficulty! Luke says that in no way at all could she lift herself up out of that position. When Jesus saw her, he called her to come to him. You can just imagine how sorry he felt for her, and in his compassion he said, "Woman, thou art loosed from thine infirmity." That means, "Woman, you are free from that sickness. It is over, the thing has gone away!" Immediately she stood up straight. Now if you, Margaret, Kirsty, Becky, Elizabeth, Natasha, Samantha, Jessica, Jandy, Fiona, Ranald or——————(*add your own name or the names of your family here*), have been leaning over, suddenly stand up. You have been trying to bend over for a few minutes, but it feels good to stand up. She had been bent over for eighteen years, so imagine how excited she must have been to be straight again, and to feel well again. No backache after Jesus had made her well! She began to glorify God. Then guess what happened. One of the scribes and Pharisees began to get mad again. It was the ruler of the synagogue this time, and Luke says he answered with indignation, a kind of anger and annoyance all mixed together. He said, "There are six days in which men ought to work: in them therefore come and be healed, and not on the day of the sabbath."

Those men were always ready to criticize in a way that made them feel proud. They had made so many extra rules that they thought they were the judges. They thought they had made all the rules in the first place. Whose rules are absolute? God's rules. Men's rules are never absolute, unless they are fitting in perfectly with God's rules.

Now men have a right to run a grocery store the way they want to. "No bare feet, and no dogs allowed," can be a sign on a bakery shop and it is up to those people to say what they want in their store. But if anyone says that is God's rule, they are all wrong. God never said it was wrong to go around in bare feet, and to have a dog with you! People can make up little rules about their own houses . . . like "Put your shoes in this basket and wear sandals in our house." They do this in Japan. It keeps mud off the floors and is a great idea. But no one should mix *that* up with God's rules. Like the Pharisees, a lot of religious people today mix up their rules with God's rules, and try to make people think their rules for people are "absolute," like God's rules. Do you understand the difference?

Let's go back to Jesus in the synagogue on that Sabbath day again. The Pharisees had not changed their way of treating him, and had not learned anything, but I'm sure a lot of other people sitting there were learning a lot. Jesus said, "You hypocrites. You teach that people should untie their animals on the Sabbath day so that they can have a drink and quench their thirst. Then don't you think this woman, a daughter of Abraham, a Jew, more important than animals, should be untied from this awful thing Satan has tied her with for eighteen years?" Jesus said it was Satan who was responsible for this woman having a disease which had kept her bent over as if she were tied in that position. Jesus was angry that these men had no compassion for a poor suffering woman.

He is angry today at people who think they are so pious in following their religious laws, that they have no compassion on people who are suffering from sicknesses, accidents, in hospitals, in prisons "bound" as if with some kind of rope, and with no one to care for them. Jesus showed us that it is part of the law of loving your neighbor to show evidence of compassion. If you are going to show compassion for poor, sick, suffering, old and unattractive people in the way Jesus told them to and as he tells us to do, it has to be in *practical* ways for the immediate need, as well as showing compassion by helping people to find the way to Heaven, to God the Father's house that has so many rooms.

Yes, it was the Sabbath day, and all the Pharisees could think of was the law to do no work. Some of them really were "hit" this time, as they thought of how they untied their animals for a drink, and saw this woman's happy face as she stood up, because Luke tells us in Luke 13:17, "All his adversaries (that is, his enemies, the ones against him) were put to shame: and all the multitude rejoiced for all the glorious things that were done by him."

≫ After Jesus had healed this poor woman, Luke says he walked through cities and villages on the way to Jerusalem. Someone said to him, "Lord, are there few that are going to be saved?" Jesus answered by telling him several things. First he said, "Strive (try hard, that is)to enter in at the strait gate!" In the book of Matthew we are told about another time when he said almost the same thing, but there he told a little more about it. In Matthew 7:13, 14, Jesus said, "Enter ye in by the narrow gate: for wide is the gate, and broad is the way, that leadeth to destruction, and many be they that enter in thereby. For narrow is the gate, and strait the way that leadeth unto life, and few be they that find it." Get out some paper and pencils, or whatever you like to use to make a picture. Draw, or paint, a wide road, with flowers and fields and an easy-looking walk. Lots of people are on this road, laughing, joking, eating and drinking. They seem to be having an easy time . . . but far off in the distance, the road leads to destruction (some sort of bad thing, a cliff, a heavy thunderstorm, whatever you want to picture). Now draw another road, a

narrow one, steep, which looks difficult to climb, with a
narrow gate at the top. On this it looks as though there are
less people, but later on you will meet many friends going
through the narrow gate too.

Perhaps in your house you have an old book of *Pilgrim's
Progress* (try to get one soon if you haven't), and it would be
a good idea to read it, and look at the old pictures of Pilgrim
going up the steep way and coming to the wicket gate. John
Bunyan had been put in prison for preaching the gospel, and
while he was there he wrote this book, picturing Pilgrim as
one who came to understand that his burden of sin would roll
away when he accepted Jesus as his Savior. We remember as
children thinking of that narrow and steep way with the wicket gate ahead, and used to put a pillow on our backs, and
climb up the stairs, and pretend the top of the stairs was
where we found the certainty that we had accepted Jesus as
Savior . . . then we'd let the pillow fall off and roll, bump,
bump, bump, down the stairs, and think . . . "There, the burdens of sin are all gone." That was a good illustration at the
age of five or six, which was taken out of *Pilgrim's Progress*
which had been read to us.

However you picture it, it is important that you understand that the compassion of Jesus is very real for people who
are burdened and bent over with sickness, like the old
woman. But he came to do more than help for a few years.
He came to roll the burden of sin away so that we could really
stand up straight, and climb that steep path as he leads us.
Does it sound too romantic to think of burdens as something
tied on your back? Some very young people who have been
caught in Satan's lies of saying drugs are all right, and running
away and living in a mess is all right, have ended up feeling a
horrible "burden" dragging them down into depressions so
deep they want to die, and making them so "bowed down"
with unhappiness that they are like old bent-over people at
the age of sixteen! It's not funny to feel like that. And it's
great news that Jesus came to do something about it.

As Jesus walked along, healing and teaching and answering questions, one of the Pharisees said to him, "You'd

227

better get out of here because Herod is going to kill you."
You see, Herod had had John the Baptist beheaded at the
request of his brother's wife. This Pharisee knew that Herod
had been asking questions about Jesus, and so he warned
Jesus. But Jesus had come to do a work on earth. In John 17:4
we know that Jesus said in a prayer to his Father, "I glorified
thee on the earth, having accomplished the work which thou
hast given me to do." That work was to make known the truth
of how glorious God the Father is, and to teach men the truth
that they might know the Way, and then to die that they
might enter the way. To run in the other direction would not
have helped that work.

But Jesus gave us some tiny idea of his compassion and
love as he approached Jerusalem and cried out with real
sorrow, "O Jerusalem, Jerusalem, which killeth the prophets,
and stoneth them that are sent to her! how often would I
have gathered thy children together, even as a hen gathereth
her chickens under her wings, and ye would not!"

Have you ever seen a hen with tiny, peeping baby
chicks under her wings? Have you seen other birds with baby
birds clustering to be protected by their wings? Have you
seen baby ducks or baby swans near their mothers, with
wings puffed out on land or in the water to protect them? If
you could get some real chicks and a chicken, it would help
to "see" the picture Jesus gave us. Otherwise, look for a
picture, or draw one now. Jesus said he would have gathered
the people of Jerusalem, the Jews, and protected them, held
them close to himself, but they would not. Who does he
mean? Pharisees, scribes, Sadducees, lawyers, the poor people, the "publicans and sinners" in eyes of men . . . he would
have gathered them *all,* but people are people. People are
personalities, who think and act and feel and have ideas and
make choices. Jesus said, "And ye would *not!*" Is Jesus
compassionate? He is so compassionate that he weeps over
people. He is so compassionate that he left heaven to be born
and live in a difficult place, for people. He is so compassionate that he came to talk to people, to explain to them, and to
stand before them even when they said sarcastic, harsh things

228

to him. He is so compassionate that he went through all those temptations for us. Don't let anyone ever tell you that God is not compassionate, that he does not love us with greater love than any human being ever has had.

But people say,"This is just Jesus. God was a harsh God in the Old Testament." Don't you believe that. God hated sin, and God had to teach people, in a variety of ways, the law that was the law of love. He had to teach them that there were no other gods, and that to follow that broad road, of those wrong paths, would lead them to destruction.

Please listen to the compassion of God in the Old Testament:

> *Deuteronomy 5:29:* "Oh, that there were such an heart in them, that they would fear me and keep all my commandments always, that it might be well with them and with their children for ever."
> *Psalm 81:10, 13:* "I am the Lord thy God, which brought thee up out of the land of Egypt: Open thy mouth wide, and I will fill it. Oh, that my people would hearken unto me (listen to me) and Israel would walk in my ways."
> *Isaiah 42:5, 6, 7:* "Thus saith God the Lord, he that created the heavens, and stretched them forth: he that spread abroad the earth and that which cometh out of it; he that giveth breath unto the people upon it . . . I, the Lord, have called thee in righteousness, and will hold thine hand, and will keep thee, and give thee for a covenant of the people, for a light of the Gentiles; to open the blind eyes, to bring out the prisoners from the dungeon, and them that sit in darkness out of the prison house."

God made a path in the middle of the Red Sea for the Israelites. God brought water out of a solid rock for thirsty people in their wanderings. The Red Sea rolled back for the need for them to get away from their enemies right then. The water was to quench their thirst right then. The manna (food

229

like little cakes) fell from heaven each day because they needed food right then. Yes, God in the Old Testament days was compassionate and loving, but he tried to show the people that the path to heaven is more important than the one through the Red Sea, the Water of Life is more important than the water they needed right then, and the Bread of Life, which is Jesus the Messiah, is most important of all.

The living God—God the Father, God the Holy Spirit, and Jesus the Son of God, the Second Person of the Trinity— is compassionate beyond anything any *man* can imagine when he feels tears for other people . . . God is perfect holiness and perfect love. Let us worship him, adore him, trust him, and love him, appreciate him, and say *thank you*. Let us not criticize and not let other people's criticism affect us . . . or cause us to doubt our Father.

17
HAVE A FEAST!

Do you know what a *motive* is? There are good motives, and bad motives, and mixed motives! Everyone has motives, from the tiniest children to very old people.

"Look daddy, look up there," said little Jessica who was not yet two years old, and when her daddy looked up, baby Jessica put her finger in the jam pot and licked it! Her *motive* in getting her daddy to look up "there" was not because she wanted daddy to see what was on a high shelf, but so that she could get her tiny finger full of sweet jam. It's amazing that at twenty months a little human being can be so clever as to have a "hidden motive," but that happens even earlier in life, and never stops happening.

Shut your eyes and try to remember when you did something with a *motive,* a reason, that was not the motive you wanted other people to know about. Can you remember? Maybe once you set the table because you hoped that your mother would tell Dad you were such a good girl he should buy you the ball you wanted. Or perhaps you cut the grass, or shoveled the snow, or weeded the garden, because you wanted to ask to go swimming or skiing or sledding and you thought your parents would agree if you did something for them. Maybe you bought a bigger present than your sister was giving your mother for Christmas, not because you loved Mother, but because you wanted everyone to think your present was better than anyone else's. Maybe you visited someone in the hospital not really because you felt sorry for that person, but because you wanted the doctors and nurses to think you were the kindest person they ever saw. Maybe as an older person you gave money to help build an orphanage for children with no parents to care for them, not because you really had compassion for the children, but because you wanted your name to be on top of a list of important people in town who were giving money too. Maybe you invited people to your party, as a child, or to your dinner, as an older person, just so you would be invited back into a house you wanted to see, or to meet a person you had no other way of meeting, and who you thought would help you in some way.

Now open your eyes. What you have done might be quite different from the things I have put in that list, but everyone has done things with hidden motives, or with motives they hope no one will find out about.

At other times we all do things with mixed motives. That means we do things for two reasons at once. We bring Mother a bunch of flowers because we love her and want to make her happy with the surprise, but also because we are bringing home a friend for supper, and we want the table to have real flowers, and we don't know any other way of getting the plastic things off the table! Or we give Father a fine new turtle neck sweater for skiing, or for walking, because we love him and want him to have something we hope he will enjoy, but also because we are ashamed of the old patched-up sweater he insists on wearing. We invite our friend over to play in our garden (if we are children) because we really do want to give that friend a good time, and we really do like that person, but because also we have heard that child has a new swing and we want to get invited to play there. We visit an old lady who we know is lonely and we want to give her a happy afternoon, but we also know that she has lovely chocolate-covered ginger and peppermint creams that she serves for tea, and we know she will let us look at her rare collection of stamps, old postcards, and books . . . and we think maybe she will even give us one to keep. Mixed motives are not always completely bad.

With our eyes open and remembering such things we have done, we can smile at each other, because we know we each have done things with mixed motives at times. But as we smile, and as we realize that we all do these things, let us think of the fact that sometimes "motives" can be very bad indeed, and sometimes "mixed motives" can be deceiving ourselves, and others, and trying to deceive the Lord. It is a very important thing to understand that underneath everything we do there is a motive, and it can be good, or bad, or mixed. It can be something we do not realize we are doing, or it can be to deceive on purpose. When we understand this, we can, if we belong to the Lord's family, ask God as we talk to him day by day, to help us with our motives.

We need to understand something about what motives are, and something about the motives we have had, to understand what Jesus is teaching in Luke chapter 14. We have already talked about the absolute law, that is, the law of God that does not change from place to place and time to time. God's law is a law of love. We are to love the Lord our God with all our hearts and all our souls and all our minds, and our neighbors as ourselves. If we were able to keep the law perfectly, then all our *motives* would be good. We would do things because we love God, and then because we love other people as much as ourselves. But no one is perfect, and no one has perfect motives in this life. People who think they are good, don't realize very much about motives, nor understand their own motives. God not only knows what we think and feel, but knows our motives.

One of the chief Pharisees had a group of guests for a meal on the Sabbath day, and Jesus was there among them. They watched Jesus very closely as a man with a disease called dropsy stood before him. Once more Jesus healed on the Sabbath day, and reminded the men again that they would do something for their animals on this day. He told them that if an animal such as an ass or an ox fell into a pit, they would pull it out on the Sabbath day. This silenced them as the man with dropsy was healed and went on his way.

While Jesus was there he noticed that there were rooms, and places at tables, where it was an honor to sit, and people were trying to sit in these. Because of this, Jesus told a parable about a man who came to a feast and sat himself at the place of honor, and then was very shamed when the host of the feast told him that place belonged to someone else, and made the man sit in the lowest place.

Jesus said they ought to learn a lesson from this parable, that it is better to choose a lower place, and then have someone tell you, "Oh, no, you must go to a higher place," than to be shamed as the man in the parable had been (in front of everyone).

Jesus then said a very important thing. Luke 14:11 states that "whoever exalteth himself shall be abased, and he that humbleth himself shall be exalted." It means that if you are proud and all puffed up and trying to make yourself the top person with high honors, you will be put down, but if you are really humble and want other people to be put ahead of you, then one day you will be honored. It is another one of those "backwards" or "upside down" sayings like "He that loseth his life findeth it," and like "If you seek first the kingdom of God, all these things (food, clothing and other material things) will be added unto you." Back in the Old Testament, in Proverbs 15:33, people had already been taught, "The fear of the Lord is the instruction of wisdom; and before honor is humility." And in Isaiah 57:15 God talks about the fact that he will specially be near to people of humble and contrite spirit, and that he will revive the spirit of humble people.

What Jesus was teaching was not easy to listen to, because it was like that mirror we looked in earlier. As people listen to these things (whether they were the people at the Pharisee's Sabbath dinner table, or whether it is people today) if they really listen and think of themselves, it is like seeing all kinds of smudges in the mirror. We, and anyone who listens, begin to realize how far are our thoughts, and actions, and feelings, and motives, from what they ought to be.

≫ Jesus then looked around the table and said to the man who had invited him, "Some time when you make a dinner or a supper for a lot of people, don't invite your friends, or your brothers and sisters, or any of your relatives, or your rich neighbors. They always invite you back again. When they come to a party, or a tea, or a luncheon, or a dinner, or a supper, they feel they should invite you to return your treat to them, and in that way you are paid back completely. Now instead of this, plan a *feast,* not just a simple meal, and invite really poor people, handicapped people, blind people. If you invite a whole group of people like this, they cannot possibly pay you back for it, and you will have given them something helpful and a happy time without wanting anything in return. This is the kind of motive you should have for giving a dinner. One day there will be a resurrection, and at that time there are going to be special rewards given for the things you have done like this, with the very honest and humble motive of helping the people you invite."

Yes, we need to try to check our motives day by day, and to ask ourselves what our underlying motives are. We are never going to have perfect motives for everything, but that does not mean we are to just shrug our shoulders, and say, "Well, I can't help it, I just can't be perfect." We are supposed to ask God to help us day by day to do his will, and to follow what he tells us his will is in the Bible. So often people say, "I don't know what the Lord's will is for me." And they sit and think, and they walk and frown, and they lie down and sigh deeply, and they say, "I can't find out what the Lord's will is for me to do. If I knew, I would do it right away." Usually they are expecting some notice to come from the Lord, some message telling them to go thousands of miles away, or to do some very new thing at least ten miles away, or to start a new kind of profession, but they have not been doing the things God had said to do—already shown in the Bible.

How long ago did Dr. Luke finish his manuscript? How long ago was the New Testament being read? How long ago was Jesus talking to people face to face so they could hear these things we have just been listening to? Nearly 2000 years ago now. For nearly 2000 years people who have believed the Bible, and people who have been born into God's family by accepting Christ as their Savior, have been told that they are supposed to be having lovely big dinners in their own homes for poor people, who are not their own relatives, nor their good friends, but people who cannot do anything in return.

Have they been doing it?

A few have. Oh, yes, a few at different points in history, and a few today do have their doors open for people to come into their homes. Some have taken refugee children into their own families. Some have taken into their own homes a mother and child without a father to care for them. Some have brought children from the slums into their homes for a meal. Some have really found poor, lame, halt, blind, and have had them to dinner over and over again. Some have opened their doors to anyone the Lord would send, and shared their food with the ones who have come. Some have done a great variety of things without any desire to be paid back by the people they are helping.

But really there are very few who have done this simple thing which Jesus outlined as important to do. Jesus took the time to put it into clear words.

Stop now, as you are reading this, and get pencil and paper, or better still a notebook. Now talk together as a family, or as friends, or as one person if you are reading alone. Consider whether you have ever done what verse 13 of Luke chapter 14 says we are to do. Have you ever made a "feast" . . . a very special meal, and invited the very poor and handicapped people of your village, town, city, or area? If you lived in Bombay—where there are over a million living on the streets in makeshift pipes, shacks made of paper, cardboard, rags, or simply lying on a few rags, it would overwhelm you to think of how many need to be invited! But even in the places of the world where there are too many, if every Christian would have a "feast" once in a while for a few of them, it would be something done for them. Perhaps in the place where you live, you don't know any people like that. But think! Are there people who work in the mines, the fields, big vegetable gardens, fruit orchards, factories, or who clean the streets, or who don't have any jobs? Are there foreigners who are lonely? Write now in your notebook, the people anywhere near you that Jesus has said are the ones we should invite. They would all be people your neighbors would be surprised to see coming to your home for a dinner, not your usual friends.

Now, on another page of your notebook, write down how often you think you should do this. Perhaps once a year? Or once in six months? Or even once every three months? Or perhaps once a month? You will have different ideas about this. Why don't you stop and pray about it! As a family ask the Lord to help you find the person of his choice, or the people of his choice, for whom you can care in this way. Now take another page, and write down ideas of what ages of people you could invite. Should there be someone of about the age of each one in the family? Should they all be children? Should they all be old? Think it out a bit, and write down some ideas, again praying for the ones the Lord wants you to have. Now on another page, make a calendar of this month. Put a circle around one day. The only way to begin to do a thing, is to begin!

How many people will you invite? Well, you know your own home. If you have a very little space, you will need to limit the number to the space you have. Is it worth inviting just two people? Of course. It is worth it if you really have only room for one. In Hong Kong some Christians live in apartments so tiny that they can never sit down together as a family for a meal, and the only way they could sit at a table together at one time, would be to go to a restaurant. If that is your situation, of course it would be difficult, but you could do something for one person! At times it is good to have just one person and to get to know that one person well.

Next, write out a menu of a very nice meal, and decide that it will be the one to share, with the prettiest tablecloth and flower arrangements you can manage to have. Is it to be just giving food to someone that is hungry, as if you were dishing out soup to flood refugees? No, you are sharing your home, so there is to be a warm atmosphere, and the conversation is to be as important as the lovely food. As Christians, you will begin by thanking the Lord for the food. And perhaps the stranger you have invited will ask a question about that.

Anyway somehow the conversation will start, and you will be talking and finding out about how this person thinks, and what this person or people, find difficult in life. Perhaps you will be seeing life through a different viewpoint. You won't be able to be as "boxed in," as if you lived in a fenced-in park with no contact with the outside people at all.

This is what Jesus taught that people should do, and I wonder what would have happened during 2000 years if every believer had done *this one* thing regularly. There are so many *other* things he taught us to do as well! Whose fault is it that so few people know that God really exists, and know about his love?

» After talking about this, Jesus told the people a parable, a story to teach a truth. This is the parable: "A certain man made preparations for a really great meal for many people, and he invited a lot of people. When it came supper time, the man told his servant to go to all the ones who were invited and tell them that everything was ready to serve, and that it was time to come. Then every single one of them gave an excuse as to why it was impossible to come. One said, 'I just bought a piece of ground, and I have to go to see it. Please excuse me.' Another one said, 'I have just bought five yoke of oxen (that would be ten oxen yoked two by two) and I have to go and try them out to see if they are all right, so please excuse me from coming.' Still another one said, 'I have just got married, so I really can't come.'

"Every single one had an excuse of something he or she felt more important than coming to the supper to which they had been invited. The servant came back to his master and told him that no one was coming, because they all had excuses. Then the master became angry and said to his servant, 'All right then, if none of the invited guests will come, just go out quickly into the streets and little lanes of the city and bring in all the poor, and the crippled ones, the blind ones.' And when the servant had all these people in the dining room, he said, 'There are still some more places left, master.' So the master said to the servant, 'Go out, past the city, out to the highways and hedges and bring in the people you find there to fill my house. I tell you, I don't want any of those people who were given the invitations and then didn't come. I don't want any of them to have a taste now!'"

Compare this for a minute with something in your own life. Suppose you were having a birthday party, or a supper for special friends on a special day of yours, and you had sent out beautiful invitations, printed and decorated in whatever would be the most polite and beautiful way to invite people in your part of the world. Then you got ready for the party. You had a flower arrangement on the table, a beautiful meal prepared, the best sort of dessert, music, or some surprise games and treats at the end, like balloons to float and play games with, or kites to fly, and a gift to take home. You had planned and prepared a *long* time, and it had cost you a great deal to get it ready . . . and then, at the last minute, excuses came from every single person. Now suppose you sent someone outside to call in all the children whom they could find playing on the streets of your village, or near your house in the city. Wouldn't they be excited to have such an unexpected treat? How they would laugh and enjoy the good food and special surprises! After they were all seated, eating the food and saying "thank you," and looking forward to the music or the balloons or the kites, or the gifts—then it would be too late for the others to change their minds, wouldn't it? Even if they began to be sorry that they had not come, it would be too late.

Jesus tells us in John 14:1, 2, 3, "Let not your heart be troubled; ye believe in God, believe also in me. In my Father's house are many mansions; if it were not so I would have told you. I go to prepare a place for you. And if I go and prepare a place for you, I will come again, and receive you unto myself, that where I am, there ye may be also." Yes, Jesus has said he is preparing a place and that he is coming back again to take us there. In Revelation we are told there will be a supper some day, one where Jesus will serve us, and we will sit together and eat as he serves. The invitation to be with Jesus at that supper, and in that place he is preparing, is

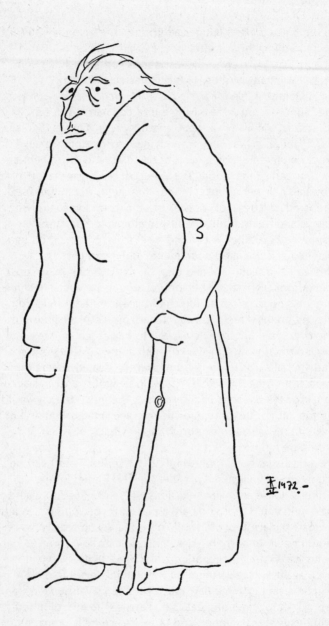

given, in the Bible, and by those of us who are his children today, to people who *will* listen and "come" to him.

The story or parable Jesus has just told is another way of explaining to us the *choice* people make to put other things in the place of first importance, to consider themselves too busy to bother, rather than taking seriously the existence of God, and his invitation to come to him. And he has made clear the *way* to come! Jesus showed in this story that the people who *will* accept the invitation of the Bible to believe and accept Christ as Savior are often not the ones you expect to accept him. Often the people who seem cultured, educated, kind and nice, and who you think would be the very first to accept the Lord's invitation will not accept Christ as their Savior because they are too busy with business, investments, sports, marrying a wife and perfecting a home, and other things which they would consider important. Boys and girls sometimes think they are too busy to bother as well, or have other things that are more important to do. There are people who always have too much to do, always have excuses that keep them from coming to discuss truth, from seeking any answers or even thinking about the questions of what life is all about. There are people too busy to read books that would give them answers from the Bible's viewpoint. There are people who always make excuses. Life goes on. A person who is ten is soon fifteen. A person who is twenty is soon twenty-five. A person who is thirty is suddenly astonished that ten years have gone by and he or she is forty! It doesn't take much time.

God says that with him 1000 years is as a day! To God, human beings' excuses must seem very tragic indeed, as he sees what he is preparing for the ones who will *accept* the invitation, and he knows the wonderful time ahead is *for ever*!

The people whom the servant brought in from the streets and highways are not the kind of people you would ever expect to find at a rich man's table. Often we find that

A beggar with a stick.   Luke 14:16–24

those who do accept Christ's invitation to come to him are not the kind of people you would expect to find at the table of the very Son of God. In the Old Testament in I Samuel 2:8 we find, "He raiseth up the poor out of the dust, and lifteth up the beggar from the dunghill, to set them among princes, and to make them inherit the throne of glory." This is what the Lord does. He does make it possible for anyone who will come to him to inherit eternal life!

Jesus speaks to people who realize their need. If they are proud like the Pharisees, or turn away from the supernatural like the Sadducees, or feel they are perfectly satisfied with piling up lands and money and things to enjoy now, like the foolish man with his barns, if they are "too busy to come," like the people in the parable and have all kinds of excuses, then suddenly the years will have gone by . . . and the time will be over, and it will be too late to "accept."

Take a card or a stiff piece of paper, the nicest thing you can find on which to write an invitation, and copy Matthew 11:28, 29, 30 on it. Let this be for you. When you have copied it, put it in your Bible, or on your desk, or somewhere which is just for you. It is the invitation of Jesus to you, and to all who will listen. Remember we read "He came unto his own and his own received him not." In a way Jesus was really refused by the people he first invited, when you think of the fact that he was the promised Messiah, and people who should have been waiting for the Messiah turned away from him. Now that invitation is to be given "in the highways and byways of the whole world." Your card can remind you that the invitation is also for others. "Come unto me, all ye that labor and are heavy laden, and I will give you rest. Take my yoke upon you, and learn of me; for I am meek and lowly in heart: and ye shall find rest unto your souls. For my yoke is easy, and my burden is light."

18
"I'LL GO BACK"

Have you ever lost a kitten, or a puppy, or your favorite dog?
If you have, you will remember how you called and whistled,
looked and looked. Perhaps you walked through the woods,
looking, or up a high hill, or all over the city streets. You
were afraid, probably, that the dog might have been hurt, run
over, attacked by an animal, lost in a place where he couldn't
get out. If you have lost a pet animal, and have then found it
again, you know what it feels like suddenly to see your kitten
trembling on the limb of a tree, afraid to come down. You
know what it feels like to climb up and perhaps scratch your
knees on the bark, slip a bit and tear your fingernail so that it
hurts, but to feel so very happy now that you have found your
pet. You will also know that you wanted someone else to be
glad with you too. You wanted the family, or some friends, to
know you had found the lost dog or cat, and you probably
called out as soon as you reached the house, "Hey, everyone,
look, he's all right, I found him, isn't that great? Let's celebrate! I thought it was lost for ever, and now I've *found* him."
If you know what that kind of relief and joy feels like, you will
understand these three parables that Jesus told.

Jesus had been talking about how believing people are
supposed to be the salt of the earth, and he said if salt had
lost its saltiness it was absolutely no good for anything. You
know that salt makes things taste better, but also salt pre-
serves things. Salted bacon, salt pork, salted meat, makes it
stay fresh even without a refrigerator. You salt cabbage to
make sauerkraut which stays fresh for a long time. Salt keeps
a lot of things from going bad. What Jesus meant was that
people who are believers, ones who are the children of the
Lord, were meant to be a help in the world, to keep things

243

from going bad so rapidly, from decay taking place so quickly. If salt is no longer *salty*, it doesn't work, and you might as well throw it out. You can't depend on unsalty salt to do any good whatsoever, either for taste, or for preserving things.

Who would have been listening to Jesus then? Who were like unsalty salt? The Pharisees, because they were supposed to be ones who were following the Old Testament and believing, but they had added *men's rules* and were so *far* from being "real" in the love of God, that they didn't recognize the Messiah at all. As "salt of the earth" they weren't at all salty. Then there were the Sadducees who also claimed to believe in God, but they did not believe in miracles, in the resurrection of the body, or in anything supernatural. They, too, were not salty salt! As Jesus gave this clear picture, we find a new understanding of why the world seems rapidly to be getting so much worse today. A lot of the "salt" is not at all salty. A lot of people who say they are Christians are not real at all because they either add things which they think are the signs of being a Christian, or subtract things from the Word of God which they say do not matter. Unsalty salt will not keep the world from getting worse and worse . . . the molding and the spoiling can move more quickly if there is *no salt* to hinder it.

The Pharisees had heard Jesus say these things and they knew he was criticizing them, and instead of wondering whether they *might* be dangerously wrong, and comparing themselves with the teaching of the Word of God, they began to mutter to each other and say, "This man talks to sinners, and lets them sit with him and eat with him." They were criticizing him again for spending time with the people they thought of as so much worse than themselves. They still felt puffed up with pride in being religious.

It was then that Jesus told them three parables, three stories to teach them why he was spending his time with sinners. Of course, these men were sinners, too. In their pride they thought they were good, but that did not *make* them good! The pride of these men kept them from realizing they needed a Savior. If someone is swimming with a good strong stroke across a river and you rush up in a row boat and shout, "I'll save you," he or she would laugh and keep on swimming. But if suddenly that person felt the pull of a whirlpool and felt afraid of being sucked in, then if you yelled and threw a rope he or she would be very grateful for the rope. The Pharisees felt perfectly safe as they were. Did they really listen to these stories, and think about them?

Many of the people Jesus talked to were shepherds, or their friends, so they knew the habits of shepherds very well. We thought about having lost a dog or cat at some time, so that if you have never had sheep, you could at least imagine something of the feelings of a shepherd.

Jesus told them to imagine what they would do if they were the shepherd of a flock of a hundred sheep. As the shepherd was out in the wilderness, a mountainside full of steep places, thorns and sharp rocks, the sheep crowded around him, following where he led, eating the bits of grass and flowers as they walked along. Suddenly the shepherd missed one of the little sheep. He looked among the flock and counted, "91, 92, 93, 94, 95, 96, 97, 98, 99 . . . " but the hundredth was not there. Jesus said that any good shepherd would do what this man did; he left his ninety-nine sheep in a safe spot there in the wilderness, and went out searching for the lost one. Can't you imagine him hunting behind rocks and prickly bushes, over steep places where the precipice started and where the sheep would be dashed on rocks below? The shepherd's hands would become scratched with thorns, and his feet torn by sharp rocks, but he would keep on searching. Jesus said that he found the sheep, and placed it on his shoulder. Can't you imagine his cry of joy, and his smile as he tenderly carried the sheep back to the fold? When he arrived home that night, he called all his friends and neighbors over for a celebration, saying to them, "Rejoice with me, be glad with me, celebrate with me . . . for I have found my sheep which was lost."

Now Jesus didn't leave the meaning of the story to the imagination of the people! Those Pharisees had been mur- muring criticisms against Jesus because he was spending so much time with sinners, and Jesus was making it clear to them that he had come to find sinful, wandering people. Jesus is the shepherd and people are the sheep, and the wandering sheep are the ones he has come to look for. In the Old Testament in Isaiah 53:6, which was written 700 years before Jesus was born, we find this: "All we like sheep have gone astray, we have turned every one to his own way: and the Lord hath laid on him the iniquity of us all."

Yes, Jesus searches for lost sinners, just as the shepherd searched for the lost sheep. Jesus made a very strong point to those Pharisees, telling them that being with sinners was exactly what he came for as it was among sinners he would find the lost sheep. Jesus suffered more than scratched hands and bleeding feet. In the same chapter in Isaiah it says, "He was wounded for our transgressions." Transgressions are sins, and as he died on the cross, he surely was wounded for our sins. Now the thing to remember is that for hundreds of years people had been reading the Old Testament, and if they had really studied it and had been thinking about it, when they heard the story Jesus was telling of the lost sheep, they could easily have thought of Isaiah's message about the sheep going astray, and the sins being taken by a person who was to be coming to do that very thing. You see, it was not something brand new, but something God had been preparing people for years to recognize and understand.

Another of the Old Testament prophets is Ezekiel, and God speaks through Ezekiel to tell of how Israel had been scattered. Here again the people are called sheep. Listen to Ezekiel 34:6: "My sheep wandered through all the mountains and upon every high hill . . . and none did search or seek after them." God goes on through Ezekiel to say that the religious leaders had not been taking care of people, and had not been teaching them properly or "feeding them good, spiritual food," so the people were like flocks that had a bad shepherd who fed himself but not the sheep. Then a promise is given in verse 11, "For thus saith the Lord God; behold, I, even I, will both search for my sheep and seek them out." And in verse 14, he says, "I will feed them in a good pasture, and upon high mountains of Israel shall their fold be: they shall lie in a good fold."

This was written hundreds of years before Jesus came, and God called the religious leaders of that time bad shepherds. He said one day he, God, will be their shepherd and lead them to a good fold. So as Jesus tells the story of the lost sheep, he makes it very clear to the ones listening who knew their Old Testaments, that *he* was the Shepherd who had come to search for the lost sheep and to carry them in his arms. He was doing what he had come to do when he spent time with sinful people, eating and drinking with them . . . and when he finds one, that is, when one person comes to believe in him and to accept him as Savior, what takes place in heaven is just like the friends and neighbors of the shepherd coming to celebrate and be glad with him after he had found his lost sheep. Jesus says, "I say unto you, that even so there shall be joy in heaven over one sinner that repenteth." It is really exciting to know that angels in heaven are happy, or have joy, when a single human repents of his sins, and accepts Christ as his Savior. It *matters* to them. Doesn't that make it both real and personal? Isn't it special to know that the angels knew about you the very moment you believed, and remarked about it, were showing some sign of joy about it? How do we know? Well, Jesus said that there is joy in heaven when one sinner repents and comes "home on his shoulder" like that sheep. We know it is true.

» Then Jesus told another story. One of you can illustrate this while we read it. Let one person go out of the room (or if you can't decide which one, let two go out!). Now those who are left, take a coin, a nice coin, and hide it on the floor, in a corner, maybe under the corner of the rug, or somewhere that you agree is a good place. If more than one person has gone out of the room, hide at least two coins. Have the lights quite dim, and the person coming back can have a flashlight, or a candle, or a little lamp with which to look. Act out the story now, with a broom and a light.

A woman had ten pieces of silver, but she lost one

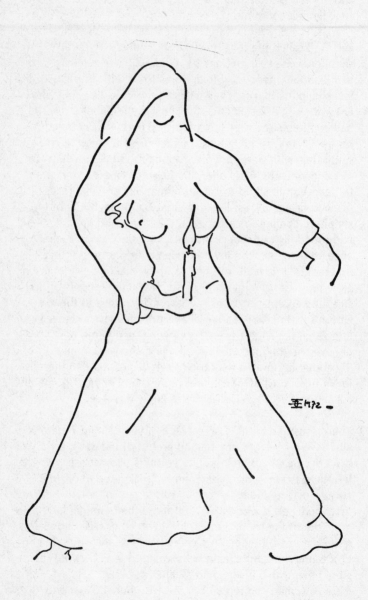

somewhere in her room. She took a candle and lighted it and
began to look everywhere on the floor. She swept every
corner and spot in the room, looking for the lost coin. Then
after a careful, hard search, she *found* it. When she found it,
she was very excited, because it meant a lot to her. It was
one-tenth of all she had. She called her friends and neighbors
in to rejoice with her, saying, "Come, be glad with me, for I
have *found* the piece of money I lost!"

The rest of you can be the friends and neighbors and
congratulate the one, or two, who pretended to be the woman. Be sure to be really happy about it. And to make it real,
the one who found the coin should be allowed to keep it!

Jesus then said, "Even so, I say unto you, there is joy in
the presence of the angels of God over one sinner that repenteth." Now remember that a parable teaches something,
but cannot be carried out to the end. For instance, when
Jesus says we are to be fishers of men, we are not expected
to eat men! He is illustrating *one thing* with a parable to make
us see it vividly, and clearly. The lost coin illustrates that some
people do not know they are lost, just as the coin does not
know it is lost. Some people are afraid, like the lost sheep,
feeling their danger and unhappiness, but the coin represents
people who do not feel lost like that. But the Holy Spirit
knows that they are lost, and searches them out, until they
are found. Jesus says that there is rejoicing in heaven over the
finding of such a one. Each found person brings joy to the
angels. The angels *care*!

In this twentieth century in so many big cities, where
the "salt has lost its saltiness," and there are not many really
salty Christians preserving things among human relationships
. . . you would not find very many neighbors and friends who
would really care if your lost sheep, or your dog or cat, or
your money or watch had been found. There are more people
who are greedily wanting to take things from other people,
than there are people who *care* about people who have lost

A woman with a candle looking for a lost coin.   Luke 15:8–10 things. Human sensitivity to other people's fears, worries, sadness and loss, has been blurred by more and more selfish feelings.

But the compassion of God, and the compassion of the angels, is so very real that they rejoice over every single one of the lost people who are found. That really is exciting! There is not one person so small, so poor, so uneducated, so uninteresting, that the angels are not excited and glad when he or she becomes a child of God by believing. There is not one single person of any tribe far off in the jungle, or of any slum in any city of the world, or of any nation no matter what the government is, nor of any language group, nor of any family line no matter how many thieves there were on the family tree, who is not recorded in the Lamb's Book of Life, and excitedly rejoiced over by the angels in heaven, and by the Trinity, when they are "found." If you ever feel that nobody loves you, nobody cares about you, nobody finds you interesting, or fun to be with, that you don't matter to anybody, then remember this—Jesus told the story of a little lost sheep, and of a tiny coin not worth much in the world's eyes, to show that in the eyes of people in *heaven*, no matter how insignificant we feel, we matter enough to bring excitement, joy, a real celebration right there in heaven itself!

The next parable Jesus told those Pharisees was to give them an opportunity to understand God the Father. Remember they had been criticizing Jesus for eating with sinners, and each of these parables is teaching something about what it means to be lost, and found! Jesus is looking for the lost!

Are all fathers good fathers? No, unhappily not, because men are sinful, and being bad fathers is one thing that happens as a result of sin, along with a lot of other things. What kind of a Father is God? Well, God is perfect in his holiness and in his love, so he is a perfectly loving Father, and he requires perfection from his children. How awful for us! We *cannot* be perfect. We might get into some very bad things because of temptation and our weakness. Will God disown us if we do? Will he cut us off and say, "Don't ever come home to me again!"?

The Bible teaches us a lot about the fatherliness of God. In Psalm 68:5, we are told that God is a Father to the fatherless. That means he will be a Father to people whose parents have died, or whose parents have deserted them. Then we find in Psalm 103:13 that he tells us, "Like as a father pitieth his children, so the Lord pitieth them that fear him. For he knoweth our frame; he remembereth that we are dust." That is exciting, because God is telling us that he is like the sort of a father that is kind and pities his children when they are dusty and dirty. Did you ever get dressed up for a picnic, or a family dinner, or to go to church on a Sunday, or to be taken to a concert, and then fall by accident into the dust and dirt? Maybe you were doing something you had been told not to do, but you didn't mean to get dirty! You meant to stay clean. You say you are sorry, and a kind father or mother washes you, dusts you off, and understands you, realizing that you are really sorry and forgiving you.

God says he doesn't forget that we are weak, sinful creatures. He remembers that we are pretty dusty people, and he pities us. He is ready to wash us and clean us and forgive us when we fall. Just before that, the Psalmist had said, "As far as the east is from the west, so far hath he removed our transgressions from us." This is as far as you *can* be removed from something! God is able to do this because Jesus died to take the punishment. God does not have to spoil his holiness by loving us that way. He can wash away our "dust." We don't have to ever be afraid of bringing people to our Father God, and of feeling ashamed of his love or of his fatherliness. His love is real, and far greater than that of any earthly father. But to experience his fatherliness, to come to know him as Father, people must come to him believing, and accept what he has prepared. So often people say, "I don't think God is loving," but they have never become his children, so he is not their father. No one knows a father the way his own children know him.

» The parable Jesus told was of a loving father who had two sons. One day the younger son came to his father and said, "Father, I know that there is a good bit of money you have that will some day be mine, and of course the rest will belong to my brother. I want my part of it now. Just divide it up and give me my part." The father must have said, "All right, then, if that is how you want it!" We are told he divided it right then, and gave the boy his share of what he would have inherited later.

As the boy took the money, he must have counted it, felt it in his hands, put it in a bag and jingled it. "Wow, what a good time I can have now, I won't have to work any more. I won't have to stay around this old place and help my father, or have him watching what I do all the time. I can do what I want and no one can stop me. I won't have to live such a dull, dumb life. I can just go anywhere I want and buy anything I like, and have a really free time . . . no rules to hold me down."

Not many days after that he gathered together all his things, and off he went. Did he have a pack on his back with everything in it? Perhaps. He went off to a far country, we are told. Of course there were no airplanes, and no automobiles to give him a lift, so although it was far from home, it wasn't as far as people today go when they go to a far country. What a feeling of freedom he must have had! "Now," he thought, "I can begin really to see the world and have an interesting time. Goodbye, everybody; goodbye, hard work. Here I go to have fun for the rest of my life!" He went far enough away from home for no one to know what he was doing, and then we are told he wasted all his money. Yes, he spent it wildly in everything he thought he wanted . . . food, drink, girls. He must have been popular for a time because he spent so freely. Then came the day when it was all gone.

If you've got a little bag or a purse around . . . empty it. Now shake and shake it, looking to see if one last penny will drop out. Maybe after he shook his money bag, this young man started scrambling through his pack of things. Maybe he sold some of his clothing for the next meal, and then something else. Finally, we are told he had nothing more and he was really hungry. What should he do? Find a job, of course. But there was a big problem—there was a famine in the land where he was.

A famine occurs when storms spoil the crops, or an earthquake destroys food supplies or a big fire burns up fields and trees, or sweeps through a city and ruins the food supplies, and there just is not enough food. There is not enough to buy even if you *do* have money, and this boy had no money. With a famine in the land it would be hard to find a job, or food. The only thing he could find was a very dirty job. Imagine feeling hungry and sick because you had lost everything, and because you had not eaten for days, and then to be given a job feeding pigs! He would have had to walk in the wet, muddy mire, throw food into the pigs' troughs, and watch the pigs pushing and shoving to eat. No one gave him anything to eat, and he was so hungry that he tried to fill his stomach with the husks given to the pigs. At first he probably felt more sick than ever, being among the pigs, but then he was glad to have even the husks. What a state he was in! He must have been not just dusty, but filthy, muddy, raggedy, sloppy and smelly. I'm sure he felt he couldn't stand the sight and feel of *himself,* let alone the food he was putting into his stomach.

Then a picture came into his mind. Something which I am sure he put side by side with the situation in front of him. Stop reading for a few minutes and prepare something for all of you to look at together. You can't fix a pigsty in your living room, but you could do something, even there. Prepare a table with a nice cloth, some clean dishes and a candle in a lovely candlestick, or a flower, or some pretty fruit, to make the table look especially nice. If it is nearly lunch time, or supper time, put some of the food you are going to eat there on the table. If it is not meal time, then get a loaf of bread, some cheese, fruit and cake, or anything that you have that looks appetizing. Near this table put another little table, or tray or board on the floor. On the table, tray or board put some garbage—old potato peelings, husks of corn or vegetables if you have them, surrounded by something dirty and spoiled (but don't wreck your family rug!). Make it as unappetizing as you can, so that it resembles as closely as possible what it would have been like to eat in that pigsty.

Now sit and look at the contrast. If you have arranged it properly, the table with the flower arrangement and the food will be perfectly beautiful, and you will *want* to sit there together soon and eat, or think of friends you would like to have there with you. And when you look at the garbage, you will feel revolted and want to say, "Take it away." It should look, feel and smell disgusting to show the real contrast.

The first thing to think about is that these two "meals" represent not just a contrast in food—but in the whole of life. You can do as this boy did, in a number of different ways, and throw your life away. Remember Jesus said, "He who loses his life for my sake, finds it, and he who grabs his life to do his own thing, will lose it." This boy had gone off to have a good time, to eat better, work not at all, to have friends: he went to do his own thing. He did his own thing in his own way. No one stopped him. He was free to choose. He thought, he chose, he acted on his choice. He was not a *puppet* tied by his father to doing that which would keep him comfortable and well fed, warm and cared for. He had freedom to choose, and to do his own thing. Utterly selfish, greedy, without obeying the law of love in any portion of it, he went off to wallow in sin, and the wallowing ended in the pig pen. He ended up eating garbage, but that was after he had been filling his mind, feelings, emotions, with garbage. Purpose in life? He had only garbage.

Jesus had said, "If you will forsake everything for my sake, if you will be willing to trust me for food, clothing, and shelter, and do what is my purpose for your life, I will add to you all things that you need." The beautiful table is what he would prepare for his children. The *garbage* is the end of rushing off away from God to do your own thing. Never forget it—the end is garbage in a pigsty.

Now go back to the boy. This is what he began to "see"

in his mind. He thought of his father's house and of all the wonderful things that were there. "Why," he thought to himself, "here I am dying of hunger, starving, and my father's servants have more than enough to eat. There is always food left over at home, even on the servants' tables. I'm being really stupid to stay here. I'll swallow my pride, and I'll go back to my father. I'll just tell him frankly that I was wrong . . . that I have sinned and I'll tell him I've sinned against heaven as well as against him. I'll tell him I am not worthy to be called his son at all. In fact, he can take me on just as a hired servant and not even say I am his son." He really was sorry, wasn't he? And he was humble and willing to apologize and also to take the consequences of going off on his own so stubbornly. He did not try to pretend that he had lost everything by accident; he spoke the truth about himself, admitting and acknowledging his sin. That isn't easy to do, but that is the way we must come to God.

Well, after thinking these things out and coming to a decision, the boy got up out of that pigsty and came the long way back. Did he take a bath first? Did he get clean clothing first? How could he clean up first? He had no money. Dirty and smelly from the pigsty, tired and dusty from the journey back, he must have been a sorry sight coming up the road in the distance, his hair and his beard sticking out, stiff with dirt, his eyes dull with lack of proper food and sleep. Not an attractive sight. Would his father even recognize him?

But when he was a long way off, the father saw him, and knew him and ran, because he had compassion. The father had compassion on his son who had gone off and wasted his whole half of the money, and who had spent it so ridiculously, had sinned in every way, and had now come back looking as if he had rolled in the pigsty. Remember, compassion is the kind of pity mixed with love that makes you want to *do* something for the person, or people, for whom you have that feeling. The father loved the son, while he was still dirty. The father loved his son while his stomach was still full of garbage and his whole body still ruined by what he had done. It was right then, in that condition, that he felt his father's arms suddenly around him. The father had run to hug him, not to yell at him. The father hugged and kissed him. Jesus says, "He fell on his neck and kissed him"—that means he put his arms around him and put his face right down in that smelly neck and kissed him. Then the son said, "Father, I have sinned against heaven, and in your sight, and I am not worthy to be called your son any more."

Listen a moment to what God tells us in the New Testament in Romans 5:8: "God commendeth his love toward us, in that while we were yet sinners, Christ died for us." You see the kind of love God the Father has for us. He sent Jesus to die for us, and Jesus loved us so much that he died for us *while we were still dirty, and full of garbage.* Not *after* we were cleaned up. It is Jesus who washes us clean, and who gives us his robes of wonderful white linen to dress us.

What did that father do in Jesus' story? After the son said he was sorry and felt he shouldn't be called a son any more, the father said to his servants, "Go, bring the very best robe we have and put it on him, put a ring on his hand, and shoes on his feet. Also, go right away and pick out a calf, a nice one that will make a wonderful roast of veal. Prepare it so that we can have a real feast, for we will eat and drink and be merry. Why? Because this my son was dead, and is alive again. He was lost and is found." And they began to be merry. This was greater rejoicing, a bigger celebration than finding the sheep. How happy the father was to have his son with him again!

The rejoicing in heaven is like this when any one sinner comes to the Lord and acknowledges that he has been doing his own thing, wasting his life, that he has sinned, and will accept what Christ has done. When we accept Christ as our Savior, God the Father answers, "You are my child now." He puts his arms about us, he cleans us up, clothes us with the righteousness of Christ, and feeds us with spiritual food, and we have fellowship with him.

19
ONE TAKEN, ONE LEFT BEHIND

Day after day Jesus taught in stories and parables. Day after
day in the sun, rain, heat, dust, in streets or by the lakes, he
walked and talked, sat and ate with people, moving around
among them. The ground is still there, the hills are still almost
the same. Some of the rocks, if they could speak, might be
able to tell what he said. What Dr. Luke recorded did not
happen on another planet, but on this earth. The sun looked
the same, at sunrise and sunset time, as it would today if you
visited Palestine, and it is the same sun and moon that you
see day after day. Jesus taught things that were important to
people living then, and made it possible for us to find out the
same things by having men write them carefully down.

Strange, isn't it, that both the ones who heard with their
ears and the ones who have read it with their eyes through
the years, have done the same thing . . . some have believed,
and others have made fun! People were just as sarcastic and
unbelieving as they stood looking into the eyes of Jesus, as
they are now when they read his Word. And the most sarcastic ones were the ones who read the Old Testament but had
lost any keen feeling about it, or had lost the sharpness of
what it said, because they had covered it up with so many
little rules of their own. Yes, those Pharisees.

The Pharisees were standing around when Jesus told a
parable about a rich man's steward who had wasted his money and had been a bad steward. And Jesus had just finished
the parable and made a strong statement. Jesus said, "No
servant can serve two masters: for either he will hate the
one, and love the other; or else he will hold to one, and
despise the other." In other words, you can't serve two men
with totally different basic principles . . . you can't be honest

and work for two men who have totally opposite ideas about what is most important. "You cannot serve God and mammon." You cannot put God first and wealth first. You cannot have money as your integration point and God as your integration point. Your integration point is that which ties your life together. It is the thing that you put first, that makes everything else worthwhile, that is so much first that you make changes in your way of living to fit into that thing.

If God is your integration point, if God comes first, then you think about him, and the things he would have you do. You decide at times to do or not to do something because it fits in with your wanting to show love to God and to trust him, or because it fits in with what God has clearly said you should do in his message to you, the Bible. To you, God is the most important Person in the universe, and serving *him* matters most of all.

If money is your integration point, then money comes first. If anything interferes with making money and having money you push it to one side. Wealth is the center of your life, and your bank book is more in your thoughts than the Bible. You don't bother even to look at what the Bible says. Either money or what money can buy is what is always in your thoughts, and the biggest comfort you can have is finding out you have made more money. Your creative ideas are not as important as the wealth they might produce.

Jesus calls it "serving God, or serving mammon," and says you cannot serve two masters. In Luke 16:14 we are told that the Pharisees who were hearing all this were covetous. These men did covet money and *things*, and they didn't like hearing what Jesus said, so they "derided him"—that means, they made fun of Jesus. It made them feel superior, better than Jesus, to make fun of him, and then they could forget what he was saying, and not let it bother them. Jesus said they were "justifying" themselves in front of other men by doing this.

Were the Pharisees ignorant of the Old Testament? No. They had it, and had studied it. And there stood Jesus saying the teaching of the New Testament to them. It was as if right there before their eyes they had the choice of God—the Word of God, and Mammon—wealth. One of you put your Bible on the table there in front of you, or on the grass . . . just there where you can see it. Now a little bit away from it, put some money, or a bank book, or all your bank books and piggy banks and a pile of coins . . . whatever you have that would give you the two opposite things. The question is, which will you *serve*? It isn't that you can't ever *have* any money if you choose to serve God. He can call you to make a great deal of money, if that is his plan for you. But the question is, which are you going to put *first,* which are you going to have as the central thing in your life?

Many centuries before, the Israelites had stood while a man named Joshua had spoken very clearly to them. Their fathers had served false gods for a period of years. Joshua reminded them that the true God had brought them out of Egypt and had done all sorts of miracles to show them that he indeed was God. And Joshua called out, "Choose you this day whom ye will serve; but as for me and my house, we will serve the Lord." And the people said unto Joshua, "The Lord our God will we serve, and unto his voice will we hearken" (Joshua 24:15, 24).

Those Pharisees stood there that day, knowing the Old Testament, and knowing these verses from their study of Joshua. Perhaps they remembered the choice Joshua had given, a choice that God clearly gives through his Word, and although they might not have seen in their imaginations a Bible looking like yours, and a pile of money looking like yours . . . still they would have had something like that in mind. The choice is always there. What will be of first importance?

Jesus went on to say something more, so that people would understand the seriousness of the Bible's teaching, on this and other things. You will find it in verse 17 of Luke 16: "It is easier for heaven and earth to pass away, than for one tittle of the law to fall."

What does that mean? Well, the law Jesus is speaking of is the Bible. Remember that the Pharisees had added their

259

own little laws to the Bible. What Jesus is saying is that their laws don't matter a bit—but that the Bible is more lasting than the earth and heaven. We look up at the sky—blue as blue today (or is it grey with rain, dark with thunder and lightning clouds?). Whether we see the sun or not, it is there, and at night the moon will be somewhere, even if it is behind a cloud. The sky was the same when your grandfather was a little boy, and many, many years before that. The earth has been the same year after year, too. Some farms have been in the same family for generations. Even some trees are hundreds of years old. If you could fly to Palestine, you could walk over the ground Jesus walked on. But we need to realize that Jesus said it is easier for the heaven and earth to pass away (that means for them to vanish like smoke in the air), than for one tiny part of the Bible to fail, even a part as small as a tittle—the dotting of an "i" or the crossing of a "t" in the original as it was given.

Then, in answer to some saucy questions, Jesus went on to give these men some more strong teaching from the Old Testament. In Matthew 19:3 it says that the Pharisees asked, "tempting him," which means that it was not an honest question but just a catch question. They asked what Jesus thought about divorce. When Jesus answered (Matthew 19:4–5), he quoted from way back in the first book of the Bible, Genesis. He said, "Have ye not read, that he which made them from the beginning (that means, *Jesus* said that God made man and woman), made them male and female (and *that* means that God *purposely* made two different sorts of people, male and female, men and women), and said (so Jesus is saying it was *God* who said the next sentence, to that first man and woman he had made), 'For this cause shall a man leave his father and mother, and shall cleave to his wife; and the twain shall become one flesh.'" (So when two people live together physically, they become, in a mysterious way, one.) Jesus said, "So that they are no more twain, but one flesh. What therefore God hath joined together, let not man put asunder." Then in Luke 16:18, Jesus said that God does not mean a man to put away his wife and marry another woman, because this breaks the whole beautiful oneness which God meant to last for a lifetime.

There is not space or time to talk about marriage in this chapter, or even in this book. But there is enough in the Bible that people do *not* know today, to make a whole book on the amazing thing God made people able to have, when he made men and women with the possibility of being one—spiritually one when both are children of the Lord, intellectually one as they share all kinds of things together, both the serious and the fun things of life, physically one as they live together and have children that belong to both of them. This *oneness* helps us to understand how we can be one with the *Lord* when we accept Christ as our Savior. When we are *one* with the Lord, we are *not ever to worship a false god.* That would be like going off with another person who is not your husband or wife, and living with them. Spiritual adultery is a very serious sin. Spiritual adultery is worshiping other gods, trying out Hindu worship, or Buddhist meditation "just for the fun of it." Physical adultery is sinful because our marriages are meant to be a tiny picture of the oneness of God's people with God.

》 You will remember what "absolute" means and what "relative" means; we talked about this earlier. They are two important ideas that we need to understand to help us to be clear, and not mixed up, as we live in the world in this century, two thousand years after Jesus spoke these things, and Luke wrote them for us.

Something that is "an absolute" is something that does not change as the years go on, or as we move from one country to another. Something that is "relative" is something that is changing from year to year, and country to country. Let's look at some examples.

What about length of hair? Men wore long hair in Jesus' time, long hair and beards. In certain parts of the world and at certain times of history, men wore powdered hair or wigs when they dressed up. Men wore short hair at another time of history, and the very daring ones had crew cuts! Then long hair began to be a "far out" thing to do, and crew cuts were called "square" in certain parts of the world. Men wore pig-tails or "queues" in the Far East at one time of history, but now in Singapore if men arrive at the airport with long hair, they have to wait for a barber to come and cut it. (We asked "why" when we saw about thirty-five boys with long hair waiting at the customs desk in Singapore airport!) The answer is that in Singapore it is against the law for men to have hair longer than a certain length. So long-haired boys are not allowed to come in.

Now—is the specific length of men's hair something the Bible teaches to be an absolute? Does the Bible say that there is an exact right and wrong length that must always be the same at every point of history, and in every part of the earth's geography? No. That is just something men make rules about, or have ideas about, that has no real right and wrong con-nected with it. The Bible says men are to be men and not to be like women, but when many men are wearing hair a cer-tain way, or are wearing certain clothes, being a *man* in that country or that period of history means that you wear that type of clothing, and wear that style of hair-do! So these things are not absolute, but relative. If someone teaches that a thing that is relative is absolute, then it mixes up everything, and spoils the Word of God. This, you see, is what the Pharisees were doing. They tried to make their rules absolute.

What about women's clothing? It changes through the years, and it changes from country to country. We were re-cently in Hong Kong. All the young, middle-aged and elderly Chinese women who were *conservative* in their clothing, wore trousers, pants, and the blouses were of the same material, with little high collars and those lovely Chinese cloth buttons. They look so much like the pants suits of the twen-tieth century that you find in other parts of the world. So in Hong Kong it is the people with dresses who look "modern," and not people with the pant suits. Among conservative Chinese you look more like someone dressed properly as a woman, and fitting into the age-old customs, if you wear a pants suit.

Again, is the *kind* of clothing an absolute? No, the Bible teaches women are to be women. There is to be a difference. God made male and female. God puposely made two different kinds of people. But the kind of clothing that is woman's clothing is "relative," it differs from century to century, and from country to country. In India women wear saris, so for each dress they need from five and one-half to seven yards of material to wrap in a certain way. Almost every woman wears a sari, and they are graceful and beautiful, but to be a woman in America you don't have to wear a sari. When people try to make just one type of clothing for women an "absolute," then they get everyone around them mixed up, just as the Pharisees did, and people stop listening and are not prepared to hear what the Bible really does say, or what God sets forth as absolutes.

Now today, you will hear taught in schools and universities, and see in the plays on TV and read in newspapers and magazines, that *there are no absolutes* and that *everything is relative.*

This is because people do not believe that God exists; they do not believe there is true *truth* that does not change. They do not believe there is an absolute. They think *everything* is "relative," and they live that way, write that way, teach that way, make music that way, and try to "feel" that way. It doesn't work out very well, because you see there *is* truth and there *are* absolutes and people get so mixed up inside that the psychiatrists are very busy trying to unmix them. But some of the psychiatrists are mixed up themselves, so they can't do so well. People do not turn out to be happy when they deny God's absolutes and try to live in quite the opposite way from what God teaches to be right and wrong, true and false.

Back to our illustrations. We have had two illustrations of things that really are relative, and I would suggest you think up more. Have a "fashion show" in your family some time and rig up as many varieties as you can of the ways women and men dress in various countries. Get five and a half yards of material and learn to wrap a sari; wear an

263

old-fashioned long dress with ruffles; get a coolie hat for the teen-age boy and pin on a pigtail! Look up old *National Geographic* magazines and talk about the variety there has always been from one part of the world to another in the "relative" things, that are not a question of right and wrong. While you are eating together, discuss things that do change, and that are not right and wrong. Try to make some explorations into ways of eating differently. Is a fork and knife the "right" way to eat? What about trying chopsticks? Buy some and try to learn to use them. Think up other different things that are really "relative," and differ from place to place, and from time to time.

We can find the *absolutes,* the things that God clearly teaches us do not change from place to place or time to time, by studying the Bible. This is why it has been so important all through history to study the Bible, but it is especially important when people are saying and living all kinds of "mixing up" things. The Pharisees were living and saying "mixing up" things right then, and it made them criticize God the Son as he talked to them. They had *added* a lot of little rules, little relative things, and made them *absolute.* And when Jesus taught them things that really *were* absolute, they criticized him.

Today people are saying there are *no* absolutes, and Christians are getting mixed up and thinking right things are wrong, and wrong things are right. Why? Because that teaching is like a thick fog getting in through your windows and doors and filling your house and you don't even know you are breathing the smog in the house! At the same time, other people are taking little rules and making them absolutes, so that everyone becomes even more confused. What can we do about it? We can read the Bible, discuss, think, and ask God to help us really to sort things out. Then, day by day, we can ask for help to live with a balanced understanding of what is an absolute and must not change, and what is relative.

Adultery is always wrong. The two kinds of adultery are always wrong. It is an *absolute* that you are to worship only the true and living God, and you are not to follow false teaching about God, or try out other religions or fool around with idols in your house, or take lightly *joking* about such things. This would be spiritual adultery. Physical adultery is sleeping with someone who is not the person with whom you are *one* for a lifetime. God has made marriage to be a very special and wonderful relationship. Is it ever perfect? *No*, because sin has spoiled everything, and nothing is perfect now. But—even though your home, your family, your relationship as sisters and brothers is not perfect, you can ask God to help you day by day to make it closer to what it could have been if sin had not spoiled everything. Learning to put the Lord *first,* and other people *second* and self last (which is one of the *absolutes* we have already studied) is one way of "losing" your life, and discovering you are "finding" it! God's "backwards rules" (backwards to the way people usually live) are rules that will bring you what you are really looking for as well as being absolute. Because, you see, *he really did make people to be people,* and he knows what will fulfil them, and make them have what they really *need*. He *knows* children need a Mother and Dad to whom they really belong, and who together care more about God than about anybody, and more about each other and the children than about themselves. He knows people need him as their Father to love with all their hearts and minds and souls, and need to be fulfilled by loving their neighbors, as well as obeying these laws as *absolute*. If it hadn't been for sin, it would have been just like that naturally!

Jesus stood there in front of those Pharisees and told them another story to emphasize the point strongly that they would *not* believe *him*, or anyone, about what is *true* and *absolute*.

He told them about a rich man who had wonderful food, magnificent clothing, and lived in a large home with a gate at the entrance of his property. All through the rich man's life, a beggar had been lying at his gate, and all *he* had to eat were "crumbs" from the rich man's leftovers. The beggar was full of diseased sores, and all the help he had was from a dog who licked the sores. Then both the rich man and the beggar died, and went to the place where people used to have to wait. It was called Hades. Now that Jesus has died to open the door to heaven, it is different for believers, for children of the Lord.

Jesus said the rich man was in the part where the unbelievers are, those who had not become children of the Lord, and the beggar was where the believers are, which Jesus called at that time, "Abraham's bosom." The rich man asked if he could come over to the better place, but Abraham told him he had had all his good things in the other life, and that now the beggar had come to where he was being comforted for the sad life he had had. Then the rich man said, "Please send the beggar back to the world again just long enough to go to my brothers' houses! I have five brothers and I want him to go and tell them what it is like if you live the life I lived!" (How had he lived? Well, we know that he had not been born into God's family; he had lived for himself; he hadn't taken care of the beggar at his gate, let alone all the other people he should have had compassion for . . . and now he wants to warn his brothers.) But Abraham said, "No. No, that would do no good at all. If your brothers do not listen to Moses (that is to all Moses wrote in the Old Testament which would teach them true truth, and would teach them to know the difference between men's rules and absolutes) . . . and if they have not listened to the other Old Testament prophets, then they won't ever listen to a man coming back to them after he has died." Now this beggar's name was Lazarus.

Do you know another Lazarus? In John 11, we have the history which John writes for us of what happened in a family who were very close to Jesus. Jesus often visited in the home of Mary and Martha and their brother Lazarus. One time Lazarus was very ill, and Mary and Martha begged Jesus to come and heal him . . . but he didn't go until Lazarus had died. The sisters were heartbroken over the death of their brother, and were weeping, as you can imagine. Jesus had made it clear to Martha that one day he would raise from the dead everyone who believed in him. He said, "I am the resurrection, and the life: he that believeth on me, though he die, yet shall he live: and whosoever liveth and believeth on me shall never die." What does he mean? Every believer will one day be raised from the dead, and there will be one generation of people who will be living when Jesus comes back, who will never have to die, but will be changed, immediately, just like that!

Now when Jesus went to the grave of Lazarus, with Mary and Martha, he wept, too. He wept with compassion for Martha and Mary, and because he loved Lazarus too, but he wept also with anger at the enemy Satan, who had brought death in the first place. Jesus is God, and he was angry at the abnormality that resulted because Satan and men turned away from God. Although he is God he was angry at the abnormality without being angry at himself. And you may be sure Jesus looked forward to the day when the last enemy, death, would be destroyed for ever. There will be a day when no one will die again! Death will be vanquished. That means that the war between God and Satan, between life and death, will be won.

Why are we telling this history John wrote about? Because Jesus had told those Pharisees so very clearly in Luke 16 that even if a man came back from the dead, they would not believe him, so that it would be no use for the beggar Lazarus to be allowed to come back to tell the rich man's brothers. And now Jesus says, "Lazarus, come forth." Remember that Martha had already said before they rolled the stone away from the door of the grave (like a cave), "He's been dead for four days; there will be a terrible odor!" You see, it was a hot country, and there was no embalming, of course. Dead four days, wrapped round and round with yards of cloth in what were then called "graveclothes." And up he got—graveclothes and all. Even his face was tied up with a cloth around it. What a sight! A walking corpse! People must have let out little screams, or maybe there was a deathly silence, because they were afraid. "Take those things off him, loosen the cloth, untie his face. . . . " That was what was needed, so he could move and see properly, and so that they could all see him. Yes, Lazarus, who had been dead for four days, had come back from the place of the dead.

What was the result? Did everybody then believe in Jesus as the Son of God? Was everybody then ready to be born again? No. Some believed, and others went running off to the Pharisees to discuss the whole affair. "What are we going to do?" the Pharisees and scribes and chief priests said, as they held a council meeting. "This man is doing too many miracles. If we don't do something about it everyone is going to believe on him, and we'll lose our places" (John 11:47, 48). It is really hard to believe that this council thought about what they could do to him, but they did. And instead of stopping to think whether they might be turning away from *truth* or not, instead of stopping to consider whether they might be being given a warning . . . they did not believe, but made a plan to kill Lazarus again. Can you imagine that? Can you imagine such a desire? You see, many people came to see Lazarus because they were curious, and they heard Jesus teaching. The Pharisees and priests thought the way to stop that would be to kill Lazarus.

So . . . although it was a *different* Lazarus, Abraham was very right. If people would not listen to God's prophets, or to the Word of God, the whole Bible, or if they would not listen to Jesus, then if someone came back from the dead, it would make no difference whatsoever to these people.

» In Luke 17 Jesus went on to tell his disciples to be careful lest they do things that will hinder people, specially little children, from understanding and believing the truth. He said that one thing to be careful about is being forgiving. Are people perfect after they become Christians? No. But should there be a difference? Yes. One of the differences should be that we learn to forgive each other.

Does this sound like anything you have ever heard? "No, I *won't* . . . I *can* have it, if I want to . . ." "Oh! Now you've gone and and pulled it *apart*!" "The wheels are coming off my fire engine! I hate you!" "I'm going to break it

some more . . . see, I'll just *jump* on it." "I don't *want* to play
with you any more . . . yaaaaaa!" And grown-ups behave this
way, too. Is this acting according to the Bible? No. Can you
always be perfect? No. But listen again.

"Give me my engine back." "No, I *won't*! I *can* have it
if I want to." "Now you've pulled it apart! You mean thing! It
is broken now and it was all your fault." "Well, I'm sorry. I
really am sorry. I won't do it again." "Well . . . if you are
sorry then I forgive you. I don't know if it can be mended,
but I forgive you anyway. Come on, let's play something
else." There could be lots of stories like this told about *every*
age group, five-year-olds, ten-year-olds, fifteen-year-olds,
twenty-six-year-olds, sixty-two-year-olds, we all have things
that make us angry or upset or annoyed, or hurt. We all find
that people do things, or say things to us, which we feel were
done on purpose, or carelessly, or because they don't care
about them. Everybody in Jesus' time and before that, *had*
these problems, just as they have now, of feeling, "Now that I
can't forget, I'll never feel the same about that person again."
People are the same. Jesus says, "After you have become my
disciples, you are to learn to forgive . . . even if the same
person does the same thing to you seven times a day, you are
to forgive him or her seven times." Did you ever keep an
account in a notebook as to whether it was more than seven
times in one day that someone did exactly the same thing,
and you forgave them? In another place in the New Testament, Jesus says we are to forgive a person "seventy times
seven"; work out how many times that is and remember it!

As people followed Jesus around listening to him, they
began to realize that following Jesus was not just a matter of
getting healed, and seeing bread suddenly multiplied. It was
not an *easy* teaching he was giving them, and gradually people turned away, unless they had really believed and been
saved.

I want you to get a globe, if you have one in the house,
and put it in front of you. If you don't have a globe, then get
an atlas, or a geography book with a map of the world in it,
or some airline maps. If you cannot find a map at all, then

draw two circles representing the world, and very roughly sketch the continents in those circles. Now you have the "world" in front of you. Now please make two little sets of two people. If you have dolls, take four of them. If you have fuzzy pipe cleaners for making things, make four little people out of the pipe cleaners. At least take a pair of scissors and cut out four small people out of paper. The arms can stick straight out and the legs be straight; it's not hard. Now take a box and put two of your people in a bed, a tiny box, with a tiny cloth (a handkerchief will do) for a blanket. Take a stone, a small stone to fit the size of your people, and a little stick, and prop two people by the stone as if it were a hand-worked grinding stone, to grind wheat.

With all this ready to look at on the table, you are ready to listen and think of what Jesus is now saying. One day when Jesus was talking about the time when he would come back again, he said that the Christians then would be so wishing they could see the day when he would be back in the world, that there would be some saying, "See here; see there he is!" But don't go after anyone who says that, don't follow them. They will not be telling the truth, Jesus warns, because when Jesus comes back again, all the Christians will know at once. They won't need anyone to tell them, "Jesus is here." He won't come first to one and then another. He is not going to come to a tiny village like Bethlehem, or be born as a baby, or just let a few shepherds know. When he comes back again, it will be very different from his first coming. His first coming was to live, and then to die . . . to do all the things we are studying now, to teach and do miracles and show people that he really *was* the Messiah. His second coming will be in *glory*, and it will be to *every* believer at once. All those who are dead will rise at once, if they have believed. All those who are *living* when he comes will be changed and taken up with him at once. It won't be slow, and we won't know a day before, or even an hour before. It will be sudden.

In this chapter of Luke (17:22–37), Jesus tells us a little of what to expect at that time. He said that when he comes back again, it will be as lightning streaking the sky, suddenly bringing light. He warned the people that first he will have to suffer many things and die, and be rejected (that means men will turn away from him) but he said that the day of his return is *absolutely certain.*

He helped the people to understand this by telling them the story of Noah from Old Testament history. He said that in the day of Noah, people were laughing at Noah for saying that a big flood would happen; they had never seen a big flood before, so they didn't believe it. They kept marrying and having babies, and eating and drinking . . . and making fun of Noah! But the day came when he went into the ark, begged them to come with him, and then God shut the door. The flood came and destroyed them all. Jesus said people will behave in the same way before he comes back. They just won't believe it, and won't live any differently.

He also told the story of Lot. In Lot's time people were eating, drinking, buying and selling, planting their gardens and building new buildings, just living their everyday lives in their homes and places of business. They would not listen to warnings; they became more and more wicked and immoral. Back in Lot's time they were living a life based on relativism and did not believe God's absolutes. And one day, God destroyed this city, after telling Lot to leave. Jesus said it will be just like this before he comes back. It will be a time when people will not be worshiping God, and will not be listening. People will laugh at Christians who try to warn them, who try to teach them what the Bible, God's Word, says.

Jesus made it very realistic, very plain, by saying that when the time comes, it will be different times of the day for different people, depending upon where they live in the world. Now look at your map. Can one of you tell the time differences in the different parts of the world? Recently we crossed the "date line" on our way to Japan, and one of us lost half our birthday, because it suddenly became the next day! When it is in the middle of the night in Switzerland, we often get phone calls from someone in America who forgets there is a difference! It's not so nice to have to get up to answer the phone at three o'clock in the morning!

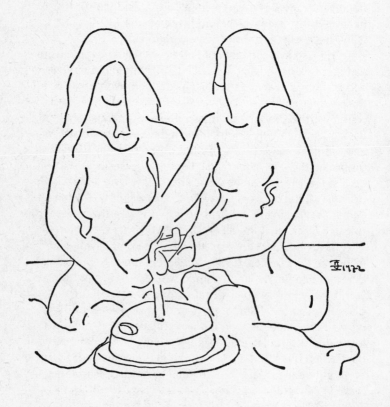

Jesus is accounting for the time difference around the world when he says, "I tell you in that night there shall be two in one bed: the one shall be taken, and the other shall be left. Two women shall be grinding together; the one shall be taken and the other left." You see, it will be the very same minute that each one will be caught up to be with him, changed in the twinkling of an eye, but in different parts of the world that minute will be a different time on the clocks, just like the clocks you see at an airport which give you the time in different countries. Jesus was speaking at a period of history when people did not have phone calls from half way round the world at the wrong hour, but he is making it plain to everyone at every moment of history that his coming back will be at a real time, it will take place in real history, but the sun will be shining for some people, and the moon for others . . . as they, as we, are caught up with him.

Why one taken and the other left behind? That is just to remind us that only believers will be taken. It *matters* whether this is true or not. It is important for us to make the truth known, and to pray for our families, our friends, the people we know, other people we don't know in our towns, and to pray for the people in places we are especially concerned about round the world. We mustn't just pray for "everyone" without it being real to us, but we must *care* and not forget to pray for the people we come to feel real compassion for.

Are you going to go? Will your family go together? It isn't necessary for anyone to be left in the bed, or in a field, *if* both in the bed, both in a field, and both grinding at the mill, are Christians, are believers.

Two women grinding together.   Luke 17:35

20
CLAP FOR GOD!

Remember we said before that there is so much to learn
about prayer that it would take a whole book to talk about
even the first things? As Jesus spoke week after week, month
after month, he taught things that have to be fitted together.
Just reading or knowing one part of what he said about
something isn't enough. To have real understanding you need
to put it together. Now in Luke 18, Jesus told a few more
things about prayer, which need to be put together with what
we have already studied. One of the many ways in which the
Bible is different from every other book is that you never
finish finding new and wonderful things that you didn't "see"
before. That is because it is really God's Word. No one but
God could give a book that keeps on being fresh and exciting
year after year. We often think of it as fresh baked bread,
warm and fragrant, smelling so good, hot out of the oven.
The Bible is our "bread," our food day by day. In one place
we are told that when we are baby Christians we are to have
the "milk" of God's Word, and also that there is "strong
meat" in God's Word. The Bible has something for every age
of person, and for every age of a person's Christian life.

Do you have a baby in your family? Put the baby's bottle
of milk on the table, or if you don't have a baby, put a glass
of milk on the table. Now next to it put a loaf of bread, a
piece of meat, or some other food a baby could not chew or
digest. Here we are, all studying the Bible together. There is
milk, bread, meat and strong food, for people who have been
Christians a little while and are like babies, for Christians who
are growing, and for people who are what we call mature
Christians. The wonderful thing is that as we listen, read,
think, and talk together, there really is something for *each* of

274

us. Whatever our age, there is something we can understand that we didn't understand before. No matter how many times a person has read the Bible, there are always fresh exciting things to learn as years go by. Part of the freshness comes from suddenly seeing how one verse fits together with another one in a way you didn't see before.

Another interesting thing is that a ten-year-old boy, who has accepted Christ as his Savior and has the help of the Holy Spirit can, if he reads and studies his Bible and talks to the Lord every day, grow faster and be an older Christian sooner than a forty-year-old person who never reads his Bible and who thinks that, because he accepted Christ as his Savior twenty years ago he is perfectly all right. It's quite amazing, but it is *possible* to grow faster spiritually than you do physically.

Also, a young person who is a Christian and *believes* the Bible, and knows God's Word, can be far wiser about what the universe really is, and about what a *person* really is, than a professor who has six Ph.D.'s and does *not* believe God exists and has no satisfactory explanation of where man's personality (love, communication, thinking, acting, feeling, having ideas, making choices, creating) came from. So as you sit and look at the milk, bread and meat, or other heavier food, remember that the people who can *digest* the food God puts in his Word, are not always divided up in the way you would divide them if you were dishing out a physical meal! God's way of judging wisdom and understanding is very different. He says in Proverbs 9:10, "The fear of the Lord is the *beginning* of wisdom." That means that recognizing the Lord as God, feeling awe and admiration for him, having some idea of his greatness and having a respect for him, is the beginning of wisdom. If people say there is no God . . . they are not yet at the *beginning* of really getting things put together!

What we are putting together here is some more understanding about prayer. Jesus told a parable to illustrate that men ought always to pray, and not to "faint" as it says in the King James (Authorized) version of the Bible. It means not to "feel it is no use," or to get so discouraged you stop praying.

But we like the word "faint" because at times many of us
feel all headachy or backachy, tired and exhausted, and our
thoughts and feelings are all full of aches and tiredness, too,
and it seems that we would almost *rather* just "faint away"
than go on praying for something that we've prayed for without an answer for months and even years! So when we read
this it seems to be saying "Keep on" to us when we feel like
that. Jesus is saying, "Keep on," to each of us, whatever our
age, wherever we are.

The story is of a widow woman who had an enemy who
had done something really wrong to her. Maybe the boy next
door has poisoned her lettuces, maybe a man had charged
her too much rent, maybe someone had made her pay for a
broken window she didn't break. Have you ever had a neighbor who was mean to you? Have you had a neighbor who
blamed you for things you didn't do? Sometimes neighbors
yell at children because they are playing ball or laughing and
having a good time! Well, this woman had someone who had
been mean to her in a really unfair way, and she needed a
judge to make this person do the right thing. Now the judge
she went to was not a sympathetic man. He really couldn't
care less about people, or about God. He didn't care about
making a wrong thing right; Jesus calls him the unjust judge.
He was the sort that would have backed up the mean enemy
just as easily as the widow woman. But, says Jesus, the
woman bothered the judge, and he said, "I'll fix up this thing
for her, I'll right the wrong against her, just so that she will
stop annoying me. Otherwise she really could become a nui-
sance and make my life miserable."

Now Jesus says, "Do you think that if an *unjust* judge,
who doesn't care about right and wrong, will help right a
wrong for such a woman just to get rid of her (you see, his
motive was wrong although he was going to do a right thing)
. . . that you can depend on the perfectly *just* God to answer
the prayers of his own children who cry to him day and night
about things that are *their* problems, about wrongs that are
being done to *them?*" Then Jesus answers his own question.
"Yes," says Jesus, "I tell you, God will answer and right the

276

wrong thing." Think back a minute. What was this parable meant to illustrate? It was to illustrate *why* we should go on praying and not be discouraged. Would you be discouraged if your prayer was always answered in a day, or in a week? No. So this story is being told to help you to keep on for a very long time. Sometimes we must wait a long while for a prayer to be answered. Why? Well, there can be lots of reasons.

One reason is this. *We have only a short time to trust God.* When Jesus comes back, or when we die and go to heaven, our time to trust God without having prayer answered right away, will be over. Our time to *trust* and *love* God even when things are difficult, even when things are going wrong, will then be over. There will be *no more fainting,* no more tiredness, no more pain, no more disappointment, no more crying, no more frustration, no more sadness, no more struggle, no more fighting, no more hurt feelings, no more feeling that no one understands us, no more loneliness, no more fears. We will be perfectly happy, perfectly fulfilled, perfectly supplied with all needs, when we have our new bodies and are never again tempted by Satan and never more in the presence of sin. Marvelous? Yes, it is marvelous, but right now our special thing is to *trust* God, and *love him,* and *believe* what he tells us, even when things are *not* easy, and when we do not see the next step, and when doors are shut in our faces, and when it is hard to pray. We can show God the reality of our love for him, we can let him know it is *real* while we are still in this life and it is hard to do this. When all the hard things are taken away, that thing, that chance to show God how we feel about him is over. *Now* is the time to make it real to *him,* and to bring you to *him.*

Think for a moment of how great God is. How wonderful it is that he has done all these things for us, and promises us that he will hear us when we call to him, and right the wrongs for us as we ask him to. Now, let's *do* something together. In Psalm 47:1, it says, "O clap your hands, all ye people; shout unto God with the voice of triumph." I want you really to clap your hands right now. What do we clap for? When we hear a piece of music we enjoy, we clap . . . it is a way of saying, "Thank you." The writer of this Psalm says, "O clap your hands, all ye peoples" . . . and it is clapping for God. God is pleased with our feeling of thankfulness, and he is pleased when we express it. Let's clap to tell him how much we love him, trust him and how thankful we are we have such a just judge in all the matters that bother us, and that we can take everything to him.

In Psalm 48:11, we are told to be glad, to rejoice because of God's judgments. We would suffer if God judged us and punished us for our wrong doing. But he has sent Jesus to take that punishment, and we can be glad and rejoice that we don't have to sit around judging other people even when they are mean to us. If we pray and cry out to God, he will help. The people harming us might become Christians and then be sorry and be our friends, or they might move to another place. But God is a *just* judge, and he can answer after long years of prayer . . . about all kinds of things we are praying about. Meantime we are to keep on, and not get discouraged in praying, and give him our trust, with clapping of hands! Clap for him when things are hard, being thankful you have him to go to, and clap for him when you have an answer to prayer. *Show* your thankfulness, and don't be embarrassed!

In Psalm 48:14, we read of another thing we can clap about: "For this God is our God for ever and ever: he will be our guide even unto death." He won't stop leading us and guiding us. As we climb with a mountain guide, we may not understand the path he takes, the rocks he chooses, the times he goes a long way around. But we trust the guide to know the mountain. God is our guide. At times we *think* his answer to prayer is taking us to a certain house, or a certain city or country, but it has only been a "stepping stone" across a rushing stream, or it has been a "long way around" to miss a sharp precipice. *He* knows why he had to take us a long way around to get to the place he was taking us, and his *reasons* are good, his reasons are perfect reasons.

Once in L'Abri we prayed ten years for a house, Chalet les Sapins, before the Lord opened up the way for us to have it. Ten years is a long time, and the things that happened in that ten years with Les Sapins, seemed a very "long way around" indeed. The person God used to buy that chalet for L'Abri was half the world away from us when we started to pray. People bought the chalet, lived in it ten years and died, before it came to us.

But another time we prayed for four years for the putting up of a new building. God seemed to be leading in giving the land, and certain amounts of money, and in an architect's plans . . . and then it all became impossible, and we were not only in danger of losing all the money paid to the architect, but forty people were going to have to leave L'Abri if we did not have more space. What happened? We had three days of prayer, crying out to the Lord. Did he give us the new building? No. His answer was clearly "no" and the money *was* paid to the architect, a lot of it, just to fold up the plans and not use them. A *waste?* No, God knows what he is doing, and he knows *why* we have to walk through all that long, long mountain path which seemed to lead to no other place than you could get to by taking a very short cut. Why not, O Father, take us by the short cuts? Because he knows the need we have to learn what it means to *trust him* and to trust his plans, and he knows how important it is for us to win a battle against Satan. Satan is trying to say . . . "Yah! See, your God doesn't answer you!" and make us stop trusting our Heavenly Father. If we keep trusting, Satan is defeated, he loses his fight in that particular thing against God.

What happened about the new building after the plans had to be folded up, and we had three days of prayer? It is a long, wonderful story, but to make it short . . . it never has been built, but the Lord showed us a very old chalet about twenty minutes' walk up the mountain, which we now know was his plan all along. It isn't new, it isn't efficient, it isn't what we pictured, but it took care of the need *then* so quickly that within a short time it had become Udo and Debby's home, and was full of students who otherwise would have been sent away. And more than that, two wandering people who were seeking an answer to life were knocking at *that* door within a week of Udo and Debby moving in. Suppose it had been a hotel still? These two people, coming at separate times, had never heard of L'Abri. They just knocked at that door because they were in trouble and saw that door from the sidewalk. Who put Udo and Debby on the other side of that door *just* in time to help someone from California one day, and someone from Chile another day? God, who had brought Udo and Debby and all of us in our decisions "a long way around the mountainside" to the older chalet, Gentiana . . . and who had also brought these two wandering ones a "long way around" in their wanderings to hear truth and to be born into his family.

Yes, even though it seems sometimes that we are going to faint because prayer does *not* seem to be answered, we need to remember to keep on, as Jesus said we were to do, and we need to remember to *clap* because we love and trust God our Father and want him to know it *before* we see where the path round the backway is leading to! He is the only Guide who knows everything.

» Remember that in our last chapter we said the world would not be getting better, but worse, before Jesus comes back again. We spoke about the "salt" (Christians) often not being as salty as they should be. Right after telling us how we should keep on praying, Jesus says (in Luke 18:8) that when he (you see, the Son of Man is another name for Jesus) comes back, there will not be many who will *truly* be believing and having real faith in him. It doesn't mean there will be *no* believers, but that many will be as we know many are today . . . many will think they are too intelligent to believe God's Word. You see, God has said, "The fool has said in his heart, there is no God!" And many men say just the opposite, "How foolish, how unintelligent, how dumb people are who believe the Bible to be true!" God says that the fear of him is the beginning of wisdom, and so many men say that no wise man believes that God is a truly personal God, who created the universe.

Remember that just as the *first* coming of Christ as a baby, came *exactly* in detail as it had been prophesied in the Bible, so Christ's *second* coming is going to be as it has been prophesied, and then it will be like the day of Noah's closing of the door of the ark. It will be too late for people suddenly to change their minds.

Jesus told another parable after this, to show another important thing to remember about prayer. He spoke about a Pharisee and a publican going up to the Temple to pray. We have talked earlier about what the Pharisees were like; now we hear the kind of prayer one made. "God, I thank thee that I am not as other men are, thieves who take too much money from people, unjust, adulterers, or even like that publican over there who gathers too much tax money, and cheats people. I fast twice every week, I give a tenth of all I have" (Luke 18:11). No wonder Jesus said about this Pharisee that he was really talking to himself (see verse 11). This wasn't prayer. This wasn't talking to God. This was bragging about how good he was, and making himself feel even prouder as he went on listing the things he thought proved he was just about perfect!

Now *no* one is good enough to come to God because of his *own* goodness. The reason we are able to step right into the presence of the living God, the Creator of the whole Universe, the perfectly holy God, is that we come in Jesus' name, we come because Jesus died for our sins, and because we have accepted what he has done for us. We come asking forgiveness, and being thankful for that forgiveness, because we know that otherwise we would not be able to be there in the same room with God.

But the publican, one of the despised tax-gatherers, knew he was a sinner. He stood apart from the other man, and with his head bowed, hit himself upon the chest. He didn't do this to show off, but because he really felt so strongly that he was a sinful man. And he said to God, "God be merciful to me, a sinner." People have to realize they need God's mercy because they are sinners. This man, as a Jew,

could connect his asking for mercy with some understanding of the Old Testament basis of mercy, as the lamb was brought by the priest.

But today we can come to God understanding that Jesus is the only one we need—he is the Lamb, and he is the High Priest. In Hebrews 4:14 and 16, we are told that since Jesus is our High Priest and he is always there in Heaven, we can come boldly to the throne of grace and obtain mercy and find grace to help in time of need. This is a tremendous promise. We don't need to be afraid that we can never be good enough to come to God the Father. We can come through Jesus and be sure of mercy, because Jesus himself was the Lamb, and did what was necessary for us.

After Jesus had told these two new parables to help his disciples understand prayer, some people came walking over toward him, carrying babies in their arms; no doubt also some little toddlers were clinging to their mothers' skirts. In Mark 10:13-16 we can find a little bit more about this than Luke tells us. Mark says that the disciples scolded the mothers and fathers and tried to stop them from coming. When Jesus saw what was happening he was very displeased: he was moved with indignation, and was really very much against the reaction of the disciples. He said, "Suffer the little children to come unto me; forbid them not: for of such is the kingdom of God. Verily I say unto you, Whosoever shall not receive the kingdom of God as a little child, he shall in no wise enter therein."

After saying that, Jesus took the babies and the little children up into his arms and put his hands on them and blessed them. We are told that the literal way of translating this would be to say, "Jesus, folding them in his arms, was blessing, putting hands upon them." To the Jews who were accustomed to a father giving the kind of blessing Isaac gave, it would have looked like a father blessing his own children. Can't you just imagine how gentle and loving Jesus was to those little children and babies, after he had scolded the

The Pharisee and the publican.   Luke 18:9–13

283

disciples, and how he wanted them to be sure of his love and accepted them right into his arms. The disciples' scolding voices must have frightened the children, but Jesus I am sure took all that fear away. Isn't it great comfort that Jesus accepted them and said, "Of such is the kingdom of heaven." Jesus was making it clear that he came to die for little children and babies, and that they were not to be shoved away like that.

Again Jesus is teaching that men are just *backwards* in their reactions. People think children must grow up to be clever enough, to be educated enough, to understand complicated things before they can be born into the family of God, or before they can be accepted into the church. Jesus says it is the other way around. Adults need to believe and accept completely, and without complicated objections and proud formulas, the Bible, the Word of God, the truth, as God has given it. In other words, adults must become as little children when it comes to the moment of being "born" into the family of God. No one is born in a more proud way than another. The birth of a baby into God's family is through understanding that Jesus, God's Son, has taken our place, has taken our punishment, and with some amount of understanding of this, accepting what he has done, bowing, as the publican bowed, without pride. Yes, Jesus said, a little child can come in the right way.

When Jesus went out into the road again, a young man came running to meet him. His colorful clothes must have blown out about him as he ran. As a rich young ruler he probably had beautiful robes, and he must have been a very handsome fellow, with a look of eagerness on his face. He would have been eager because he had a question, and he expected an answer which he could then act upon. Mark says he not only ran up to Jesus but then knelt before him saying, "Good Master, what shall I do that I may inherit eternal life?" The first thing that Jesus said to him was, "Why do you call me good? There is no one good except one, and that one is God." He wanted the young man to realize that only God is good, that Jesus is God, and that the young man himself was a sinner. You see, Jesus can do more than hear the *words* of a person's question; he knows what the person is thinking, and he knew that young man thought of himself as good. As the young man asked what he could do to have eternal life, Jesus could tell that he thought he was capable of doing whatever it was that was needed.

Then Jesus listed some of the commandments, such as "Do not commit adultery, Do not kill, Do not steal, Do not bear false witness (tell lies), Defraud not (don't cheat people), Honor your father and your mother." Well, the young man said he had done all these things since he had been very young. Of course, we know that no one can keep the ten commandments perfectly, but this young man thought that he had. As Jesus looked at him, we are told he really loved him. Mark especially speaks of Jesus' love for the young man, and we can just imagine the loving voice with which Jesus said, "You lack one thing; go now and sell everything you have, give to the poor, and you will have treasure in heaven. Come and follow me." The young man became very sad when Jesus said this, because he had so very much; he was very wealthy. Mark says, "He went away grieved because he had *great* possessions."

Amazing, isn't it? Yet it is so very true for every human being. It is even easier for a person who is a Christian to give everything to the Lord, when that person does not have very much in the way of money and material possessions. So often the more money a person has, the less he gives. Why? Because it is harder to give proportionately when a person has much, than when he has little. It is just the way human beings are. Possessions get such a hold on us that they make it hard for us to keep a balance.

» Way back in Genesis, Abraham gave a tenth of all his possessions to God, and that amount was considered in the Old Testament as the minimum proportion for a believer to give to the Lord. What is a tithe? I want you to get ten oranges, twenty apples, fifty walnuts, or ten potatoes, twenty carrots, fifty radishes, or ten tomatoes, twenty lemons, fifty

onions, or ten bananas, twenty tangerines, fifty turnips . . .
whatever you have in the house that you can put on your
table right now. Now get some pennies, or some paper
money, ten or twenty or thirty pieces of each kind of coin.
And—if you can—get ten tins of soup, or packages of rice,
macaroni . . . or whatever packaged food you have in the
cupboard with ten of the same kind.

So we have a variety of things in front of us on the
table. Put it all over on one side, and have the other side of
the table empty. Now . . . of the ten oranges, take one and
put it over on the empty side of the table. This is the Lord's
pile. Put a little card that one of you will make right now
saying, "the tithe for the Lord," on that side of the table. Now
where you have twenty carrots, or apples or whatever, take
two out of the twenty, and put in the Lord's tithe. If you have
fifty walnuts, or onions or turnips, or fifty of something else,
put five in the Lord's pile. Keep on with everything you have
put on the table. Put one-tenth, one out of every ten, of each
thing, and one out of ten pieces of money.

Now sit there and look at the two piles. Think of a few
things together. First, think how much there is for you, when
you give one out of ten to the Lord. You have nine left . . .
plus the promise of the Lord that the one you gave to him is
now a treasure in heaven! Secondly, think of *all* the people
who have been the Lord's children from Abraham's time
down to our own, and think especially of all the Lord's children from the time Jesus was living on earth down to our
own. If every single person had given one out of ten of
everything they had to the Lord, a lot of things would have
been different. A lot of poor people would have had more to
eat.

Then if you think of the disciples going out two by two
to tell people about the *truth*, about the true and living God,
and how to come to him, please do this arithmetic problem.
If everyone gave one-tenth to the Lord, how many people
would it take to give one person the one full average salary?
Well, it would only take nine people to take full care of one
person. So the number of "candles" that would be lit all over

the world would increase, if the Lord's children were taking care of sending "candles" or "beans" or whatever you used when we put the two by two going out in that earlier chapter. Think of another thing, however, that if the treasure in heaven is the pile on the side marked "the Lord's tithe," the treasure on earth is still nine times as much. So, even when we give one-tenth to the Lord, we are taking less to heaven with us than we have spent on earth.

How do you give to the Lord? The first thing to do is to separate your money or your apples or whatever into different piles. Put a tenth aside in a box, or a little piggy bank, or a bank account, and tell the Lord that it is his. If you made those "bags that wax not old," you have been putting money in a separate place for some weeks now. Then pray, asking the Lord what *he* would have you do with it, asking for guidance as to where to give it. You could give it to buy a Bible for someone who hasn't one, or you could use it to buy shoes for someone. You could use it to provide food or clothing for someone, or you could use it to help pay rent for a room for discussions about Christianity and Bible studies. You could use it to help people who are teaching or preaching the Bible to others, or you could use it to help people who have lost their homes in a flood. The good Samaritan took care of a man who had been beaten and robbed. Jesus told the rich young ruler to give his money to the poor.

It is really truly separating an amount of money that is not going to be for yourself, and praying that God will help you know what to do with it, that is the first step in following his clear teaching to lay up treasures in heaven and not on the earth. If all the Lord's children would really do what he teaches in the Bible, people would only have to *pray* about money and not have to ask for it in churches. People ought to be praying that the Lord would show them what to do with what they have put aside, to be put in heaven!

After that rich young ruler walked away so sadly because he had too much to give away all of it, Jesus looked around at his disciples and said, "How very hard it is for rich people to enter into the kingdom of God!" It is really a difficult thing

287

for a rich person to be free to make the decision to put the Lord first. Remember our study about serving God or Mammon, God or wealth, God or riches? Money is a strange thing. The more a person has, the more it shifts over into the center.

Try taking a pile of beans, or walnuts, or peas, or stones . . . whatever you have a lot of, two or three hundred. Now put ten on the table. Take one and put it aside, then add ten more, put one aside . . . Keep doing this, but after a while only take one out of twenty, then one out of thirty . . . and as you get the whole three hundred or so dried beans there, shift the pile to the center instead of on one side. It may not picture it to you, but try hard to realize that, after a while, it is the *pile* that becomes interesting in itself. A person can only sleep in one bed at a time, eat one meal at a time, read one book at a time, be in one place at a time . . . and life can only take seventy-five or a hundred years to be finished, at the most . . . but the "pile" becomes like a kind of hypnotism, it fascinates a person, and it is almost like getting your fingers in sticky glue and trying to pick up peanuts and drop them. They won't drop off!

The disciples looked astonished when Jesus finished explaining how difficult it was for a rich man to be a follower of his, to be born into the family of God. So Jesus said it a bit differently: "It is hard for them that trust in riches to enter into the kingdom of God." You see, you cannot trust in God, and in riches at the same time. People as they get older and richer trust to their riches for more and more things. If you trust in riches to provide you with food, clothing, a house, cars, trips by air, vacations, sports, toys, money for dentists' bills, expenses for all of your children, there is less to trust God about.

When someone has a large bank balance and sufficient investments, it is more difficult for him or her to feel the reality of having a Heavenly Father who provides. But someone who hasn't "riches" needs to ask God for money as a part of guidance when he or she wants to know whether to buy a house, or go on a journey, or go to medical school. It is very hard to know you are trusting God unless there is a very real place or portion of your life where you can understand that you are completely dependent on God. Riches make people independent of other people, and all too often they make people independent of God. Remember the "weeds" we thought about earlier, weeds that choke the plants, weeds that make it hard to have a fruitful Christian life? They were the "cares" of this world (being too poor, having dreadful troubles) on one side, and the riches on the other. Both are dangerous. Both hinder people from coming to the Lord, or from growing as Christians. Jesus says riches are the hardest problem of all.

Do you have a needle in the house? Do go and get a needle. One with a big, long eye like a carpet needle would be good. Pass it around and look at the eye of the needle. Jesus says, "It is easier for a camel to go through the needle's eye than for a rich man to enter into the kingdom of God"! Some people say Jesus meant a low gate that was called the Needle's Eye, but there is no reason to think he meant anything less impossible than going through the needle you are passing around. A camel could not go through a needle's eye. Then the disciples were "astonished out of measure" . . . which means they were so absolutely flabbergasted that you could not measure their surprise! And they began to say among themselves, "Who then can be saved?" And Jesus looked at them and answered that question by saying, "With men it is impossible but not with God: for *with God all things are possible.*" Jesus said that *God is able to perform the great miracle of all miracles and that is the change of the human heart* . . . God is able to open eyes spiritually blind and to remove the sticky glue from people's fingers, and make it possible for some rich people really to put him first.

Then (because Peter had just watched the rich young man leave to go back to his houses and lovely *things* rather than to follow Jesus) Peter began to say, "Lord *we* have left all and have followed you." And Jesus said, "Verily, I say unto you, there is no man that hath left house, or brethren, or sisters, or father, or mother, or wife, or children, or lands for my sake and the gospel's, but that he shall receive an hundredfold now in this time, houses, and brethren and sisters, and mothers and children and lands, with persecution; and in the world to come, eternal life." The promise is that God does *not* let his children suffer loss . . . he will give back to you *in this life* (although there will be persecutions and hardships) all you willingly give over to *him*, with trust *in him* . . . and then there are the eternal things *too.*

Then Jesus says another "backwards" thing, which is upside down from a human viewpoint. "Many that are first shall be last, and the last first." Poor, sad, young rich ruler . . . a ruler, rich in this world . . . who turned his face away from the Lord, and gave up eternal treasures and joys to put his "things" and money first! Poor man who ended up with only sadness in this life, too, because he had so much!

21
TAKE OFF YOUR SCARVES

What is it like to be blind? Perhaps you know someone who is blind—maybe someone in your own family—so that blindness is not a strange thought to you but something you have understood for a long time. There are two basic kinds of blindness: physical blindness, when for some reason your eyes cannot see; and spiritual blindness, which means you are unable to understand about God and the universe and are "blind" to truth. Of course, people also speak of someone being "blind" to another person's faults when they are in love, or of parents being "blind" to their children's actions when they don't know what their children are doing or thinking. We use the word in a number of different ways to express the fact that people are *not* seeing things as *they really are.* "She is *so* blind as to how she irritates people," someone may say.

Do you have some black cloth, a navy blue, black or brown scarf, a dark square handkerchief, something that can be folded in a bias fold to tie around a person's head? Get enough for the whole family, one apiece, except for the person who is reading this. If the cloth is not long enough to tie into a knot, you'll have to get some safety pins to pin them. Now while everyone else is getting fixed up with cloth folded and tied over their eyes so that they cannot see, you (the person reading this book) think of something in the house that no one has seen. Do you have any new book, a new tin of biscuits or chocolates, a new vase, a new dress, a new plant, a new broom or a dust brush no one has seen yet? If not, just get something and don't tell anyone what it is, a rock or a box of salt—anything!

Of course the person who is going to read the book can

help the others to get fixed up so that they cannot see, and help each one to find a spot to sit. Then that one can go and get the thing he or she thought of—preferably something that people have never seen before. Put that thing on the table, or somewhere in the room. Now, first, everyone think for a minute what it would be like always to be in the dark in this way, even when the sun is shining and the sea is splashing against rocks with the spray catching the light. You could hear the sound of the waves, but you couldn't see the sea. You could imagine it, if you had seen it before, but if you had always been blind, you would imagine something quite different perhaps.

Think of a few things it would be hard to have any idea of if you were blind. Perhaps you can remember seeing something for the first time. We remember some boys from Malaysia seeing *snow* for the first time in their lives. They had always lived where it was hot, and where there were flowers all year long. For them to see snow, all white and fluffy falling from the sky, to feel the cold in it, to make it into balls and throw it, to get a sledge (a sled in America) and slide down a hill because it was slippery under them, to see the amazing sight when it stopped snowing and the sun came out and made it look like a million diamonds scattered over everything, was all a fantastic, exciting surprise to them. No one can perfectly imagine snow if they have never seen it. No one can imagine the *quietness* in deep woods when snow is falling and so silently covering everything with whiteness, and muffling the sounds—if they have only experienced rain pattering down with a noise! The silence of snow is very hard to describe so that someone can imagine it. To hear silence, and not to see the snow "making the silence" would be very difficult for the blind.

As you sit there blinded with the cloth over your eyes, try to think of things you know by sight, which it would be hard to describe to a blind person who *always* had to be in the dark, as you are now. How would you describe a London street, a subway train coming into the station, a field of flowers in Sussex, the soft, rolling hills and trees somewhere in Hampshire, people living on junks in Hong Kong harbors, houses up on stilts in Malaysia, a rock cave temple in India, a village in the Alps, a small midwestern American town, a farm in rural France compared with a huge dairy farm in Michigan in the United States! How would you describe a butterfly, a giraffe, a cow, a tiny mouse, an elephant, a parrot and a sparrow, a swan with the light brown babies swimming behind her and the duck some distance away, the difference between sunrise and sunset? Think of things in the room you cannot see now, and how you could describe them to a blind person.

Now, one at a time, try to walk around the room. Is it easy to walk without seeing? Do you feel a little out of balance? Think for a minute how it would be to walk along a *path* you could not see. Now let someone *lead* you. (Now the person reading should stop and try to describe the thing he or she brought into the room, *without* saying *what* it is. Something like this, "It is round, it is hard, it can be eaten. . . . " or "It is soft, it is six feet long, it is blue. . . . " After just a little description, the person who is reading can go around to everyone else with a pad and pencil, and get them to write down their guess, as to what the thing is. Or whisper their guess to the person who can see, so that she or he can write them down. Now put that paper aside for a while, and keep the cloth on your eyes, while the next bit is read. We'll tell you when you should take the cloth off.)

Jesus, in Luke 18:31-34, had again been telling his twelve apostles that they were on their way to Jerusalem. He told them plainly that the reason they were going to Jerusalem was so that all that the prophets had written in the Old Testament, should be fulfilled, should all be done exactly as it had been written about, ahead of time.

Jesus said that the things that were written by the prophets concerning the Son of Man would be accomplished. And then Jesus told them what those things were to be. That is, that he would be given to the Gentiles (people who are

not Jewish) and would be mocked, spat upon, spitefully en-
treated, whipped with whips, and put to death. Jesus said that
the third day he would rise again.

Please listen carefully and think as you are listening. In
Isaiah 53, much of what was going to happen to Jesus had
been written about seven hundred years before. Read the
whole chapter sometime (now, if there is time). Isaiah said,
"He is despised and rejected of men; . . . wounded for our
transgressions, bruised for our sins, . . . with his stripes, we
are healed." The bruises and stripes were the marks from his
being whipped. All that was in Isaiah. In Psalm 22, written
long before Isaiah, David wrote about the death of the
Messiah who was to come, "All they that see me laugh me to
scorn, they shoot out the lip, they shake the head saying, he
trusted on the Lord that would deliver him, let him deliver
him, seeing he delighted in him . . . My strength is dried up
like a potsherd, my tongue cleaveth to my jaws, and thou hast
brought me into the dust of death."

All this and more had been written, and these Apostles
were *Jews* who *had* the Old Testament, just as we have the
whole Bible. They should have *remembered*, and understood
and have "seen" with the eyes of their understanding what
Jesus was talking about. But as they walk along the dusty road
to Jerusalem, Jesus tells them clearly what is ahead, and they
were as "blind" to what he was saying, as you are right now
with your eyes tied up. They just did not *really see*. That is,
they did not take it in to their thinking, and believe it to be
what was coming, and accept it, and *expect* it. We will find
out later how true it is that they did not expect Jesus to die.
They loved him, he was doing marvelous things, they believed
he had come from God . . . and they just could not *imagine*
him dying. So they heard with their ears, but did not really
listen to what it meant at all. They were blind to the truth
Jesus told them.

It took a long time in those days to go from one place
to another. There were no trains or automobiles, and Jesus
walked almost everywhere he went. All along the way as they

went toward Jerusalem he was talking to people, healing
people, answering questions.

Luke says that as Jesus was getting close to Jericho, a
poor, blind man was sitting by the side of the road begging.
People passing by would splatter him with dirt, and often I'm
sure they didn't look twice at his hand sticking out hoping for
some money. All his food and all his living would have come
from begging. As Jesus came along there was a crowd following him, so the blind beggar would have heard more of the
noise of footsteps than usual, and he asked someone why
there was such a crowd of people going in that direction.
They told him, "Jesus of Nazareth is passing by." So the blind
man cried out, "Jesus, thou son of David, have mercy on
me." Did he *see* Jesus? No, he couldn't see, but he believed
what he had been told. He must also have believed what he
had heard about Jesus before, because he immediately asked
him for help. People said, "Oh! keep quiet, stop bothering
him," but he cried out more loudly, "Thou son of David, have
mercy on me!"

Jesus asked someone to help the man over to him, and
when he stood there, Jesus asked him what he wanted. The
answer came quickly, "Lord, that I may *see*!" And Jesus said
to him, "Receive your sight, your faith has saved you."

Now all of you take off your blindfolds, and you will
have a tiny idea of how the man felt. He had been without
light and had been shut out from everything, not just for a
few minutes, but for years. How excited he was. Lots of
things he had imagined must have surprised him by looking
different. Look . . . here is the thing you guessed about. Let's
read your guesses. You had more of a possibility of guessing
what was described because you have seen things all along.
Imagine trying to figure out anything if you had never seen
anything but darkness, and just had to guess by feeling.

But there is a blindness that is worse than blindness of
the eyes, and that is the blindness spiritually that keeps people from "seeing" (that means understanding and knowing)
the truth about God, about the universe and about them-

selves. Satan is the one who likes to tie dark cloth around people's "spiritual eyes" if we can think of it that way. He wants people to be in the dark, and not see the truth, even if it is right in front of them. Paul in the letter he wrote to people in Corinth said, "But and if our gospel be veiled, (gospel is the good news about Jesus' coming to take away people's sins) it is veiled (or hid) to them that are perishing: in whom the god of this world hath blinded the minds of the unbelieving that the light of the gospel of the glory of Christ who is the image of God, should not dawn upon them" (2 Corinthians 4:3, 4). It is as if Satan, who is the god of this world, got thousands of black or navy blue or brown scarves to tie around the "spiritual eyes" of people. The gospel is not hid by hiding it in the ground somewhere, but hid because people's eyes are blinded. There are *two* ways of hiding things; one is to put the things where they can't be found, the other is to tie something over people's eyes so they can't see them. And *this* is the way Satan hides the truth from people, so Paul says.

Then Paul says that, for those of us who do believe, God who commanded light to shine out of darkness in the first place, has shined in our hearts (our minds, our under-standing now clear) to give the *light* of the *knowledge* of the glory of God in the face of Jesus Christ.

That is *exciting.* Here is Satan going round tying up people's eyes, to stop them from seeing and yet believers have light that should be so bright that it will penetrate. Back, in the third chapter of 2 Corinthians, Paul is talking about how Moses put a scarf over his face after he had been with God getting the Ten Commandments, because Moses' face was so bright that people couldn't look at it. Christians should have a special glow that people can notice. Christ has come so that the veil, the scarf, the blindfold can be taken off, spiritually, so that people will *see.*

We are, as Christians, not to have a blindfold on our eyes any more, but in 1 John 2:11 we have a warning. We are warned that there is something that will be *like* a scarf tied back over our eyes so that we would stumble around in our

Christian life, and not really see clearly at all, when new things are being held up in front of our eyes. What is that dark scarf that blinds us? It is hating a fellow-Christian, instead of loving him. Here is how John puts it, "He that hateth his brother is in the darkness, and walketh in the darkness, and knoweth not whither he goeth, because the darkness hath blinded his eyes." (Tie up one person's eyes again, and pin one word on the cloth, "HATE." Then spin that person around a bit and let him stumble around the room . . . this is what John is saying.) "He that hateth his brother is in the darkness, and walketh in the darkness, and knoweth not whither he goeth." But (let someone else walk around without the blindfold) "He that loveth his brother abideth in the light (give that one a candle and light it, too, so as to make the contrast as it should be) . . . and there is no occasion of stumbling in him."

Yes, we are to love our neighbors, and do good to them. But we are to have a special love for our brothers (and sisters) who are all other Christians, of any nation, kindred, tribe, tongue . . . of any color, any race, any nationality, any country. Wherever there is a believing, born-again child of the Lord, *that* one is our brother and we are to love *that* one. We must ask that the brown, black, navy, dark scarves be untied and ripped away from our eyes if we want to *walk in the light of the candle we are meant to have*!

We must go back to Jericho now, because we left the blind man just as Jesus had told him, "Receive thy sight: thy faith hath saved *thee*." And *immediately* he received his sight. When Jesus does something, he can do it so quickly . . . one minute blind, and the next seeing, one minute dead, the next alive . . . and when the *final* moment comes, and Jesus comes back, it is to be quickly that our bodies will be changed . . . Jesus works speedily when the right moment arrives. The man who had been blind followed Jesus, glorifying God: and all the people when they saw it gave praise to God.

Notice two things: Jesus told the man that his faith had saved him. Faith in what? Saving faith, faith that really saves people, is always faith in Jesus, the Son of God, and Jesus who could see inside this man's thoughts, knew he had *come to him* believing. He had come believing in the right way, and he could "see" in *both* ways at once. Isn't it a fantastic double thing? He could see with his eyes—the trees, the people, the blue sky, the birds flying—and he could see spiritually, that he was a sinner and needed to come to Jesus. That man really saw. So no wonder he went prancing around glorifying God, and no wonder the people who saw the change in him were full of praise, too.

» All this was taking place on the road just in front of Jericho. Now Jesus entered the city with the crowd still thick around him. A very tiny person—perhaps as short as a child of ten or twelve, but a mature man—named Zacchaeus, had been waiting to get a glimpse of Jesus. He was a chief among the publicans, and he was rich. You remember that the publicans were tax-collectors and that the system was that they paid the government, and then *collected* as much as they could. So they often cheated people a lot. As the crowd began to surge into the city like a wave foaming up on the beach, Zacchaeus realized that he could never get through all that mass of people to see Jesus and that it would be hopeless to try to get near him. So he had a bright idea, and ran ahead in *front* of the crowd. He saw a sycamore tree, and his idea was to hurry up and climb it, so that he'd be fixed there on a branch looking down, by the time Jesus passed. Can't you imagine him scrambling up the tree, and panting a bit as he carefully fixed himself so that his robes wouldn't trip him, and he could get properly turned in the right direction before it was too late? Perhaps he heaved a big sigh, put his hands down the branch, one on each side of him, and then leaned over to watch intently.

But what was happening? Wasn't that Jesus? Why he was walking over to stand directly under the tree! As soon as he arrived there, with Zacchaeus looking down at his head through the leaves, Jesus looked up, and saw him, and said to him, "Zacchaeus, hurry up and come down; for today I must stay at your house."

Can you imagine Zacchaeus's surprised reactions? His mouth must have dropped open. He must have thought, "*How* did he know my name? I can't imagine, because I haven't been introduced to him   and how did he know I was up here?" Surely something like this was going on in his mind, as Zacchaeus hurried up, and, gathering his robes over one arm, climbed back down the tree. Off he would go to his house, breaking into a run probably. He would prepare the house so that Jesus could eat and sleep there. There would be water made ready in a basin for Jesus to wash his feet, as men wore barefoot sandals in those days. There would be the couch made ready for Jesus to lie down at the table to eat, and a place for him to sleep. Zacchaeus, being a rich man, would have someone to cook and serve a meal. So he would tell them what to have, and make everything as comfortable as possible. How excited he must have been . . . he had been trying so hard to just get a *glimpse* of Jesus, and here Jesus was coming to have supper with him. Imagine Jesus coming to your house to have supper with you! But did you know that in Revelation 3:20 Jesus, the Second Person of the Trinity, the Son of God says, "Behold, I stand at the door, and knock: if any man hear my voice and open the door, I will come in to him, and will sup (eat) with him, and he with me." Yes, it is a definite statement of fact, a promise given by God. What does it mean? It means that Jesus is giving an invitation that helps us to understand what happened that day when he went to eat with Zacchaeus. It means that when we understand about Zacchaeus, we will also understand this promise of fact given to us in the book of Revelation.

What happened as Jesus walked on to Zacchaeus's house and knocked there? First of all the crowd started murmuring—a rumbling sound of talking in complaining and critical tones. "What is Jesus going to eat with that man for? He's just a cheat of a tax-gatherer! Surely there are good religious people here in Jericho who would be much more suitable hosts for him! Huh, imagine *him*, going to be the guest of a sinner. I surely don't approve of that." This is the sort of thing they were saying. We could have told them what Jesus

had said before, couldn't we? About coming to save sinners who know they are sinners, and not people who think they are righteous. These men were always the same . . . patting themselves on the back. Talking to themselves about how good they were, even when they called it prayer! They didn't really talk to God, nor did they *listen* to what God said to them. They were too busy listening to themselves.

When Jesus had come into Zacchaeus's home, Zacchaeus came and stood in front of him and began to speak with very real honesty and humility. Such a little man, he'd been such a clever little crook getting money out of people and piling up wealth . . . but now, suddenly, he isn't blind any more to his sin. Suddenly he really sees himself as God would see him . . . and I am sure he had an intense look of being ashamed, maybe even with tears in his once hard eyes . . . he is standing there, thinking how terribly wrong and sinful he had been. How do we know? Well, first by what he said: "Look, Lord, the first thing I want to do is this. I want to give half of everything I have to the poor; and if I have taken things from any man by overcharging him, by falsely telling him to pay more than he should, I want to give back four times as much as I have taken from him." Do you have those apples, carrots, potatoes, walnuts or whatever you used to show what a tenth or a tithe is? Remember we put a pile on one side, and put one-tenth for the Lord's tithe on the other? Well, put out your things, and the money you used, on the table again. This time separate it in half, half and half. Half of everything Zacchaeus had went immediately to the poor. Then of the half he had *left* he gave four times as much to any man as he had cheated him of. I am sure that took a lot more than half of the other pile. It was greatly diminished anyway. I wouldn't be surprised if Zacchaeus had only about ten percent left to live on for himself.

What had happened to Zacchaeus? Was that *natural*?

First, let's listen to what Jesus said to him. "Today is

---

*Zacchaeus in a tree, and Jesus telling him to come down.
Luke 19:1–10*

salvation come to this house, forasmuch as he also is a son of
Abraham. For the Son of man came to seek and to save that
which was lost."

Why did Jesus say salvation had come to Zacchaeus, and
his house, that day? Not because he gave the money away,
but because he had understood that he was a sinner and had
believed in Jesus. Zacchaeus was now "found"—like the lost
sheep, the lost coin, and the lost boy. Jesus connects
Zacchaeus with all the lost and found ones, making it clear
that Zacchaeus had been found by Jesus. Jesus saw what was
going on inside Zacchaeus. In fact, Jesus had seen what
Zacchaeus *really* was seeking when Jesus called him down
out of the tree. So the *order* of things is that, first, a person
truly sees he is a sinner, and comes to believe that God the
Father, God the Son and God the Holy Spirit exist, and comes
to accept Jesus as Savior. It is *after* this that a change is seen
in what he does. Jesus spoke to Zacchaeus as being one who
had salvation, right after Zacchaeus had so eagerly and earnestly told Jesus that he wanted to give away his money, that
he wanted to make things right, and had showed he was
more interested in following the Lord than in wealth. This
change was an enormous change, because money had been
his biggest interest in life before, and he had piled it up by
being dishonest. So he had cared more about wealth than
about honesty.

» Let's go back to the rich young ruler, and put him beside
Zacchaeus *in our imagination.* The rich young ruler had been
asking Jesus his question just a short time before, on the road
as Jesus was starting his long walk to Jerusalem. Jesus had
loved the attractive Jewish ruler who had tried so hard to
keep the Ten Commandments. He wasn't hard like the
Pharisees, yet *he was so sure he was all right in himself* that
he very quickly claimed to have kept all the Ten Commandments ever since he had been a boy, and acted as if there was
very little more he needed to do, by his own strength and
goodness, to get eternal life in heaven. He *never* said, "What
will I do about my awful sin and guilt?" Jesus saw inside this

man's mind and heart and saw these things. It was easily proved that he preferred his earthly pile of wealth to taking any chances of losing it, even though Jesus said he would have treasure in heaven. Jesus was giving the young ruler an opportunity to get the "scarf" off his blind eyes, to see how very much he really had put wealth first. What is the greatest commandment? "Love the Lord your God with all your heart and with all your soul and with all your mind." The rich young ruler showed clearly that he loved his money first of all . . . he turned "sorrowfully away" because he did *not* love God first—yet he had just claimed to have kept all the commandments perfectly. Do you see? Jesus was pointing out his weak place. But the man didn't want to be disturbed in his way of life.

Now here stands Zacchaeus in contrast to the rich young ruler. What had Jesus said? It is harder for a rich man to become a Christian, to be born again, than for a camel to go through a needle's eye. Do you still have your needle to look at? All right, look at it closely. Zacchaeus is rich. Zacchaeus is hated by the others because they think of him as a cheat and a thief and a terrible sinner. Zacchaeus has proved in his life-style that he has a wrong view of money, and has had for a long time. *But* as a sinful publican he began to be troubled by his sin, and his attitude was that of the publican praying. Those two men we saw praying—the Pharisee bragging about his goodness, to himself, and the publican crying out for mercy because he knew he was sinful—are like the rich young ruler and Zacchaeus. Both men are Jews. Both know the law. The rich young ruler puffed himself up because he had made his own little standards about what it meant to keep each of the Ten Commandments. Zacchaeus knew he had not kept the law, and was overwhelmed with his sin, and began to seek for mercy, for forgiveness, and he really wanted to see Jesus.

Didn't Jesus say that all things are possible with God? This is just what he meant. Of course, there will be rich men who will have the blindfolds fall away from their eyes so they can see themselves as God sees them, at least in a small measure. Such men *can* go through a needle's eye, so to speak! Zacchaeus was so changed when he came to the Lord in faith, believing, that he did—without even being asked— what you would expect it to take a very long time for him to do. He said, "I want to be rid of it, and let you lead me as to what to do, Lord." That was the depth of what he was saying. "Anything, Lord, I want your plan for my way of life, for the kind of house I live in, for what to do with my time, for what to do for other people . . . I'll give most of this away, then you show me what you want me to do with whatever time I have left in life."

Why did Jesus speak of Zacchaeus as being a son of Abraham, when he said he had come to seek and to save that which was lost? Let's look at what another Jew, Paul, said: "For I am not ashamed of the gospel: for it is the *power of God* unto salvation to everyone that believeth; to the Jew *first*, and also to the Greek" (Romans 1:16). The Messiah had been promised to the Jews for centuries. The Old Testament had been read and studied by the Jews, as they looked forward to the coming of Messiah. At the beginning, all the people who believed and formed the early church were Jews. Jesus is saying to Zacchaeus and to any who are listening, that salvation has come that day to a descendant of Abraham, to one of the very lost sheep he came to find. Then Jesus says again that he has come to seek and to find, to save that which was lost. That would mean *anyone* who is lost.

Just before Jesus says in the book of Revelation that he stands at the door and knocks, listen to what he says to the people who are wealthy and religious like the rich young ruler—wealthy and religious like the Pharisees who felt proud because they were keeping all sorts of little rules and regulations and whose prayers were not even real. Note this carefully, because there are many people like this today. See them standing, with brown, black, navy blue scarves around their eyes, blindly staggering around in the dark, thinking they are so fine, thinking they are finding their way. Jesus says to them:

"Because thou sayest, I am rich, and have gotten riches,

and have need of nothing; and knowest not that thou art the wretched one and miserable and poor and blind and naked: I counsel thee to buy of me gold refined by fire, that thou mayest become rich; and white garments, that thou mayest clothe thyself, and that the shame of thy nakedness be not made manifest; and eyesalve to anoint thine eyes, that thou mayest see. As many as I love, I reprove, and chasten: be zealous therefore, and repent" (Revelation 3:17, 18, 19).

God is saying, "Please look at yourselves; don't wait until it is too late . . . if you feel so good in yourself, and think you have everything in this world plus everything in a religious life, and you haven't discovered that you are sinful and wretched and miserable, and that as far as treasures in heaven are concerned you are really *poor*, and as far as having clothing which should be the white clothing Jesus gives us, which is his righteousness when we accept him as Savior—you are without that really naked." "Blind ones, take the scarves from your eyes," is what he is saying when he says, "Put some sort of ointment on your eyes." He is speaking about eyes to see and understand and know that God is God indeed, and that we must come to him in the way he has opened up to himself.

Then listen again to the beautiful words of Jesus who knocked on Zacchaeus's door and went in and ate with him, talked with him, accepted him, forgave him . . . because Zacchaeus repented, believed, accepted, bowed, and was born again. Jesus says to *all* who will listen to him: "Behold, I stand at the door and knock; if any man hear my voice, and open the door, I will come in to him, and sup with him, and he with me."

It is a true offer. We need to examine ourselves, to know whether we are running away with sorrowful faces, like the rich young ruler, or hurrying to prepare for Jesus to come in, hurrying to prepare by being sorry for sin and accepting him as Savior, and preparing *space* in our lives to be with him.

22
DON'T WRAP UP YOUR LIFE!

Isn't it wonderful the way the Bible combines history with the teaching of deep truths that are unchangeable, and also gives us the instruction we need for living right *now*, and tells us how to prepare for the future, *and* tells us something of what the future is going to *be*? We have such a fantastic combination of things in the Bible. How can people think it is dull and old-fashioned?

Today we went to a second-hand store that a friend in Montreux had introduced to us, and because chapter twenty-one had just been written last night, the second-hand store made us think of the Bible as it appears to be in so many homes.

Here is a store, if you can call it that, which looks more like a whole series of people's attics. Chairs, tables, chests, couches, old stoves to heat old-fashioned irons, benches from a country railroad station, a tricycle over a hundred years old, pillows, and lamps, things piled up on top of each other, and in a number of old buildings so that you have to go from room to room. And you look and look among every-day things that people don't need any more but are still all right, wonderful antiques which only need sanding and polishing, rubbing with oil and loving appreciation to become marvelous things of beauty in someone's home. Some people have no understanding of the beauty of wood, brass and copper that lies under the dust, nor do they see the artistic lines and curves of things which show forth the wonder of the artist who designed them in the first place. People look at something, walk away, and want new stuff . . . cheap, veneered and varnished stuff that looks shiny and clean and will take no trouble or time simply to push into a spot and be used, but is not lasting in beauty of line or wood.

A real work of art does not get "old" in the sense of wearing out like an old dish towel or broom. Oil paintings, sculpture, etchings, woodcuts, great music, instruments like violins and pianos, literature, beautiful porcelain, become more attractive as the years go on. People look for rare old things in attics as if they were searching for treasure chests buried by pirates!

The Bible is full of the rarest treasures of understanding, and yet sometimes there it sits in people's houses, stuffed in with other books, and unread, and only the new books, shiny with the varnish of twentieth-century language and *ideas*, are read. Often people fill the "houses" of their minds and the balconies of their feelings with the things they can push in without any effort. They don't have to look for twentieth-century thinking or philosophy, or ideas, because they are right there in all the cheap stores, so to speak. A philosophy is made of the explanations you or anyone gives as to where everything came from, what life is all about, the values of life and what may be expected in the future. Everyone has a philosophy which they live by, even if they never have heard of the word.

As we were saying, these twentieth-century ideas and philosophies can be just picked up cheap in any magazine, newspaper, novel, school text book, TV program, movie (cinema), comic book, and in songs and music as well as in art. The modern answer to life is that there are no answers.

So it is that the greatest book of *all* history, the most fantastic treasure-chest that *ever* existed, the book that *can* give people knowledge of the things that happened before human beings existed, the *only* book that *can* tell about the future, the only book that gives a complete understanding of all of history and *where* we fit into it all, this book which is never out-of-date, is treated as if it were too *old-fashioned*, and full of ideas *too worn out* to bother with. It is the book that has answers.

As we study it together, you and we (because in a real

way we feel a togetherness with you right there reading)—we need to take the soft dust cloth of our *minds*, and the oil of our *feelings*, and the hard work of our *time* to do something about it, and just polish and rub away together until we find the exciting truths with fresh understanding. Is the Bible old? Yes, it is old, and it is rare, with the beauty of a work of the art of the masters. The difference is that in the realm of art, whether painting, photography, furniture, music or writing, people *are* able to do as great work in this century as in any other. It *is* possible for a man or a woman to do something greater in our time than the greatest of the masters of creative art of the past. *But* there is no book that will be written like the Bible. God gave it to us, to give us all we need to know, until Jesus comes back. It is always *old*, and always *new* in a way only God could produce with his perfect creative ability. Peter says that the Bible is a more sure way of finding out about things than even being an eyewitness. He says we should pay attention to it, because it is like a light that shineth in a dark place until the dawn, and the day star arises in your heart (2 Peter 1:19). Those are not just beautiful words—they should make us want really to take time to *discover* what we are meant to have from the Bible.

In the last chapter, we saw how a lot of exciting things fit together, as we saw the connection between Old Testament and New Testament, and between what Jesus taught on the road to Jericho, and what he says in the book of Revelation. But, all the time while we are discovering the more complete picture of what the *whole* Bible teaches, we must remember that Luke is also giving a history of the time of Jesus' life on earth. The next bit of history was that, after Jesus had eaten and refreshed himself at the home of Zacchaeus, and had had the joy of knowing that Zacchaeus had believed and was a changed man, he prepared to leave the city on his climb up the mountain road toward Jerusalem.

Before Jesus left, he told the people a parable in order that they would be better prepared for what was coming. You have been hearing how the crowds were following him down the roads, and up the hills. They liked to hear him speak and

were, of course, fascinated by the way he healed people.
Although he had said he would suffer and die and be raised
from the dead, you remember even the apostles seemed
quite blind to that and couldn't believe that was *really* what
would happen next. People thought he would be King *right
away*. They were mixed up between the Old Testament
prophecies which told of the Messiah coming to suffer, and
those which spoke of the Messiah coming to be King. Remember when Jesus read to them in the synagogue from the book
of Isaiah? He stopped in the middle of a verse, didn't he?
That was because at that time he was only going to fulfil the
first half of the verse. He had come to teach and preach the
good news to the poor and to heal people, but also to die. It
is not until he comes back a *second* time that he will be King.

The parable, Dr. Luke tells us in chapter 19 verse 11,
was to help them and us to understand that he is *not* going to
rule as King until after he has gone far away for a long time. It
is also a parable to teach us what we are meant to be doing
until he comes back and to prepare us for the day when he
does come back.

Jesus told of a man of a noble family who was going on
a long journey into a very distant country, and who, when he
came back, would be king. Now the Jews would *not* think this
a strange story, because they *had* kings ruling over them, and
when it was time for a new king to take over the kingdom, he
had to make a long journey to Rome. In Rome he would
become king, and then would return to rule over the Jews.
The people in Jericho were very familiar with all this. When
the man who was at that very time their king had made *his*
trip to Rome, the Jews had sent a message to Rome saying
that they did not want him for their king.

Jesus *always* used something people would understand
when he told a parable to teach an important truth. He spoke
in the language *they* used, so that they understood the *words*,
and he used illustrations from the kind of things *they* were
familiar with—like sowing seed, finding sheep, fishing, and so
forth. People were meant to understand with their *minds*, and
not just be filled with a big emotion. In this parable that Jesus

told in Jericho, he used this example of something familiar to them, to show that he was going to be King, but that first he was going to a far off place for a long, long time before he would return. Because, of course, he was going to die, and then go to heaven, where he would spend many years before he would come back as King. He has been gone now nearly 2000 years, and we do not know how much longer it will be before he comes back. He wanted the people then to know that he was not going to set up his kingdom right away, and he also wanted them (and all who would be his followers from that time on) to know what he expected them to do between the time of his leaving them and his coming back as King.

In his story, or parable, Jesus told of a nobleman who called his servants before him and gave them a special task to do while he was gone. What was this task? Well, first of all, the nobleman gave some money to the servants, one pound apiece. Each one received the same amount. Then the noble-man said to them, "Trade ye herewith till I come."

He didn't tell them when he was coming back; he just gave them each a pound and said, "Trade till I come." What does that mean? It means that they were to *use* that which he had given them for their master's interest, so that when he returned he would have as much as possible. It meant that they were to do all that they could do for their master while he was gone. That was their job, their task, their work, the thing that was supposed to take up their time and energy and interest. They were to use their brains to think of ideas, and then to choose to do something they thought of, and really to do something that could be shown to the master. It took ideas, choice, and action to carry out the master's request.

Perhaps to make this real to you, you could each have the same amount of money, or *something*, and be given some time to "increase" it, not for yourself, but for your mother or dad or friend. At least, *think* about what you would do. If each one is given an English pound or two or three American dollars, or a smaller amount of some kind of money (depend-ing on where you live), in this time limit you can decide upon among yourselves, how could you *increase* it? Well, you could buy sugar, milk, cocoa, and margarine and make some chocolate fudge. Then cut it in bars or squares and sell it, figuring out how much you would have to sell it for to pay for your work and give profit.

Now remember that as a servant of the nobleman your *time* really belongs to *him*. Or you could buy cards and paint brushes and paint, and make Christmas or birthday cards to sell. Or you could buy a chicken and, if you knew how to care for it, gather eggs and sell them. Or you could plant seed, care for a vegetable garden, and sell the vegetables, or grow flowers and sell them. As you are pretending to be the nobleman's servants, you could take a small amount of money and come back together in a month or so to see whether you had "increased" it or not! The girls could buy material and sew something to sell, or buy wool and knit something to sell. The boys could make something out of wood, or something out of leather. You would have ideas of one kind or another, and one might have more success than another with his or her ideas.

If you decide to have a "thing" instead of money, maybe you could *each* take a pound of flour, a pound of margarine, a pound of sugar, some eggs, raisins, nuts and some milk. See what cookies (or biscuits, as we say in England) or cup cakes you could make out of these! Maybe you'll have better ideas, but at least *think* about it, and *pretend* to be servants of the nobleman (who will be the one chosen for that part?) and understand one thing, that *each* one is given the *same* amount to start with. Now as Jesus went on with this parable, he told of the day this nobleman returned as king!

If you decide to spend some time trying to "increase" one franc, twenty pence, or a large amount, such as a pound, of course that would take a week or a month or more to do, and you would be discussing the whole thing—that is you would spend time talking about just what that project is illustrating. However, please just get some things to illustrate the story now. Give each one a penny, or an apple, or a walnut, or some sort of thing. Have some more of whatever you give out, to show the "increase." Now, as you pretend the noble-man has gone away, one of you take some more of the apples, or nuts or money, so that that one has ten. Another one take five. And another person should get a napkin and wrap it around the *one*. Sit there now with these on your lap.

So, the nobleman stands before the servants as he has called them to him. He wants to find out just how wisely each one had used his money, and how much each one had gained for him. Remember he is the king now. They are standing in front of the king. He was coming with a very different kind of power from that which he had when he was with them be-fore.

As they stood before him, one servant stepped forward and placed ten pounds before the master who was now king. (The one of you who has ten of the things, put them on the table; if two of you took ten, then both put them on the table now.) "Lord," this man said, "thy pound has gained these ten pounds." How pleased the king was! "Thou good and faithful servant," he said as he praised this man, "you have been very faithful in this small thing; now you shall be ruler of ten cities." The master was now king; he had come back with power to rule over the land and he was giving rewards to his servants for what they had done while he was away. This man was now no longer a lowly servant; he was a ruler over ten cities.

Now remember that Jesus is talking to Jews who knew quite a bit about the Old Testament. Perhaps they remem-bered that after the wall of the city had been rebuilt, Nehemiah had said, "I gave my brother Hanani, and Hananiah the governor of the castle, charge over Jerusalem: for he was a faithful man, and feared God above many" (Nehemiah 7:2). Then, (see Nehemiah 9:8) Nehemiah spoke of how God had given Abraham the land he promised him because Abraham was faithful. Perhaps in the synagogue from sabbath to sab-bath, they had often heard the words from Psalm 101:6, "Mine eyes shall be upon the faithful of the land, that they may dwell with me. . . . "

If they knew and remembered the teaching of the Word of God, the Bible, they could have connected what Jesus was teaching now with what they already knew, and understood much more what the parable meant. I wonder what was going on in their minds as they listened. So often people push away out of their minds anything that might change their way of life. They don't *want* to understand.

Jesus then told of the next servant who also stepped up with his pounds. He said, "Lord, thy pound hath gained five pounds." He had done something with his pound to make it five times as much. The king gave him his reward, too, and made him now ruler over five cities. (The one of you who has five things, put your things on the table now.) Just for a minute put *out* from among the things (money, apples, walnuts or whatever you used to represent the pounds) one for each person who has put things there; that is, if one put ten pounds and one put five, take away from the fifteen the original two. Now you can see the increases. Jesus wants us to see it this way; the *increase* means something. We'll explain it later, but look now as the last servant came up to the master who is now king. This one said, "Lord, here is thy pound, which I kept laid up in a napkin." He talked about being afraid, as if he thought it would be a good excuse to say that he didn't really know what to do to please his master, so he didn't try. He hadn't even *tried* to carry out his master's command. What an unfaithful servant! (Now whichever of you has the thing wrapped up in the napkin, put it up there on the table.) There is the pound, not used in any way for the master. The king did not praise him at all for keeping the pound so protected. Instead, he took his pound away and gave him no reward at all. The king gave his pound to the one who had ten.

Now what is Jesus teaching in this story? You know from what he has said earlier, that he is not teaching that anyone who makes a lot of money will be given extra money that is taken away from the poor people! A parable is a story that teaches something, but we must be careful to realize *what* it teaches. Always remember that Jesus uses word-pictures to help us to understand, and that when, for example, he says we are to be fishers of men, he does not mean us to eat men!

So what *was* Jesus teaching here, as he prepared to leave Jericho? *First,* he was teaching the people who were listening that day in Jericho that he was *not* going now to Jerusalem to become their king, but that what he was going to do would be *like* going to a far-off country. He was going to die. He had told them that before. And he was going to rise from the dead. But he was now telling them that he would be going away for a length of time. He was going to heaven for some time, but he did not tell them for how long.

Secondly, he was teaching that all those who believed on him, his disciples, Zacchaeus, all who have lived since, we too, are meant to take those things that he has given us, and use them well for him while we are on this earth. We are expected to do *something* with what he has given us that will be an *increase* to his glory. We are his servants. (Are we not in the *family*? Are we not sheep of the Lord's pasture, one of his flock? Are we not a part of the bride of Christ? Yes, all those things, but we are also his servants.) As his servants, he wants us to know something is *expected* of us.

What *is* expected? Are we to make a lot of money so that we can hand over a pile ten times as much? Are we to grow a lot of apples so that we can hand over ten times as many? What is he talking about?

He means *something.* He does not mean *nothing.* We cannot just shrug our shoulders, turn the page a little bit uncomfortably and say, "What is the next story?" Some day we will be reminded that we were told this parable in Luke, and we will be asked what we have done about it. Jesus warned all *those* people, but he is warning us too.

What is it that the Lord gives *one* of to each of us? What is it each person has been given right from that day there in Jericho, and long before that, down to each one of us now? A house? No. Lots of people never have a house to live in; they sleep on the ground, in an empty drain pipe, under a tree, in a cave. A special talent to do something better than other people? No. Lots of people have no special talent that they know of at all. Health? No. Some people are ill all their lives, others are blind and lame. Freedom to do what we will? No. Some people are in prisons and concentration camps, some have been sent to Siberia away from their families. Lots of people have no freedom at all. What does each of us have *one* of? A life, a body, and soul and some length of time during which we will live before the King comes back.

» When this book is being read out loud, some will be gathered together in a family circle, with children of five, ten, fifteen or twenty years of age, and parents of many ages from twenty to sixty. But some who are gathered together will be in a hospital ward, listening from their beds to someone reading aloud. Some will be hearing this read in an old folks' home, sitting in chairs, some needing hearing aids. Some will be hearing this as they sit in their wheelchairs unable to walk, and finding it hard to write because their hands don't work properly. Some will be hearing this read, because they are blind and cannot see to read it for themselves. Some will be listening, or reading alone in a cell, in a prison. Some will be hearing this read after they have had very great tragedies happen, like an earthquake destroying their house, or a flood ruining their place of business. Some will be reading this book after some desperate unhappiness has made them feel that life is not worth anything. Some will be in a very happy, excited state, others will be despondent and desperate. Some will be wondering what to do with all their wealth, and still be following the Lord; others will be so poor they will need to pray for their food for supper. Some will be sharing the book with friends and family and *feeling* the togetherness . . . and some will be all alone somewhere *feeling* the aloneness.

What is the one thing each one has, no matter what the circumstances? A life in the body for a period of time. How long? We do not know, any one of us. We do not know when Jesus will come back as King, and we do not know whether we will die first, so that we will be one of the ones raised from the dead in the twinkling of an eye. *But* we are expected to be doing something with the one life the Lord, the Master has given us, and he is the one who will be giving out the rewards as King.

"But," perhaps you are saying, "I can't make my life into ten lives, I can't do a thing here in the hospital, in prison, in the old folks' home, in a boarding school, as a ten-year-old, as a busy mother, as a man with a business to take care of, as a blind person, as someone so poor I have nothing to share, as someone dying of cancer! What does Jesus mean? He can't be talking to me; I can't do anything to increase the effect of *my life.*"

How can this be fair? Remember that Jesus told his disciples that the little widow had given *more* by dropping her mite into the box than the rich Pharisees had? It is the same with time, energy, trust, love and all our attitudes to other people. Someone in a lonely bed-sitter in London, in a prison, a hospital, a room in a city slum, *can* be laying up more treasure in heaven than people who seem to have much more opportunity. One day we shall *see* the contrast in a different direction. Perhaps the people who had the most here will be almost sorry that God is so fair!

God really is just, you see, fair to each one. After we have accepted Christ as our Savior, and we are in this sense his servants, we have our life for a month, a week, a day, a year, ten years, forty years . . . however long it is. We are meant to ask his help to show us what we are to do to use it as he means us to. But we have one place to find something out about how to use it, and that is the Bible. So listen carefully, if you are in the hospital, or the old folks' home, or in a wheelchair. God says that the first commandment is to love him with all your heart and soul and mind. We are to trust him. Satan comes to God and points a finger as he did at Job (in the book of Job in the Old Testament) and says, "That person doesn't love you, that one in the wheelchair, the hospital, the old folks' home, the prison, the person living in the cave, having terrible headaches . . . " and you, and you, and you and we, when we are in one of those places, just love God, and say, "I trust you, dear Heavenly Father, and if I can do more now, please show me. But I love and trust you right here even though I don't understand all this pain and suffering and loneliness." What is that? Well, that is like being *ten* people fighting against Satan, because a victory has been won in the battle up there in the heavenlies where Satan is fighting God; that is the victory for the Lord. But it needed *you* to have the victory, not in your *own* strength, but because Jesus died to give you salvation and the possibility of having a victory in the battles day by day. Why you see, it is so fair that it is *possible* for people who have no money, no strength, no talents to use or no way of using them still to be multiplying their lives by ten!

Does it only mean winning battles against Satan's temptations to us not to love God, and not to love our neighbors? No, but that is part of it. When we have a victory over being selfish, and give a lot of what we have earned to feed people who are starving, or for spiritual food, then we, too, are multiplying our one life by ten.

Don't you see, it all fits together with the things Jesus has already been teaching? We are meant to see how it fits together with other parts of the Bible. You want to use your life the way the Master has asked you to do, to increase it? You can invite the poor, blind, maimed and halt in for a feast (as we thought about before) or you can go and help people who need you to bring them a meal, a bunch of flowers, a book, or a painting to give them beauty in their home or sickroom. You can be sensitive to the needs of your neighbors near you, and your "neighbors" across the world. You can spend time praying for people, no matter where you are—in a cave, a hospital, a wheelchair, or washing dishes, scrubbing floors, or doing some work that does not use your brain all the time.

You can earn a million dollars as the Lord helps you, *not* putting money first, but being like a camel going through a needle's eye; you can give that money-making ability to the Lord and ask *him* to show you what he means you to do. Maybe he wants you to have a large home to fill with those poor people for feasts! Or maybe you are the one he expects to lead to do his work with your millions in India, China,

Africa, or Idaho or Hampshire. Maybe he wants you to become a great author to *his* glory, with your *motive* being what
he would have it be. The motive of loving him in the midst of
your creativity can be such a victory over Satan's temptation
to puff you up, you can be as ten men or women. As a child,
you know that God has said to obey your parents, so as a
five-year-old you can tell the Lord that you love him and want
to do the hard thing of picking up the toys, setting the table,
keeping quiet when Dad is working at his desk. And as you
do it, obeying your parents, you are using your life to be like
the life of ten five-year-olds, because it is so amazing that you
are being so obedient.

The whole teaching of the New Testament on our needing to ask the Lord to use our lives, to give us guidance and
strength to do what he would have us do, fits in to this
parable. But the warning is: *Do not wrap up your life in a
crisp linen napkin and save it.* "He that saveth his life, will
lose it." You are not to spend your life saving your life so
carefully that it is just like wrapping yourself up to protect
yourself. Some people spend their whole lives "wrapped up."
They spend their thought and time in taking care of their
bodies (sleeping, eating, exercising, having recreation, im-
proving their minds, caring for all kinds of things so as not to
waste any of their energies). Is it wrong to have sleep and
food and exercise and recreation, and to read books that will
educate you and go to lectures that will give you more knowledge and not to get ill by being careless? No, but there is a
delicate balance between taking some care of one's "life" in
this way, and just making one's own body and life the center
of everything, so that you have wrapped a napkin around
yourself.

Look now at the money, or apple, or whatever you
used. Wrap it back up in the napkin. Then take a white sheet,
and wrap it around one of you who is listening. There both
the "pound" and the *person* are wrapped up. Just look and
think a minute. Are you, am I, are any of us in danger of
wrapping up our lives and "saving" them in a wrong sort of
way, always putting our "rights" first, being so afraid some-

one is going to take advantage of us that we are afraid to invite anyone in, or afraid to give anything away, or afraid to use our time for people, or afraid to use our "talents" without being paid properly for them? Are we wrapping up our health, our energies, our money, our talents, our homes, our emotions (that is, we don't let ourselves have compassion, for fear it might make us sad), our time . . . all that makes up the whole person, that makes life now, are we wrapping it all up as if in a sheet? Look at the person in the sheet. What good can he or she do for anyone else in the room?

When the King comes back again, our lives should have been such that there are very many more *people* who will have believed and been born into his family, being servants in his kingdom, but the multiplying of the use of our lives *is not only counted when other people can see it.* This is what is so fair. Yes, the world would change if every Christian unwrapped himself, or herself, and stopped saving herself or himself, and really let his or her life be used for the Master, but the effect would not all be where it could be seen. The effect would be in the heavenly battle too.

But there is a *third* lesson that Jesus was also teaching from this story. He told of certain citizens who did not want that nobleman for their king at all. These citizens were punished when the king came back to rule. Jesus is teaching here that those who do not want him as their King—who do not accept him as their Savior—will one day have to stand before him when he comes to the time of judging. They will receive their judgment and be shut away from the wonders of God.

≫ After telling this parable of the pounds, Jesus started up the mountain road for the climb toward Jerusalem, along with his disciples. When they came close to Bethphage and Bethany at a place called the Mount of Olives, Jesus spoke to two of the disciples and gave them an errand to do for him. "Go," he said, "into that village over there; in that village you will find a colt tied. No one has ever ridden this colt, no man has ever sat on him. When you untie him, bring him here to me. If any man stops you and asks you why you have untied this colt,

simply say to him, 'The Lord hath need of him.'" The two
men went obediently off and found the colt exactly as Jesus
had told them they would. They began to untie the animal,
but while they were doing this the owners came to ask what
they were doing. They answered exactly as Jesus had told
them to, "The Lord hath need of him." This was enough! You
may be sure that the owners had been prepared in their
hearts to give anything to Jesus that he might need. They
were ready to say "yes" without asking questions. Really this
is the way we should be with our possessions, and our energies and time, not just when *people* tell us what we ought to
do, but when the Lord asks us something. They didn't say,
"Oh! A colt isn't anything big and fine to give!" They gave
what they had and didn't wait until they had a glamorous gift
to give to the Lord.

Think of giving a colt for the Lord to ride upon! Clop,
clop, went the hoofs of the colt as they walked along back to
Jesus. No man had ever sat upon this colt, he had no saddle,
but the disciples spread their coats upon his back, and the
colt allowed Jesus to mount him and ride quietly on his back.
Jesus, who made all things and who could speak to the waves
and the wind and command them to be still, did not need to
tame a colt, for the colt would obey his voice, as all nature
does.

As Jesus rode along, the people spread garments and
branches of palm trees along the path, so that the colt, bearing Jesus, walked on a path covered with clothing and green
branches. Now, as he came close to Jerusalem and began to
come down from the Mount of Olives, a huge crowd began
to rejoice and praise God with loud voices. "Hosanna to the
son of David!" they shouted. "Blessed is he that cometh in
the name of the Lord." Some sang out, "Hosanna in the
highest!" What a great wave of shouts there must have been,
just like the pounding of waves on the seashore and rocks! A
tremendous rolling of voices in praise! But not all the voices
were praising him. Some asked, "Who is this?" while others
of the Pharisees came boldly right up to Jesus and told him he
should scold his disciples for praising him that way. Jesus

answered the pious, proud Pharisees by telling them that if the disciples had stopped praising him that day, the very *stones* would immediately cry out! For this one short moment in Jesus' life, he was to have the praise that *all* the world *should* have been giving him then, and should be giving him now.

When Jesus came near the city and saw it stretched out before his eyes, he began to weep. "Oh, Jerusalem," he wept, "If only you had known the truth, but your eyes have been blind to it. (Poor, blinded, spiritual eyes, as if scarves were tied over them.) Now you must go through terrible days, for one day this city will be destroyed, and the stones of the buildings will all be cast down upon the ground."

The people of Jerusalem should have known that Jesus was the Messiah, the Son of God, and they should have accepted him as their Savior and King. A crowd was following Jesus that day, shouting his praises, but even many people in this crowd did not believe that he was the Messiah; and there were very many others who lived in Jerusalem who were not even in the crowd which shouted his praise for that short moment.

The city had rejected him. "He came unto his own and his own received him not." In a short time the people of this city would be shouting something else. They would be shouting that they wanted Jesus killed. Jesus knew this, and as he rode into the city on the colt among the palm branches and shouting people, he wept for all the hundreds in that city who were so blind that they could not "see" that he was God, and their Messiah. Jesus wept for the lost.

Then Jesus went to the Temple. We find what happened there in Matthew 21:12, 13; Luke 19:45–48; Mark 11:15, 17 and John 2:13–17. We are told that, as he came to the Temple, he found it full of people selling things. They had turned it into a market place. They had oxen, sheep and doves and tables where men were changing money. This was the place for worship, and Jesus cried out that they were just making it into a place of business. You can imagine his face: those eyes that had just been filled with tears of sorrow over Jerusalem

DON'T WRAP UP YOUR LIFE!

were now burning with righteous anger. They must have been flashing with fury, a truly righteous fury. Here is Jesus, the Messiah, coming to *die* for men, and right here where the Pharisees made so much fuss about his healing people on the sabbath, the whole place was full of animals being bought and sold, and money being exchanged, a real hubbub of noise and business going on.

Jesus made a whip of small cords and lashed out at them, driving them out of the Temple. He also overthrew the tables, so that the money rolled everywhere and the tables crashed to the floor. The chairs of the money-changers he also threw over. He shouted at them, "Take these things away from here, and don't you make my Father's house a place of buying and selling." And then we are told that his disciples suddenly remembered a verse they knew, Psalm 69:9, "For the zeal of thine house hath eaten me up; and the reproaches of them that reproached thee are fallen upon me." David had written this centuries before, but the disciples recognized that it was going on right then. Jesus was feeling the awful way in which God's house had been treated and feeling the reality of the way men had turned away from his Father.

Jesus had just explained in Jericho about his going away for a long time, before he would come back as King and Judge. The people were soon going to see him die, and they would be confused by seeing him so weak and humble as he was taken to die. But on this day, on his way to Jerusalem, during his entrance into Jerusalem—for two short periods of time, he has shown the disciples two things, just for a little while, but both very vividly.

First, they saw him riding on a colt and being praised as a *King* would be on entering the city. Secondly, they saw him make a whip and throw out the money-changers and the marketing business in the Temple as a *judge* would do. He was giving a vivid lesson for us to remember, as well as for the men there. Jesus *will* be King one day. Jesus *will* be Judge

Jesus chases the money-changers out of the Temple. Luke 19:45

one day. "And (God) hath given him authority to execute judgment also, because he is the Son of man" (John 5:27). Right *now* his invitation to us is gentle, and he weeps for the lost, as he says, "Let not your heart be troubled: ye believe in God, believe also in me. In my Father's house are many mansions: if it were not so, I would have told you. And if I go to prepare a place for you, I will come again, and receive you unto myself, that where I am there ye may be also."

If we are believers, and have come to him and accepted what he has done for us, he will come again for us to take us to the fantastic home he is preparing. But remember we are either his people and he our King—or he comes as Judge.

23
THE OWNER'S SON

You will remember that Jesus has now come to Jerusalem. He
rode on the colt with a crowd of people following him, strew-
ing his path with palm branches and clothing as they shouted
praise to him. But many of them were just caught up in the
excitement of the crowd. You know so often people just
follow along because it seems everyone else is doing something and they don't really pay much attention to what it is all
about. Many of these people were not really praising Jesus as
the Son of God, the Messiah, because many of them did not
believe. Remember we saw that Jesus, as he came into Jerusalem, gave people the opportunity to see for a very brief
moment the fact that one day he would be coming to be *King*
and *Judge.* Now, after chasing out of the Temple the men who
were selling animals and changing money, Jesus stayed there
at the Temple, healing people and teaching.

People gathered around him, and were listening carefully. But even as they were listening, the chief priests and
scribes were plotting and planning as to how they could
destroy Jesus. Now these leaders began to try to ask catch
questions, hoping they could "trip up" Jesus and get him to
make an answer that would make it possible for them to
accuse him of some terrible thing. They wanted to find something that would be a crime against either the Jewish or
Roman law—and then accuse Jesus of this crime.

Jesus was and is God, even though he had put aside his
glory, to walk on the earth and just be in *one* place at *one*
time, healing *one* person at *one* time, talking to *one* group at
one time, limiting himself—still he was God. Jesus knew all
things. Therefore he could read the thoughts and minds of
those priests and scribes, and he knew exactly what they

thought as they were plotting behind his back. No one can do anything against anyone *behind God's back*! God knows all men's secret plots. No matter what anyone does in dark and hidden places, God knows about it. People may fool each other, they may fool the government, they may fool their parents, they may even fool themselves, but they can never fool God—because they cannot hide anything from him.

Because Jesus knew what was in their minds, he told them a parable to warn them about what would happen to them if they succeeded in carrying out their plans. It really gave them fair warning—and a chance to change their minds. This is the story that he told.

He said that there was a certain man who had a very fine piece of land on which he planted a vineyard. Have you ever seen a vineyard? In Switzerland they are planted on the sides of steep hills, made into terraces with stone walls. Neat rows of grape vines are tied, each vine to a tall, straight stick, so that they rather look like an army standing at attention. The rows upon rows of brown branches tied to the sticks grow green as spring grows into summer, and the leaves spread out almost completely covering the sticks. Always you see people bending over, working among the vines, weeding the earth to keep it brown and fresh to catch the raindrops, spraying vines with a blue-green spray to kill the bugs, covering them with a spider-web-thin net to keep off the birds as summer turns into autumn and the grapes begin to appear. By October, when the summer is a memory, and though days are golden, the nights are frosty, the grapes are ready to pick. Then the men and women, boys and girls, hired to pick, come with their huge baskets to go up and down the long rows, filling the baskets so full that the grapes spill over the top.

Perhaps you would like to put a basket of grapes on your table as you are reading this. Maybe you would like to, but you don't *have* any grapes, so you can't do that! Well then, get some paper and drawing pencils or crayons and draw a vineyard with people working in it, or draw some grapes. As you concentrate for a while on grapes and vines and vineyards with your pencil, you may think of some little stick men you can draw *as* the parable goes on, to illustrate what happened.

In this story that Jesus told, the owner went away to a far country for a long time. Before he went, he arranged for other men to take charge of his vineyard. When it came time to harvest the grapes, and the grapes were hanging heavy on the vines, the owner sent one of his servants with a basket, to ask for a portion of his fruit.

Can you imagine what those ungrateful men did? It seems hard to believe, but although they had rented the vineyard, and the other man was the owner, instead of giving him some of his own grapes, they beat his poor servant. Not only did they not give the servant any grapes, but they hit him over the head with sticks, stones and whips! Off he went back to his master with an empty basket, and probably wounded.

After a while the owner sent another servant to get some grapes, and these same men (Jesus called them "husbandmen") beat him too, and sent him away with empty baskets. When a third one came, he had the same horrible treatment. In Mark 12 we are told they threw stones at him and beat him up. Mark also tells us that many servants were sent and that they either beat up or killed them. They never treated anyone that the owner of the vineyard sent with any attention; they simply threw each one out. Then the owner of the vineyard said to himself, "What shall I do? I know what I shall do . . . I will send my beloved son, and maybe when they see him, the people will have some respect for him, and treat him kindly."

But when the vineyard keepers saw the son coming, they talked among themselves. "Here comes his son," they said. "He is the heir—he is the one to whom all these beautiful vineyards will belong some day. Come on, men, let's grab him and kill him—*then* the whole vineyard will belong to us." So the wicked men seized the son roughly, threw him out of the vineyard, and killed him.

"Now what," said Jesus, "shall the owner of the vine-

327

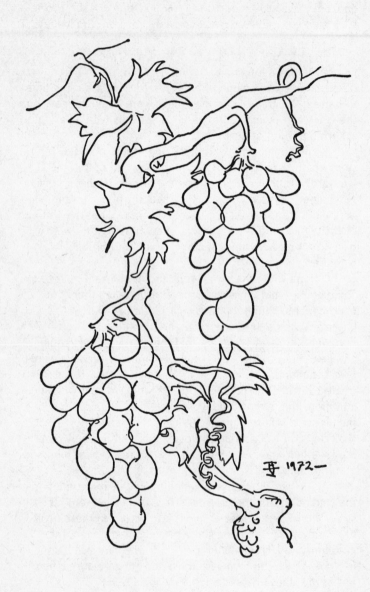

yard do when he returns? He shall destroy these husbandmen (the men who had been doing all this) and give the vineyard to others."

Remember that Jesus was giving a warning in this parable to the chief priests and scribes, the men who were plotting and planning to kill Jesus. What did Jesus intend to teach by this story? Something they should have understood very easily. These priests and scribes were men who knew the Old Testament, and they should have remembered what had happened to the prophets through the years. Jesus was reminding them of something they had studied, of the fact that for hundreds of years God in his great love had been sending prophets to the Jewish people.

What are prophets? A prophet is a man whom God sends with a message to people. A prophet gives a message directly from God. We don't need prophets in the same way now, because God has given us the complete message he wants us to have right in the Bible. He has given us all the history we need, to have an understanding of the past. He has given us sufficiently clear instructions as to how we are to live now, after we are born into his family (and, of course, he has told us clearly how to be born again). He has given us in very clear and strong language all the *warnings* we need to have, and he has given the prophecy of the future, so that we know enough about what is coming next to be careful to be ready for it. We can see where we "fit in" to all this. We need to be careful continually to read the Bible, to discuss it together and to pray, asking the Holy Spirit to help us to be refreshed and helped by it, and to ask to understand it more all the time, and also that we will do what it says. It is no use looking at the Bible as a wonderful work of art, and not *doing* what it says.

During the Old Testament days, God sent many prophets like Isaiah, Ezekiel and Malachi. The prophets warned people to turn away from their sin and to worship and serve the true and living God. Over and over and over again, in-

---

Parable of the vineyard.   Luke 20:9

stead of listening to the prophets, people hurt them and some of them they killed. These men listening to Jesus would have known that. In fact, maybe as they listened to the story, they thought of 2 Chronicles 24:20, 21, where it tells what a prophet said, and then what they did to him: "And the Spirit of God came upon Zechariah the son of Jehoiada the priest, which stood above the people and said unto them, *Thus saith God*, Why transgress ye the commandments of the Lord, that ye cannot prosper? because you have forsaken the Lord, he hath also forsaken you. And they conspired against him, and stoned him with stones at the commandment of the king in the court of the house of the Lord."

I want you to put on the table there a basket of grapes (or some other fruit or some vegetables . . . something to represent a harvest from the land) and next to the basket put some sticks, stones and some sort of a whip or club, if you have it. (Maybe a baseball or a cricket bat!) Look at these. The prophets were sent to "gather grapes" or to bring some "harvest." How? Well, God speaks of the grapes or harvest as a way of picturing people turning to him, people believing and being a "crop" of fruit in his kingdom. It is something like the fish being a picture of people being "fished for" for the Lord. So there you have a picture before you on your table—grapes (or something) in a basket or a bowl, and next to that the stones, sticks, whip or clubs. Instead of the prophets being able to "gather grapes" for the Lord, they were attacked with the stones, sticks, whips, clubs . . . and sometimes were killed. On your table you have a picture of *history*! This is how God's prophets were treated time after time. Over and over again as the prophets warned people, they did not listen to them, but hurt them. Now—right in front of the chief priests and scribes, stood the Son of God himself.

Don't you see? Jesus told a parable to show these men that they were about to plot and plan to kill the Son of God who had been *sent to them* to give them an opportunity really to be sorry and *listen*, and to believe. He warned them that, just as in the parable the owner of the vineyard would give the land to someone else, so God would give away what they could have had to other people.

Then Jesus quoted to them from the Psalms, as he spoke of the stone which the builders rejected being something that will fall on them (Luke 20:17). "I will praise thee: for thou hast heard me, and art become my salvation. The stone which the builders refused is become the head stone of the corner. This is the Lord's doing; it is marvelous in our eyes" (Psalm 118:21–23).

What Jesus told them was that when they kill the Son, they will be the ones to be hurt and turned away in the end, and others, who are not Jews, will be the ones to be given "the vineyard"—or a place in the Father's household.

» Now all the first Christians *were* Jews. Not *all* Jews rejected Jesus. But as many of them did reject him, the gospel was preached to the Gentiles right away. That, however, is *no* reason for Gentiles to be proud, or to think they are superior in any way. There is no difference between Jew or Gentile when we become born into God's family through accepting the Messiah. Any people who are *against* the Jews, and use the name "Christian" to boast that they are better than the Jews, are either not Christians at all, or are being very wrong as Christians. What is a Christian? Just a person who has recognized that he or she is guilty of sin, and needs some way of getting rid of it, and who has come to believe in the existence of the Triune God, and has accepted Christ as Savior, as the Messiah. "Christian" is *not* a word meant to separate races of people from other races. Christians are supposed to *love* their neighbors, no matter what their race or background, and are supposed to love other Christians, who are their brothers and sisters in Christ. So *that* doesn't leave anyone left over to hate! Christians can hate the Devil and demons, and hate sin, and hate the things people do that are sinful, but hating a group of people of any sort is *not* a mark of being a Christian.

Paul, a Jew who was an apostle and wrote much of the

New Testament, wrote a warning to Gentiles in Romans 11. He says that if you think of all the Jews as being a tree, then you must think of the root being God, and the branches being the Jewish people who believe. The Jews, then, are God's chosen tree. Paul says that, if the Jews do not believe, then they are cut off—like a branch cut off from the tree. Now, where that branch is cut off, the branch of another tree is grafted *in*. (That is a thing you can do with trees, if you know how, to make a branch from a red cherry tree grow on a white cherry tree.) Paul says that Gentiles are like branches grafted in. Well, says Paul, if God will cut off the original branches, he will also cut off the grafted-in branches, and for the same reason—*unbelief*. So it is no better to have the *name* "Christian," than the *name* "Jew." It is believing inside, in your mind and heart, that God is really there, and that his word the Bible is true, that counts.

Jewish people in the Old Testament threw stones at the prophets, but people who call themselves by the name "Christian" and who are Gentiles, often throw stones just as much at the Bible, which is what God has given today to tell us his message. There is no difference between throwing stones at the prophets, and throwing stones at the Bible. Finally, the leaders of the synagogues and Temple plotted to kill the Son of God, but that is no worse than leaders of religious groups called "Christian" plotting and planning to destroy the *truth* concerning the Son of God, and telling people he is only a good man, and not God, telling people he is not the Creator who had no beginning and made all things, telling people he is only a son of Joseph, and not born of a virgin with God as his Father, telling people he died but did not rise again physically but only in some misty, moisty, mystical, meaningless way. Some people say that the resurrection of Jesus was not a physical resurrection. They call it a resurrection but they teach that his body stayed dead and only his spirit rose. As you will see, Jesus himself took great trouble to prove that it was his body that had risen.

No, Paul warns, the branches that were cut off the

natural tree because of unbelief, will also be cut off the grafted-in ones, because of *unbelief*! Do you know that a branch cut from an apple tree may be placed against a cut in the right place on another apple tree of a different variety? If it is done correctly, this branch will grow and produce apples. This is called grafting. Do some grafting of a tree if you live where you can. If not, take something and pretend it is a graft; tie with sticky tape, or glue together, a branch you have fixed to look like a tree, and put it on your table for a period of time (until it gets too dusty or falls apart!). *Talk about this* together at your mealtimes for a while. None of us has any reason for "pride" and we need to be certain we are not just going by a "name," when inside we are something else. Be reminded by the branch!

What happened when Jesus finished explaining his parable to the leaders? Did they remember Old Testament warnings and become worried about themselves? *No*, unhappily no. They became angrier than ever, and plotted and planned all the more to kill Jesus because even this story made them more furious.

They sent spies to question Jesus, pretending that they wanted to find out some things, though they did not really want to find out anything. When they first started to talk to Jesus, they tried to flatter him because they thought that this could make him proud, and that that would make him give a foolish answer. This was impossible. Jesus could not be flattered, as he is greater than anything any man can say about him. He is God. He cannot be made to give a wrong answer, because he knows the right answer to *every* question that can be asked. The question they asked him at this time was, "Is it lawful for us to give tribute to Caesar or not?" What does that mean? Well, they meant, "Should we pay taxes to the Roman government which rules over us?" They thought that surely this would catch him. If he said, "No," then they could get him arrested by the Roman government for speaking against the government. If he said, "Yes," they thought they could say to the Jewish people, "See, we told you he is not the

Messiah. He isn't trying to help you to get free from the pagan Roman government." How *would* Jesus answer? Would he get caught?

Jesus had a wonderful answer. He asked someone to show him a penny; then he held it up. (Do you have some coins in the house? If you have some from a number of countries, put a variety of coins out so that you can pass them around and examine them.)

Jesus asked, "Whose picture is on this coin?" "Caesar's," the men answered. "Well," said Jesus, "you must give to Caesar the things which belong to him, and you must give God the things that belong to him."

Whatever country you are in, look at a coin from your *own* country, and then if you have them, look at coins from *other* countries. If people are in Finland they do not buy things at the stores with French francs; they need Finnish marks, and that proves that the Finnish government rules there, and that people must pay taxes to that government. If people are in England, they use pounds to buy things in the markets, and not Dutch guilden, and that shows they are ruled by the British government, and pay taxes to that government.

We must give the Lord our worship, and our supreme highest and first loyalty. No human government has a right to these things. But as long as we live in earthly countries, we must pay taxes where we live. We are heavenly citizens when we accept Christ as our Savior. Yes, that is another thing we are . . . we are sheep of the Great Shepherd's flock, we are children of the Lord's family, we are servants of the Master, we are a part of the bride of Christ, and we are also citizens of the heavenly country! But—we are not yet living in heaven, are we? If we are Americans living in Switzerland, we must pay taxes to Switzerland. We must use Swiss money and pay their taxes and keep their laws. As citizens of heaven, living in an earthly country, we should pay the taxes of the country in which we live and be good, honest citizens of that country.

However, our two citizenships are not equal. Our loyalty to God is first. We must always remember that the first place must be given only to God. Jesus showed that there is the higher loyalty to the Lord, but that there is to be a separation, so that we can be also loyal, earthly citizens and not refuse to pay our taxes wherever we live. This answer of Jesus was so perfect that the men had nothing to say. They just kept quiet.

» Soon after that, Jesus was sitting over beside the treasury, which is where people dropped in their gifts for the Temple. It was the way they gave what they wanted to give to God. Jesus, so Mark tells us (Mark 12:41–44) as well as Luke, watched while a lot of rich men came and put gold pieces into the treasury. Jingle, jingle went the gold into the box, but jingle, jingle went their purses or money bags as they walked away. They had given only a small portion of a lot of money. It looked like a big gift, but they had a lot left over.

Then a poor widow came to the box, and she had two mites (much less than a penny). Will she put one in? Oh! She put *both* in. She put in all she had.

I wonder what she had for supper? She has put everything she had at that time in the box for the Lord. As he saw her, Jesus called his disciples over to him and said, "See this poor widow? She has put in more than *all* the other people put together have put in the treasury." What? Two little mites are *more* than all that gold put together? Yes, because you see God's way of counting is another of those "backwards" things. He doesn't count the amount; he counts the *proportion.*

We want you to show yourselves what this means by putting some money, or other things, on the table again. Let's count out money for each person here in a pile. Ten pennies in this pile, ten dollars or ten pounds in this pile, a thousand dollars or pounds in this pile. Now this does not have to be real money, but can be pieces of paper representing money. Find a box to use as the treasury box. If the person with ten dollars or ten pounds puts in one dollar, or one pound, and

the person with a thousand dollars or a thousand pounds puts
in twenty dollars or twenty pounds, but the person with ten
pennies puts in five pennies, who has put in the most?
According to man's way of thinking, you get one answer;
according to God's way of thinking, you get another. Two
different sets of accounts. The arithmetic for the bank in
heaven where the treasures are kept is a very different kind of
arithmetic. The *treasures* in heaven are added up by *proportion.* So a poor person who gives what looks a small
amount may be giving half, or sometimes all of what he or
she has, whilst the person who has more, and gives one of
every ten things, is giving ten percent, and the person who
makes larger gifts and has so very much more left, is really
giving the least. Very often the people who are poor here
have the largest accounts in heaven. It is "backwards" again,
you see. "He that is first shall be last." "He that loseth his life
for my sake findeth it." It is *that* kind of thing. We need to
learn to see things from a *different* perspective.

This widow, or *any* poor person who has given *all* that
he has, has given *as much* as if the rich young ruler had given
everything, and followed Jesus. And some day, everything he
has that he kept in exchange for following Jesus, will seem
like *less* than the two mites!

One of the disciples started talking to Jesus about the
Temple, because of course they were right *there.* As the
disciple looked around, he remarked about how beautiful the
precious stones were, and Jesus said that the day was coming
when not a stone would be left in this Temple. "When will
that be?" they asked. Another man said, "Can you give us
signs to look for?" So Jesus spoke of some of the things that
would happen in the following years . . . the years between
that day and his coming back again. We are still living in
those years, so we should listen to what he said, because he
was saying it to us, too.

He said, "Don't be fooled by people coming and saying
'I am Christ.' Don't follow such people! And when your hear
of wars and commotions, don't be terrified: for there will be
such things, and the end will come later." Then he said that

nation would rise against nation, and kingdom against kingdom. There would be earthquakes in a lot of different places, and famines and plagues of various kinds, and some fearful sights and signs in the heavens. "But before these things happen," said Jesus, "people will persecute you because you are believers. They will bring you up before synagogues and put you in prisons, and make you stand before kings and rulers for my name's sake. When you are dragged before men like this because of your belief, don't worry about what you will say, for I will give you wisdom and words that your enemies will not be able to contradict or deny. And because of sin some Christians will cool off toward the truth. Many will betray one another and hate one another, and false prophets will arise and fool a lot of people. But he that shall endure to the end shall be saved. And this gospel of the kingdom shall be preached in all the world for a witness, to all nations; and then shall the end come."

All these things have happened in history, and are still taking place. Jesus is saying, "Don't be discouraged. The end *will* come. I *will* come back. And when you see these things happening, don't think that Satan has won. Even when all men hate you for my sake, I can protect you—have patience." Jesus then told them how Jerusalem would be destroyed and Gentiles would take it over. That time came. For years the Jews were *not* in Jerusalem, and even fifty years ago it seemed *impossible* ever to think of Israel being a nation again. But more recently, the prophecy that Israel would be a nation, that one day the Jews would go back to Jerusalem *in unbelief*, has been fulfilled. We can remember seeing the first issue of stamps from Israel. What a thrill!

We live a long time from the days when the prophecies about Jesus being born in Bethlehem came true, but we don't live so far away from the time when Israel became a nation, and that came true. What comes next? No one can know when Jesus will come back again. He warned us that things would get worse, and that men's hearts would be filled with fear. Nations would be distressed in many ways, and there would be calamities of all sorts. Jesus can come at any moment. No one can know the day or the hour when he will come back.

Jesus then told another parable, about how a fig tree has little leaves which tell you that summer is coming near. He said, "Don't be foolish about not recognizing things as the world gets worse, because the Kingdom of God is coming nearer." He reminded people then, and us now, that God's Word, the Bible, *is* going to be fulfilled. It is true. It is not to be just put aside on a shelf, or in our minds, along with other books.

Jesus was soon to be dragged off by the men who were going to kill him. He was so close to his death on the cross, but he was saying *very* important things. We can know they were important because he was very careful to make his warnings plain and clear, so that people would not get mixed up and throw their lives away. What are these strong warnings about how people should use their lives and how they should be ready for the coming of Jesus? They are warnings that take us back to the weeds that choke out the growing plant, the Christian life. He says that we are to watch out that we don't let ourselves be all taken up with the worries of this life, and with drunkenness and having too much. Worries—about health, money, pressures of all kinds—worries about people taking advantage of us, about getting our share of power, attention, success—can so use up our thoughts and energies that we have nothing left over to do what the Lord really has for us to do. He says that having too much can do the same, and he doesn't just mean being drunk with wine, or high on drugs, but being drunk with success or high on power. *Watch out*, says Jesus, that his second coming doesn't take you unawares.

That is the negative. That is what not to do. What is the *positive*? What *should* we do? We are to *watch*. Watch for what? For his coming. "Watch" means to *do* the things that we are learning that he wants us to do. It does not mean that we stand at the window and look for him. We are to be hospitable to people, invite them in for food if they need it, for conversation, for care—in other words, to show love to

338

people, and to the Lord as we study the Bible to find out how. We are to *pray always*. That means we are to pray every day, many times a day. About what? Well, about everything. We are to ask the Lord to help us, to guide us, to give us courage to do his will, and to give us his strength when we are weak. We are to pray for our needs, and to pray for other people. We are to ask for things, *with thanksgiving*. We are to pray that we will *understand* what his Word is saying to us, and to ask him that he will help us to see if we are in any way being like the Pharisees, being hypocritical. Yes, Jesus said, "Watch ye therefore and pray always, that ye may be accounted worthy to . . . stand before the Son of Man."

And then they shall see the Son of Man coming in a cloud with power and great glory. What will be the thing we are doing in that minute?

We are to *watch* and *pray*, not to be like the men in the vineyard who never paid any attention to the owner's servants *or* son! God *has* sent his prophets in the Old Testament days; then he *had* a clear record written so that people through the years could read it. Then he *sent* his Son to give the spoken warning, and now we have the written record both of what the prophets said, and of what his Son said. For people today to throw stones at the truth of the warning that God's prophets and Son spoke, by denying the truth of the Bible, is to put themselves in the place of those men working in the vineyard.

24
A BREATHLESS MOMENT
IN THE UNIVERSE

As those days in Jerusalem passed, the time when Jesus could be free to move among the people was getting very short. The plots and plans were increasing. However, Jesus went on telling people important things as he spoke daily at the Temple and spent his nights out on the mountain.

Early each morning people came to hear him at the Temple. It was just coming up to the time of the Passover when the chief priests and scribes met together to figure out how they could kill Jesus without stirring up the people to riot. They were afraid of the ordinary people. You remember that they had been trying to make Jesus say something that they could use against him, but that they hadn't succeeded. So now they were thinking of some other way to arrest him.

Before Jesus allowed himself to be arrested, there were some important things he had to do. He had to finish the Passover, and begin the communion service. What is the Passover? What is the communion service? Really to understand that, we need to go back to the Old Testament and read Exodus 12.

One thousand and five hundred years before Jesus came to be born and live on earth, the Israelites were slaves in Egypt. What was it like for the Israelites to be slaves to the Egyptians? It was something like being in a concentration camp. The Egyptians made them work very hard, and killed many of them. God warned the Egyptians over and over again to let his people go, but they wouldn't. Moses was the one whom God prepared to speak to the Pharaoh the ruler of Egypt to tell him to let the Israelites go free. Nine times

Moses told Pharaoh that God would bring plagues upon Egypt if the Israelites were kept there, and nine different plagues came. But after each plague was over, the Israelites were still kept as slaves. Finally God provided a way of escape. The only way the Egyptians could ever be persuaded to let the Israelites go, would be to have the angel of death come over Egypt, so that the first-born son—that is, the eldest son—in every Egyptian family would die.

God told Moses to tell the Israelites that they would have to prepare very carefully so that *their* first-born sons did not die. This thing that God was going to ask them to do was to help them to *understand* more about the Lamb of God that was coming, the Messiah they were to look forward to. Moses told them that they were to take a lamb for each house. If there were not enough people in the family, two houses could share a lamb. The lamb had to be without any blemish or spot, and it had to be kept for fourteen days so as to make sure that it was perfect. Then everyone had to kill their chosen lamb the same evening, and take the blood of the lamb and mark the doorposts and top of the door with it. Then they were to roast the lamb over a fire and prepare to eat it. While they were eating the roast lamb meal, they were to be prepared to go out, to escape from Egypt, with their shoes on, and a staff in their hands, not lingering over the meal but eating it quickly.

During that night, the angel of death passed over Egypt, and the first-born son of every house died—except in the houses which had the blood of the lamb on the doorposts! The first-born sons were safe, and lived, in the houses where people had believed and obeyed what God had told them to do.

Then the Jews were free to go out, and it was as they went away and came to the Red Sea that the Lord did the miracle of causing the water of the sea to pile up in a fantastic manner like two water walls, so that they could pass through! They were free from the power of Egypt.

This is true history. It really happened. It is *not* a parable. But God did this for several reasons. First, to show the

341

way for the Jews to escape from the slavery of Egypt, and start their journey to the promised land. Secondly, God did it to teach those Jews who took part in that actual time of the Passover—that is, the passing over of the angel of death—that there was a Messiah coming who would be the Lamb of God. All Jews were to keep the Passover as a feast each year, a time when they ate unleavened bread and remembered the passing over of the angel of death, and the fact that their sons were living! Just think if you had been through that experience! You would never forget the connection between the lamb dying, and the son living! The lamb had taken the place of a first-born son dying. You would eat your unleavened bread, and thank God for that. Then you would be thankful that you were out of slavery and on your way to a land promised by God as a beautiful land.

Do you have unleavened Jewish bread, matzi, in your stores? It would be good to have some of it, eat it, and think of living in that period of history when you would be looking back to the Passover and forward to the Messiah. How fantastically God gave a *picture* in this thing he told them to do to be free of the slavery in Egypt! It all fits together so perfectly, you see.

As the little lamb was to be without blemish, so Jesus was "without blemish" because he was without sin. The little lamb represented Jesus, the Messiah. Jesus lived and was tempted and proved to be perfect, even as the lamb was kept for fourteen days to see if it was perfect. The little lamb died. Jesus died to take our places. That is, Jesus died to take the place of each one who would believe in him, so that each one would escape death and live, and also escape the slavery of Satan and sin. After the little lamb died, the blood had to be put on the door as God commanded. And now that Jesus has died, we must do what God tells us to do—that is, to believe that Jesus died for us.

After the Jews ate the lamb they had to flee from Egypt. And after we have been set free by the lamb, we go out in haste to be pilgrims! No bone of the little lamb was to be broken, and no bone of Jesus was to be broken when he was crucified. You see, God was giving a picture that people would be able to think about for many years, to prepare them to understand more when Isaiah told them eight hundred years later, "He is brought as a lamb to the slaughter . . . " (Isaiah 53:7) and "Surely he hath borne our griefs and carried our sorrows: . . . But he was wounded for our transgressions, he was bruised for our iniquities" (verses 4 and 5). This also gave them more understanding of other Old Testament prophets' writings.

All these people in Jerusalem at that time were keeping the feast of the Passover. Just think of it! The Son of God was right there. For fifteen hundred years, generation after generation had been explaining to their children why they were eating unleavened bread for the Passover, and what had happened in Egypt, and that they were looking forward to the Messiah. For fifteen hundred years, they had told the story of the lamb, so perfect a picture of what the Messiah was going to do one day. They had been singing the Psalms since David's time—with great music and marvelous arrangements of singing back and forth. They were divided into parts and sang as a chorus. They sang for instance, Psalm 22: "All they that see me laugh me to scorn: they shoot out the lip, they shake the head saying, commit thyself unto the Lord, let him deliver him, . . . I may tell all my bones . . . they look and stare upon me . . . they part my garments among them, and upon my vesture do they cast lots." Think of the fact that many in Jerusalem had heard these words over and over again, and were even at that very time going to eat the Passover.

Before we go on to find out what Jesus did during the Passover, please do listen to some music. If you don't have the entire *Messiah,* an album of records of the oratorio by Handel, do get it as a family project. And as you listen, try to imagine that you have heard these words handed down by generations of ancestors who believed them, yet—there you are in Jerusalem, *blind* to what was about to take place!

If you do have the *Messiah,* select some of these extracts to listen to now: from Part 2, Chorus, "Behold the

343

Lamb of God"; Aria, "He was despised and rejected of men";
Chorus, "Surely he hath borne our griefs"; Chorus, "And
with his stripes we are healed"; Chorus, "All we like sheep
have gone astray"; Tenor solo, "All they that see him laugh
him to scorn"; Chorus, "He trusted in God that he would
deliver him"; Tenor Solo, "Thy rebuke hath broken his
heart."

If you haven't time to listen to all that now, please do
when you reread this chapter another time. Perhaps take a
whole Sunday afternoon to listen, read and discuss. Read it
over and listen, then continue reading. These words were in
the minds of many in Jerusalem. God had given the words to
prepare people.

Imagine Jews coming into Jerusalem from *all* over Palestine to celebrate the feast of the Passover, *so* many in fact
that, when Jesus told Peter and John to find a place for them
to prepare the Passover and eat together, they asked him
where he thought they could find room. They had no house
in Jerusalem. So Jesus told them, "When you get inside the
city, you will meet a man carrying a pitcher of water; follow
him into the house and say to the owner of that house, 'The
Master asks you, Where is the guestroom where I shall eat
the Passover with my disciples?' And he will show you a large
upper room furnished: there you can make things ready."

Peter and John went and found that things happened
just as Jesus said they would, and they made all the preparations for the Passover, in the big upstairs room.

Jesus ate the Passover in that upper room with his
apostles, but that was a very special moment in history, as it
was the last time after 1500 years, that God wanted anyone to
eat the Passover. You see, its purpose was finished. That
purpose had been to look forward to the Lamb of God coming to die for the sins of people. He had come, and soon he
was going to die. This was the end of the Passover, because
Jesus wanted to introduce that which was to take its place for
the next period of history, the one we are living in! By the
time Passover time came the following year, the death of the
Lamb of God would be past history, and not something to

look forward to. Jesus sat there, eating the last Passover feast looking forward to his *own* death!

In 1 Corinthians 5:7 we are told that Christ is *our* Passover, sacrificed for us. And in the tenth chapter of the book of Hebrews we are told that year after year the sacrifices were made at Passover time, but that it wasn't possible that the blood of animals could take away sin. It was necessary for Jesus to come in a body to do God's will. Listen to verse 10: "By the which will we have been sanctified (or made clean) through the offering of the body of Jesus Christ, once for all." Then, in verse 12, we find it clearly explained that Jesus, after he had offered *one* sacrifice for sins for ever, sat down on the right hand of God. You see, the Passover took place year after year looking forward to the time when the Messiah would come. *But when the moment came in history,* the death of the Son of God made perfect, or made worthwhile, made valid, kept the promise of all those who through the years, had done what God told them, because they believed God. Think of the perfect timing of Jesus' death at Passover time! It was timed so that it would be as clear as possible to anyone who wanted to find out, that he was the Messiah to whom all these years of the Passover had been pointing forward.

There Jesus, sitting with twelve apostles eating, said, "I have desired to eat this Passover with you before I suffer." Then he told them he would not be eating in this way with them again, nor drinking the fruit of the vine, until the kingdom of God came.

Then he taught these men what would, from that time on, take the place of the Passover. He took bread in his hands, gave thanks to God the Father, and then broke the bread. As he broke it, he said, "This is my body which is given for you: this do in remembrance of me." In the same manner he also took the cup saying, "This is the New Testament, (or new covenant, the new contract I am making with you) in my blood, which is shed for you." In 1 Corinthians 11:26, it is explained that as often as we eat this bread and drink this cup, we are remembering Jesus' death for us until he comes back again.

345

What does it mean? Well, it means that right at Passover time Jesus made it very clear that his death was what had been pointed forward to by the Passover through 1500 years, and that now he would die. He made it clear that after his death, people were not meant to keep the Passover, but to take bread and what he called the fruit of the vine, the juice of the grape or wine, and in eating and drinking together, they were to *remember* his death for them, and also look forward to his coming back. Some Christian churches and groups take communion every Sunday, some one time a month or less often. But it is important to remember that Jesus said that we really were to do this.

The communion service is not to be just a kind of solemn religious moment when we hear music and have a spiritual feeling. We are really meant to think and to remember that Jesus' body was broken for us so that we could have eternal life and not need to be punished for our sins. We are really to remember that he gave his blood, dying for us, so that we could live with him. Also we are meant to think back over our sins and to ask the Lord's forgiveness, not just shrugging our shoulders and thinking, "Oh, I'm all right because I'm a Christian. It doesn't matter that I have really hated another Christian this past month, and planned all sorts of things to hurt or annoy him. I don't have to worry about my coveting or my putting money first this past week. I'm O.K." We are told in 1 Corinthians 11:28 to examine ourselves and as we come to communion to *tell* the Lord we are sorry, and are *thankful* for what he did for us; we are to be glad that we know we *can* be forgiven because of what he did. And we are to think of his coming again and be glad about that, believing that it is true and that he will come some day.

We are not meant to take communion with our minds filled with other things. God has given it to us to help us remember. We should think of all those 1500 years of Passover feasts, with people waiting for Jesus the Messiah to come, and then of all the nearly 2000 years during which people have been glad he did come and die for them, and have looked forward to his second coming. All this should be more real to us time after time as we take communion. We are not meant just to do it with our hands and lips and mouths, while our minds and feelings are all filled with a lot of everyday worries or ambitions or plans. Nor is it some sort of magic. But we are to be *remembering* and *looking forward* (which are things we do with our *minds*) and we are to be *thankful* for Jesus' death for us, and full of hope and expecting his second coming. And thankfulness and hope fill us with *feelings* as well as thinking.

People who do not believe that God exists, people who do not believe the universe is anything but atoms, plus time plus chance, people who do not believe that God is three Persons, Father, Son and Holy Spirit, and that Jesus really *is* God the Son who was promised for so many centuries as the coming Messiah, should not take communion. The communion is for the believer to take. It cannot be said too strongly that communion is not something like singing a hymn or reading part of the service responsively from Psalms. Jesus has made an absolute, something that doesn't change, when he says, "You do this to remember me until I come back again."

》 Right in the midst of the solemn time when Jesus had eaten the last Passover and had then had the first communion with his twelve apostles, Jesus looked round the table and said clearly that among them there was one who did not love him. There was one who was only pretending to be faithful to Jesus. This one had talked to the chief priests and scribes and had promised them he would help them to catch and arrest Jesus. Everyone looked around the table, wondering who it could be. But, of course, Judas knew. Judas Iscariot had thirty pieces of silver jingling against each other in his pocket. He knew very well that he had secretly promised those plotting scribes and chief priests that for that much money he would lead them to Jesus. Judas had planned to betray him. The other eleven discussed among themselves who the betrayer might be.

Somehow, there have been so many paintings of the last

Passover and the first communion time, showing men sitting
in robes, one pictured as Jesus, that it all becomes a sort of
religious airy-fairy kind of idea to many people, just a kind of
a symbol, a sort of religious flag to wave. People don't seem
to think of these men as *men* who had families, mothers and
fathers, sisters and brothers. We know that Peter, at least, was
married. They had friends—Matthew's were publicans, Peter's
would have been fishermen. They had come to this moment
which was right in the middle of history, but to them it was
really just a day in the midst of their own lives. How many
years had they behind them? Each one of them had once
been five, ten, fifteen years old. They had had toothaches,
appendix pains, sore throats, and fevers. They had loved
others in their families, and still did. They had ambitions to
do or be something special. They knew people they liked and
people they didn't like. They had itchy places that they
wanted to scratch suddenly, they yawned with sleepiness,
they wondered how long it would be before they could go to
bed. They thought of people they would like to prove something to, so that thoughts of being leaders came into their
minds. They were men in their twenties, thirties, forties? We
don't know their ages, but each had a birthday coming some
time.

Some painters have painted this picture to look as if it
were floating in air. Salvador Dali has a painting of this supper
and you can see sky under the table, and you can see through
Jesus. People often feel that this supper was real and yet not.
It was so very real that God took the trouble to put in details
to help us feel that reality. He made sure that we know it was
a borrowed upstairs room in a man's house, for instance, as
well as making sure that we know that they used real food for
the Passover, just as everyone else in Jerusalem was doing—
and were then the first people ever to have communion
together, to start the whole next long period of history.

Another thing shows us how very human these men
were. They began to have an argument. Yes, an argument
right there at this stupendous moment in history. What was
the argument about? It was about which one of them would

be the *greatest*. And if that makes you think, "How *could* they?" try to remember the conversations and arguments *you* get into when it is an important moment in your family. At someone's birthday dinner, or at a wedding reception, or when you are about to go to the hospital, and it seems that everyone should be concentrating on the person who needs our love, or our sharing of joy, or our sympathy, suddenly people begin to start an argument because of some personal thing that looms up as much more important. You suddenly *feel* as if where you *sit* at the birthday supper, or the wedding luncheon, or in the taxi to the hospital, is more important than the big thing that is taking place. "I *want* that," you whisper, or scream, and your thoughts and feelings are all turned in that direction. You hadn't planned it that way, but that is how it turned out.

So these men suddenly began to think of reasons why one or another should have first place! And Jesus said, "Anyone who is the oldest of you and thinks that should make him a leader, let that one be as if he were younger. He that feels he should be chief, let him serve and wait on others."

And to illustrate what he meant, Jesus washed the disciples' feet. As you know, they wore sandals in those days, and their feet got dirty from the dusty roads. Washing a person's feet meant kneeling and actually washing the dirt off with your hands. It was a humble kind of work to do for someone else. Jesus went to wash Peter's feet and Peter said, "Oh, no." Jesus had laid aside his garments, John 13 tells us, and had wrapped a towel around himself, and took a basin of water. Jesus explained to Peter that he, Peter, didn't understand, but that he would understand later on just what Jesus was doing. Peter answered impulsively, "You will never wash my feet." I'm sure that although they had been arguing about who was greater, Peter knew that Jesus was greater than all of them, and that washing someone's feet was a servant's job. But Jesus answered him by saying, "Peter, if I don't wash your feet, you won't have any part with me." Then Peter quickly said, "Oh, wash me then, not just the feet but my hands and head too."

After that Jesus went back to the table and used the washing of their feet as a real lesson to teach them, and us something. It is all part of the "backwards" teaching God has given us all through our study of Luke. In this case, Jesus was showing that the greatest ones are the ones who are willing to serve. He says, "Now you wash each other's feet, because I have given you an example." He said that he, the Son of God, the Creator of all things, the Ruler of the universe, Lord of Lords, King of Kings, who is coming back in glory some day to be King and Judge, was *willing* to wash the feet of his disciples. Then he said we should wash each other's feet, that is, we should not be worrying all the time as to who is leader, who is on the committee, who is elected president of the society. We are not to care about being first. We are to be perfectly content to take the lowest place, and even to wash people's feet.

Every day each of us ought to ask ourselves, "What is my opportunity today to wash feet?" We don't mean you to literally take a basin of water and go around getting people to put their feet out for you to wash them. No. But there must be some real things that we can do that are serving in that low a place. Suppose Mother says, "Pick up those toys and brush the floor," and your sister doesn't do a thing, but you do it all, and you don't get the credit for it. What do you do? Yell about it? If *this* is your chance to do what Jesus means by washing feet, you go ahead and pick up the mess and tidy it all up, and tell Jesus you did it for him, and ask him to make you glad you could do it. If you do all the dishes while everyone else is talking, and no one seems to notice, you tell the Lord *this* is your foot-washing for today, and you love him and have done it for him. You scrub the floors? Wash out the toilets? Peel the potatoes? Get up in the night to change the baby's diapers (or nappies if you live in England)? You weed the garden? You paint the room? You type all the letters? You carry the heavy things? You clean the furnace and separate the clinkers? And all the time, other people are reading books, listening to music, taking a walk or sleeping. And are they going to get some of the credit that these things are done? You are going to feel *you* want the credit and praise. But you have to be so careful, or you can get proud of your humility. You have to be careful not to want to be the most "servingest" person anyone has ever seen, and to be praised by people for that. We never get to the end of needing the Lord's help hour by hour to live directly for him, and not to earn praise from other people.

After Jesus told the disciples to live this way, and to be serving each other, he said, "If you know these things, you will be happy if you do them." Let's each take a little notebook, or a piece of paper and keep a little account for a while that no one else will see but the Lord. Let's keep whispering a question to ourselves, just when we are tempted to say, "Who do they think I am?" When someone asks you to give a bed bath to a sick old woman, or to sit up all night in a hospital, or when someone asks you for help you think someone else should give. That question should be, "Lord, is this my foot-washing for today?" and the notebook should help you to check up on yourself. When did I last wash someone's feet by doing a job that was dirty or that I didn't want to do, or that I didn't get any credit for? Ask yourself, and when God sends you a thing to do, try to recognize it!

To remind yourself about this right *now*, you could get a basin of water and wash the feet of someone in the room. It will help you to see how real it was that Peter was a bit shocked when Jesus did this for him. It will help you to remember to do the kind of work Jesus means us to do as "servants."

And while someone is washing someone else's feet, get one other person in the room to wrap himself or herself up in a blanket or sheet. Remember how the man wrapped up his pound, and that we showed that the pound represented a "life"? This is the *contrast* today. One washing feet, loving the Lord, and caring for the other person. Another wrapping himself or herself up to protect herself or himself from being asked to do something that they would scream at as being unfair and would refuse to do. Amazing, isn't it, that Jesus taught this lesson so strongly just before he was to take all the punishment for us? Jesus said, "Verily, verily, I say unto you . . ." or "Truly, I say this to you, Anyone who receives, welcomes, someone I send to them, receives me, and whoever receives me, receives the One who sent me" (John 13:20). It should make us very serious about praying each day, "Help me to *do* whatever you *mean* me to do. Help me so that I won't say 'That's too much to do for you, Jesus, and for the Heavenly Father who sent you.'" Let's get used to thinking to ourselves, "Whose feet have I washed today?" But none of us should judge each other about this, or check up on each other. We should just pray that the Lord will help us to *notice* our *own* opportunity!

Jesus turned to his disciples after he had returned to the table, and told them they were not going to give him all the help he needed in those next days, and that they would just scatter as sheep. Peter boasted that he was ready for anything. He said he would follow Jesus to prison and even to death. The other disciples said the same sort of thing. But Jesus told Peter that before the rooster or cock would crow early the next morning, Peter would already have denied three times that he even knew Jesus.

» After this Jesus went into the garden at the Mount of Olives. It was a garden where he had often gone, so Judas and the other apostles knew it well. It was night now, and perhaps a soft moonlight would be the only light for their feet as they walked along the paths, shadowy and calm. Probably they would hear a few twitters of birds getting ready to sleep, a night owl in the trees somewhere, crickets making their special noises. The smells and soft sounds of night in a garden would have been the same as at any time in that land. A bush would have caught on their robes, a thorn or broken stick scratched them. A mosquito might have buzzed in their ears, and a night moth flown against a cheek. A spider web across the path from tree to tree could have tangled in their eyelashes and beards, causing them to brush their faces in that way that you do to push the unseen threads away.

At one place, Jesus told eight of the apostles to wait,

and to pray for themselves, that they would not enter into temptation. He took Peter, James and John a little further on. Then he left them to go about a stone's throw away from them to be really alone, and pray. We're told that he knelt down and began the most agonizing time of prayer in all history. This was the Son praying to the Father at the moment in history that had been looked forward to for centuries. This was Jesus, who was truly Man as well as truly God, facing the most agonizing choice that has ever been made.

Stop and think a moment. Have you ever asked, or has anyone ever asked you, "Couldn't there be other ways of salvation? Why only one way? Surely there are many paths to heaven, aren't there?"

We want you to try to forget everything else right now, except that you can begin to understand about Jesus' prayer. The Trinity throughout all history has made it clear that there is no other way to get rid of sin, no other way for people to be forgiven, except for the Son of God to come and be the Lamb of God and die. All the lambs for centuries had made this clear, at the time of Abel, Noah, Abraham, Moses and Isaiah, and even that very night in Jerusalem when all the Jews had been eating the passover.

Jesus was now facing the final decision. It was really his choice. He was man and God. He was facing bodily suffering, and separation from the body. He was facing spiritual suffering that was beyond anything we can imagine—the Trinity, which had always been together, was about in some real way to be separated. The agony of taking our filthy sins upon him on the cross was ahead of him. It was *real*. There was Jesus in the quiet of nighttime sounds and smells and amid the softness of the air in that garden, with the men asleep instead of praying . . . so very alone, faced with being more alone than anyone has ever been or will be, the most alone moment of all history for eternity.

In the midst of this, Jesus cried out to his Father with the question, the question that everyone asks, but the question only he had a right to ask. The answer to this question was going to cost him the greatest suffering, suffering beyond any human imagination. He knew the answer but, as he faced the reality of that moment, the question was real. It was not a play or a piece of theater. Jesus the Son of God was asking with tears, with sweat pouring down his body, with blood sweating from his pores because of the intensity of his feelings. He asked: "Father, if it be possible, remove this cup from me." He asked three times. And we believe it is a correct understanding of this question and prayer to say it in these words:

"Father, can't there be another way? Father, can't you think of another way of salvation for the people? Father, is this really the only way to save people from the results of their sin?"

It was a breathless moment in the universe. The angels had been waiting for the victory to be won over Satan. The people who had died through the centuries were waiting in Hades for the price actually to be paid, and the door to be opened for them to go out to Paradise. Satan and the demons had tried to hinder Jesus from living, tried to kill him as a baby, tried to tempt him to sin. This moment of decision, the importance of the answer, meant total defeat to Satan.

Yes, it was a breathless moment. A question was being asked. A prayer was being honestly made. *Is* there another way? *Is* there another door to life? *Is* there another *truth*? The answer came three times . . . always the same, and Jesus knew there was no way for you or me, for all who have lived before and believed, for all who are alive today, for those in the future who will believe, and for the Jews who will turn to him in the future. Jesus knew there was no other way for any human being to be rid of sin, to have eternal life, to have a resurrected body, to enjoy the preparations he would be making for them in heaven. So Jesus bowed and said, "Thy will be done." He said that although his prayer was not answered as he pleaded for another way, he was willing to do God's will. He was willing to suffer, so that we would not have to suffer. He was willing to die, so that we would have life. He was willing to take our filthy sin so that we would be cleansed. He was willing to be separated so that we would never have to be separated from God. He was willing to go naked to the cross so that we could be clothed in the white linen of his righteousness. You can be sure there was and is no other way, or all this would have made no sense at all. If there were any other possible way, God the Father would have revealed it to the Son at that moment.

He went to find the others after this stupendous moment of suffering and final decision, and found all of them sleeping. Imagine having gone through that, to find your closest friends calmly snoring in the bushes, sleepily stretching themselves with waking-up questions. They had been too discouraged and sad to stay awake and pray, but their awakening would not have been much comfort to Jesus. For, just as Jesus spoke to them, a noisy crowd came up, shattering the quietness. Judas was just in front of them, and he came to Jesus and kissed him, because that was the sign he had arranged with the soldiers. Jesus said to Judas, "Are you betraying the Son of Man with a kiss?"

At that point, one of his disciples said, "Lord, shall we slice them with a sword?" And one of them cut off the ear of the high priest's servant with a swipe of the sword! But Jesus touched the man's ear and it became perfectly all right again. Then Jesus said, "Why are you coming to capture me with swords and staves as if I were a thief? I taught in the Temple every day, and you didn't touch me. But this is the hour of darkness, it is your time." After that the men took Jesus, and he told them to leave his disciples alone.

Matthew tells us that Jesus had said that, if he had wanted to, he could have called seventy-two thousand angels and more to help him. But he went willingly to suffer for our sakes. He let them bind him and lead him away to the high priest's house to begin his trial.

As the crowd went up the road with Jesus, Peter followed, but far enough away so he wouldn't be seen. Peter followed right into the high priest's open courtyard, or hall, and as some people had built a fire there, Peter came near it to warm his hands. A girl who was standing among the people looked at Peter and said, "This man was with Jesus also."

"Oh, no," Peter quickly said, "I don't even know Jesus."
What had Peter done? He had already denied Jesus. Soon
after that, Peter was asked twice more about knowing Jesus
and each time he said absolutely that he didn't know what
they were talking about, that he didn't know Jesus at all. The
third time this happened, a rooster began to crow, the first
crow of the morning. Peter suddenly remembered what Jesus
had said, "Before the cock crows this day you will deny me
three times." How terrible Peter felt as he realized he had
done this very thing. He was so sure he was going to be very
brave and follow Jesus even to the death, and here already he
had replied with fear to all three questions, and each time
had denied his Lord. Peter went outside the high priest's
house and wept bitterly.

The people that followed Jesus then were ordinary people, just as we are, with fears and doubts and weaknesses.
Moreover, they still had not really understood about Jesus'
death and resurrection. It must have been very hard to watch
the person you expected to be King, suddenly taken off and
tied up and treated roughly. And as the next hours came
along, it was even harder.

Today, we have the help of the whole Bible to make it
clear to us. We also have the help of the Holy Spirit in a way
that these men did not. Yet . . . we also have a struggle to be
faithful to Jesus when other people are mocking and laughing
and saying that none of it is true. We need to pray that we
will never deny him.

Jesus is betrayed with a kiss.   Luke 22:47–48

25
RIPPED FROM TOP TO BOTTOM!

In the last chapter, we left Peter crying in the garden because he had denied Jesus three times. But what was going on inside the high priest's house? The men who were holding Jesus were being very cruel to him. They mocked him and hit him. Then they blindfolded him and slapped him on the face, saying sarcastically, "Who is it that hit you?" And you can imagine their horrible laughter, taunting him to guess who they were. "Aaaa . . . tell us who hit you that time!" All the time Jesus was keeping as quiet as a lamb, although he knew well enough who had hit him. Just think, he knew not only their names; he could have told the family history of each one, and could have told every man exactly what he had done all through his life. He knew their ugly thoughts against him, because all men's thoughts are known to him. Yet he didn't say a thing. Of course, he also knew what was coming to him in the next awful hours. Having said to his Father, "Thy will be done, not mine," he intended to go quietly through all that was ahead of him, and to do it thinking lovingly of those for whom he was going to suffer.

Being God, Jesus knew *exactly* the ones for whom he was dying. Jesus is infinite, and just as God the Father is able to be alone with each of us when we pray, and hear all the details of our thanksgiving, our praise, our love, our requests, and desires, and is able to answer us individually . . . so Jesus was able to suffer all this torture, and to die for each one of us really thinking of each one personally. That is what it means to have a personal and infinite *Savior* who did all this for each one personally. We have a personal and infinite Father who can hear each child of his. He does not get impatient when a five-year-old talks to him, because he has time for people of every age-group. And we have a personal and infinite Holy Spirit, who can dwell in each Christian, and not only choose a few.

When the sun streaked its first rays across the morning sky, and the light softened the blackness of that night, all the religious leaders began to arrive at the high priest's house. Jesus had not had any sleep, and he had been taunted and tortured all night. These scribes and elders had probably just rolled out of their beds and had a good breakfast when they came to hold Jesus' trial. They were not coming to try to find out the truth about Jesus, and to do justice. They had only one idea and that was to find some excuse for killing him.

Now as they gathered together, and placed Jesus in front of them, they were a religious court, a court made up of religious leaders trying Jesus for a religious crime. Think of it! God the Son on trial for doing a religious crime! All through this book, we have seen how the Pharisees had become so blinded to the truth of the Bible, that their little rules were like dark glasses, or a smoked-up pane of glass, through which they looked at God's Word. They carried on criticizing Jesus until the end, when they were ready not only to try to do something like killing Lazarus again, but actually to kill the Messiah.

The question they asked was, "Art thou the Christ? Tell us." They were asking if Jesus claimed to be the Messiah prophesied in the Old Testament. He answered, "If I tell you, you will not believe." This was true, wasn't it? He had been telling them, and making it clear by doing miracles and by teaching from the Old Testament and telling them about the future . . . but they had not listened, and they certainly would not have listened now. So he said to them clearly, "Some day (hereafter) you will see the Son of Man sitting on the right hand of power and coming in the clouds of heaven" (Matthew 26:64). It makes shivers go up your spine when you think of those men looking so sneeringly and boldly into the face of the Son of God, and staring at him with hate and scorn, as he told *them* they would see him come back as King and Judge. Some day those men will see those same eyes judging *them,* and they were warned! The high priest said to the other religious leaders, "He has spoken blasphemy." And they all answered together, "He is guilty of death."

We must always remember that the real reason the men were killing Jesus was because he had told them he was God. How much opportunity those men had of knowing the truth! They had seen him raise Lazarus from the dead; they had heard his teaching; they could have checked up on the Old Testament prophecies and seen that they had come to pass. They heard him speak, preach, teach over and over again. What they threw into his face was their thought that he was *not* God. That was why they killed him. Today people do not have Jesus on trial in front of them in the same way, but when they laugh the Bible to scorn, and turn away from the teaching of the Old and New Testaments as if the Bible is only one more of men's books, when they say that Christianity is only one among many religions, when they say there are many roads to heaven—don't you *see* that they are judging Jesus just as much as these men were that day. They, too, are saying he is a liar and has not spoken true things.

Yes, it is like the parable Jesus told these people before about the owner of the vineyards who sent his servants and then his son. God sent prophets, and now his Son . . . and the men who that day could have accepted Jesus, will be one day judged by him. Here is another "backwards" thing: if people judge Jesus by saying he is not God, they will one day be judged *by* him. This is part of what Jesus meant in his sermon on the mountain when he said, "Judge not, that ye be not judged." Yes, he was talking about us judging other people with motes in their eyes while we have beams in our own. Remember we drew those pictures of eyes? But Jesus was also speaking about people who judge the Bible, and the God of the Bible—people who think they are better than God, just like those men who stood in front of Jesus that day. People think they are more loving, more compassionate, and have better ideas about how people should get to heaven— they judge God, and one day they will be judged by Christ. If we believe God, and his word to us, and accept Christ, then we will not be judged among the lost.

So the religious leaders had decided that Jesus must die. But they did not have the power in their court to put a man to death. So they had to go to a Roman court, to have Jesus condemned there by the Gentiles. The Roman court had the power to put a man to death. So the whole crowd rose up and led Jesus before Pilate, accusing him as they went along. They said to Pilate, "This fellow has been hurting our nation, and telling people not to give tribute to Caesar, not to honor Caesar properly. He goes around saying he is King." When Pilate turned to Jesus and asked, "Art thou the King of the Jews?" Jesus said that was right, but Pilate told the men he saw nothing wrong with that. Pilate knew that Jesus was not trying to overthrow the government. He knew that Jesus was speaking of an entirely different kind of kingdom. Remember that Jesus had said very clearly that they were to pay taxes when he said, "Render to Caesar the things that are Caesar's." Pilate could see no reason for killing Jesus; he did not think he had done anything wrong.

When the Jews told Pilate that Jesus came from Galilee, he thought that would be a good excuse for getting out of judging Jesus. So he said, "Take him to Herod; he's the one to judge people from Galilee." So Jesus was taken before Herod that day.

Herod had been wanting to see Jesus do some miracles, but that was not the time for miracles. That time was over. Jesus just stood silently, although he could have stopped the trial. He was silent as a lamb, the way Isaiah said he would be, and we can hear that in the words sung by the chorus in the *Messiah*. He didn't open his mouth.

Then Pilate said to the Jews, "I haven't found anything wrong with this man, and Herod hasn't either." Pilate knew that, to be a fair and just judge, he should simply let Jesus go, but to be a popular ruler, he needed to keep the Jews happy and he felt the Jews would be angry with him if he did the fair thing. So instead he said, "I'll just turn Jesus loose, as it's always my custom to turn one prisoner loose at Passover time." But when he suggested this, the mob cried out in a roar of angry voices, "No, no! Away with this man! Let Barabbas go." Barabbas was a murderer and a criminal.

Pilate again tried to release Jesus, but this time the mob cried, "No. No!" again. The wild shouts went out into the air, "Crucify him, crucify him." And all this so soon after those streets had heard him being praised! Now many had turned against him, and any friends he had had kept away. The third time Pilate said, "Why, what evil has he done? I find no wrong in him; I will just whip him and let him go." But the voices became even louder, shouting for Jesus to be crucified.

So Pilate took out a bowl of water. You might get a bowl of water, and show everyone in the family how it was. He washed his hands in front of everyone, just like that. It was his way of saying that the death of this man wasn't his idea, and he didn't want the blame. Have you heard people say, "I wash my hands of the whole affair"? Well, that is what Pilate was saying. But look, as one of you washes his or her hands in front of the others, that isn't a very effective way of getting rid of the guilt of sending the Son of God to his death, is it? You can't get rid of *any* sin by just washing your hands, and saying, "It isn't my fault."

Pilate was not a Jew; he was a Gentile. And as he now agreed to send Jesus to his death, it meant that both Gentiles and Jews shared together the responsibility of putting Jesus to death.

Remember our talk about motives? Neither Pilate's motive of wanting to satisfy the Jews so that he could be popular, nor his going through a little ceremony like washing his hands, was enough to free him from his guilt.

If someone is asking you to do something, and you know it is very wrong, but you go ahead and do it, just so that they won't be mad at you—can you just go over to that bowl of water, and wash your hands and say, "I wash my hands of the responsibility," and then do the bad thing and not be punished? God does not give any such stupid "ways out" anywhere in his Word, and if anyone tells us ways to "get around" right and wrong, they are making up "relative" things. Do you remember what we said about relatives and absolutes? Pilate was wrong. And that is an absolute!

» Then—as Matthew tells us—it was the rough Roman soldiers who grabbed Jesus, and took him into the big hall, where they took his clothes off and put a scarlet robe on him. They had the idea of taking branches from a thorn bush and weaving a crown out of them, so that the thorns would stick in his head. They forced it down on his head, saying in loud, mocking, sarcastic voices, "Hail, King of the Jews." They put a reed in his hand as if it were a king's scepter, but one of them pulled that out of his hand and used it to hit him with. How these Roman soldiers seemed to enjoy thinking things up in order to torture the Son of God! And after mocking him they led him out to crucify him.

One day, every one of these men will stand before Jesus the King and Judge. Seven hundred years before, Isaiah had written about Jesus, "I gave my back to the smiters and my cheeks to them that plucked off the hair: I hid not my face from shame and spitting" (Isaiah 50:6). Here stood men who knew that verse. Wouldn't you think those religious rulers would have thought of it? Jesus is now being spat upon, struck with the reed, and he is letting them do it. And the Jews had been told for centuries that this would happen to the Messiah. When Handel wrote the *Messiah* he used this quotation from Isaiah . . . which means that thousands of people are hearing the words, and should be understanding how the whole of history fits together.

Do you have a jigsaw puzzle, a good big one? Do put it out, and start it there on a tray or board so you can keep it around for a few days to remind you of something. All through the centuries from the time that Abel had stood there with the sacrifice that God had told him to bring, and Cain had turned away and judged that God's way was not as good as his own idea of bringing fruit—all this time God's teaching had been like fitting jigsaw pieces together. Maybe you don't see it all at once, but gradually you see where all the little pieces fit. And as we study this book of Luke and see where some of the other "pieces" fit in, it is very much like doing the puzzle. But the complete picture which we are going to see one day, can't be finished until Jesus comes back. Then it will be far more exciting than when you finish your jigsaw puzzle; it will be the most marvelous moment in all history. But lots of the pieces have been given to us—enough to get us excited about it all. Let's pray that more people will realize they are just kicking the pieces of a marvelous puzzle that will give them all the answers, and give them *hope.* Let's pray they'll start *doing* the puzzle.

We could think of it also as a tapestry, as it is really rather more like many threads woven into a marvelous picture, each thread of which is necessary for the perfection of the picture. A puzzle is easier for you to find and do as an illustration, but if some of you do needlepoint, or if you weave cloth with a special picture pattern in it, you can think of how God weaves the whole of history together, and remember that you are one of the threads! Even a five-year-old can have a small weaving frame. But, whether it is jigsaw puzzles you do, or weaving, or needlepoint, do remember that in this book we have only seen a very small part of all the things that fit together in the Bible. And everyone in the family of God who has lived since then—including each one of us who are in his family—"fits in" somewhere in the picture.

As they started on the road, when they had come out of the high priest's house, they saw a man named Simon, a Cyrenian. The soldiers pulled him into the procession, and forced him to carry the big heavy wooden cross upon which Jesus was to die. This man followed Jesus, carrying the cross, and the whole crowd of people followed after them.

When they arrived at a place called Calvary, they nailed Jesus to the cross, naked and with his head bleeding already from the thorns, and placed the cross between two others with a thief on either side of him. They put a sign over Jesus'

head in the three languages used most widely at that time—
Greek, Hebrew, and Latin: "This is Jesus of Nazareth, the
King of the Jews."

The first thing he did as he hung there was to pray in
agony, "Father, forgive them for they know not what they
do." What compassion he had! He had known this was going
to happen to him when, in the garden, he had prayed that
there might be another way. But now he had done what
Isaiah 50:7 says: "I have set my face like flint, and I know that
I shall not be ashamed." Jesus was not ashamed to hang
there, taking *our* shame upon him. He was naked for us,
bearing our shame . . . so that he could give us clothing
which is his righteousness. It is all so amazing! In Revelation
(3:18) we read, "I counsel thee to buy of me gold refined by
fire, that thou mayest become rich; and white garments, that
thou mayest clothe thyself, and that the shame of thy nakedness be not made manifest."

Historically, the Roman custom of crucifying was crucifixion completely without clothing. The humiliation included
being naked. It is amazing that in Psalm 22, before crucifixion
had ever been used as a means of death, the description of it
is so clear. People try to make the Cross just nice and religious and in so doing often remove the reality of the shame.
A pretty little gold cross does not represent what happened.
The Trinity had chosen and planned the manner and time of
the death that Jesus would die when he died that we might
live. He suffered that we might be comforted. He was rejected
that we might be accepted. He was separated from God the
Father that we might be forever with God. He bore the shame
of our sin and suffered that shameful death in front of people
that we might be rid of sin and shame forever. He was crucified without clothes in front of men and angels and demons,
that we might be given the clothing of righteousness which
we will wear before all people and angels. This is an *exchange*. Yes, he really hung there, making all these exchanges
possible. And while he was suffering, he prayed for the men
who put him there.

365

The Roman soldiers sat in front of the cross where Jesus was dying, and began to divide up his clothing among them. Each one took something, but when it came to his coat they decided not to cut it up into four pieces but to gamble for it, and give the coat to the winner. So they sat and gambled for a coat which would last only a few years, when if they had only lifted up their eyes to Jesus, and believed him, they would have received life everlasting, and a coat that would never grow old. Today, in the same way, people look "down" at houses, cars, airplanes, boats, jewels, collections of a great number of things which will not be lasting, and they waste their whole lives with their eyes turned "down," just as these soldiers were wasting their time when they could have realized that Jesus the Son of God was dying and that his death *could* make such a difference to them.

What were others doing at the foot of the cross? Some were making fun of Jesus, saying, "Himself he cannot save. . . ." (This was also prophesied in Psalm 22, and if you have bought records of the *Messiah,* this is one of the choruses you could listen to again now.) This must have been one of the most difficult tortures of all—to be taunted when he was suffering so terribly, and to know that he could have come down, he *could* have called on thousands of angels, and frightened them all. But if he had come down, we could not have been saved, we could not have been born again, we could not have become children in the Lord's family. It was for us that he just stayed there.

» One of the thieves who was dying beside Jesus made fun of him, saying, "If thou be the Christ, save thyself and us." So often people say this kind of thing to God today . . . acting as if God ought to prove to them in some direct way that he is God, and asking for something that would be contrary to his plan. The other thief was quite different; he showed he was sorry for his sin, and also that he realized that Jesus was God and that he believed that he could save him. While Jesus was dying there beside him, this thief cried out very earnestly for his own salvation, "Remember me when thou comest into thy kingdom." Jesus tenderly turned to him and told him that that very day he would be with him in Paradise. Just think, the thief was dying in agony for the sins he had committed. He had no time to go back and live a good life now. His life on earth was over, but because at that moment he accepted Jesus as Savior, in just a little while, when he had died he was going to enter Paradise. When he got there that very same day before sunset, Jesus would be waiting to welcome him.

At every point of history, there were *some* who believed, and others who mocked. Some at the foot of the cross may have believed, too, while others mocked or just stared. The women who had loved Jesus stood afar off, watching from a distance. They were deeply shocked, grief-stricken, sad, crushed, sick about what was happening. Yes, he had told his disciples that he would die and rise again, but his death had made them despondent and no one was thinking of his rising. We really cannot imagine what it was like to see him die, so we mustn't blame them for being sad and confused.

Suddenly a great darkness came over all the earth, and the sun did not shine. It was a supernatural darkness that God sent during Jesus' most difficult time of suffering. The pain of the crucifixion was very great, but it was not that which was the hardest for him to bear. At that point, as he became sin for us, the Father became separated from the Son, and he called out to God the Father, "My God, my God, why hast thou forsaken me?" God the Father could not look upon sin, and at that moment Jesus really did become sin for us. That was the worst suffering of all. In Psalm 22:1, written a thousand years before, this cry of Jesus, "My God, my God, why has thou forsaken me," was prophesied. Christ's work on the cross was over. He had paid the price for our sin.

Now, as we learn from John and from Luke, he cried, "It is finished. Father, into thy hands I commend my spirit." Again he had called God the Father, *Father,* and because Jesus' work on the cross was now complete, he *willed* to die and died. This made his death very different from the death anyone else has ever died. To all others, death comes without their being able to do anything about it. But in John 10:18 we are told that Jesus said, "I lay down my life, that I may take it again. No man taketh it from me, but I lay it down of myself. I have power to lay it down, and I have power to take it again." Just before that Jesus had said, "I am the good shepherd: the good shepherd giveth his life for the sheep."

Here is another perfectly fitting piece of the gigantic puzzle—or another thread that was so wonderfully woven by God into history. What am I talking about? About a supernatural event that only God could have made to happen, and it was stupendous because it should have proved to all the Jews that Jesus really was the Messiah. The thing that happened was this: just as Jesus cried with a loud voice and gave up his spirit, and died, there was a tremendous earthquake and rocks were split in half, graves opened and some of the Old Testament believers arose, and a very thick curtain in the Temple which separated the most holy place from the other room, a curtain called the veil of the Temple . . . suddenly ripped from top to bottom! It was so thick that no person could have torn it, and it ripped down by itself . . . ziprip . . . like that, and the holy of holies was no longer hidden.

Why? Each of these things that happened was to prove that the moment of history that everyone for centuries had waited for had taken place. Some of the believing dead came forth, to show forth the reality of what they had been waiting for. And the earthquake showed that nature has been waiting, too, as God tells us. And then in the Temple, the most exciting thing of all took place. I can't understand how anyone would know about it and not believe—especially the Jews then or now!

In Hebrews 9:3, 7, 11 and 12, and in Hebrews 10:18, 22, we have the teaching about what happened. In the tabernacle and in the Temple, there was a place called the holy of holies. In it was the ark of the covenant, and the tablets with the Ten Commandments. Over the tables of law, that is, the Ten Commandments, there was the mercy seat. Now this holy of holies was the place where God's presence was. God came there to meet with men. But because of sin, and because this place was really to be filled with God's presence, only one man could go there, the high priest, and he could go only once a year, as a representative of all the people. He had to bring the blood of the lamb, and sprinkle it on the mercy seat. That was like a lid that covered the box with the law in it. It was a picture of the fact that God's mercy "covered" the law. What does that mean? That when God forgives, he forgives all we have done in breaking the law, in sinning. But he can forgive only on the basis of the blood of the lamb. And, as you know, the lambs throughout all the Old Testament days, and right up through the life of Jesus, were *pointing ahead* to the day when Jesus would die. The lambs were a picture of Christ dying on the cross.

But the exciting part was this. Just at the very minute when Jesus actually died, God caused that veil, or very thick curtain, to split down so that the holy of holies was no longer hidden away. *Why*? Because now the real *Lamb of God* had died. Now sins could be forgiven, and no one had to come through a human priest any longer. In Hebrews 9:11, 12 we are told, "But Christ having come a high priest of the good things to come, through the greater and more perfect taber- nacle, not made with hands, that is to say not of this creation, nor yet through the blood of goats and calves, but through his own blood, entered in once for all into the holy place, having obtained eternal redemption."

What does that mean? It means that our detail-perfect Heavenly Father actually opened up the holy of holies in the Temple to prove that Jesus, who is now the High Priest, died himself, and that his blood opened up the holy of holies for ever, giving us all the right to enter into the presence of God when we accept Jesus as our Savior. Any person who accepts Christ as Savior and is thus born again, can now call out to God the Father at any time, and can be in his presence as if he is in the same room with him. The death of Christ on the cross opened up the holy place of being with God—for any of us who believe. The death of Christ gave a victory over Satan, who had separated us from God in the first place. But isn't it fantastic that the same God, who planned to have the baby

Jesus born in a stable so that it would be detail-perfect, perfectionist-perfect as the place for a lamb to be *born*—also planned to have the actual material veil split in half to make it *clear* that there was no use for a holy of holies any more, no need of lambs' blood any more—because Jesus had just that very second died!

We often wonder what people in the Temple thought. What could they have said about it? To fool themselves, people make up excuses for everything. Often they are so blinded by their own stubbornness.

We do know that the centurion, and those with him who were watching Jesus die, saw the earthquake, and the things that happened, and that they were very much afraid, saying, "Truly this was the Son of God." So, you see, some did believe.

Why don't you fix up a place maybe by putting two blankets or pieces of cloth or knitted afghans, or sheets, across chairs, making a closed-in place. Probably you won't want to rip a cloth in two, which is why I say fix two pieces of something, like blankets; though if you didn't mind ripping it, one would be better. Now, in this closed-in place, just put a box to represent the things that were in the holy of holies. Now let's read Hebrews 10:19–22 together, and while we are reading, darken the room and read by flashlight or candle. While one person ripzips (or pretends to ripzip) the cloth down from top to bottom to make the place open, try to have some small idea at least of what someone would feel like when they saw the veil of the Temple rip during an earthquake and darkness, after it had been in one thick piece for all those centuries! "Having therefore, brethren, boldness to *enter* into the holy place by the blood of Jesus, by the way which he dedicated for us, a new and living way through the veil, that is to say his flesh; and having a great high priest over the house of God; let us draw near with a true heart in fullness of faith, having our hearts sprinkled from an evil conscience and our body washed with pure water."

What's it about? Well, we are told we can enter into the holiest place . . . that means we can now pray, and be with

God right away when we talk to him. It means that we can do this because Jesus lets us in through the veil, which is his flesh, or his body. It was when his body died that the curtain ripped down. You see, the *real* ripping was the ripping apart of his body and soul, and that opened the way for us to come right into the presence of God, without being afraid and without having a bad conscience. We have a *way* to be washed clean as we come.

So as we come to God in prayer, we can think of coming right *through* that curtain, the curtain that only a high priest used to be able to come through!

26
"I JUST CAN'T BELIEVE IT!"

So the greatest moment in history had taken place, as the veil in the Temple had split and all the ones who had waited for centuries where the believing dead had been waiting, *knew* that they had been redeemed. And the angels in heaven, who had rejoiced for centuries over each person who had believed, knew that now the price had been paid for all these people's sins and those recorded names were *safe* for eternity, God the Father had seen his Son be faithful to the end. He had seen Jesus endure all the suffering until it was all over. The Trinity had accomplished what had been necessary for the victory over Satan, and Satan had failed to stop it. After all the years of looking forward in faith, Jesus had come as the Lamb of God. The time had *come* when people could begin to look back to what he had done and be absolutely sure that everything that needed to be done to open the way to God, had been finished. Yes, the veil was torn as a middle point of history; what happened when Adam and Eve had been turned out of the garden had now really been reversed. Instead of a division which could not be crossed, instead of a ravine which had no bridge, instead of a wall too thick to come through, the way was now open to anyone who would believe. Already the thief who had been hanging next to Jesus had found out what it was like to go not to Hades, but straight to Paradise.

But what about the apostles, and all the disciples who had followed Jesus, who had believed in him and loved him and spent all their time with him? Did *they* feel any joy because of what Jesus had done for them? Did they realize it was a victory over Satan? Did they talk about the exciting fact that the veil in the Temple had been split in two? Did they connect that with all they knew about the Old Testament and

372

the high priest only going into the holy place once a year? Did they remember what Jesus had explained to them about his death? Did they remember John the Baptist saying, "Behold the Lamb of God that taketh away sin of the world," and talk about how that had now taken place? Did they talk about their salvation now being sure and certain? Did they remember that Jesus was going to rise again, and plan to go and see that happen? Were they full of hope, expectation and excitement, realizing that they were living in the midst of the greatest moment of history?

The answer to each question is the same. No, no, no. Why? Because they were very human men and women. They had seen him roughly taken away by soldiers. They knew he had been tortured, spat upon, made fun of, paraded around in king's robes with a crown of thorns. They had seen him nailed naked to a cross, with his bones all out of joint and a face that must have horrified and shocked them because he was suffering so much. They were brokenhearted because they had watched all this happen to One they loved so much, but One whom they also expected to be their King. Yes, we know he had told them, but when people are filled with sadness and grief, when they are crying so hard they can't think of a thing, the pictures in their minds' eyes, the things they "see" inside their heads are all the awful things they have just seen and heard, so we can sympathize with them, and understand that everything else was blotted out altogether.

Take from a magazine a picture of something beautiful, like fields of flowers, sunshine on trees that have turned red and gold in the autumn, a seashore with gnarled cypress trees, or a garden full of flowers and birds. Now put this picture on a big baking tin with sides, or a washable tray so that you don't spoil things outside that area. Pour over this picture some sticky black treacle or molasses, or some dark sticky glue, the kind that carpenters use. Just let this dark, sticky stuff ooze over the beautiful picture, and into the sticky stuff sprinkle some bits of dirt, sand, ashes, coal dust, whatever you have around somewhere. Now can you see the picture? This is what happened to the disciples! Watching Jesus die, seeing him suffer, watching people treat him so sarcastically as well as cruelly, made it seem as if he had failed. Their thinking of him as the Messiah and King, the pictures they had had in their minds of his promises, were *all covered up* now by fears, doubts, sadness, despondency, and depression as sticky as that glue with dirt in it.

If you had heard their voices, I don't think you would have recognized them even as the same voices. I am sure they were so full of despair that even their voices were flat, listless, and without any note of music left. If they thought anything about the future during those hours at all, it would have been about going back to fishing, or tax-gathering, or whatever they had done before. They felt crushed. They walked with dragging steps, wondering how to pick up the pieces of their lives.

Have you ever had something happen that made you forget the good things that are coming? Even, perhaps, to forget something like a good dinner! But I also mean this: have you had things that made you so sad, so disappointed, so crushed and confused because it was *not* what you expected, that you have forgotten that this life is short—and that God has promised us fantastic things ahead? Each of us has moments of forgetting the real wonders ahead. This gives a very tiny idea of how the disciples felt. Their black disappointment was black indeed. Their minds were filled with sticky, dark, dirty pieces of despair.

Jesus had died. What was going on now at the foot of the cross? There was a member of the Jewish Sanhedrin who had not voted for Jesus to be put to death. Joseph, who lived in Arimathea, was a Jew who was among the leaders, but he had believed Jesus, and now he wanted to do something for him. Joseph was very rich and influential; so when he went to request something from Pilate, Pilate paid attention to him. "Jesus has died," Joseph said, "and I would like permission to bury his body in my private tomb." Pilate was surprised that Jesus had already died, because there had not been time enough yet for death to come. Remember that Jesus had willed to die, and had said, "It is finished," when his work was complete. Pilate did not believe he could be dead yet. So he asked the centurion, the Roman officer who had charge of Christ's crucifixion, "Is it true?" When the centurion assured Pilate that Jesus was truly dead, then Pilate gave Joseph, this rich man of Arimathea, this Jewish leader, permission to take Jesus' body. Joseph tenderly took the body of his Lord to a nearby garden, where his tomb was cut out of a huge rock.

As he carried him there, I wonder if he was remembering the verse in Isaiah, "And he made his grave with the wicked, and with the rich in his death" (Isaiah 53:9). Because, of course, Jesus died with a criminal on either side of him, and was now being buried in a rich man's grave. You see, God's details are all being taken care of. God does not make promises and tell things about the future without remembering to take care of them. It is like seeing an intricately hand-made piece of silver, with every tiny detail included by the artist . . . tarnished through the years . . . and suddenly polished! If you have some silver or brass thing—perhaps a large vase or jug or teapot, or a tiny spoon or fork, or a little sugar bowl—with a design in it, that is dull and dirty, it would be great to polish it *now*. This would be a small way of illustrating to yourself how brightly the details come out, when it is God's time to bring things to pass, or for what we like to call, "polishing the prophecies." God gives us his prophecies in detail. But, as years go on, people do not "see" them. The things they read are read as if they were covered with tarnish and green mold. Then God's moment comes to fulfull the prophecy, and as if good polish and cleaning fluid and a soft cloth and much rubbing were being given to each detail, suddenly it shines with brilliance, and you realize it was there all the time. You realize that what God said was important enough to fulfill in each tiny detail. It is beautiful, the work of an Artist, and nothing was too small to leave out!

From now on, the rest of your life, every time you polish silver, brass, bronze, copper, no matter how small the piece is, think of the prophecies that are already fulfilled and *thank* God for doing it all so carefully. Then think of all the prophecies of the future, and tell him you are really excited as you look forward to them all coming true in each shining detail.

Back to Joseph, as he came to the tomb cut in a rock; it was his own tomb, prepared for the time when he would die. Now he was giving it to Jesus. No one had ever been buried in it before. As Joseph and those helping him carried the body of Jesus to the tomb, some of the women followed to see where the body was laid. It would soon be the Jewish Sabbath day, and so everything had to be done in a hurry. The Jews were not allowed to bury the dead on the Sabbath day. The women planned to come back after the Sabbath day was over to place sweet-smelling spices in the tomb. When they had seen the spot, they knew just where they must come on the next day, the first day of the week.

Do you have any sweet spices in the house? If you have a little lavender in a sachet (or some cloves) you could put it in an envelope, or wrap it in a soft linen handkerchief, and pass it round for everyone to smell.

In John 19:38–42, we are told that Nicodemus came to help Joseph prepare Jesus for the burial. Nicodemus had brought with him a hundred pounds of aloes and myrrh. These were the spices which he and Joseph placed in the folds of the fine linen cloth as they wound it lovingly around the body of Jesus. This was the custom in those days, and the women had planned to bring some more on the first day of the week. As they were doing this, Nicodemus may have mentioned to Joseph what Jesus had told him one night as they talked together. You can read about this in John 3. Nicodemus had come to Jesus at night, because as a Pharisee and a ruler of the Jews, he didn't want people to gossip about his coming in the daytime. It was to Nicodemus that Jesus had so very clearly explained how to be born again. Nicodemus seemed mystified as he questioned Jesus, but Jesus was very patient in explaining that just as the serpent was lifted up when Moses was with the Israelites in the wilderness, so would the Son of Man be lifted up. Nicodemus, you see, would have known well the story of the time snakes were biting the Jews, when they had murmured against God, and Moses was told by God to lift a snake made of brass up on a stick. Anyone who looked at the brass snake would be healed of their snake bites. Jesus said this was a picture of what believing in him and being born again meant. Anyone who would look with faith, believing him and accepting him as he, Jesus, was lifted up on the cross, would be healed of their sin. I think the fact that Nicodemus came bringing a hundred pounds of spices to help Joseph, means that both these Jewish leaders loved Jesus and believed. So, you see, not all of the Pharisees turned away. You always find that out of *every* group of people, *some* do believe, while others turn away.

≫ As they laid the body of Jesus away, silent and cold, and as the face which had been so dear to them was covered with a linen cloth, they rolled a great stone in front of the door-like opening to the rock grave, and walked dejectedly away from the garden to mourn because they, too, thought that their Redeemer had been defeated. What a very sad and dreary Sabbath day these disciples must have spent! The putting away of a body in the grave seems so final, and is never easy. But they had had such different expectations about Jesus, so this was more than the usual mourning.

Strangely, another group of men were at that very moment remembering that Jesus had said he would rise again. All those who believed in Jesus and loved him had forgotten this, because it seemed so impossible to them, and it was all covered up in their minds by the dark memories, so now all they thought about was Jesus in that tomb, with the awful suffering before that. The women were planning to take some more spices because that gave them something they could do. It is like people taking flowers to put on a grave; it is comforting to the person who puts them there. They needed comfort; they were not planning to do anything to fool other people. All the disciples were planning to go back to their other work; no one expected them to make any new kind of start. It would be the last thing in the world any of them would have thought of, to try to fool anyone into thinking Jesus had risen.

But another group of men who did not understand anything about Jesus or his disciples, hated him, and were afraid that the disciples might be going to try to start something that would upset their position. As you will have guessed, they were the scribes and Pharisees who had wanted Jesus killed in the first place. These men came to Pilate and said something like this to him: "You know, Pilate, that man told the people that he would rise from the dead after three days. Of course, that was just a lie, but we are afraid that the people who followed him will come to the tomb where he has been laid, and steal his body away. Then they could just hide it and tell everyone he had risen from the dead. Pilate, would you make sure that the tomb is well guarded, so that this can't happen?"

Pilate answered something like this, "All right, go ahead and seal up the tomb yourselves, and get a watch put on the place." So they went and sealed that big stone with the mark of Pilate's authority, so that no one could open it up. Now no one could roll the stone away. Not even the women could have asked anyone to help them to put spices there. In addition, they put strong Roman soldiers as guards near the stone, so that no one could possibly steal the body of Jesus. Can't you just imagine the way they pulled their lips down at the corners and nodded their heads at each other, and winked their eye and rubbed their hands together, as they said, "There now, we've fixed them; they can't make up any fancy stories now. This business of following Jesus will end, because we've ended it once and for all. We will always have the proof that his body is right here in this tomb. We will keep it well guarded all the time, and we will stop any nonsensical stories because we can always show his dead body to people." Never forget that the tomb of Jesus was sealed tightly by the government and the army as well as by religious men, and that the guards were right there.

Very early the following morning, on the first day of the

week, on Sunday, the women came walking together and carrying the spices they had prepared. There were quite a few with them, in the early morning coolness of the garden as the first light streaked the sky. They must have been very heavy-hearted and sad as they talked together, hoping to do the last thing they thought they could ever do for Jesus. But when they arrived at the tomb, they found that an astonishing thing had happened—the great sealed stone had been rolled away, and the tomb was open! They entered the tomb, and found—it was empty! The body of Jesus was not there! Greatly astonished, they looked at each other. *What* could have happened? Where *was* the body of Jesus? Luke tells us they were "greatly perplexed," very puzzled. We can imagine that at that moment their faces were frowning and anxious. Then they saw what they thought were two men standing near them in shining garments. Afraid of what they saw, they bowed their faces to the ground. But these were angels who spoke to them in this way, "Why are you looking for a living person among the dead? Jesus is not here, he has risen. Don't you remember what he told you when he was still in Galilee? He told you that he must be delivered into the hands of sinful men, and be crucified, and he told you that he would rise again the third day."

How could they have forgotten! What a widening of their eyes there must have been as they looked at each other, and then hurried as fast as they could go, carrying the spices, which were of no use now. They wanted to get back to the eleven apostles and tell them what had happened. Now they were remembering. What an excitement must have been bubbling inside them! Can you imagine how they tried to tell the joyful news? "Jesus was not there! The stone was rolled away! Jesus has risen! We know, the shining men told us! He arose!"

I'm sure they could hardly get the words out . . . but what was the reaction, a shout of joy? No. The disciples scoffed at them. "You crazy women, you are really out of your minds," was the sort of thing they must have said. They

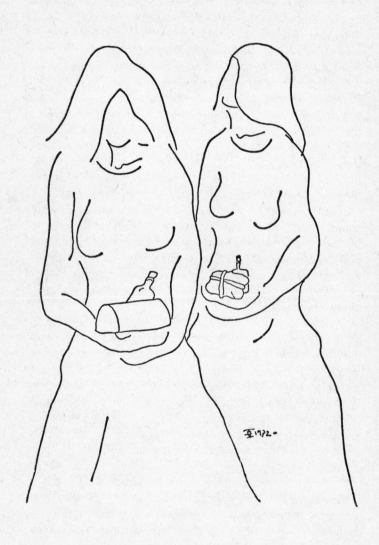

thought they were telling some sort of fanciful story. They just did not believe that the broken, torn, dead body of Jesus could possibly have risen from the tomb.

Peter and John were curious, however, and thought they would go see for themselves. John ran ahead and got there before Peter but, as John was peering in from the opening, Peter ran right inside and looked around. They saw the linen grave clothes neatly folded in a pile, and the cloth that had been over his face folded a little away from the rest. There was no sign of rush; no one had torn the clothing from Jesus to steal the body. No, Jesus had risen from the dead. He had simply stood up. His body was alive once more, and he had carefully left everything in perfect order before he stepped out of the tomb. Peter wondered what had happened, but John saw and believed the truth. John was the first of the disciples to believe the glorious fact that Jesus, his Redeemer and Lord, had risen from the dead.

In John we are told that, after the disciples went away again, Mary Magdalene stood outside the sepulchre weeping. As she wept, she stooped down and looked into the sepulchre, and saw two angels in white sitting, one at the head and one at the foot of the place where the body of Jesus had been lying. The angels said to her, "Woman, why are you weeping?" and she answered, "Because they have taken away my Lord, and I know not where they have laid him." And when she had said this, she turned away from the tomb, and saw Jesus standing there, but she didn't know it was Jesus. Jesus' risen body had some different qualities, so that people didn't always recognize him immediately. She thought it was a gardener, so she said to him, "Sir, if you have taken him away, tell me where you have laid him, and I will take him somewhere else." And Jesus said to her, "Mary." She recognized his voice, for she turned toward him and said, "Rabboni" which means "Master." Then Jesus said, "Don't touch me, because I have not yet ascended to my Father." That means

The women brought spices to the tomb.   Luke 24:13

he wanted to go to heaven in his risen body and be with his Father before anyone touched him.

Can you imagine the entrance of Jesus into heaven in his resurrected body? His body was the first resurrected body. He raised other people from the dead, like Lazarus and the son of the woman who was being taken to be buried outside the city, and the daughter of Jairus, but their bodies were just the same kind of bodies that would get sick, be hurt, get scratched and burned and have illnesses and die again. Jesus was in the first body to be a body to live for ever and ever. We will hear more about what a resurrected body is like in a little while. But first let's keep thinking about how amazing it would have been for all the angels to have Jesus back to heaven after his life on earth, and then his death and resurrection.

Jesus made it clear to Mary that, until he had been with his Father, no one else was to touch him. Then Jesus said, "Go to my brethren." (Isn't that great that he now calls them his brothers? It is a special new name, now that his death for them and for us is over, and so sin is truly cared for, and we can be his brothers and sisters in a real way.) "Say to them that I ascend to my Father, and your Father, to my God and your God." You see, he is making it very clear that they are in the family with him now, and that God the Father is both Father and God to them. What a message for her to carry to the others! She was the first person to see Jesus in his new body, his risen body, and to hear his voice again. She knew without a shadow of doubt that he had risen! And Mary Magdalene went and told the disciples that he had spoken these things to her.

》 That same day, two of the disciples were walking from Jerusalem to a nearby village called Emmaus. As they walked along the road, they talked together about the things that had happened during the previous few days. Their faces were sad, and their conversation was without joy. While they were talking, the risen Lord Jesus himself came near to them, and asked, "What sort of a conversation are you men having to make you so sad?" But we are told they didn't recognize Jesus. Thinking him to be a stranger, they began to tell him all about Jesus. They told the story of how the chief priests had delivered him to be crucified. "We had thought he would redeem Israel," they said as an explanation of their sadness. "Then a most extraordinary thing happened this morning. Some of the women who are in our group went to the tomb very early, and when they came back, they told us they didn't find Jesus' body, and also had a vision of angels who told them that Jesus was alive. And some of the men who were with us went to the tomb, and found it to be just as the women had said."

Then Jesus said to them, "You men have slow hearts to believe. Don't you *know* the things the prophets told concerning Christ? Don't you *know* that Christ had to suffer all these things and then to enter into his glory?" Then for the rest of the walk Jesus began with the books of Moses and explained the Old Testament to them. What a wonderful "polishing of the prophecies" that must have been! Think of having Jesus himself tell how all the threads of the Old Testament fit together, and how recent events had been exactly as God had told them this would be. They must have marveled at the brilliance of this Bible study as the "stranger" unfolded so much to them of the prophecies about the Messiah.

As they came to the house in Emmaus, they invited him in to have supper with them, still not knowing who he was. But when Jesus took some bread as he sat at the table, and broke it and blessed it, suddenly they knew who it was who was eating with them. We are told that "their eyes were opened." But as soon as they knew who he was, he vanished from their sight.

They got up and went off immediately to Jerusalem to tell the others what had happened; they could not see him now. When they reached Jerusalem they found the apostles gathered together, and others with them, saying, "The Lord is risen indeed, and has appeared to Simon." Then they told the others all about their walk, and how they didn't know him until he broke bread with them. Just as they were talking excitedly about all this, suddenly Jesus himself stood there among them. They were terrified, and thought they were seeing a ghost. So Jesus said to them, "Why are you so troubled? Why do these thoughts arise in you? Look at my hands and my feet, it is I myself. Handle me, and see, for a spirit hath not flesh and bones as ye see me have." And when he explained this, he showed them his hands and feet.

We want you to notice that he did not say just "Look." He told them to *touch* him. They were able to shake hands and feel him now, so he must have gone to his Father and have come back. He did not get impatient with their doubts and fears. Notice that Jesus wanted them to be sure he had risen in the body. Jesus wanted them to know he was not a ghost, not a spirit, but that his was a resurrected body. He showed them the scars the nails had made in his hands and feet. He wanted them to know the truth about the resurrection, so that they could explain it to others, and be certain themselves.

Now we are told that they "yet believed not for joy." It was the sort of thing that happens when people hear some marvelous piece of news, or are given a very unexpected surprise, and they keep saying, "I just can't believe it." They were so happy and excited that they felt they couldn't believe it could be real.

Suppose we who are reading this together had not been together for a long time, and had been afraid we would never see each other again, and suddenly we looked up and saw each other. We'd want to hug each other, or shake hands or something, to be sure we were actually seeing each other. Right now shake hands all around! Can't you sense the difference between shaking hands—Margaret and Elizabee, Kirsty and Becky, Fiona and Jandy, Ranald and Jessica, Natasha and John, Lydia and Samantha—and just *seeing* each other when you didn't expect to? Yes, shake hands now and think of how the disciples must have felt when *they* actually realized *by touch* that Jesus had risen in his body.

But because they still had that feeling of unreality, of it not being possible that it could be real, Jesus very patiently said they were to do something else that would help. He said, "Have you anything here to eat?" So they brought him some boiled fish and some honeycomb. Now a spirit without a body cannot eat. Jesus is showing them that he is able to eat in this resurrected body, so that when he talks to them about the resurrection of all the rest of us, they and we will understand that we will be able to eat, too. The resurrection is a bodily one.

Do you have a honeycomb? or some honey? or fish? If so, fix a plate for each person with honey and perhaps a scone (or biscuit) to put it on, and some fish, or a bit of other food. Have some refreshment *right now*, remembering that you are going to be able to eat like this when your body is raised from the dead, or when you are changed in a twinkling of an eye before you die—if Jesus comes back first. Paul says we are going to meet him in the air, and then come back with him. Let's try to feel how fantastically excited the disciples must have been when they saw him bite into the fish and chew it and swallow it. Yes, indeed he is risen! He is our living Lord.

But Thomas, called Didymus, was not with them when Jesus came. The other disciples said to him, "We've seen the Lord, Thomas." But he said, "I won't believe it, unless I myself see in his hands the print of the nails and thrust my hand into his side." (Jesus had a big gash in his side, made when one of the soldiers pushed a spear into him on the Cross.) And eight days after this, the disciples were in the room, with Thomas there, too, and Jesus came. The doors were shut, and he suddenly stood in the middle of the room, and said, "Peace be unto you." Then Jesus said directly to Thomas, "Reach out your finger, and see my hands, and put out your hand and push it into my side: and don't be without faith, but believe." And Thomas answered and said to him, "My Lord and my God."

Then Jesus said to him, "Thomas, because you have seen me, you have believed. Blessed are they that have *not* seen, and have believed." Jesus is speaking about those who looked forward to his coming and believed without seeing him, and about those who have believed since he went back to Heaven, without seeing him. Today *we* are in that class . . . we have not seen him . . . and we can have that special blessing as we come to believe, without seeing. Do you believe? You see, Thomas should have believed what the others told him about seeing Jesus after he had risen.

If you now have Handel's *Messiah,* do select the aria from the third part, the soprano solo, "I know that my Redeemer liveth," and listen to it. Job, who lived before Moses, believed this . . . all those centuries before. But God did not let Job believe in vain. Job's certainty has been fulfilled thus far . . . and both Job and all the others who are looking to the day when our bodies shall be raised, will not be disappointed. God's promises do not fail. God keeps his promises. Jesus is saying, "Blessed is Job," because Job believed without seeing. Are *you* blessed?

Later, on another day, Jesus came to the disciples on the sea of Tiberias. The ones there that day were Simon Peter, and Thomas, and Nathanael of Cana in Galilee, and the sons of a man called Zebedee, and two other disciples. Simon said to them, "I'm going fishing." And they said, "We'll go with you." So they went out and got into a ship right away, but all night they didn't catch a thing. When the morning came, Jesus stood on the seashore, but the disciples didn't know it was Jesus. Jesus called to them, "Children, have you caught anything?" and they answered, "No." So he said, "Cast your net on the right side, and you'll have some." So they cast where he said, and they had so many fish that they could hardly draw up the net for the large number of fish.

Then the disciple whom Jesus especially loved, John, said, "It is the Lord." And Peter grabbed up his coat and pulled it around him, for he had been fishing naked, and he jumped into the sea and waded to the shore. They were close to land, about three hundred feet away, and the other disciples came into shore in the little ship, dragging the net with fish. As soon as they came to the land, they saw a fire had been built, and on the hot coals some fish had been laid to broil, and there was bread! Now Jesus told them to bring the fish they had just caught. Simon Peter drew in the net which was full of really big fish, and when they were counted there were a hundred and fifty-three of them, yet the net had not broken. Then Jesus said, "Come and eat." So Jesus, the risen Lord, had cooked a meal for them, and now he was serving them bread and fish!

Paul says that Jesus was seen after his resurrection at one time by more than five hundred people (1 Corinthians 15:6). He appeared to very many people, and not just to the twelve apostles. Many knew that Jesus had risen, and that he had a victory over death. No longer were they crushed and depressed and in despair over a dead Christ. They knew they had a risen Savior, and they were ready to listen to what he would have them do.

We need to be sure he is our Redeemer . . . so that we can sing "I know that my Redeemer liveth," and *mean* it! He can be yours, he can belong to you in a very real way . . . as soon as you accept that he suffered and died for you. He rose for us, too . . . so that we can rise!

27
EVERYBODY CAN KNOW

This is the last chapter of this book, though there is so much we want to tell you about the wonder of all that God has given in the Bible that it would take hundreds more pages before we felt that it was really finished. John, who wrote the fourth Gospel, felt this much more than we could feel it. When he came to the end of his chapter 20, John said that there were many other proofs that Jesus did that were not written down. But John said that what he had written was written that everybody who reads and finds out about these things might *believe* and *know* that Jesus is the Christ, the Son of God, and that believing, then they might have life through his name.

The whole purpose, you see, is that God gave enough reasonable proof so that people could believe and *know* and have *life* for ever. At the end of his 21st chapter, John said that there were so many other things that Jesus did that he supposed that, if every single thing were written down, the world wouldn't be big enough to contain all the books! But God gave *enough* so that people could understand with their *minds*, and see how logical it all is, how it answers the questions we naturally have about things, and how fantastically it all fits together, like the jigsaw puzzle and the weaving of a tapestry. God gives enough so that we can be excited and hopeful about the future. God gives enough for us to be able to explain it to other people, so that they can know, too. God has made it all fit into one book that can be carried around.

If, as John said, everything Jesus did when he was on earth had been written down, and if, as John thought, that would make so many books that the world couldn't hold them—think how many books it would have taken to explain

in detail the way God *created* everything! Think how many
books it would have taken if God had explained all nature and
science from his perfect knowledge of it all! But God made it
possible for every person to have this one important book
with *just* enough so that we could know all we *need* to know,
to believe and to have everlasting life, and everything we
need to know until Christ comes back again. This book does
not need a library to contain it! No palace, house, tent, hut,
cave, spot on the sidewalk or pavement or under a tree, is
too small to contain this one book. It can be carried about in
the pocket. It is in nearly all languages. It can be read over
and over again in a lifetime. People can read it through once
every ten months if they read four chapters a day.

I want you to take that Bible of yours and put a lot of
books on the table and floor . . . and the Bible beside them
. . . *or* carry your Bible around, and stand in front of the book
cases if you have any. Some day this week, take your Bible
with you and stand in a library in your village, town, city,
university—wherever you can walk into a library. Walk into a
book store with your Bible. Compare wherever you can the
size of that one little book, with all the books in the world!
Yet it contains *truth*, and it is the entire condensed history
God wants us to understand, and the entire condensed teaching of the way of life we are meant to follow, and the entire
condensed prophecy of the future ahead of us. On top of
that, it tells us how to be rid of our sin, so that we can be
sure of eternal life.

We have understood and come to "see" some things
very clearly, as we have discovered things together during
these chapters. We have found fresh things ourselves. It is
exciting to feel that some things are becoming clear, like
freshly washed and polished crystal. But please do something
together right now. Get a piece of glass. Do you have a part
of a window pane, broken but too big to throw away? No?
Well, do you have a piece of glass of some size, the bigger
the better? If not, do you have a window that opens on to a
balcony or porch? A window you can stand on both sides of?
What we want you to have is some piece of clear glass. Smear

the glass with streaks of cleaning powder mixed with water, or something that will smear it up and make it hard to see through, but *not* so that you can't see *anything*. If you have a piece of dark glass, or very dark glasses . . . you could add a bit of smeared-up soap to those. Now—hold the glass in front of you, one at a time. Or put on the glasses that have been smeared up, or stand one at a time on the other side of the window. Can you really *see* each other, or the things that you want to show each other? Looking through the dark, smeared-up glass, how sure can you be of the details of each other's faces, or of something you have in your hands?

Now . . . take a well-polished, clean, clear piece of glass, or glasses, and look through them. Some difference! One more thing: take two of the nicest clear or crystal glass dishes or drinking glasses or whatever shape of glass you have, smear *one* up with something to make it dirty (but not so as to ruin it), and wash and rub the other one till it shines. Put these in front of you now, and let's go on.

In 1 Corinthians, Paul says, "For now we know in *part*, and the day is coming when we shall know perfectly . . . for now we see *through a glass darkly* . . . but the day is coming when we shall see face to face. . . . " No matter how wonderfully we begin to understand, no matter how real things become to us, it all is as though we were seeing it through dark or smeared-up glass, compared with the marvelous way we are going to see and understand when we see Jesus face to face. Yes, from time to time as you walk in the woods, or by the sea or a lake, or in a park where there are birds and trees . . . look at the beauty, the details, and then put on smeared-up glasses and see the difference.

Yes, God polishes up prophecy when he brings it to pass . . . so that there are shining details being understood, as the disciples understood after Jesus rose again, and as we can understand as we read about it now. *But* there is much, much more ahead of understanding, and of seeing, and of beauty—beauty beyond anything we can imagine. If we could see now—we would burst! In these bodies, we couldn't stand the wonder of it all. We need our resurrected, changed bodies, like Christ's resurrected body, to be able to stand the clear, clear view, to stand the brilliance of seeing face to face.

Paul saw things very clearly, and he said that there was danger of his being exalted above measure because of all the wonderful things he was seeing and understanding (2 Corinthians 12:7, 9, 10). He called them revelations. What does it mean? Well, that God was making things so very clear to Paul, that Paul could have been too excited to go on and do what he needed to do here on earth! When you get too excited about what is coming, you can't go on with what you have to do, can you? Paul said he had to have a "thorn in the flesh"—that means poor eyesight or some sickness, or lameness, or headaches, or pains in the joints, or some kind of trouble—and he had this "thorn" so that he could keep his excitement from ruining what he needed to do. When he prayed that God might take away his "thorn," God's answer was "My grace is sufficient for thee, for my strength is made perfect in weakness." It is not the time *now* for everything to be perfect, for all our prayers and desires to be answered, or for all our difficulties to be taken away. That time is *coming*, and we need our new bodies to be able to stand the excitement and joy. But what we can have now, that we won't have then, is his strength in our special weakness right now. What we have now is the opportunity of seeing how he can give us just the strength we need a minute at a time for whatever is happening that very minute.

Now let's go back to that time when Jesus was with his disciples in his resurrected body. They have seen him, touched him, watched him eat, eaten food he had cooked and handled with his own hands . . . and we are told in Luke 24:44, 45 that he took time with them to go back over everything in the Old Testament about himself, so that they would understand it clearly. He said, "I told you while I was teaching you day by day, that all the things written by Moses would come to take place now. I told you that the things the prophets wrote were going to come to pass. I talked to you about what David wrote in the Psalms about me." Then he went on patiently and taught them from the Psalms, the prophets, and

Moses' books again and showed how it all fitted together. He opened their understanding so that they might understand the *Scriptures.*

How marvelous it would have been to have heard him! Is that what you think? Yes, but you must not forget that he stuck to the Scriptures. They did not have an edge on us. He stuck to what God had written for his people through all the ages. He polished it for them, but it was not something new; it was what had been there for them to discover before, and is still there *now*. We have the Old Testament which Jesus explained, and we have the New Testament which God gave to complete all we need to know now. We have even more than they had that day, because we have *all* the New Testament, including the book of Revelation, which takes us right into heaven, with some description of the heavenly city, too! That was given to John later on an island where he was shut up in a kind of concentration camp.

No, that day they didn't have as much as we have now as we stand in front of all the books with our Bible in our hands! Jesus showed them how the living history of that time fits in with the Old Testament Scriptures. But with all that has been added in the New Testament now we can understand much more of the present and the future.

At last the disciples saw the whole picture clearly. No longer were they confused. Now they knew that Jesus, the Son of God, had not failed, had not been defeated because he was tortured and put to death. Now they realized and understood that in dying he had fulfilled all the prophecies given through the centuries about the Lamb of God who would suffer for the sins of his people.

» Jesus gently gave time for all this to be very real to these disciples who were so dear to him. He understood that they had been through terrible fears and doubts and that they needed reassurance and time to be *very certain* of his resurrection. He knew they were going to face all kinds of persecution in the future, and that they needed strong certainty that it really was true that there had been a victory on the cross, and not a defeat. So Jesus stayed for forty days on the earth, coming to various people at different times, talking to them and explaining things. Forty days—a month and ten days, quite a long time. It doesn't seem like just a dream if you are with someone from time to time during a forty-day period, whereas it might if you only saw someone once.

Once during the forty days, that time on the seashore, John tells us that after they ate, Jesus called Simon Peter to him and asked him, "Do you love me more than these?" (that is, more than all the fishing and everything?), and Peter answered, "You know that I love you." Jesus said, "Feed my lambs." (That means he wanted Peter to give spiritual food to people who would be accepting Jesus as Savior. Jesus wanted Peter to teach the Scriptures to people, and to explain things to them.) Then Jesus asked a second time, "Simon son of Jonas, do you love me?" And again Peter answered, "You know that I love you." And Jesus said, "Feed my sheep." Jesus was making it clear that the *motive* for telling others the truth and explaining the Bible to people, and telling them about himself, is love for him. To show our love for him, we are to give "food" to other people—spiritual food.

Then a third time Jesus asked, "Simon, son of Jonas, do you love me?" And this time we are told Peter became sad because he was being asked again whether he loved Jesus. So this time Peter replied, "You know all things, Jesus. You know that I love you." So Jesus said, "Feed my sheep." But then Jesus went on to tell Peter that he was going to be very persecuted for telling people about the Bible, the truth and about Jesus himself. He told Peter that one day he would be stretched out and carried off. He meant that Peter would be crucified, killed as a martyr. There have been many martyrs in history, martyrs for the Christian truth, people who have been killed rather than give up their faithful declaration that Jesus is God, and that the Bible is true.

When Peter heard this, he first looked around him, and asked "What is going to happen to John? Will he suffer like that too?" Now Jesus' answer to Peter is what we *each* need to hear. He said, "If it is my will for him to live and be around until I come back again, that is nothing for you to worry about. You are to follow me." In other words, Jesus did not say John *would* live until he came back, but that for each one of God's children, for each person who is a Christian, there is only one main concern, one important thing to do, and that is to follow the plan of God for his or her life. The plan God has for each person is also important in the jigsaw puzzle of the whole of God's history. The plan he has for each one is a thread, that would cause a raveling to take place in the cloth, if it were cut out.

Take your jigsaw puzzle now. Put it together, if it still needs that. Then take out a few pieces from here and there; put them aside in a box. Now look at it—the total of the picture isn't there. Take a piece of cloth—not a good tapestry, of course, but some cloth with a pattern, or even an old sweater you are going to use as a dust cloth—something that won't matter spoiling. Take some threads out and make it ravel in a few places. Now this is nothing compared with the beauty of the tapestry God is weaving, but can't you imagine a gorgeous work of art with raveled bits, threads missing right in the middle of it?

Yes, each person's part is important to the entire picture. And each person's victory is important in the battle against Satan. The total battle is made up of millions of attacks and defenses and skirmishes. The total victory is made up of millions of little victories. Each victory is important to the whole thing—to the defeat of Satan. Satan is to be defeated in every single *kind* of thing he attempts to do against God, including whatever he attempts in each of our lives.

What do I mean? Well, let's look at the 11th chapter of Hebrews. Read it all some time. If you are sitting under the trees in the summer, or by a roaring fire in the fireplace in the winter, or out on a balcony, or inside an apartment in the fog—if you have time right now, read it. Otherwise read Hebrews 11 later together, and then read this chapter over again.

Hebrews tells of many of the things that people who are believers have done during the centuries of history. It tells of

Daniel in the lion's den, believing God and having faith, and experiencing the wonder of an answered prayer, keeping the lions from eating him. It tells of Abel who believed God and by faith brought the right sacrifice. It tells of Abraham who had such trust in God that he took Isaac up the hill to sacrifice him at God's command, and of the marvelous substitute that God provided, the ram in the thickets which took Isaac's place so that Isaac did not have to die. It tells how Joshua by faith marched the men around Jericho's walls until they fell down.

Just as John said that, if he wrote all the things Jesus had done the books would be enough to fill the world, so the man who wrote to the Hebrews said that there was not enough time to tell of all the people who had done fantastic things by faith. But you will notice that another list of people starts in verse 35, and tells of those who were tortured, mocked, persecuted, stoned, sawn in two—and that these are said to be just as important as Daniel and Abraham; they had a victory of faith, because they loved God and trusted him, although no miracle happened to deliver them from the pain of death.

Jesus told Peter not to think about John. Actually John went to an island and wrote the book of Revelation and lived to be an old man. Peter had a tremendous work to do preaching, and finally he was killed because he taught the truth. Which of them was more important? Both were important.

Now add this to what we are thinking about. There is Job. We just talked about how fantastic it was that he believed in the resurrection and expected to be raised, way back all those years before Christ. Job was accused by Satan of not loving God. Satan went to God and said, "Look at Job! He only loves you for what he can get . . . for all the fine houses, lands, cattle, health, wealth . . . Let me spoil all that and Job will hate you." Well, Satan did spoil all that Job had, and Job ended up sitting in ashes, full of boils and with everything gone. But he still loved and trusted God. Satan was defeated. A victory had taken place in the heavenlies—Satan was trying to win a point against God, and because Job trusted God,

God won the point. The victories of each person just in loving and trusting God when it is hard to do so, when we can't understand the reason for some suffering or disappointment, are just as important as the wonderful answers to prayer that do come.

God does not promise to treat each of his children the same in this life. God does not say that each one of his children will have the same pattern of living or follow the same plan. God is a God of diversity. God can make trees—but among the trees are hundreds of kinds of trees. God can make apple trees but among the apple trees are hundreds of kinds of apples. God can make one apple tree, but among the apples on that tree no two look identically alike. God is able to make snowflakes, and make each snowflake differently. God has a different plan for each of his children—but it all fits together.

What about Peter and John? What about all those people who were persecuted? What about the people in Chinese prisons today, or in Siberia, or in other places where Christians are not free? What about Christians in hospitals with cancer? We could make a list pages long of all the difficulties and problems people have—people who are the Lord's children.

Do you think God is ashamed of having people have such different lives? In that same chapter in Hebrews, in verse 16, we read, "Wherefore God is not ashamed to be called their God: for he hath prepared for them a city." No, God is not ashamed to be called the God of Job, or of Peter, or of the people who suffer today, because he has prepared a marvelous city that is so wonderful that we will all forget our sufferings. We are told that the wonders of what is ahead of us are so amazing that they cannot be imagined, and that our present suffering will be just for a tiny moment as compared with the eternity ahead.

Jesus told the disciples—and us—in John 14 that we are not to let our hearts be troubled because we believe in God, and there are many dwelling places in his Father's house. He said, "I go to prepare a place for you. And if I go and prepare a place for you, I will come again, and receive you unto myself, that where I am, you may be, too." That was a promise that fits in perfectly with the information we get in Hebrews that God is preparing a city. The Father and the Son are preparing places of magnificent beauty for us in a marvelous city!

Jesus also said in John 14, "I will pray the Father and he shall give you another Comforter, that he may abide with you for ever." That means that this Comforter will always stay with us. Who is the Comforter? The Holy Spirit, the Third Person of the Trinity, will always be in us once we have accepted Christ as Savior. We have the Father to talk to at any moment of the day or night, we have the Holy Spirit living in us, and both the Father and the Son preparing a place for us. In Isaiah 64:4 we are told this: "For from of old men have not heard, nor perceived by the ear, neither hath the eye seen a God beside thee, which worketh for him that waiteth for him." That is an exciting promise from the Creator of all the beauty in this universe that we have seen and heard. He promises that we have never heard music, or birds, or water beating on rocks, or words or ideas that will compare with what we are going to hear one day. He promises that we have never seen sunsets, or moon on snow peaks, or flowers in the spring, or butterflies, or forests of trees, or star-studded skies that can be compared with the beauty that he is preparing for us. *If* we are *waiting* for him, this is what we can look forward to. Are we waiting for him? That is the only question.

» At the beginning of the book of Acts, we are told what took place toward the end of that forty days. We are told that during the forty days Jesus showed himself alive, in his body, resurrected, by many infallible proofs. What is "infallible"? That which is perfectly right and cannot be a little bit wrong. Are you ever infallible? No, because you can make mistakes. Are we infallible? No, because we can make mistakes. God is infallible. He never makes mistakes. God's Word, the Bible, is infallible because it is the Word of the infallible God. Now God tells us that the proofs of the resurrection of Jesus, in his body, are infallible, and that Jesus gave not just a few, but many infallible proofs to the disciples during those forty days. Also Jesus spoke about many things that had to do with the kingdom of God.

As Jesus talked to them all together at one time, he told them they should wait in Jerusalem until the promise that he had made to them came to pass. What was the promise? Well, the one we just talked about . . . that he would send the Comforter, the Holy Spirit, after he left them. He said he would not leave them as orphans. They were to wait in Jerusalem for the Holy Spirit to come to them. Then someone asked Jesus a question. "When will you restore the kingdom of Israel?" They wanted to know when he was going to be King. And Jesus said that no one was to know that except God the Father. God the Father is the only One who knows when Jesus is to come back again.

"But," Jesus said, "you will receive power when the Holy Spirit comes to be in you, and after that you shall be witnesses unto me in Jerusalem, Judea, and Samaria, and unto the uttermost parts of the earth."

They were standing on a hill opposite Bethany when he said this. He held up his hands to bless them, and while they were looking right at him . . . he started to rise up from the ground. Up and up he went. Can't you imagine them turning their heads up, leaning back a bit to watch as he went up higher, and then disappeared into a cloud! You cannot blame them for keeping their heads turned up, in case they would catch another glimpse. This was the first time anyone had seen anyone go up like that since Elijah went up. And Elisha was the only one who had seen Elijah go up to heaven in a fiery chariot. Now all the disciples are watching Jesus go. He did not have a chariot or anything . . . he just went off into a cloud. He had appeared and disappeared for forty days, but this was his official departing, just as his baptism was the official beginning of his ministry. While they were still looking up, two men stood by the disciples in white clothing. Were

---

The disciples gazing into heaven.   Acts 1:9–11

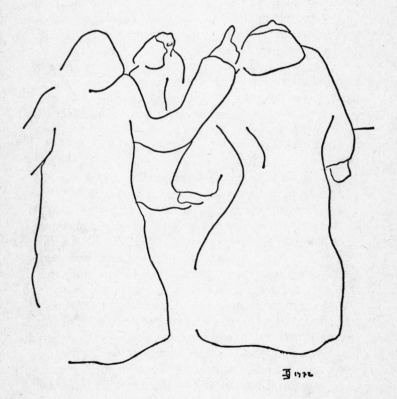

they the same two angels who had come to the tomb? We don't know, but anyway they were two angels with a message from God. They said, "Why are you standing there gazing up into heaven? This same Jesus, who was just taken from you up into heaven, will come exactly in the same manner as you have seen him go into heaven."

Yes, he is coming again, this very same Jesus, down from the clouds. And we? We are going up to meet him, to meet him in the air. In a moment, in a twinkling of an eye, when that trumpet sounds that we were told about in 1 Corinthians 15:51, 52: "Behold, I show you a mystery; we shall not all sleep but we shall all be changed, in a moment, in the twinkling of an eye, at the last trumpet: for the trumpet shall sound and the dead shall be raised incorruptible, and *we shall be changed.*" (Listen to it now from Handel's *Messiah*, the bass solo, part three.)

Yes, we have exciting things ahead of us. We are to be changed. And some people will be living when Jesus comes again, just as definitely as some people were living when Jesus first came. Those are the ones the New Testament means when it says we shall not all "sleep."

1 Corinthians 15:20, 21, 23, 26 explains a bit more. It tells us that Christ rose from the dead and is the "firstfruits" of all others who have died. What does "firstfruits" mean? Do you have a fruit tree in your garden, or a berry bush? Or can you go somewhere and see a lemon or orange tree, an apple or cherry tree, tangerine or mango tree, peach or plum tree, or raspberry or blackberry bushes? If you can look at a fruit tree or berry bush—or even better, bring a small branch to the place where you are reading this—then look at the fruit that is on that tree. Maybe it is just in bloom, and you have to wait to see the fruit later on. If you can't look at fruit on a tree, get a picture, or draw a picture, of a tree with fruit on it. If the first fruit on a tree is an orange, you know that when it has fruit again, they will not be cherries. If the first fruit on a tree is an apple, you know the next fruit will not be bananas. In other words, God is making it plain that when Jesus rose

from the dead, his body was like a first fruit, and our bodies when we rise from the dead will be the other fruit.

What does that mean? That means our bodies will be just like Jesus's body. We will be able to eat, to shake hands, to make a fire and cook, to walk as usual, to talk, to do all the other things we have done, but so very much more. We will never be able to be sick, to get hurt, to die, to be tired, to be sad. We will be able to go "up" as Jesus went up, and to have a whole new set of experiences. We cannot imagine the amazing things we will experience for ever in our new bodies, as we learn and discover what God will show us about his creation, about the universe, and, most of all, about himself.

Who will take part in this resurrection? Who will be able to have this wonderful new body and live for ever and ever? All who have believed and accepted Christ as their Savior. All who have believed God as he speaks to them through his Word, the Bible. All who believed in Abraham's time. All who believed back in the days of Moses. All who believed in David's time as they sang the Psalms. All who in the time of the prophets believed as they knew more and more about the coming Messiah. All who believed when Jesus was on the earth. All who have believed during the centuries since then. All who believe today.

Do you believe? Have you really accepted Christ as your Savior? Don't be stubborn like many of the Pharisees and the Sadducees were. Don't keep black, navy blue and brown scarves tied around your eyes—when the truth is so crystal clear! Hurry and believe, and come to Jesus. Don't be ashamed of the gospel of Christ, because it really is a power! It is a "power unto salvation." When you belong to him, don't be ashamed to tell others, because they need you to tell them to come too.

If it is at all possible for you to get Bach's Cantata 78, "Hasten to Jesus," and listen to it, it is a really joyous music that Bach wrote with tremendous understanding of the importance of hastening to Jesus. What is everything else, money, the houses, the lands, the jewels, the things, the waste of time, the selfish protection of your own belongings so that you aren't being imposed upon—what is it all worth if you are going to miss out on the eternity that is open to you? And if what interests you is freedom to roam and do nothing . . . what is sitting under a tree doing nothing in a pair of blue jeans worth, if you are going to miss out on an eternity that will give a freedom to roam through the universe and the new heavens and the new earth? Freedom here is a prison by contrast! People have been so blind and wretched, miserable, poor and naked, without realizing it . . . thinking they are rich, and have need of nothing! And people have also put themselves into a prison of believing lies about the universe and about themselves, rather than stepping out into the freedom of truth and through the open door that is Christ.

One day all who have believed will be there together. And together we will sing a new song of praise, saying, "Thou art worthy to take the book, and to open the seals thereof, for thou wast slain, and hast redeemed us to God by thy blood out of every kindred, and tongue and people and nation: And hast made us unto our God kings and priests: and *we shall reign on the earth*. And I beheld, and I heard the voice of many angels round about the throne and the beasts and the elders: and the number of them was ten thousand times ten thousand, and thousands of thousands: saying with a loud voice, '*Worthy* is the *Lamb* that was slain to receive power, and riches, and wisdom, and strength, and honor, and glory, and blessing'" (Revelation 5:9, 10, 11, 12).

"After this I beheld, and lo, a great multitude, which *no man could number*, of all nations, and kindreds, and people, and tongues stood before the throne, and before the Lamb, clothed with white robes, and palms in their hands, and cried with a loud voice, saying 'Salvation to our God which sitteth upon the throne, and unto the Lamb'" (Revelation 7:9, 10).

Yes, there will be so many there that no man can number them. There will be ten thousand times ten thousand and then thousands and thousands more. They will be from *every single* tribe and nation and language-group and family line. Satan will not have been able to seal off any one kind of people. The whole tapestry will be completed. The Lamb will open the book. The Lamb will receive our praise. The Lamb of God, promised from the very time Adam and Eve sinned, will have brought the final victory over death.

Adam was the first man to bring death to men, and we are told that the contrast is that in Adam all died, and in Jesus we are made alive. The victory will be total—and the struggle will be ended.

Remember something that we did together—we clapped. I think we should clap again. It is something anyone can do. Then I feel the only music on earth that can really give us *some* idea of the "new song" is Handel's Hallelujah Chorus from the *Messiah*. Do play it now. Listen to the words, sing it if you can, feel it in your chest, in your bones feel the absolute *wonder* of the fact that this is all true. It is not religious gobbledegook—it is true truth and it is going to come to pass. The future prophecy will be polished brilliantly by God at the exactly right moment, and every detail will be seen in all its perfection.

Listen: "Hallelujah, Hallelujah, Hallelujah, Hallelujah . . . Hal-le-lu-jah; for the Lord God omnipotent reigneth. Hallelujah . . . Hallelujah, Halle-lu-jah . . . The Kingdom of this world is become the kingdom of our Lord, and of his Christ, and of his Christ. And he shall reign for ever and ever, and he shall reign for ever and ever . . . Hal-le-lu-jah, Hal-le-lu-jah, King of Kings, and Lord of Lords, King of Kings, and Lord of Lords . . . Hallelujah, Hallelujah . . . Hal-le-lu-jah!"

Sing it now—believe it now—feel it now. *Know it now, and be there too*!

3/18/80 Trade 5⁹⁵